Search Engine Optimization

FOR

DUMMIES®

...ITION

Search Engine Optimization

FOR

DUMMIES®

4TH EDITION

by Peter Kent

WILEY

Wiley Publishing, Inc.

Search Engine Optimization For Dummies®, 4th Edition

Published by
Wiley Publishing, Inc.
111 River Street
Hoboken, NJ 07030-5774
www.wiley.com

Copyright © 2011 by Wiley Publishing, Inc., Indianapolis, Indiana

Published by Wiley Publishing, Inc., Indianapolis, Indiana

Published simultaneously in Canada

For general information on our other products and services, please contact our Customer Care Department within the U.S. at 877-762-2974, outside the U.S. at 317-572-3993, or fax 317-572-4002.

For technical support, please visit www.wiley.com/techsupport.

Wiley also publishes its books in a variety of electronic formats. Some content that appears in print may not be available in electronic books.

Library of Congress Control Number is available from the Publisher upon request.

ISBN: 978-0-470-88104-0

Manufactured in the United States of America

10 9 8 7 6 5 4 3 2

WILEY

About the Author

Peter Kent is the author of numerous other books about the Internet, including Pay Per Click Search Engine Marketing For Dummies, the best-selling Complete Idiot's Guide to the Internet, and the most widely reviewed and praised title in computer-book history, Poor Richard's Web Site: Geek Free, Commonsense Advice on Building a Low-Cost Web Site. His work has been praised by USA Today, BYTE, CNN.com, Windows Magazine, Philadelphia Inquirer, and many others.

Peter has been online since 1984, doing business in cyberspace since 1991, and writing about the Internet since 1993. Peter's experience spans virtually all areas of doing business online, from editing and publishing an e-mail newsletter to creating e-commerce Web sites, from online marketing and PR campaigns to running a Web-design and -hosting department for a large ISP.

Peter was the founder of an e-Business Service Provider funded by one of the world's largest VC firms, Softbank/Mobius, and VP of Web Solutions for a national ISP, and founded a computer-book publishing company launched through a concerted online-marketing campaign.

Peter now consults with businesses about their Internet strategies, helping them to avoid the pitfalls and to leap the hurdles they'll encounter online; he has helped Amazon, Zillow, Lonely Planet, and Tower Records, along with hundreds of small and medium businesses in a wide range of industries. He can be contacted at `Consult@PeterKentConsulting.com`, and more information about his background and experience is available at `www.PeterKentConsulting.com`.

Dedication

For David Spencer, my best friend, who left too soon

Author's Acknowledgments

I'd like to thank all my clients, who have given me an opportunity to play with search-engine optimization in a wide variety of businesses. I'd also like to thank Kyle Looper, my Acquisitions Editor, and my editor, Susan Christophersen, who as usual were both patient and helpful. And, of course, the multitude of Wiley staff involved in editing, proofreading, and laying out the book.

Publisher's Acknowledgments

We're proud of this book; please send us your comments at http://dummies.custhelp.com. For other comments, please contact our Customer Care Department within the U.S. at 877-762-2974, outside the U.S. at 317-572-3993, or fax 317-572-4002.

Some of the people who helped bring this book to market include the following:

Acquisitions and Editorial

Project and Copy Editor:
Susan Christophersen

Acquisitions Editor: Kyle Looper

Technical Editor: Paul Chaney

Editorial Manager: Jodi Jensen

Editorial Assistant: Amanda Graham

Sr. Editorial Assistant: Cherie Case

Cartoons: Rich Tennant
(www.the5thwave.com)

Composition Services

Project Coordinator: Sheree Montgomery

Layout and Graphics: Joyce Haughey,
SD Jumper

Proofreader: Christine Sabooni

Indexer: Slivoskey Indexing Services

Publishing and Editorial for Technology Dummies

   Richard Swadley, Vice President and Executive Group Publisher

   Andy Cummings, Vice President and Publisher

   Mary Bednarek, Executive Acquisitions Director

   Mary C. Corder, Editorial Director

Publishing for Consumer Dummies

   Diane Graves Steele, Vice President and Publisher

Composition Services

   Debbie Stailey, Director of Composition Services

Contents at a Glance

Table of Contents

Introduction

Welcome to *Search Engine Optimization For Dummies,* 4th Edition. What on earth would you want this book for? After all, can't you just build a Web site and let your Web designer get the site into the search engines? Can't you simply pay someone $25 to register the site with thousands of search engines? I'm sure you've seen advertising stating, "We guarantee top-ten placement in a gazillion search engines!" and "We'll register you in 5,000 search engines today!"

Well, unfortunately, it's not that simple. (Okay, fortunately for me, because if it were simple, Wiley wouldn't pay me to write this book.) The fact is that search engine optimization is a little complicated. Not brain surgery compli-cated, but not as easy as "Give us 50 bucks and we'll handle it for you."

The vast majority of Web sites don't have a chance in the search engines. Why? Because of simple mistakes. Because the people creating the sites don't have a clue what they should do to make the site easy for search engines to work with. Because they don't understand the role of links pointing to their site, and because they've never thought about keywords. Because, because, because. This book helps you deal with those becauses and gets you not just one, but dozens, of steps ahead of the average Web-site Joe.

About This Book

This book demystifies the world of search engines. You find out what you need to do to give your site the best possible chance to rank well in the search engines.

In this book, I show you how to

- Make sure that you're using the right keywords in your Web pages.
- Create pages that search engines can read and will index the way you want them to.
- Avoid techniques that search engines hate — things that can get your Web site penalized (knocked down low in search engine rankings).
- Build pages that give your site greater visibility in search engines.
- Get search engines and directories to include your site in their indexes and lists.

✔ Get into the product and shopping indexes.

✔ Get search engines to display your site when people search locally.

✔ Encourage other Web sites to link to yours.

✔ Make the most of social networking and video.

✔ Keep track of how your site is doing.

✔ And plenty more!

Foolish Assumptions

I don't want to assume anything, but I have to believe that if you're reading this book, you already know a few things about the Internet and search engines. I presume that you

✔ Have access to a computer that has access to the Internet

✔ Know how to use a Web browser to get around the Internet

✔ Know how to carry out searches at the Web's major search engines, such as Google and Yahoo!

Of course, for a book like this, I *have* to assume a little. This is a book about how to get your Web site to rank well in the search engines. I have to assume that you know how to create and work with a site or at least know someone who can create and work with a site. In particular, you (or the other person) know how to

✔ Set up a Web site

✔ Create Web pages

✔ Load those pages onto your Web server

✔ Work with HTML (HyperText Markup Language), the coding used to create Web pages

In other words, you're not just using some kind of simple Web-page creation program that isolates you from the underlying HTML code; and you, or your geek, understand a little about HTML and feel comfortable enough with it to insert or change HTML tags.

I don't go into a lot of complicated code in this book; this isn't a primer on HTML. But to do search engine work, you (or someone on your team) need to know what a <TITLE> tag is, for instance, and how to insert it into a page; how to recognize JavaScript (though not how to create or modify it); how to open a Web page in a text editor and modify it; and so on. You need basic HTML skills in order to optimize a site for the search engines. If you need more information about HTML, take a look at *HTML 4 For Dummies,* 5th Edition, by Ed Tittel and Mary Burmeister (Wiley Publishing, Inc.).

How This Book Is Organized

As are all good reference tools, this book is designed to be read when needed. It's divided into several parts: the basics; building search engine–friendly Web sites; getting your site into the search engines, including the product and shopping indexes; what to do after the search engines index your site (such as creating links, working with video, and using social networking); and the Part of Tens. If you just want to know how to find sites that will link to your Web site, read Chapter 15. If you need to understand the principles behind getting links to your site, read Chapter 14. If all you need is to figure out what keywords are important to your site, Chapter 5 is for you.

However, search engine optimization is a pretty complex subject, and all the topics covered in this book are interrelated. Sure, you can register your site with the search engines, but if your pages aren't optimized for the search engines, you may be wasting your time. You can create pages the search engines can read, but if you don't pick the right keywords, it's a total waste of time. So I recommend that you read everything in this book; it will make a huge difference in how well your pages are ranked in the search engines.

Part I: Search Engine Basics

In this part, I provide, yep, the basics — the foundation on which you can build your search engine optimization skills. Which search engines are important, for instance? In fact, what *is* a search engine? What's a *search directory?* And why am I using the term *search system?* In this part, you find out the basics of sensible site creation, discover how to pick the keywords that people are using to find your business, and discover how to do a few quick fixes to your site. You also find out how to create a basic strategy for your Web site and search engine campaign.

Part II: Building Search Engine–Friendly Sites

Do you have any idea how many sites are invisible to the search engines? Or, if they're not invisible, are built such that search engines can't see the information needed to index the site the way the site owners would like?

Well, I don't know an exact number, but I do know that most sites aren't optimized for maximum search engine indexing. If you read Part II, you'll be way ahead of the vast majority of site owners and managers. You discover how to create techniques that search engines like and avoid the ones they hate. You also find out about tricks that some people use — and the dangers involved.

In addition, you find out how to add content to your site (search engines love content) and the best way to get your site found through local-search services.

Part III: Adding Your Site to the Indexes and Directories

After you've created your Web site and ensured that the search engines can read the pages, somehow you have to get the *search systems* — the engines and directories — to include your site. That's hard if you don't know what you're doing. In this part, you find out which search systems are important, how to register, and how to find other search engines and directories that are important to your site. You also find out why registering sometimes doesn't work, and what to do about it, as well as how to get your site listed in the product and shopping indexes.

Part IV: After You've Submitted Your Site

Your work isn't over yet. In this part, you find out why links to your site are so important and how to get other sites to link to you. You also learn about using video to get traffic to your site, and you see how to use social networking for SEO purposes. And, just in case, I include a chapter about what happens if things go badly wrong and your site is penalized by Google!

Part V: The Part of Tens

All *For Dummies* books have the Part of Tens. In this part, you find a chapter that covers the ten things to consider when looking for an SEO firm and a chapter about common SEO myths and mistakes. In addition, you get ten ways to keep up-to-date with the search engine business, and ten services and tools that will be useful in your search engine campaign.

Icons Used in This Book

This book, like all *For Dummies* books, uses icons to highlight certain paragraphs and to alert you to particularly useful information. Here's a rundown of what those icons mean:

A Tip icon means I'm giving you an extra snippet of information that may help you on your way or provide some additional insight into the concepts being discussed.

The Remember icon points out information that is worth committing to memory.

The Technical Stuff icon indicates geeky stuff that you can skip if you really want to, although you may want to read it if you're the kind of person who likes to have the background info.

The Warning icon helps you stay out of trouble. It's intended to grab your attention to help you avoid a pitfall that may harm your Web site or business.

Don't forget to visit the Web sites associated with this book. At www. dummies.com/go/seofd4e, you find all the links in this book (so that you don't have to type them!). At www.SearchEngineBulletin.com, you find the aforementioned links along with additional useful information that didn't make it into the book.

Part I
Search Engine Basics

The 5th Wave   By Rich Tennant

"Well, heck — all the boy did was launch a search on the Web and up comes Tracy's retainer, your car keys, and my bowling trophy here on a site in Seattle!"

In this part . . .

The basics of search engine optimization are surprisingly, um, basic. In fact, you may be able to make small changes to your Web site that make a huge difference in your site's ranking in the search results.

This part starts with the basics. I begin by explaining which search engines are important. You may have heard the names of dozens of sites and heard that, in fact, hundreds of search engines exist. You'll be happy to hear that the vast majority of search results are provided by no more than four systems, and 70 percent or more of all search results come from a single company, Google.

You also discover how to make some quick and easy changes to your Web site that may fix serious search engine problems for you. Sites can have a number of common problems that, if present in your site, must be resolved before you have any chance of getting into the search engines at all, let alone ranking well.

This part of the book also includes information on developing a search-engine strategy for beating your competition, and discusses how to create a Web site that works well for both visitors and search engines.

Chapter 1

Surveying the Search Engine Landscape

In This Chapter

▶ Discovering where people search

▶ Understanding the difference between search sites and search systems

▶ Distilling thousands of search sites down to four search systems

▶ Understanding how search engines work

▶ Gathering tools and basic knowledge

You've got a problem. You want people to visit your Web site; that's the purpose, after all — to bring people to your site to buy your product, or find out about your service, or hear about the cause you support, or for whatever other purpose you've built the site. So you've decided you need to get traffic from the search engines — not an unreasonable conclusion, as you find out in this chapter. But there are *so many* search engines! You have the obvious ones — Google, AOL, Yahoo!, and MSN/Bing — but you've probably also heard of others: HotBot, Dogpile, Ask.com, Netscape, and EarthLink. There's also Lycos, InfoSpace, Mamma.com, WebCrawler, and many more. To top it all off, you've seen advertising asserting that for only $49.95 (or $19.95, or $99.95, or whatever sum seems to make sense to the advertiser), you, too, can have your Web site listed in hundreds, nay, thousands of search engines. You may have even used some of these services, only to discover that the flood of traffic you were promised turns up missing.

Well, I've got some good news. You can forget almost all the names I just listed — well, at least you can after you read this chapter. The point of this chapter is to take a complicated landscape of thousands of search sites and whittle it down into the small group of search systems that really matter. (Search sites? Search systems? Don't worry; I explain the distinction in a moment.)

Index envy

Late in 2005, Yahoo! (www.yahoo.com) claimed that its index contained information for about 20 billion pages, along with almost 2 billion images and 50 million audio and video pages. Google (www.google.com) used to actually state on its home page how many pages it indexed — they reached 15 billion or so at one point — but decided not to play the "mine is bigger than yours" game with Yahoo! and removed the "mine is bigger than yours" boast. Still, in 2008 Google reported that it had one *trillion* URLs in its index!

If you really want to, you can jump to the "Where Do People Search?" section (near the end of the chapter) to see the list of search systems you need to worry about and ignore the details. But I've found that when I give this list to someone, he or she looks at me like I'm crazy because they know that some popular search sites aren't on the list. This chapter explains why.

Investigating Search Engines and Directories

The term *search engine* has become the predominant term for *search system* or *search site,* but before reading any further, you need to understand the different types of search, um, thingies that you're going to run across. Basically, you need to know about four thingies.

Search indexes or search engines

Search indexes or engines are the predominant type of search tools you'll run across. Originally, the term *search engine* referred to some kind of search index, a huge database containing information from individual Web sites.

Large search-index companies own thousands of computers that use software known as *spiders* or *robots* (or just plain *bots*) to grab Web pages and read the information stored in them. These systems don't always grab all the information on each page or all the pages in a Web site, but they grab a significant amount of information and use complex *algorithms* — calculations based on complicated formulae — to index that information. Google, shown in Figure 1-1, is the world's most popular search engine, closely followed by Yahoo! and MSN/Bing.

Figure 1-1:
Google,
the world's
most
popular
search
engine,
produced
these
results.

Search directories

A *search directory* is a categorized collection of information about Web sites instead of containing information from Web pages.

The most significant search directories are owned by Yahoo! (`dir.yahoo.com`) and the Open Directory Project (`www.dmoz.org`). (You can see an example of Open Directory Project information, displayed in Google — `dir.google.com` — in Figure 1-2.) Directory companies don't use spiders or bots to download and index pages on the Web sites in the directory; rather, for each Web site, the directory contains information, such as a title and description, submitted by the site owner. The two most important directories, Yahoo! and Open Directory, have staff members who examine all the sites in the directory to make sure they're placed into the correct categories and meet certain quality criteria. Smaller directories often accept sites based on the owners' submission, with little verification.

Figure 1-2:
Google
also has
a search
directory,
but it
doesn't
create the
directory
itself; it
gets it from
the Open
Directory
Project.

Here's how to see the difference between Yahoo!'s search results and the Yahoo! directory:

1. **Go to** www.yahoo.com.

2. **Type a word into the Search box.**

3. **Click the Search button.**

   The list of Web sites that appears is called the Yahoo! Search results.

4. **Look for Directory above the Search box.**

   Above the Search box you'll see either a Directory link or a More link that opens a drop-down menu with the Directory option inside the menu; either way, click Directory and you'll end up in Yahoo! directory. (You can also go directly to the directory by using dir.yahoo.com.)

Nonspidered indexes

I wasn't sure what to call these things, so I made up a name: *nonspidered indexes.* A number of small indexes, less important than major indexes (such as Google), don't use spiders to examine the full contents of each page in the index. Rather, the index contains background information about each page, such as titles, descriptions, and keywords. In some cases, this information comes from the meta tags pulled off the pages in the index. (I tell you about meta tags in Chapter 2.) In other cases, the person who enters the site into the index provides this information. A number of the smaller systems discussed in Chapter 12 are of this type.

Pay-per-click systems

Some systems provide *pay-per-click* listings. Advertisers place small ads into the systems, and when users perform their searches, the results contain some of these sponsored listings, typically above and to the right of the free listings. Pay-per-click systems are discussed in an additional chapter posted at www.SearchEngineBulletin.com.

Keeping the terms straight

Here are a few additional terms that you'll see scattered throughout the book:

- **Search site:** This Web site lets you search through some kind of index or directory of Web sites, or perhaps both an index and directory. (In some cases, search sites known as *meta indexes* allow you to search through multiple indices.) Google.com, AOL.com, and EarthLink.com are all search sites. Dogpile.com and Mamma.com are meta-index search sites.

- **Search system:** This organization possesses a combination of software, hardware, and people that indexes or categorizes Web sites — the system builds the index or directory you search at a search site. The distinction is important because a search site might not actually own a search index or directory. For instance, Google is a search system — it displays results from the index that it creates for itself — but AOL.com and EarthLink.com aren't. In fact, if you search at AOL.com or EarthLink. com, you actually get Google search results.

  Google and the Open Directory Project provide search results to hundreds of search sites. In fact, most of the world's search sites get their search results from elsewhere; see Figure 1-3.

- **Search term:** This is the word, or words, that someone types into a search engine when looking for information.

- **Search results:** Results are the information (the results of your search term) returned to you when you go to a search site and search for something. As just explained, in many cases the search results you see don't come from the search site you're using, but rather from some other search system.

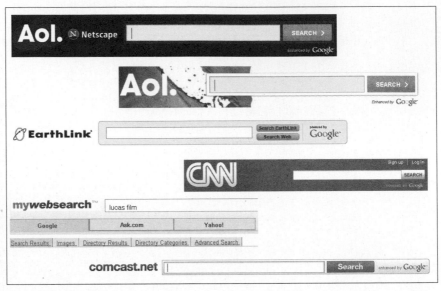

Figure 1-3:
Look
carefully
and you'll
see that
many
search
sites get
their search
results
from other
search
systems.

- ✔ **SERPs**: I don't use the term much, but you'll hear others in the business talking about the *serps*. It simply means *search engine results page,* the page that appears after you search.

- ✔ **Natural search results:** A link to a Web page can appear on a search results page two ways: The search engine may place it on the page because the site owner paid to be there (pay-per-click ads), or it may pull the page from its index because it thinks the page matches the search term well. These free placements are often known as *natural search results;* you'll also hear the term *organic search results* and sometimes even *algorithmic search results.*

- ✔ **Search engine optimization (SEO):** Search engine optimization (also known as *SEO*) refers to "optimizing" Web sites and Web pages to rank well in the search engines — the subject of this book, of course.

Why bother with search engines?

Why bother using search engines for your marketing? Because search engines represent the single most important source of new Web site visitors.

You may have heard that most Web site visits begin at a search engine. Well, this isn't true, though many people continue to use these outdated statistics because they sound good — "80 percent of all Web site visitors reach the site through a search engine," for instance. However, way back in 2003, that claim was finally put to rest. The number of search-originated site visits dropped below the 50 percent mark. Most Web site visitors reach their destinations by either typing a *URL* — a Web address — into their browsers and going there directly or by clicking a link on another site that takes them there. Most visitors don't reach their destinations by starting at the search engines.

However, search engines are still extremely important for a number of reasons:

- The proportion of visits originating at search engines is still significant. Sure, it's not 80 percent, but with billions of searches each month, it's still a lot of traffic.

- According to a report by comScore, Internet users in the United States carried out over 16 billion searches at major search engines in June of 2010.

- comScore also reported that in the same month, U.S. Internet users carried out another 9 billion or so searches in other search sites, such as map sites, video sites, Amazon, eBay, YouTube, Craigslist, and so on. In total, comScore counted 25 billion searches, 2–3 searches every day for every man, woman, child, and baby in the United States.

- Of the visits that don't originate at a search engine, a large proportion are revisits — people who know exactly where they want to go. This isn't new business; it's repeat business. Most *new* visits come through the search engines — that is, search engines are the single most important source of new visitors to Web sites.

- It's also been well established for a number of years that most people researching a purchase begin their research at the search engines. (Except for those who don't. As I discuss in Chapter 13, many, perhaps most, product searches actually begin in sites such as Amazon, eBay, and Craigslist. But then, I think it's important to understand that these sites *are* search engines; they are, in effect, product-search engines.)

- Search engines represent an inexpensive way to reach people. Generally, you get more bang for your buck going after free search engine traffic than almost any other form of advertising or marketing.

Here's an example. One client of mine, selling construction equipment to the tune of $10,000 a month, rebuilt his site and began a combined natural-search and paid-search campaign, boosting sales to around $500,000 a month in less than two years. It's hard to imagine how he could have grown his company, with relatively little investment, so quickly without the search engines!

Where Do People Search?

You can search for Web sites at many places. Literally thousands of sites, in fact, provide the ability to search the Web. (What you may not realize, however, is that many sites search only a small subset of the World Wide Web.)

However, *most* searches are carried out at a small number of search sites. How do the world's most popular search sites rank? That depends on how you measure popularity:

- Percentage of site visitors *(audience reach)*
- Total number of visitors
- Total number of searches carried out at a site
- Total number of hours visitors spend searching at the site

Each measurement provides a slightly different ranking. Although all provide a similar picture with the same sites generally appearing on the list, some are in slightly different positions.

The following list shows the United States' top seven general search sites in March of 2010 — almost 10 billion searches — according to a Nielsen study:

Google.com	65.7%
Yahoo.com	13.4%
MSN/Bing	12.2%
AOL.com	2.5%
Ask.com	1.9%
My Web Search	1.2%
Comcast Search	0.5%

Remember that this is a list of search sites, not search systems. (It's a bit of a strange list, though, because the last three are not general-search sites.) In some cases, the sites own their own systems. Google provides its own search results, but AOL doesn't. (AOL gets its results from Google.) My Web Search is a meta-search engine getting results from Google, Yahoo!, and Ask.com.

On the other hand, Yahoo! gets its results from MSN/Bing, thanks to a Yahoo!/Microsoft partnership — known as the *Yahoo! and Microsoft Search Alliance* — that was implemented in August of 2010. (Look for the little *Powered by Bing* notice at the bottom of Yahoo! search pages.)

The fact that some sites get results from other search systems means two things:

- **The numbers in the preceding list are somewhat misleading.** They suggest that Google has around 65 percent of all searches. But Google also feeds AOL its results — add AOL's searches to Google's, and you have 67.7 percent of all searches. Additionally, Google feeds Comcast (another 0.5 percent, according to Nielsen). Furthermore, My Web Search is a meta-search engine; therefore, if you search at My Web Search, you see results from Google, Yahoo!, and Ask.

✔ **You can ignore some of these systems.** At present, and for the foreseeable future, you don't need to worry about AOL.com. Even though it's one of the world's top search sites, you can forget about it. As long as you remember that Google feeds AOL, you need to worry about Google only. You don't really need to worry about Yahoo!, either; as long as MSN/Bing feeds Yahoo!, you can think of the two as essentially the same index.

Now reexamine the preceding list of the U.S.'s most important search sites and see what you can remove to get closer to a list of sites you care about. Check out Table 1-1 for the details.

Table 1-1		The Top Search Sites
Search Site	*Keep It On the List?*	*Description*
Google.com	Yes	The big kid on the block. Lots of people search the Google index on its own search site, *and* it feeds many sites. Obviously, Google has to stay on the list.
Yahoo.com	No	Yahoo! is obviously a large, important site, but it gets its search results from MSN/Bing, so as long as you're in the MSN/Bing index, you're in Yahoo!.
MSN/Bing	Yes	MSN/Bing creates its own index, and gets many searches, and at the time of writing at least, is growing in popularity (thanks to all those cool TV ads, I imagine). *And* it feeds data to Yahoo!. So Bing is critical.
AOL.com	No	Fuggetaboutit — AOL gets search results from Google and from the Open Directory Project.
Ask.com (previously known as AskJeeves.com)	Yes	It has its own search engine and feeds some other systems — MyWay, Lycos, and Excite. Keep it, though it's small.
MyWebSearch.com	No	This system simply searches through other systems' search indexes (Google, Yahoo!, and Ask). Forget it.
Comcast Search	No	Again, results come from Google, so forget it.

Based on the information in Table 1-1, you can whittle down your list of systems to three: Google, MSN/Bing, and Ask. The top two search systems are very important, , accounting for 95 percent or more of all search results, with a small follower, Ask, which provides results to many smaller search sites. There's one more system I want to add to these three systems, though. Very few people search at the Open Directory Project (`www.dmoz.org`). However, this directory system feeds data to hundreds of search sites, including Google and AOL.

To summarize, four important systems are left:

✔ Google

✔ MSN/Bing

✔ Ask

✔ Open Directory Project

That's not so bad, is it? You've just gone from thousands of sites to four.

Now, some of you may be thinking, "Aren't you missing some sites? What happened to HotBot, Mamma.com, WebCrawler, Lycos, and all the other systems that were so well known a few years ago?" A lot of them have disappeared or have turned over a new leaf and are pursuing other opportunities.

For example, Northern Light, a system well known in the late 1990s, now sells search software. And in the cases in which the search sites are still running, they're generally fed by other search systems. Infospace, Dogpile, and MetaCrawler get search results from the top four systems, for instance, and HotBot gets results from MSN/Bing and Ask.com.

AltaVista, the first big search index, is now owned by Yahoo! and is really just a different Web design displaying Yahoo! search results. (It remains to be seen how the Yahoo!/Bing partnership will affect AltaVista.) The same goes for AllTheWeb, for the geeks among you who remember it. If the search site you remember isn't mentioned here, it's either out of business, being fed by someone else, or simply not important in the big scheme of things.

When you find a new search system, look carefully on the page near the search box, or on the search results page — perhaps at the bottom of the page in the copyright message — and you may find where the search results are coming from.

You'll also want to work with some other search systems, as you find out in Chapter 12. In some cases, you need to check out specialty directories and indexes related to the industry in which your Web site operates, or submit your site to Web directories in order to build links back to your site. In addition, in Chapter 13 you find out about the product search sites; hugely important for those of you selling products. And in Chapter 18, I tell you about the video sites — YouTube, for instance, is the world's third most important

search engine, after Google and MSN/Bing. However, the preceding systems —
Google, MSN/Bing, Ask.com, and the Open Directory Project — are the most
important general-search systems.

Google alone provides over 70 percent of all search results. Get into *all* the
systems on the preceding list, and you're in front of probably more than 98
percent of all searchers. Well, perhaps you're in front of them. You have a
chance of being in front of them, anyway, if your site ranks highly (which is
what this book is all about).

Search Engine Magic

Go to Google and search for the term *personal injury lawyer*. Then look at the
blue bar below the Google logo, and you see something like this:

```
Results 1 - 10 of about 8,790,000 for personal injury
        lawyer
```

This means Google has found almost 9 million pages that contain these three
words. Yet, somehow, it has managed to rank the pages. It's decided that one
particular page should appear first, and then another, and then another, and
so on, all the way down to page 8,790,000. (By the way, this has to be one of
the wonders of the modern world: Search engines have tens of thousands of
computers, evaluating a trillion pages or more, and returning the information
in a second or two.)

How do they do it?

How on earth does Google do it? How does it evaluate and compare pages?
How do other search engines do the same? Well, I don't know *exactly*. Search
engines don't want you to know how they work (or it would be too easy to
create pages that exactly match the search system, "giving them what they
want to see"). But I can explain the general concept.

When Google searches for your search term, it begins by looking for pages
containing the exact phrase. Then it starts looking for pages containing the
words close together, and for synonyms; search for *dog* and Google knows
you may be interested in pages with the word *canine*, for instance. (One
Google source claims that synonyms come into play in around 70 percent of
all searches.) Then it looks for pages that have the words scattered around.
This isn't necessarily the order in which a search engine shows you pages;
in some cases, pages with words close together (but not the exact phrase)
appear higher than pages with the exact phrase, for instance. That's because
search engines evaluate pages according to a variety of criteria.

Search engines look at many factors. They look for the words throughout the page, both in the visible page and in the nonvisible portions of the HTML source code for the page. Each time they find the words, they *weight* them in some way. A word in one position is worth more than a word in another position. A word formatted in one way is worth more than a word formatted in another. (You read more about this in Chapter 5.) There's more, though. Search engines also look at links pointing to pages, and use those links to evaluate the referenced pages: How many links are there? How many are from popular sites? What words are in the link text? You read more about this in Chapters 14 through 16.

Stepping into the programmers' shoes

There's a lot of conflicting information out there about SEO. Some of it's good, some of it's not so good, and some of it's downright wrong. When evaluating a claim about what search engines do, I sometimes find it useful to step into the shoes of the people building the search engines; I try to think about what would make sense from the perspective of the programmers who write the code that evaluates all these pages.

Consider this: Say, you search for *personal injury lawyer*, and the search engine finds one page with the term in the page's title (between the `<TITLE>` and `</TITLE>` tags, which you read more about in Chapters 2 and 6), and another page with the term somewhere deep in the page text. Which do you think is likely to match the search term better? If the text is in the title, doesn't that indicate that page is likely to be related in some way to the term? If the text is deep in the body of the page, couldn't it mean that the page isn't directly related to the term, but that it's related to it in some incidental or peripheral manner?

Considering SEO from this point of view makes it easier to understand how search engines try to evaluate and compare pages. If the keywords are in the links pointing to the page, the page is likely to be relevant to those keywords; if the keywords are in headings on the page, that must be significant; if the keywords appear frequently throughout the page, rather than just once, that must mean something. Suddenly, it all makes sense.

By the way, in Chapter 7 I discuss things that search engines don't like. You may hear elsewhere all sorts of warnings that may or may not be correct. Here's an example: I've read that using a refresh meta tag to automatically push a visitor from one page to another will get your site penalized, and may even get your site banned from the search engine. You've seen this situation: You land on a page on a Web site, and there's a message saying something like, "We'll forward you to page *x* in five seconds, or you can click here." The theory is that search engines don't like this, and they may punish you for doing this.

Now, does this make any sense? Aren't there good reasons to sometimes use such forwarding techniques? Yes, there are. So why would a search engine punish you for doing it? They don't. They probably won't index the page that is forwarding a visitor — based on the quite reasonable theory that if the site doesn't want the visitor to read the page, they don't need to index it — but you're not going to get punished for using it.

Remember that the search engine programmers aren't interested in punishing anyone; they're just trying to make the best choices between billions of pages. Generally, search engines use their "algorithms" to determine how to rank a page, and they try to adjust the algorithms to make sure "tricks" are ignored. But they don't want to punish anyone for doing something for which there might be a good reason, even if the technique could also be used as a trick.

What would the programmers do? I like to use this as my "plausibility filter" when I hear someone make some unusual or even outlandish claim about how search engines function.

Gathering Your Tools

You need several tools and skills to optimize and rank your Web site. I talk about a number of these in the appropriate chapters, but I want to cover a few basics before I move on. It goes without saying that you need

- Basic Internet knowledge
- A computer connected to the Internet
- A Web site
- One of these two things:
  - Good working knowledge of HTML
  - Access to a geek with a good working knowledge of HTML

    Which path should you take? If you don't know what HTML means (HyperText Markup Language), you probably need to run out and find that geek. *HTML* is the code used to create Web pages, and you need to understand how to use it to optimize pages. Discussing HTML and how to upload pages to a Web site is beyond the scope of this book. If you're interested in finding out more, check out *HTML, XHTML, & CSS For Dummies*, by Ed Tittel and Jeff Noble, and *Creating Web Pages For Dummies*, 9th Edition, by Bud E. Smith (both published by Wiley Publishing, Inc.).

✔ Firefox Web browser

Okay, you don't have to have Firefox — you can use Internet Explorer or another browser — but many in the SEO business love Firefox for its fantastic add-ons. If you do use Firefox, then I'd suggest you install the following, or similar, add-ons (go to `addons.mozilla.org` to search for new add-ons).

- *NoDoFollow:* A tool that quickly indicates the presence of "nofollow" links (see Chapter 14).

- *DT Whois:* Click a button on your toolbar to retrieve information about the domain of the site you're viewing. Great for digging up info on competitors.

- *Firebug:* A fantastic little tool for examining the code underlying a Web page. Right-click a component on the page you're looking at, select Inspect Element, and you see a frame that shows you how the component was created.

- *Google Global:* Handy if you want to see Google search results in different countries.

- *Compete Browser Extension:* Provides information, in the status bar, about the popularity of the site you are visiting, from Compete.com.

Dig around in the Firefox add-ons and you'll soon be addicted. The preceding are merely some of the add-ons I use more frequently, but Firefox has hundreds of cool toys for you to try.

✔ Toolbars

Install the Google toolbar in your Web browser . . . and perhaps the Alexa toolbar; maybe even the Yahoo!, MSN/Bing, and Ask.com toolbars, too. You may want to use these tools even if you plan to use a geek to work on your site. They're simple to install and open a completely new view of the Web. The next two sections spell out the details.

Search toolbars

I definitely recommend the Google toolbar, which allows you to begin searching Google without going to the Web site first (if you use the Firefox Web browser, the built-in Search Engine box does the same). It also allows you to see a page's PageRank (see Chapter 14), and whether the page is cached (see Chapter 2).

I also like to use the Compete.com and Alexa toolbars, too, as they provide some idea of how popular the Web site you're looking at is; great for competitive research.

Geek or no geek

Many readers of this book are business people who don't plan to do the search engine work themselves (or, in some cases, realize that it's a lot of work and need to find someone with more time or technical skills to do the work). However, having read the book, they understand far more about search engines and are in a better position to find and direct someone else working on their site. As one reader-cum-client told me, "There's a lot of snake oil in this business," so his reading helped him understand the basics and ask the right questions of search engine optimization firms. (See Chapter 20 for more information on that subject.)

You might also want to use the Yahoo!, MSN/Bing, and Ask.com toolbars. Additionally, these toolbars have plenty of extras: auto form fillers, tabbed browsing, desktop search, spyware blockers, translators, spell checkers, and so on. I'm not going to describe all these tools, as they aren't directly related to SEO, but they're definitely useful.

You really don't need all of them, but hey, here they are if you really want to experiment. You can find these toolbars here:

- ✔ toolbar.google.com
- ✔ alexa.com/toolbar
- ✔ toolbar.yahoo.com
- ✔ toolbar.bing.com
- ✔ toolbar.ask.com

You can see the Google and Alexa toolbars (at the bottom left of the browser window) in Figure 1-4. Don't worry; you don't have to have all this clutter on your screen all the time. Right-click a blank space on any toolbar, and you can add and remove toolbars temporarily; simply open a toolbar when you need it. I leave the Google toolbar on most of the time, and open the others now and then.

One thing I do find frustrating about these systems is the pop-up blockers. Yes, they can be helpful, but often they block pop-up windows that I want to see; if you find that you click a link and it doesn't open, try Ctrl+clicking (which may temporarily disable the pop-up blocker), or disable the blocker on the toolbar.

Figure 1-4:
The toolbars
provide
useful
information
for search
engine cam-
paigns; the
Google bar's
PageRank
button is
shown
open.

I refer to the Google toolbar here and there throughout this book because it provides you with the following useful features:

✔ A quick view of the Google PageRank, an important metric that I explain in Chapter 14

✔ A quick way to see whether a Web page is already indexed by Google

✔ A quick way to see some of the pages linking to a Web page

The Google toolbar has a number of other useful features, but the preceding features are the most useful for the purposes of this book. Turn on the PageRank button after installing the toolbar:

1. **Click the "Adjust Google Toolbar options" button (currently a picture of a little wrench, on the right end of the bar).**

2. **Click the Tools button at the top of the Toolbar Options dialog box.**

3. **Enable the PageRank check box and click OK.**

Alexa toolbar

Alexa is a company owned by Amazon.com and is a partner with Google and Microsoft. It's been around a long time, and millions of people around the world use it. Every time someone uses the toolbar to visit a Web site, the toolbar sends the URL to Alexa, allowing the system to create an enormous database of site visits. The toolbar can provide traffic information to you; you can quickly see how popular a site is and even view a detailed traffic analysis, such as an estimate of the percentage of Internet users who visit the site each month. (There's also a Firefox add-on called *Alexa Sparky* that displays Alexa data in the status bar.)

Work with the Alexa toolbar for a while and you'll quickly get a feel for site popularity. A site ranks 453? That's pretty good. 1,987,123? That's a sign that hardly anyone visits the site. In addition, it provides a quick way to find information about who owns the site on which the current page sits, and how many pages link to the current page. You can find the Alexa toolbar (refer to Figure 1-4) at `toolbar.alexa.com`.

I've been criticized for recommending the Alexa toolbar in earlier editions of this book: Some people claim it is spyware. Some antispyware programs even search for the toolbar and flag it as spyware, though others don't. As I mention, the toolbar sends the URLs you're visiting. However, Alexa states on the site (and I believe them) that "The Alexa Toolbar contains no advertising and does not profile or target you." I know for sure that it doesn't display ads. Alexa doesn't steal your usernames and passwords, as is occasionally claimed. Alexa does gather information about where you visit, but it doesn't know who you are, so does it matter? Decide for yourself.

Chapter 2

Your One-Hour, Search Engine–Friendly Web Site Makeover

A few small changes can make a big difference in your site's position in the search engines. So instead of forcing you to read this entire book before you can get anything done, this chapter helps you identify problems with your site and, with a little luck, shows you how to make a significant difference through quick fixes.

It's possible that you may not make significant progress in a single hour, as the chapter title promises. You may identify serious problems with your site that can't be fixed quickly. Sorry, that's life! The purpose of this chapter is to help you identify a few obvious problems and, perhaps, make some quick fixes with the goal of really getting something done.

Is Your Site Indexed?

It's important to find out whether your site is actually in a search engine or directory. Your site doesn't come up when someone searches at Google for *rodent racing*? Can't find it in Bing? Have you ever thought that perhaps it simply isn't there? In the next several sections, I explain how to find out whether your site is indexed in a few different systems.

Some of the systems into which you want to place your Web site aren't household names. If I mention a search system that you don't recognize, page to Chapter 1 to find out more about it.

Google

I'll start with the behemoth: Google. Here's the quickest and easiest way to see what Google has in its index. Search Google, either at the site or through the Google toolbar (see Chapter 1) for the following:

```
site:domain.com
```

Don't type the www. piece, just the domain name. For instance, say your site's domain name is *RodentRacing.com*. You search for this:

```
site:rodentracing.com
```

Google returns a list of pages it's found on your site; at the top, underneath the search box (or perhaps somewhere else; it moves around occasionally), you see something like this:

```
2 results (0.16) seconds
```

That's it — quick and easy. You know how many pages Google has indexed on your site, and can even see which pages.

 Well, you may know. This number is not always accurate; Google will show different numbers in different places; the number you see in the first page of search results may not be the same as the number it shows you on, say, the tenth page of search results, nor the same as the number it shows you in the Google Webmasters Console (see Chapter 11).

Here's another way to see what's in the index, in this case a particular page in your site. Open your browser and load a page at your site. Then follow these steps:

1. **Click the PageRank button on the Google toolbar.**

   I'm assuming that you've downloaded the Google toolbar — as I suggested in Chapter 1, and available at `toolbar.google.com` — and installed it in your browser. If you don't have the toolbar, don't worry; I explain a nontoolbar method in a moment.

2. **Choose Cached Snapshot of Page from the drop-down list that appears.**

   If you're lucky, Google loads a page showing you what it has in its cache, so you know Google has indexed the page (see Figure 2-1). If you're unlucky, Google tells you that it has nothing in the cache for that page. That doesn't necessarily mean that Google hasn't indexed the page, though.

 A *cache* is a temporary storage area in which a copy of something is placed. In the context of the Web, a cache stores a Web page. Google, MSN/Bing, and Ask.com keep a copy of many of the pages they index, and they all also tell you the date that they indexed the cached pages.

Figure 2-1:
A page
stored in
the Google
cache.

If you don't have the Google toolbar, you can instead go to Google (www. google.com) and type the following into the Google search box:

```
cache:http://yourdomain.com/page.htm
```

Replace *yourdomain.com* with your actual domain name, and *page.htm* with the actual page name, of course. When you click Search, Google checks to see whether it has the page in its cache.

What if Google doesn't have the page? Does that mean your page isn't in Google? No, not necessarily. Google may not have gotten around to caching it. Sometimes Google grabs a little information from a page but not the entire page.

By the way, you can open a cached page saved by Google, Yahoo!, or MSN/ Bing directly from the results page when searching; look for the Cached or Cached Page link after a search result.

You can search for a Web site at Google another way, too. Simply type the domain name into the Google search box and click Search. Google returns that site's home page at the top of the results. (Searching like this through the Google toolbar currently redirects your browser to the specified domain name rather than displaying search results.)

Yahoo! and MSN/Bing

And now, here's a bonus. The search syntax I used to see what Google had in its index for RodentRacing.com — `site:rodentracing.com` — works on not only Google but also Yahoo! and MSN/Bing. That's right, type the same thing into any of these search sites and you see how many pages on the Web site are in the index (though doing this at Yahoo!, of course, gets you the MSN/Bing results because they share the same index). There's one caveat: MSN/Bing's results are a little flaky. For instance, it may initially show, say, 750 results, but as you move through the results pages, MSN/Bing then shows a different number — 546, perhaps. Sometimes that number increases, sometimes it decreases. MSN/Bing has been acting like this for years, so it may — or may not — be fixed at some point. (Yes, Google has the same problem, but not as bad.)

Yahoo! Directory

You should check whether your site is listed in the Yahoo! Directory. You have to pay to get a commercial site into the Yahoo! Directory, so you may already know whether you're listed there. Perhaps you work in a large company and suspect that another employee may have registered the site with Yahoo!. Here's how to find out:

1. **Point your browser to** `dir.yahoo.com`.

   This takes you directly to the Yahoo! Directory search page.

2. **Type your site's domain name into the Search text box.**

   All you need is *yourdomain.com*, not `http://www.` or anything else.

3. **Ensure that the Directory option button is selected and then click Search.**

   If your site is in the Yahoo! Directory, your site's information appears on the results page. You may see several pages, one for each category in which the site has been placed (although in most cases, a site is placed into only one category).

Open Directory Project

You should also know whether your site is listed in the Open Directory Project (`www.dmoz.org`). This is a large directory of Web sites, actually owned by AOL although volunteer run; it's very important, because its data is "syndicated" to many different Web sites, providing you with many links back to your site. (You find out about the importance of links in Chapter 14.)

If your site isn't in the directory, it should be. Just type the domain name, without the www. piece. If your site is in the index, the Open Directory Project will tell you. If it isn't, you'd better register it; see Chapter 12.

Taking Action If You're Not Listed

First, if your site isn't in Yahoo! Directory or the Open Directory Project, you have to go to those systems and register your site. See Chapter 12 for information (including a discussion on whether it's worth the $299 a month for Yahoo!). What if you search for your site in the search engines and can't find it? If the site isn't in Google or MSN/Bing, you have a huge problem.

Here are two possible reasons your site isn't being indexed in the search engines:

- ✔ **The search engines haven't found your site yet.** The solution is relatively easy, though you won't get it done in an hour.
- ✔ **The search engines have found your site but can't index it.** This is a serious problem, though in some cases you can fix it quickly.

For the lowdown on getting your pages indexed in search engines — to ensure that the search engines can find your site — see the section "Getting Your Site Indexed," later in this chapter. To find out how to make your pages search engine–friendly — to ensure that when found, your site will be indexed well — check out the upcoming "Examining Your Pages" section. But first, I tell you how to check whether your site *can* be indexed.

Is your site invisible?

Some Web sites are virtually invisible. A search engine might be able to find the site (by following a link, for instance). But when it gets to the site, it can't read it or, perhaps, can read only parts of it. A client of mine, for instance (before he was a client), built a Web site that had only three visible pages; all the other pages, including those with product information, were invisible.

How does a Web site become invisible? I talk about this subject in more detail in Chapter 7, but here's a brief explanation:

- ✔ The site is using some kind of navigation structure that search engines can't read, so they can't find their way through the site.
- ✔ The site is creating dynamic pages that search engines choose not to read.

Unreadable navigation

Many sites have perfectly readable pages, with the exception that the *search-bots* — the programs search engines use to index Web sites — can't negotiate the site navigation. The searchbots can reach the home page, index it, and read it, but they can't go any further. If, when you search Google for your pages, you find only the home page, this is likely the problem.

Why can't the searchbots find their way through? The navigation system may have been created by using JavaScript, and because search engines mostly ignore JavaScript, they don't find the links in the script. Look at this example:

```
<SCRIPT TYPE="javascript" SRC="/menu/menu.js"></SCRIPT>
```

In one site I reviewed, this was how the navigation bar was placed into each page: The page called an external JavaScript, held in menu.js in the menu subdirectory. Search engines generally won't read menu.js, so they'll never read the links in the script.

Try these simple ways to help search engines find their way around your site, whether or not your navigation structure is hidden:

- **Create more text links throughout the site.** Many Web sites have a main navigation structure and then duplicate the structure by using simple text links at the bottom of the page. You should do the same.

- **Add an HTML sitemap page to your site.** This page contains links to most or all of the pages on your Web site. Of course, you also want to link to the sitemap page from those little links at the bottom of the home page.

Dealing with dynamic pages

In many cases, the problem is that the site is *dynamic* — that is, a page is created on the fly when a browser requests it. The data is pulled from a database, pasted into a Web page template, and sent to the user's browser. Search engines sometimes won't read such pages (though this is nowhere near as serious a problem as it was a few years ago), for a variety of reasons explained in detail in Chapter 7.

How can you tell if this is a problem? Take a look at the URL in the browser's location bar. Suppose that you see something like this:

```
http://www.yourdomain.edu/rodent-racing-scores/march/
        index.php
```

This address is okay. It's a simple URL path made up of a domain name, two directory names, and a filename. Now look at this one:

```
http://www.yourdomain.edu/rodent-racing/scores.php?prg=1
```

The filename ends with `?prg=1`. This *parameter* is being sent to the server to let it know what information is needed for the Web page. If you have URLs like this, with just a single parameter, they're probably okay, especially for Google; however, a few smaller search engines may not like them. Here's another example:

```
http://yourdomain.com/products/index.html?&DID=18&CATID=13
         &ObjectGroup_ID=79
```

This one may be a real problem, depending on the search engine. This URL has too much weird stuff after the filename:

```
?&DID=18&CATID=13&ObjectGroup_ID=79
```

That's three parameters — `DID=18`, `CATID=13`, and `ObjectGroup_ID=79` — and that's too many. Some systems *cannot* or *will not* index this page.

Another problem is caused by *session IDs* — URLs that are different every time the page is displayed. Look at this example:

```
http://yourdomain.com/buyAHome.do;jsessionid=07D3CCD4D9A6A
         9F3CF9CAD4F9A728F44
```

Each time someone visits this site, the server assigns a special ID number to the visitor. That means the URL is never the same, so Google won't index it.

Search engines may choose not to index pages with session IDs. If the search engine finds links that appear to have session IDs in them, it quite likely will not index the referenced page, in order to avoid filling the search index with duplicates.

If you have a clean URL with no parameters, the search engines should be able to get to it. If you have a single parameter in the URL, it's probably fine. Two parameters may not be a problem, although they're more likely to be a problem than a single parameter. Three parameters may be a problem with some search engines. If you think you have a problem, I suggest reading Chapter 7.

Picking Good Keywords

Getting search engines to recognize and index your Web site can be a problem, as the first part of this chapter makes clear. Another huge problem — one that has little or nothing to do with the technological limitations of search engines — is that many companies have no idea what *keywords* (the words people are using at search engines to search for Web sites) they should be using. They try to *guess* the appropriate keywords, without knowing what people are really using in search engines.

In Chapter 5, I explain keywords in detail, but here's how to do a quick keyword analysis:

1. **Point your browser to** `https://adwords.google.com/select/ KeywordToolExternal`.

   You see the Google AdWords Keyword Tool. AdWords is Google's PPC (pay per click) division.

2. **In the search box, type a keyword you think people may use to search for your products or services and then click Search.**

3. **Click the Get Keyword Ideas button.**

   The tool returns a list of keywords, showing you how often that term and related terms are used by people searching on Google and partner sites. See Figure 2-2.

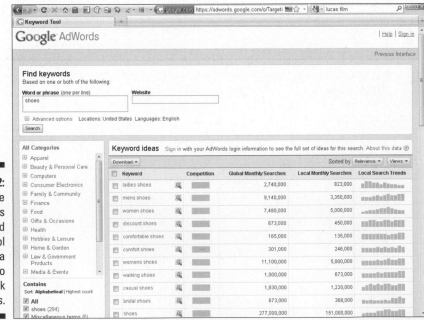

Figure 2-2:
The Google AdWords Keyword Tool provides a quick way to check keywords.

You may find that the keyword you guessed is perfect. Or you may discover better words, or, even if your guess was good, find several other great keywords. A detailed keyword analysis almost always turns up keywords or keyword phrases you need to know about. Just recently, I spoke with someone whose site was ranking really well for his chosen keywords, but he was totally unaware that he was missing some other, very popular, terms.

Don't spend a lot of time on this task right now. See whether you can come up with some useful keywords in a few minutes and then move on; see Chapter 5 for details about this process.

Examining Your Pages

Making your Web pages "search engine–friendly" was probably not uppermost in your mind when you sat down to design your Web site. That means your Web pages — and the Web pages of millions of others — probably have a few problems in the search engine–friendly category. Fortunately, such problems are pretty easy to spot; you can fix some of them quickly, but others are more troublesome.

Using frames

To examine your pages for problems, you need to read the pages' source code. Remember, I said you'd need to be able to understand HTML! To see the source code, choose View➪Source or View➪Page Source in your browser.

When you first peek at the source code for your site, you may discover that your site is using frames. (Of course, if you built the site yourself, you already know whether it uses frames. However, you may be examining a site built by someone else.) You may see something like this on the page:

```
<HTML>
<HEAD>
</HEAD>
    <FRAMESET ROWS="20%,80%">
        <FRAME SRC="navbar.html">
        <FRAME SRC="content.html">
    </FRAMESET>
<BODY>
</BODY>
</HTML>
```

When you choose View⇨Source or View⇨Page Source in your browser, you're viewing the source of the *frame-definition document,* which tells the browser how to set up the frames. In the preceding example, the browser creates two frame rows, one taking up the top 20 percent of the browser and the other taking up the bottom 80 percent. In the top frame, the browser places content taken from the `navbar.html` file; content from `content.html` goes into the bottom frame.

Framed sites don't index well. The pages in the internal frames get *orphaned* in search engines; each page ends up in search results alone, without the navigation frames with which they were intended to be displayed.

Framed sites are bad news for many reasons. I discuss frames in more detail in Chapter 7, but here are a few quick fixes:

✔ Add `<TITLE>` and `DESCRIPTION` tags between the `<HEAD>` and `</HEAD>` tags. (To see what these tags are and how they can help with your frame issues, check out the next two sections.)

✔ Add `<NOFRAMES>` and `</NOFRAMES>` tags between the `<BODY>` and `</BODY>` tags, and place 200 to 300 words of keyword-rich content between the tags. The `NOFRAMES` text is designed to be displayed by browsers that can't work with frames, and search engines will read this text, although they won't rate it as highly as normal text (because many designers have used `<NOFRAMES>` tags as a trick to get more keywords into a Web site, and because the `NOFRAMES` text is almost never seen these days, because almost no users have browsers that don't work with frames).

✔ In the text between the `<NOFRAMES>` tags, include a number of links to other pages in your site to help search engines find their way through.

✔ Make sure every page in the site contains a link back to the home page, in case it's found "orphaned" in the search index.

Looking at the <TITLE> tags

`<TITLE>` tags tell a browser what text to display in the browser's title bar, and they're very important to search engines. Quite reasonably, search engines figure that the `<TITLE>` tags may indicate the page's title — and, therefore, its subject.

Open your site's home page and then choose View⇨Source in your browser to see the page source. A window opens, showing you what the page's HTML looks like. Here's what you should see at the top of the page:

```
<HTML>
<HEAD>
<TITLE>Your title text is here</TITLE>
```

Here are a few problems you may have with your <TITLE> tags:

- **They're not there.** Many pages simply don't have <TITLE> tags. If they don't, you're failing to give the search engines one of the most important pieces of information about the page's subject matter.

- **They're in the wrong position.** Sometimes you find the <TITLE> tags, but they're way down in the page. If they're too low in the page, search engines may not find them.

- **There are *two* sets.** Now and then I see sites that have two sets of TITLE tags on each page; in this case, the search engines will probably read the first and ignore the second.

- **Every page on the site has the same <TITLE> tag.** Many sites use the exact same tag on every single page. Bad idea! Every <TITLE> tag should be different.

- **They're there, but they're poor.** The <TITLE> tags don't contain the proper keywords.

Your <TITLE> tags should be immediately below the <HEAD> tag and should contain useful keywords. Have 40 to 60 characters between the <TITLE> and </TITLE> tags (including spaces) and, perhaps, repeat the primary keywords once. If you're working on your Rodent Racing Web site, for example, you might have something like this:

```
<TITLE>Rodent Racing Info. Rats, Mice, Gerbils, Stoats,
       All Kinds of Rodent Racing</TITLE>
```

Find out more about keywords in Chapter 5 and titles in Chapter 6.

Examining the DESCRIPTION tag

The DESCRIPTION tag is important because search engines may index it (under the reasonable assumption that the description describes the contents of the page) and, in many cases, use the DESCRIPTION tag to provide the site description on the search results page. Thus you might think of the DESCRIPTION tag as serving two purposes: to help with search rank and as a "sales pitch" to convince people viewing the search-results page to click your link.

Open a Web page, open the HTML source (select View↻Source from your browser's menu), and then take a quick look at the DESCRIPTION tag. It should look something like this:

```
<META NAME="description" CONTENT="your description goes
       here">
```

Sites often have the same problems with DESCRIPTION tags as they do with <TITLE> tags. The tags aren't there, are hidden away deep down in the page, are sometimes duplicated, or simply aren't very good.

Place the DESCRIPTION tag immediately below the <TITLE> tags (see Figure 2-3) and create a keyworded description of up to 250 characters (again, including spaces). Here's an example:

```
<META NAME="description" CONTENT="Rodent Racing - Scores,
        Schedules, Everything Rodent Racing. Whether
        You're Into Mouse Racing, Stoat Racing, Rats,
        or Gerbils, We Provide Everything You Need to
        Know about Rodent Racing and Caring for Your
        Racers.">
```

Figure 2-3:
A clean
start to your
Web page,
showing the
<TITLE>
and
DESCRIP-
TION tags.

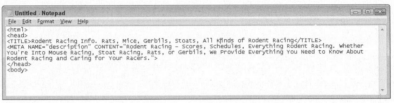

Sometimes Web developers switch the attributes in the tag, putting the CONTENT= before the NAME=, like this:

```
<META CONTENT="your description goes here"
        NAME="description">
```

Make sure that your tags do *not* switch the tag attributes. I don't know whether the order of the attributes causes a problem for Google or the other big search engines (probably not), but it *does* confuse some smaller systems. There's no reason to do it, so don't.

Giving search engines something to read

You don't necessarily have to pick through the HTML code for your Web page to evaluate how search engine–friendly it is. You can find out a lot just by looking at the Web page in the browser. Determine whether you have any text on the page. Page *content* — text that search engines can read — is essential, but many Web sites don't have any page content on the front page and often have little or none on interior pages. Here are some potential problems:

✔ Having a (usually pointless) Flash intro on your site

✔ Creating a totally Flash-based site

✔ Embedding much of the text on your site into images, rather than relying on readable text

✔ Banking on flashy visuals to hide the fact that your site is light on content

✔ Using the wrong keywords (Chapter 5 explains how to pick keywords.)

If you have these types of problems, they can often be time consuming to fix. (Sorry, you may run over the one-hour timetable by several weeks.) The next several sections detail ways you might overcome the problems.

Eliminating Flash

Huh? What's Flash? You've seen those silly animations when you arrive at a Web site, with a little *Skip Intro* link hidden away in the page. Words and pictures appear and disappear, scroll across the pages, and so on. These are Adobe Flash (formerly Macromedia Flash) files.

I suggest that you kill the Flash intro on your site. They don't *hurt* your site in the search engines (unless, of course, you're removing indexable text and replacing it with Flash), but they don't help, either, and I rarely see a Flash intro that actually serves any purpose. In most cases, they're nothing but an irritation to site visitors. (The majority of Flash intros are created because the Web designer likes playing with Flash.) And a site that is nothing but Flash — no real text; everything's in the Flash file — is a disaster from a search engine perspective.

Replacing images with real text

If you have an image-heavy Web site, in which all or most of the text is embedded onto images, you need to get rid of the images and replace them with real text. If the search engine can't read the text, it can't index it.

It may not be immediately clear whether text on the page is real text or images. You can quickly figure it out a couple of ways:

✔ Try to select the text in the browser with your mouse. If it's real text, you can select it character by character. If it's not real text, you simply can't select it — you'll probably end up selecting an image.

✔ Right-click the text, and if you see menu options, such as Save Image and Copy Image, you know it's an image, not text.

Using more keywords

The light-content issue can be a real problem. Some sites are designed to be light on content, and sometimes this approach is perfectly valid in terms of design and usability. However, search engines have a bias for content — that is, for text they can read. (I discuss this issue in more depth in Chapter 9.) In general, the more text — with the right keywords — the better.

Using the right keywords in the right places

Suppose that you do have text, and plenty of it. But does the text have the right keywords? The ones discovered with the Google AdWords Keyword Tool earlier in this chapter? It should.

Where keywords are placed and what they look like is also important. Search engines use position and format as clues to importance. Here are a few simple techniques you can use — but don't overdo it!

- ✔ Use keywords in folder names and filenames, and in page files and image files

- ✔ Use keywords near the top of the page.

- ✔ Place keywords into <H> (heading) tags.

- ✔ Use bold and italic keywords; search engines take note of these.

- ✔ Put keywords into bulleted lists; search engines also take note of this.

- ✔ Use keywords multiple times on a page, but don't use a keyword or key-word phrase too often. If your page sounds really clumsy through over-repetition, it may be too much.

Ensure that the links between pages within your site contain keywords. Think about all the sites you've visited recently. How many use links with *no* key-words in them? They use buttons, graphic navigation bars, short little links that you have to guess at, *click here* links, and so on. Big mistakes.

Some writers have suggested that you should never use *click here* because it sounds silly and people know they're supposed to click. I disagree, and research shows that using the words can sometimes increase the number of clicks on a particular link. However, for search engine purposes, you should rarely, if ever, use a link with only the words *click here* in the link text; you should include keywords in the link.

To reiterate, when you create links, include keywords in the links wherever possible. For example, on your rodent-racing site, if you're pointing to the scores page, don't create a link that says *To find the most recent rodent racing scores, click here* or, perhaps, *To find the most recent racing scores, go to the scores page.* Instead, get a few more keywords into the links, like this: *To find the most recent racing scores, go to the rodent racing scores page.* That tells the search engine that the referenced page is about *rodent racing scores.*

Getting Your Site Indexed

So your pages are ready, but you still have the indexing problem. Your pages are, to put it bluntly, just *not in the search engine!* How do you fix that problem?

For Yahoo! Directory and the Open Directory Project, you have to go to those sites and register directly, but before doing that, you should read Chapter 12. With Google, MSN/Bing, and Ask.com, the process is a little more time consuming and complicated.

The best way to get into the search engines is to have them *find* the pages by following links pointing to the site. In some cases, you can ask the search engines to come to your site and pick up your pages, but you face two main problems with this:

- ✔ If you ask search engines to index your site, they probably won't do it. And if they do come and index your site, doing so may take weeks or months. Asking them to come to your site is unreliable.

- ✔ If you pay search engines to index your site, you have to pay for every URL you submit. The problem with paying, of course, is that you have to pay.

If you want to submit your site to the search engines for indexing, read Chapter 11, where I provide all the details for submitting your site.

So how do you get indexed? The good news is that you can often get indexed by some of the search engines *very* quickly. I'm not talking about a full-blown link campaign here, with all the advantages I describe in Chapters 14 through 16. You simply want to get search engines — particularly Google, MSN/Bing, and Ask.com — to pick up the site and index it.

Find another Web site to link to your site, right away. Call friends, colleagues, and relatives who own or control Web sites, and ask them to link to your site; many people have blogs these days, or even social-networking pages they can link from. Of course, you want sites that are already indexed by search engines. The searchbots have to follow the links to your site.

When you ask friends, colleagues, and relatives to link to you, specify what you want the links to say. No *click here* or company name links for you. You want to place keywords into the link text. Something like *Visit this site for all your rodent racing needs - mice, rats, stoats, gerbils, and all other kinds of rodent racing.* Keywords in links are a powerful way to tell a search engine what your site is about.

By the way, I recommend that you use simple characters in your link text; use a single hyphen to separate words, as I did here, not typographic characters such as em dashes or en dashes.

After the sites have links pointing to yours, it can take from a few days to a few weeks to get into the search engines. With Google, if you place the links right before Googlebot indexes one of the sites, you may be in the index in a few days. I once placed some pages on a client's Web site on a Tuesday and found them in Google (ranked near the top) on Friday. But Google can also take several weeks to index a site. The best way to increase your chances of getting into search engines quickly is to get as many links as you can on as many sites as possible.

You should also create an XML sitemap, submit that to Google and MSN/Bing, and add a line in your `robots.txt` file that points to the sitemap so that search systems — such as Ask.com — that don't provide a way for you to submit the sitemap can still find it. You find out all about that in Chapter 11.

Chapter 3

Beating the Competition : Planning a Powerful Search Engine Strategy

Search Engine Optimization is getting tougher all the time. Not because the techniques are any harder than they used to be (although in a sense, they are — after all, the tricks people used to employ don't work as they did; see Chapter 8), but because it's getting so much more competitive. As more and more people learn about SEO, more and more of your competitors are doing a better and better job at SEO, so it gets harder and harder to compete for those top spots.

There's much to find out about generating traffic from search engines, and sometimes it's hard to see the forest for the trees. As you discover in this book, there are page optimization and link strategies and index submissions and directory submissions and electronic press releases and blogs and this and that — it goes on and on. Before you jump right in, I need to discuss the big picture (to give you an idea of how all this fits together) and help you decide what you should do when (to help you plan your strategy). In this chapter, I show you how a search engine campaign works overall.

Big doesn't always equal better

By the way, don't imagine that just because you're working with a large Web-design team with extensive programming experience, such a team understands search engines. In fact, the more sophisticated design teams are sometimes the ones that get into the most trouble, building complex sites that simply won't work well with search engines. I consult with companies big and small, so I've advised large design teams made up of very good programmers. I can assure you that large, sophisticated teams often know as little about SEO as the independent Web designer who's been in business a few months.

Don't Trust Your Web Designer

Let me start with a warning: Don't rely on your Web designer to manage your SEO project. In fact, I know that many of you are reading this book because you did just that and have realized the error of your ways.

Here's one of the more egregious cases I've run across. The owner of a small e-commerce store came to me for help. He had paid a Web-design firm $5,000 to build his site, and before beginning, he had asked the firm to make sure that the site was search engine–friendly. Unfortunately, that means different things to different people, and to the design firm, it didn't mean much. The site it built definitely was *not* optimized for search engines. The owner asked the firm what it was planning to do about the search engines. It told him that would cost him another $5,000.

This unusual case is more egregious than most, but the first part — that your Web-design firm says it will handle the search engines and then doesn't — is *very* common. When I hire a Web designer to build a site for me, I explain exactly what I want. And you should do the same. (Thus, this book can help you even if you never write a line of HTML code.)

The problem is twofold:

- ✔ Web designers pretty much *have* to say they understand search engines, because all their competitors are saying it.

- ✔ Many Web designers think they *do* understand, but typically, it's at an "add some meta tags and submit to the search engines" level. It won't work.

Sorry, Web designers. I don't want to be rude, but this is a simple fact, attested to by many, many site owners out there. I've seen it over and over again. Not trusting your Web designer or team — even if it claims it knows what it's doing — is probably the first step in your search engine strategy!

Understanding the Limitations

You've probably received spam e-mails guaranteeing top-ten positions for your Web site in the search engines. You've probably also seen claims that you'll be ranked in hundreds or thousands of search engines. Most of this is nonsense — background noise that creates an entirely false picture. As one of my clients put it, "There's a lot of snake oil out there!" Here are the facts.

Typically, getting a high position isn't that easy. You try a couple of techniques, but they don't seem to work. So you try something else, and maybe you achieve a little success. Then you try another thing. Search engine optimization can often be *very* labor intensive, and you may not see results for weeks, and more likely, months.

The degree of work required depends on the competitiveness of the keywords you're going after. Some keywords are incredibly competitive: *mortgage, insurance, attorney, real estate,* and so on are highly competitive, with millions of people wanting some of the action. Other phrases are very easy — such as *rodent racing,* for instance. If you're in the rodent-racing business, you're in luck because you can probably rank right at the top very easily!

Although how search engines function is based on science, search engine optimization is more art than science. Why? Because the search engine companies don't want us to know exactly how they rank sites. You have to just experiment. Ranking a site can be very difficult and tremendously laborious. After all, why should it be easy? There is huge competition, so it *can't* always be easy. If it were easy for your site, then it would be easy for your competitors' sites, wouldn't it? And, after all, there can only ever be one number one.

Top two in four

Sometimes, it's easy to get a very high position in the search systems. For instance, a client wanted to be positioned in Google for six important key phrases. I built some pages, ensured that Google knew where those pages were (find out how to do this in Chapter 11), and waited. In just four days, the client didn't just have a top-ten position or even just a number-one position, but the top *two* positions for five of the six key phrases. But this situation is very unusual. More commonly, the game takes much more work and much more time.

Eyeing the Competition

Some search terms are incredibly competitive. That is, many, many sites are competing for the top positions. Other search terms are far less competitive. How can you tell just how competitive your search terms are? Let me show you a few ways to figure it out:

✔ **Search for your terms.** This is not a terribly good method, but so commonly recommended that I want to explain it. Go to Google and search for a few of your terms. (I discuss keywords in more detail in Chapter 5.) For instance, search for *personal injury lawyer*, and Google reports, under the search box:

```
About 8,930,000 results
```

This tells you that almost 9 million pages in the Google index match the search terms. Actually, most of these pages don't match well. Most of the pages don't actually have the term *personal injury lawyer.* Rather, as explained earlier, they have the words *personal, injury,* and *lawyer* scattered around the page.

✔ **Search for your terms by using quotation marks.** Type search terms in quotation marks, like this: *"personal injury lawyer."* This time, Google searches for the exact phrase and comes back with a different number. When I searched, it came back with 1,820,000 because Google ignores all the pages with the words scattered around the page, and returns only pages with the exact phrase.

Here's the problem with these two techniques: Although they show you how commonly used the words are, they don't show you how well the pages are optimized. Remember, you're not competing against every page with these terms; you're really competing with pages that were optimized for search engines. There may be millions of pages with the term, but if none of them has been optimized, you can take your newfound SEO knowledge, create your own optimized pages, and have a good chance of ranking well.

So here's another quick technique I like to use — a simple way to get a feel for competitiveness in a few seconds. (If you use the Google toolbar, you might want to click the Highlight button so that the words you search for are highlighted in color, not just bolded, on the results page.) Search for a term and then scan down the page looking for the number of

✔ **PPC ads on the page:** For instance, in Figure 3-1 you see search results for the phrase *personal injury attorney.* As you look down the page, you see three PPC ads at the top of the page, and then more ads all the way down the right side of the page. Lots of PPC ads indicate lots of interest in the phrase. If people are spending money on PPC ads, many are also probably spending money on SEO.

✔ **Bold and highlighted words on the page:** You also notice that Google bolds the words that you searched for (and, if you're using Highlight on the Google toolbar, the words are also colored). All the major search sites do this. Lots of bold words often mean well-optimized pages.

✔ **Bold words in the links (page titles):** Bold words in each page result's link indicate that someone has been optimizing the pages. The links are the page titles, so the more bold text you see as you scan down, the more often site owners have been placing the keywords into the `<TITLE>` tags and the more competitive the search terms are likely to be.

✔ **Complete phrases on the page:** The more frequently you see the full phrase you searched for, the more competitive the terms are likely to be. If the search engine returns mostly pages with the words scattered around, it's not very competitive.

Here's another example. Search Google for *rodent engineering*. What do you see? Something similar to Figure 3-2. (Okay, I admit, I've doctored the results just a little to show you what *would* have been displayed had I not muddied the rodent-engineering waters over the last few years by using the term as an example in my books.) First, notice the absence of PPC ads; apparently, nobody's willing to *pay* to rank high for this term!

Figure 3-1: Searching for *personal injury attorney* brings up lots of bold text.

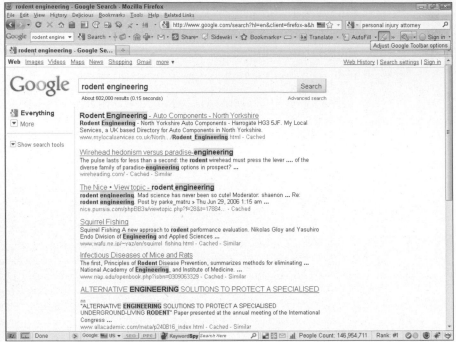

Figure 3-2:
Searching
for *rodent
engineering*
brings up
very little
bold or high-
lighted text.

Next, notice relatively little bold or highlighted text on the page, and just one of the page titles (the links at the top of each search result) contains the full phrase *rodent engineering*. You can see the difference between these two pages. The first search term, *personal injury attorney,* is far more competitive than the second, *rodent engineering.*

How important is competitiveness? When targeting search terms that aren't very competitive, you may be able to create a few optimized pages and rank well. In very competitive areas, though, creating a few nicely optimized pages isn't enough. You *must* have links pointing to the site (perhaps many of them), and you may also need large numbers of pages. In some really competitive areas, it may take hundreds, if not thousands, of links.

Why is my competitor ranking so high?

I get this question all the time. A client points out a competitor's site and asks why the competitor ranks so high. "His site is not even as well optimized as mine, yet he's still above me!" I often hear. And now and then I hear something like, "this guy was nowhere five months ago, and now his site is higher than mine!"

Get your rodent running

Here's an example of how uncompetitive the phrase *rodent engineering* actually is. I created a page optimized for the term and posted it to my Web site (http://Rodent-Engineering. PeterKentConsulting.com). Within a few days, the page was ranked number one on Google for *rodent racing* and has remained there for several years. There you have an example of how quickly things can happen for noncompetitive terms. (In the real world, for competitive terms, things are far more difficult.)

The answer to the "why is my competitor ranking higher" question is almost always that the competitor has done a better job at creating links. So if you are in this situation, do a link analysis on the competitor (see Chapter 15 for information on how to do that). You'll see how many links that site has, what keywords are being used in its links, and what sort of sites it's getting hits from. It's all useful information, and information that will give you an idea at how much link work you have to do.

Going Beyond Getting to #1

Everyone wants to rank #1 for the top keywords. Lawyers want to rank #1 for *attorney* or *lawyer*. Real estate agents want to rank #1 for *real estate*. Shoe stores want to rank #1 for *shoes,* and so on.

But what does being #1 achieve? You're trying to get the right people to visit your Web site, not to get any particular position, right? Getting ranked in search engines is merely a way to generate that qualified traffic to your site. People often assume that to generate traffic, they have to get the #1 position for the top keywords. That's not the case. You can generate plenty of traffic to your site without ever getting to #1 for the most popular phrases. And in many cases, the traffic arriving at your site will be better — the visitors will be more appropriate for your site. To draw the best types of visitors for your site, you have two things to understand: *highly targeted keyword phrases,* and the *search tail*.

Highly targeted keyword phrases

If your keywords are very competitive, look for keywords that aren't so sought after:

✔ **Go local.** One common strategy is, of course, to focus on local keywords. If you're a real estate agent, don't target *real estate*. Instead, target real estate in your area: *Denver realtor, Chicago real estate, Dallas homes for sale,* and so on.

✔ **Focus on more specialized search terms.** A realtor might target traffic on keywords related to commercial real estate, or condos, for instance.

✔ **Incorporate spelling mistakes.** Some realtors target the very common misspelling *realator*, for instance. This technique isn't as effective as it once was, because the search engines adjust for spelling mistakes, but it still works to some degree.

Specialized search terms are hidden away in the search *tail,* so I explain that concept next.

Understanding the search tail

The *search tail* is an important concept to understand. Although the first few top keywords may get far more searches than any other search, when you look at the total number of searches, the top terms actually account for only a small percentage of the searches.

Look at Table 3-1 for search terms taken from Wordtracker, a great little tool that shows what search terms people are typing into search engines. I searched for *video games,* and Wordtracker returned 300 results containing that term. I don't have room for 300, so I show the first few.

Table 3-1	Search Terms for *Video Games*		
		Searches/ Day	Cumulative Searches
1	video games	9,132	9,132
2	music video games	859	9,991
3	adult video games	621	10,612
4	used video games	269	10,881
5	video games xbox	240	11,121
6	video games playstation 2	237	11,358
7	violent video games	230	11,588
8	online video games	229	11,817
9	sex video games	209	12,026
10	free video games	194	12,220

		Searches/ Day	Cumulative Searches
11	history of video games	186	12,406
12	xxx video games	151	12,557
13	video games game cube	145	12,702
14	trade video games	134	12,836
15	violence in video games	128	12,964
16	cheap video games	128	13,092
17	nude video games	103	13,195
18	video poker games	101	13,296

Look at the Searches/Day column. It starts at 9,132 searches per day for *video games,* but immediately drops to 859 for *music video games.* By the time you get to the eighteenth search term, it's down to just 101 searches a day. Position 300 gets only 7 searches a day. This fact leads people to focus on the top phrases, where, it appears, most of the searching is going on.

However, look at the Cumulative Searches column. As you go down the list, you see the total of all searches from position one down to the current position. The first 18 keyword phrases account for 13,296 searches a day, of which 9,132 — 69 percent — are the top phrase *video games.* As you continue down, the cumulative number continues growing, of course. By the time you reach 300, the cumulative number has risen to 18,557, of which only 49 percent is the top phrase.

As you can see from the numbers in Table 3-1 and Figure 3-3, there's this long "tail"; the searches tail off. Wordtracker gave me only the first 300 search phrases; certainly thousands more contain the phrase *video games.*

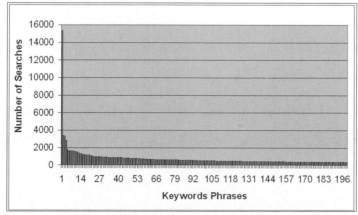

Figure 3-3:
Searches
tail off.

For each phrase, Wordtracker gave an estimate of how often the phrase is searched upon every day. And even in these first 300 searches, most are *not* for the term *video games* but are for phrases *containing* the term *video games.*

There's more, of course. What if you look, for instance, for the term *computer games*? How about *online games*? How about searching for the term *online video games*? You get a completely different set of 300 keyword phrases from Wordtracker.

Thus, if you get matched only with the exact phrase *video games,* you're missing 49 percent of the first 300 phrases, many of which — perhaps most — would be useful to you. Add the thousands of other related phrases, and the primary term becomes less and less important.

It's essential that you understand that most of the action is not at the top; it's in the search tail! This means two things:

- ✐ Even if you can't rank well for a primary term, there's still plenty of room to play.
- ✐ If you focus *only* on a primary term, you're missing most of the action.

Controlling Search Engine Variables

You have control over five basic variables, and a sixth that waits for no man. Everything in this book fits somewhere into one of these six categories:

- ✐ Keywords
- ✐ Content
- ✐ Page optimization
- ✐ Submissions
- ✐ Links
- ✐ Time

Everything you do will be with the intention of affecting in some way one of the first five variables, and as you work, the sixth, time, will keep on ticking. Here's a quick summary of each.

Keywords

As you read in Chapter 5, and as I discuss earlier in this chapter, keywords are incredibly important. They're the very foundation of your search engine strategy. Keywords target searchers. You place keywords in your pages and in links pointing to your pages as bait to attract people to your site. Pick the wrong keywords and you're targeting the wrong people.

Content

Content, from a search engine perspective, really means text, and as you read in Chapter 9, you need content, and a lot of it. Search engines index words, and you want them to index the keywords you're interested in. The more words you have on your site — the more pages of text content — the more times your keywords can appear.

Think of a page of content as a ticket in the lottery: The more pages you have, the more lottery tickets you have. One common SEO strategy is to build huge sites, hundreds of thousands of pages, with vast amounts of text with keywords scattered through. Because of the nature of the search tail explained earlier in this chapter, each page has a chance to match a search now and then. The site has hundreds of thousands of lottery tickets.

You can play the content game a couple of ways:

- ✔ Create thousands of pages and hope that some of the text matches searches now and then.

- ✔ Create pages optimized for specific phrases that you know are used frequently.

Page optimization

Content is just a start. Content has to be placed onto the pages in the correct way; the pages must be *optimized* to get the most out of the keywords. As you read in Chapters 2 and 6, you must place the words onto the pages in the correct places and formats.

If a search engine finds the relevant keywords on your page, that's good. If it finds the keywords in the right places on the page, that's a really powerful thing that differentiates your page from your competitors'.

Submissions

In some ways, *submissions* — submitting information to the search engines; telling them where your pages can be found; and asking them, in effect, to come to your site and index it — aren't as important as many people imagine. This may be one of the biggest scams in the business (a business replete with scams!) — the idea that you have to *submit* your pages to thousands of search engines, when in fact, up until mid-2005, it really didn't matter much. You could submit, but the search engines would quite likely ignore the submission; links are what really counted.

However, in 2005, Google introduced a new concept, the *XML sitemap*, and was quickly followed by Yahoo! and MSN/Bing. This sitemap file is placed into your Web site's root directory containing a list of links to all your pages so that the search engines can more easily find them. (In effect, now, there are two different types of submissions; one, the one many companies are still selling as a service, is still a scam, while the other is essential.)

These days I recommend that you assume that submitting to the search engines will not get you indexed — that the way to get indexed is by making sure that the search engines find links to your site — but that you also provide Google, and MSN/Bing ((no need to worry about Yahoo!, because its data comes from Bing) with the XML sitemap they want so that those search engines can use them if they decide to (they may not). In addition, you'll add a line to your `robots.txt` file so that other search engines, such as Ask. com, can find the sitemap even though you don't submit it to them. You read more about working with the `robots.txt` file in Chapter 11.

Links

Links pointing to your Web site are incredibly important in a competitive keyword market. If you're targeting *rodent engineering,* you probably don't need to worry too much about links (although every site needs at least some incoming links — links pointing to your site from other sites). But if you have lots of competition vying for your keywords, you won't win without links.

Links are so important, in fact, that a page can rank in the first position in any of the three major search engines even if the page doesn't have the keywords that have been searched for — as long as links pointing to the page have the keywords. I explain links with keywords in Chapter 15. The more competitive your area, the more important links become.

Reading history

We don't know exactly how Google handles all this, of course, but you can be fairly sure that Google uses some kind of historical data to help rank pages. In fact, there's even a patent application submitted in the names of various Google employees (although, strangely, without Google's name itself on the patent) that discusses the idea of using historical data. (A long, complicated URL takes you to the patent, so I've provided the link at `www.search enginebulletin.com`.) This document is wonderful bedtime reading if you're looking for a way to get to sleep without drugs. You won't find an explanation of how Google ranks Web pages, but you will find a lot of interesting possibilities.

Time and the Google sandbox

Finally, the one factor you have little control over. You really have control over time only in the sense that the sooner you get started, the older your search engine project becomes. Age is critical because the older the site, the more credibility the search engines give it.

There's something known as the *Google sandbox* or *aging delay*. (Some people will tell you that these are actually two different types of time-related effects.) The idea is that when Google first finds your site, it puts it into a sandbox; it may index it, but it won't necessarily rank it well to begin with. It may take months before the site comes out of the sandbox. (People talk about the *Google sandbox,* but it's likely that, in theory at least, other search engines have something similar.) That's the theory, anyway.

There's a lot of debate about the effect of age; some say it's critical, and that for about eight months your site hasn't a chance of ranking well (I'm not in that camp), and others say that although search engines may take age into account to some degree, it's by no means an overwhelming factor (that's where I sit).

My belief is that if there are time-related weighting mechanisms, even a sandbox of some kind, they are not as powerful as many in the business claim. I've seen sites move upward in the search results very quickly. Time is certainly an issue; it takes time for the search engines to index your pages, it takes time for you to create links to your site, it takes time for the search engines to find the links, and so on. But having seen sites move quickly in some circumstances, I don't worry too much about the "sandbox."

It comes down to this: The longer your domain has been registered, the better, and the longer your site has been up, the better. So you have control over this essential factor in just one way: The sooner you get started, the better. Register your domain name as soon as possible. Get a site, even a few pages, posted as soon as possible, and get links pointing from other sites to your site as soon as you can. Get new content posted as soon as possible. The sooner you start, the sooner you'll start ranking well.

Determining Your Plan of Attack

Now you know what you're facing. As you read in Chapter 1, you can more or less forget those thousands of search sites and focus on no more than five search systems. And, as I explain in this chapter, you have six essential factors to play with: keywords, content, page optimization, links, submissions, and time.

Forget about time — all I'll say is, get started right away! As for the other factors, how do you proceed? It depends to some degree on your budget and the competitiveness of the area you're working in.

- ✔ **Do a keyword analysis.** Regardless of competition or budget, you have to do one. Would you study for an exam without knowing what the exam is about? Would you plan a big meal and then send an assistant to the grocery store without explaining which supplies you need? If you don't do a keyword analysis, you're just guessing; you will definitely fail to pick all the right keywords. See Chapter 5 for the lowdown on how to do this analysis.

- ✔ **Create readable pages.** If you want your site to appear, you have to create pages that the search engine spiders or bots can read. You may be surprised to hear that millions of pages on the Web cannot be read by search engines. For the lowdown on determining whether your pages are being read, see Chapter 2; to find out how to fix the problem if they're not, see Chapters 6 and 7.

- ✔ **Create keyworded pages.** Having readable pages is just a start. Next, you have to put the keywords into the pages — in the right places and in the right format. The more keyworded pages, the better, too. See Chapters 6 and 9 for details.

- ✔ **Consider "Local."** If your business sells locally, rather than Web-wide, you really should read Chapter 10 to find out what you need to do to your site to get it to rank when people search locally.

- ✔ **Register with the search systems.** When your pages are ready to be indexed, you need to do two things:

  - • Let the search systems know where those pages are.

  - • Get the search systems to include the pages in their indexes and directories.

  Sometimes these tasks are harder than you might expect. You can get into the search systems in various ways, as described in detail in Chapters 11 and 12.

- ✔ **Get other sites to link to your site.** Check out Chapters 15 through 17 to find out how the number and type of links pointing to your site affect your rank.

The preceding strategies are the basics, but you may want — or even need — to go further. I cover these additional techniques in detail later:

- ✔ **Register with other places.** You may also want to register at specialized sites that are important for your particular business. See Chapter 13.

- ✔ **Register with the shopping indexes.** If you're selling a product, it's a good idea to register with the product indexes. In fact, most product searches are probably not even carried out through the general search engines, so you really need to read Chapter 17.

But there's more. If you're in a very competitive market, you may want to really push two techniques:

- ✔ **Create large amounts of content.** Make hundreds, perhaps thousands, of pages of content. (It may take a major effort, of course, and months, even years, to make it work.)
- ✔ **Go after links in a big way.** You may need hundreds, perhaps thousands, of links to rank well if your competitors have done the same.

In some cases, you may also want to consider the following techniques:

- ✔ **Social networking.** Twitter, LinkedIn, Facebook, MySpace, and so on. Social networking can be a powerful marketing technique for some businesses. See Chapter 18.
- ✔ **Video.** You can use video in various ways to bring visitors to your site, too, and in some cases to help push your site up in the search ranks. See Chapter 19 for information.

Two Things to Remember

Before I leave this chapter, I want to tell you about two things that are really worth remembering.

The first is that the ideal situation is to have a site that is so useful or cool or wonderful in some way that people naturally link to it. That's really what search engines are looking for, and much of what is done in the SEO field is intended to *simulate* this situation. People find ways to create links to their Web site to make the search engines *think* that the site is so useful or cool or wonderful in some way that thousands of people are linking to it. Of course, the real thing is better than the simulated thing, but quite frankly it's very difficult to pull off. If you're selling ball bearings, just how useful or cool or wonderful can you make your site? There's a limit to anyone's imagination, after all, so you may have to play the simulation game — but keep in mind what the search engines *really* want.

The other thing I want you to know is that a site's position in the rankings has a tendency to bounce around in the search engine field. Your site probably won't be on an arrowlike upward trajectory, constantly improving in its search engine position — rather, it goes up, and it goes down. Here's an example.

I have a client selling industrial equipment who really wanted to rank well for two particular terms (among many others); I'll say phrase A and phrase B. Well, for a long time he was ranked pretty well, near the top of the search results, for both phrases. Then, sometime in the summer of 2007, things got "all shook up." Not just his site but thousands of sites. Google changed something, and continued changing that something over a period of weeks, and people found their search results dropping and then rising and then dropping again. Talk about a roller coaster. . . .

Phrase A dropped like a stone. Once at position #3, it disappeared: It wasn't in the first 100 search results. It was gone for several days and then suddenly reappeared for a few days. Then it disappeared again — in fact, it did this several times, bouncing up and down, sometimes near the very top of the search results and then completely unfindable. Meanwhile, through all this, phrase B remained rock solid, moving up and down, as search results tend to, among the first five results.

Then phrase B disappeared, too, and played the same game for a while. Then both bounced around, and finally everything settled down and both phrases ended up back where they were in the first place. Today, phrase A is in position #2 (right behind Wikipedia) and phrase B is in position #4; in both cases, the site ranks ahead of *all* the competitors (in the second case, the phrase has another meaning, and most of the sites ahead of his are government and education sites, which are often hard to beat).

Now, this sort of fluctuation is terribly frustrating, frightening even. If your business depends on a high rank, any day your rank drops is a bad day! (You can level these fluctuations by getting traffic to your site in other ways, by the way; through PPC advertising, for instance, or affiliate marketing.)

When you drop in the rank, it's tempting to blame yourself (or your SEO consultant); you figure that whatever you last did to the site, that's what caused the problem. But it's very hard to correlate any particular action with a particular increase or decrease in search engine rank. Often when a rank drops, it's because of something that Google has done, not anything you've done. Perhaps Google decides that a certain type of link — reciprocal or paid links (see Chapter 15) — should no longer be of much value. Or perhaps it gives more weight to a particular page tag, or to another form of link. You may have changed something completely different, see your site drop, assume it's because of the action you took, and be totally unaware of the real cause of the drop. In the preceding example, my client decided that he was being punished for creating links in Craigslist.com back to his site — then, later, being punished for *not* creating links in Craigslist.

Sometimes you just have to wait and let the situation settle down, and *keep on keeping on!* Keep on creating well-optimized content, and keep on creating links (and various, different types of links) back to your site. This stuff really does work; you just have to work at it.

This chapter provides an overview of the search engine battle you're about to join. Now it's time to jump in and make it all happen, so Chapter 4 explains what search engines really like to see: Web sites that people on the Internet believe are really useful.

Chapter 4

Making Your Site Useful and Visible

· ·

· ·

*O*bviously, it's important to create Web pages that search engines will read and index, pages that you hope will rank well for important keywords. But if you're going to build a Web site, you need to step back and figure out what purpose the site should serve and how it can accomplish that purpose.

Creating a *useful* site is the key. Even if your sole aim is to sell a product online, the more useful the site is to visitors, the more successful it's likely to be. Take Amazon.com, for instance. It certainly wasn't the first online retailer of books and music, or any of the other products it offers. But one of Amazon's real strengths is that it doesn't just sell products; it's a really *useful* site, in many ways:

✔ It provides tons of information about the products it sells. The information is useful even if you don't buy from Amazon.

✔ You can save information for later. If you find a book you're interested in but don't want to buy right now, save it in your Wishlist and come back next month, next year, or five years from now.

✔ You can read sample chapters, look at tables of contents, listen to snippets of music, and so on.

✔ You can read product reviews from both professional reviewers and consumers.

Would Amazon be so successful if it just provided lists of the products it sells, instead of offering visitors a veritable cornucopia of useful stuff? Absolutely not.

Having done a little consulting work for Amazon, I've spent some time looking at the site from an SEO perspective, and what interests me are the many ways in which Amazon drops keywords into their pages. As you discover elsewhere in this book, keywords on Web pages are a huge part of SEO — and Amazon's pages are scattered with keywords. Take a look at the books pages, for instance, and you'll find the following:

- **Editorial Reviews:** These are descriptions of the book by the publisher, stacked full of keywords related to the subject covered by the book.

- **Customer Reviews:** When someone reviews a book about, say, Search Engine Optimization, they tend to use words related to the subject, such as *websites*, *SEO*, *programming*, *PHP*, *sitemaps*, *link bait*, and so on.

- **Statistically Improbably Phrases:** These are unusual phrases that appear in the book, which makes them great keywords, of course.

- **Capitalized Phrases (CAPs):** A CAP is a list of capitalized phrases in the book (often very relevant keywords).

- **Tags customers associate with this product:** The tag list is essentially a list of keywords that other customers associate with the book.

- **Books on Related Topics:** Other books will often have titles containing relevant keywords.

However, many of these features (and the other useful features on Amazon product pages) were added *without* SEO in mind. Amazon added most of these things to make the site *useful* — SEO was an afterthought. Reviews, for instance, certainly do add keywords to the page, but they also help buyers make a decision (and can dramatically increase *conversion rates* — that is, converting shoppers to buyers). So creating a useful site often serves two purposes: It generates traffic through non–search engine channels *and* it helps your site rank well in search engines.

Consider this: The more useful your site is, the greater the chance of success. The more useful or interesting your site, the more people will talk and blog about it, the more they are likely to "bookmark" it in the social-networking sites (see Chapter 17), the more likely journalists are to write about it, the more likely it is to be mentioned on radio or TV, the more people will link to it from their Web sites, and so on. Search engine marketing and non–search engine marketing are both important because either form of Web site promotion can lead to more links pointing to your site. And, as you find out in Chapters 14 and 15, links to your site are critical to search engine success.

With all these by-products of having a useful Web site in mind, this chapter focuses on the basics about what you need to do to create a successful Web site.

Revealing the Secret but Essential Rule of Web Success

Here's a simple rule to success on the Web:

Make your site useful and then tell people about it.

That's not so complicated, really. Figure out how your site can be useful and then find as many ways as possible to let people know about it. You'll use search engines, of course, but you should be using other methods, too. Remember, search engines are not the only way to get people to your site. In fact, many Web sites have succeeded without using search engines as their primary method of attracting visitors.

Many successful companies have done little or nothing to promote themselves through search engines, yet they still turn up at the top when you search for their products or services. Why? Because their other promotions have helped push them higher in the search engines by creating thousands (even tens or hundreds of thousands) of links to them around the Internet.

The evolving, incorrect "secret"

Over the last 15 years, a number of popular ideas about what makes a successful Web site have been bandied around, and all are wrong to some degree. Here are some of those dated secrets to successful Web sites:

- **Links:** When the Web began booming in 1994, it was all about *links.* You would hear in the press that the secret to a successful Web site was linking to other sites.

- **Cool:** Then people started saying that the secret of success was to make your site *cool.* Cool sites were more entertaining and more likely to attract repeat visitors.

- **Community:** Then people started talking about *community;* yeah, that's the ticket! The secret to a successful Web site was creating a community where people could meet and chat with each other.

- **Content:** Then around 2000, people discovered that the secret was *content.* By putting more stuff, particularly textual information, on your site, you could be more successful.

- **Blogging:** At some point it was decided that the real secret was having a blog on your sites.

- **MySpace, Facebook, and Twitter:** Later, the secret became having associated MySpace, Facebook, and Twitter accounts.

Amazon — Success sans search

It's unlikely that search engines were a large factor in Amazon's success; Amazon grew rapidly mainly because of the enormous press attention it received, beginning in 1994. Today, I'd bet that relatively few people arrive at Amazon.com through search engines. Rather, they already know the Amazon brand and go straight to the site, or they go through the hundreds of thousands of Amazon affiliate sites.

Specific, one-size-fits-all secrets to success never make sense.

The most harmful of the preceding ideas was that your site had to be cool. This silly idea led to the expenditure of billions of dollars on useless but pretty Web sites, most of which (thankfully!) have since disappeared. Unfortunately, some of the *it's-all-about-cool* crowd is still in the Web business and still convincing businesses to spend money on ridiculous, wasteful things, such as Flash intros for their Web sites.

Uncovering the real secret

Ready to hear the real secret of site-creation success? Your Web site has to be *useful*. The problem with the secrets I just mentioned is that they're too specific, leading people to build sites that were in many cases inappropriate. Sure, links are important to directory sites, but they're much less important to the vast majority of Web sites. If you own an entertainment site, you may want to make it cool and entertaining. Certainly, community can be an effective tool, but not every site has to have it. Content is very important, too — especially from a search engine perspective — but many successful Web sites don't have much content. (I talk in more detail about content in the next section because it's a special case.) As for MySpace, at one point it was common knowledge that "if you want to do business online you *have* to have a MySpace site." You don't hear that often today, and it was nonsense back then.

I've been writing this since 1997: *Forget cool; think useful.*

When you're planning your Web site, think about what kinds of folks you want to attract to the site. Then try to come up with ideas about what features and information might be *useful* to them. Your site may end up with a lot of link pages, providing a directory of sorts for people in your industry. Or maybe you really need a cool and entertaining site. Or, if you decide to use discussion groups and chat rooms as a way to build community and pull the crowds into your site, that's fine. Or maybe you decide to create a huge repository of information to attract a particular type of customer. That's okay, too. Maybe your target audience hangs out in MySpace; if so, perhaps you do need a MySpace site. . .and Facebook and Twitter accounts, too. Maybe you do *all* these things. But the important first step is to think about what you can do to make your site more useful.

Showing a bias for content

Content is a special case. Search engines are biased toward ranking content-heavy Web sites well for a couple of reasons:

- ✔ Search engines were originally academic research tools designed to find *text information*. Search engines mostly index text — *content*.
- ✔ Search engines need something to base their judgments on. When you type a term into a search engine, it looks for the words you provided. So a Web site built with few words is at a disadvantage right from the start.

As you discover elsewhere in this book — such as in the discussion of PageRank in Chapter 14 — search engines do have other criteria for deciding if a Web site matches a particular search (most notably the number and type of links pointing to the site). But search engines do have a huge bias toward textual content.

Unfortunately, this bias is often a real problem. The real world simply doesn't work the way search engines see it. Here's an example: Suppose your business rents very expensive, specialized photographic equipment. Your business has the best prices and the best service of any company renting this equipment. Your local customers love you, and few other companies match your prices, service, or product range. So you decide to build a Web site to reach customers elsewhere, and ship rentals by UPS and FedEx.

Search engines base your rank partly on the number and type of keywords in your pages.

To rank well, a competitor has added a bunch of pages about photography and photographic equipment to its site. To compete, you have to do the same. Do your customers care? No, they just want to find a particular piece of equipment that fills their need, rent it, and move on quickly. All the additional information, the content that you've added, is irrelevant to them. It's simply clutter.

This is a common scenario. I once discussed the content issue with a client who was setting up a Web site at which people could quickly get a moving-service quote. The client wanted to build a clean, sparse site that allowed customers to get the quote within a couple minutes. "But we don't want all that stuff, that extra text, nor do our clients!" he told me, and he had a good point.

You can't ignore the fact that search engines like content. However, you can compete in other ways. One of the most important ways is getting links from other sites, as you discover in Chapter 14. Search engines like to see links on other sites pointing to your site. Sites that have hundreds or thousands of other sites linking to them often rank well. But they still need at least *some* content for the search engines to index. And the best situation is to have lots of useful content with lots of incoming links.

Making Your Site Work Well

I've been writing about site design for almost seven years, and I'm happy to say that many of the rules of good site design just happen to match what search engines like. And many of the cool tricks that designers love cause problems with search engines. So I want to quickly review a few tips for good site design that will help both your site visitors and the search engines to work with your site.

Limiting multimedia

Much multimedia used on the Web is pointless because it rarely serves a useful purpose to the visitor. It's there because Web designers enjoy working with it and because many people are still stuck in the old "you've got to be cool" mindset.

Look at the world's most successful Web sites (with the exception of sites such as YouTube.com, of course, which are all about multimedia), and you'll find that they rarely use multimedia — Flash animations and video, for example — for purely decorative purposes. Look at Amazon: Its design is simple, clean, black text on white background, with lots of text and very little in the way of animations, video, or sound (except, for instance, where it provides music samples in the site's CD area and, more recently, videos demonstrating products). Look at Yahoo!, Google, CNN, or eBay — they're not cool; they just get the job done.

You can employ multimedia on a Web site in some useful ways. I think it makes a lot of sense to use Flash, for instance, to create demos and presentations. However, Flash intros are almost *always* pointless, and search engines don't like them because Flash intros don't provide indexable content. Anytime you get the feeling it would be nice to have an animation, or when your Web designer says you should have some animation, slap yourself twice on the face and then ask yourself this: Who is going to benefit: the designer or the site visitor? If that doesn't dissuade you, have someone else slap you.

Using text, not graphics

A surprising number of Web sites use graphics to place text onto pages. Many pages *appear* to have a lot of text, but when you look closely, you see that every word is in an image file. Web designers often employ this technique so that all browsers can view their carefully chosen fonts. But search engines don't read the text in the images they run across, so this page provides *no* text that can be indexed by search engines. Although this page may contain lots of useful keywords (you find out all about keywords in Chapter 5), the search engines read nothing. From a usability perspective, the design is bad, too, because all those images take much longer to download than the equivalent text would take. Avoiding the urge to be too clever

I advise people to stay one step behind in Web technology and try not to be too clever. From a usability standpoint, the problem is that not all browser types work the same; they have different bugs and handle technical tricks differently.

If you're always working with the very latest Web-development technology, more of your visitors are likely to run into problems. Cool technology often confuses search engines, too. As an SEO friend likes to say, "Google likes black text on a white background." In other words, search engines like *simple.* The more complicated your Web pages are, the harder it is for search engines to read and categorize them.

You must strike a compromise between employing all the latest Web-design technology and tools and ensuring that search engines can read your pages. From a search engine perspective, in fact, one step behind probably isn't enough!

Don't be cute

Some sites do everything they can to be cute. The Coca-Cola site was a classic example of this a few years ago, though it finally got the message and changed. The site had icons labeled *Tour de Jour, Mind Candy, Curvy Canvas, Netalogue,* and so on. What do these things mean? Who knows? Certainly not the site visitor.

This sort of deranged Web design is far less common now than it used to be, but you still see it occasionally — particularly in sites designed by hip Web-design firms. One incredibly irritating technique is the hidden navigation structure. The main page contains a large image with hotspots on it. But it's unclear where the hotspots are, or what they link to, until you point at the image and move the mouse around. This strikes me as the Web-design equivalent of removing the numbers from the front of the homes in a neighborhood. You can still figure out where people live; you just have to knock on doors and ask.

Sweet and sickly cuteness doesn't help your site visitors find their way around and almost certainly hurts you with the search engines.

Making it easy to move around

Web design is constantly getting better, but it still surprises me that designers sometimes make it difficult for visitors to move around a Web site.

Think carefully about how your site is structured:

✔ Does it make sense from a visitor's standpoint?

✔ Can visitors find what they need quickly?

✔ Do you have *dangling* or *orphaned* pages — pages where a visitor can't find a link to get back into your main site? Search engines don't like dangling pages, and consider what happens if someone on another site links directly to the page: Visitors can get to the page but not to the rest of your site.

Providing different routes

People think differently from each other, so you need to provide them with numerous avenues for finding their way around your site. And by doing so, you're also giving more information to search engines and ensuring that search engines can navigate your site easily.

Here are some different navigational systems that you can add to your site:

✔ **Sitemap:** This page links to the different areas of your site, or even, in the case of small sites, to every page in the site. See `www.peterkent consulting.com/sitemap.htm` as an example.

✔ **Table of Contents or Index page:** You can sort the page thematically or alphabetically.

✔ **Navigation bars:** Most sites have navigation bars these days.

✔ **Navigation text links:** These are little links at the bottom of your pages, or along the sides, that can help people find their way around — and help the search engines, too.

Using long link text

It's a proven fact that Web users like *long link text* — links that are more than just a single word and actually describe where the link takes you. Usability testing shows that long link text makes it much easier for visitors to find their way around a site. It's not surprising, if you think about it; a long link provides more information to visitors about where a link will take them.

Unfortunately, many designers feel constrained by design considerations, forcing all navigation links, for instance, to conform to a particular size. You often see buttons that have enough room for only ten or so characters, forcing the designer to think about how to say complicated things in one or two words.

Long links that explain what the referenced page is about are a great thing, not only for visitors, but also for search engines. By using keywords in the links, you're telling the search engines what the referenced pages are about.

You also have a problem if all the links on your site are on image buttons. Search engines can't read images, so image buttons provide no information about the referenced page. You can't beat a well-keyworded text link for passing information about the target page to the search engines.

Don't keep restructuring

Try to ensure that your site design is good before you get too far into the process. Sites that are constantly being restructured have numerous problems, including the following:

- ✔ Links from other Web sites into yours get broken, which is bad for potential visitors as well as for search engines (or, more precisely, bad for your position in the search engines because they won't be able to reach your site through the broken links).

- ✔ If you don't restructure carefully, all the pages you have indexed in the search engines may be lost, so you have to start over from the beginning — and it may take weeks or months to get fully reindexed.

- ✔ Anyone who has bookmarked your page now has a broken bookmark.

On the other hand, you can resolve these problems through the use of a 301 redirect; see Chapter 23 for information.

It's a good idea to create a custom 404 error page, which is displayed in your browser if the server is unable to find a page you've requested. (Ask your Web server administrator how to create this page; the process varies among servers.) Create an error page with links to other areas of the site, perhaps even a sitemap, so that if visitors and searchbots can't find the right page, at least they'll be able to reach some page on your site.

Editing and checking spelling

Check your pages for spelling and editing errors. Error-free pages not only make your site appear more professional but also ensure that your valuable keywords are not wasted. If potential visitors are searching for *rodent racing,* for example, you don't want the term *rodint racing* in your Web pages. (Except, that is, if you are trying to catch traffic from oft-misspelled keywords, which I discuss in Chapter 5.)

Ugly doesn't sell

Before I move on, I really have to cover this, um, sensitive subject, because I've run into a lot of people wasting money on SEO that would be better spent on Web design.

You see, I often get e-mails from people saying that they've had their site up "for months now, and haven't sold a thing; can you take a look and tell me why?" I type the URL into my browser, wait for the page to load, and I'm then knocked out of my chair by the unadulterated grotesqueness of the page. (I now keep a pair of very heavily shaded sunglasses — polarized, UV-filtered, glare-protected glacier glasses — for these very cases. If I get a feeling about the site I'm about to see, on go the glasses.)

I don't get it. I know some people are colorblind, but are some ugly blind? Can't they *see* the ugliness? During my phone-consulting sessions, I'll sometimes have to load my client's site into a browser window, load a competitor's site into another window, and ask the client, "Now which site would you rather buy from?" (For example, the site in Figure 4-1 or the site in Figure 4-2?)

Here's the fact: Ugly doesn't sell. By *ugly,* I mean a range of problems:

- Awful color combinations that just don't work
- Terrible typeface choices that make the pages close to unreadable
- Combinations of fonts and colors that make the text close to unreadable — such as white text on black backgrounds (no, it's *not* cool; ask yourself, why do virtually all the world's top Web sites use black text on a white background?)
- Cutesy backgrounds that look. . .cutesy, not professional
- Incredibly clunky images that look as though they were created by an amateur in front of the TV one evening
- Messy page layouts that look amateurish

Figure 4-1:
Would you
buy from
this site . . .

Figure 4-2:
. . .or this
one?

I sometimes help clients build Web sites, but I know my limitations. I'm not a graphic designer and don't pretend to be one; I'll build sites but find an expert to do the graphic design. Way too many people out there have decided to play graphic designer. If you're not one, don't try to act like one.

Having said that, be careful with graphic designers. Too many people in the Web business build beautiful pages that aren't particularly functional, and some of them like to use every graphic design tool in the box, making your site beautiful but unusable.

This is not merely a matter of aesthetics. In fact, I'm not saying that you need a beautiful Web site — just a professional-looking site. The fact is, sites that look unprofessional, as though they were built by a couple of guys who just learned HTML last week after they got home from work in the evenings, have trouble converting visitors to buyers. Would you buy from a site that looks as though it were built by one-handed gnomes? Well, if you wouldn't, why would other people? They don't.

By the way, I do understand that many small businesses have money issues; they can't afford a top professional designer. But there is actually no direct correlation between good Web design and dollars. It's possible to pay very little and get a decent site or to pay a lot and get garbage.

If, thanks to budgetary considerations — you're stone cold broke and plan to pay the designer with food and beer — you have to use Cousin Joe, the fire-man, to create your site, or perhaps your sophomore daughter, Jenny (I've seen both situations), and if Joe or Jenny has, let's say, less-than-adequate design skills, what do you do? Buy some templates! Search online for *Web page templates* and then spend a few hours looking for something nice. Even if you have the slimmest of budgets and have to use a nondesigner to create your site, you still shouldn't settle for bad design.

There's a level below which you must not go. Remember the phrase, "the kingdom was lost for the want of a nail"? Or, "penny smart, pound foolish"? Well, no amount of search engine optimization will make up for bad Web design. You might have the best SEO in the world and rank #1 for all your keywords — but if your visitors land on a dreadful site, all is for naught.

Part II
Building Search Engine–Friendly Sites

The 5th Wave   By Rich Tennant

"Look, I've already launched a search for 'reanimated babe cadavers' three times and nothing came up!"

In this part . . .

Time for the details. In this part, you discover strategies that help your site rank well in search engines — and circumstances that almost guarantee that your site won't do well in search engines. Understand the information in this part and you're way ahead of most Web site owners, designers, and developers.

You begin by learning about keywords, the very foundation of a search-engine campaign. If you don't understand your keywords, you're wasting your time.

You also discover what search engines like to find in your Web pages that are likely to help your site rank well — simplicity, text content with the right keywords, keywords in heading tags and bold text, and so on. You also discover what type of content has the opposite effect, making search engines stumble when they reach your site or even leave the site without reading any pages. From frames to dynamically generated pages to session IDs, these characteristics can be the kiss of death if you're not careful.

I also let you in on a few secrets that search engines hate, techniques that people often use to "trick" the search engines but that can also be dangerous. Many folks in the search engine optimization business shy away from using these techniques for fear of having their pages penalized or entire sites banned from the search engines.

This part shows you how to quickly build the content on your site (content is king as far as the search engines are concerned), and discusses how to make your site appear in *local* searches.

Chapter 5

Picking Powerful Keywords

1 was talking with a client some time ago who wanted to have his site rank well in the search engines. The client is a company with annual revenues in the millions of dollars, in the business of, oh, I don't know . . . staging rodent-racing events. (I've changed the details of this story a tad to protect the client's privacy.)

I did a little research and found that most people searching for rodent-racing events use the keywords *rodent racing.* (Big surprise, huh?) I took a look at the client's Web site and discovered that the words *rodent racing* didn't appear anywhere on the site's Web pages.

"You have a little problem," I said. "Your site doesn't use the words *rodent racing,* so it's unlikely that any search engine will find your site when people search for that."

"Oh, well," was the client's reply, "our marketing department objects to the term. We have a company policy to use the term *furry friend events.* The term *rodent* is too demeaning, and if we say we're racing them, the animal rights people will get upset."

This is a true story; well, except for the bit about rodent racing and the furry friends thing. But, in principle, it happened. This company had a policy not to use the words that most of its potential clients were using to search for it.

You may be asking yourself how a company could possibly build a Web site only to discover later that the keywords its potential clients and visitors are using are not in the site. Well, I can think of a couple of reasons:

✔ Most sites are built without any regard for search engines. The site designers simply don't think about search engines or have little background knowledge about how search engines work.

✔ The site designers do think about search engines, but they guess, often incorrectly, what keywords they should be using.

I can't tell you how the client and I resolved this problem because, well, we didn't. (Sometimes company politics trump common sense.) But in this chapter, I do tell you how to pick keywords that make sense for your site, as well as how to discover what keywords your potential site visitors are using to search for your products and services.

Understanding the Importance of Keywords

When you use a search engine, you type in a word or words and click the Search button. The search engine then looks in its index for those words.

Suppose that you typed *rodent racing*. Generally speaking, the search engine looks for

✔ Pages that contain the exact phrase *rodent racing*

✔ Pages that don't have the phrase *rodent racing* but do have the words *rodent* and *racing* in close proximity

✔ Pages that have the words *rodent* and *racing* somewhere, though not necessarily close together

✔ Pages with word stems; for instance, pages with the word *rodent* and the word *race* somewhere in the page

✔ Pages that have links pointing to them, in which the link text contains the phrase *rodent racing*

✔ Pages with links pointing to them with the link text containing the words *rodent* and *racing,* although not together

The process is actually a lot more complicated. The search engine doesn't necessarily show pages in the order I just listed — all the pages with the exact phrase, and then all the pages with the words in close proximity, and so on. When considering ranking order, the search engine considers (in addition to hundreds of secret criteria) whether the keyword or phrase is in

✔ Bold text

✔ Italicized text

✔ Bulleted lists

✔ Text larger than other text on the page

✔ Heading text (<H> tags)

Despite the various complications, however, one fact is of paramount importance: If a search engine can't relate your Web site to the words that someone searches for, it has no reason to return your Web site as part of the search results.

Picking the right keywords is critical. As Woody Allen once said, "Eighty percent of success is showing up." If you don't play the game, you can't win. And if you don't choose the right keywords, you're not even showing up to play the game. If a specific keyword or keyword phrase doesn't appear in your pages (or in links pointing to your pages), your site *will not* appear when someone enters those keywords into the search engines. For instance, say you're a technical writer in San Diego, and you have a site with the term *technical writer* scattered throughout. You will *not* appear in search results when someone searches for *technical writer san diego* if you don't have the words *San Diego* in your pages. You simply will not turn up.

 Understanding how to search helps you understand the role of keywords. Check out the bonus chapter I've posted at www.SearchEngineBulletin.com to find the different ways you can search by using search engines in general and Google in particular.

Thinking Like Your Prey

It's an old concept: You should think like your prey. Companies often make mistakes with their keywords because they choose based on how they — rather than their customers — think about their products or services. You have to stop thinking that you know what customers call your products. Do some research to find out what consumers really do call your products.

Do a little keyword analysis. Check to see what people are actually searching for on the Web. You'll discover that the words you were positive people would use are rarely searched, and you'll also find that you've missed a lot of common terms. Sure, you may get some of the keywords right; however, if you're spending time and energy targeting particular keywords, you may as well get 'em all right.

The term *keyword analysis* has several meanings:

- ✔ When I use it, I'm referring to what I'm discussing in this chapter — analyzing the use of keywords by people searching for products, services, and information.

- ✔ Some people use the term to mean *keyword-density* analysis — finding out how often a keyword appears in a page. Some of the keyword analysis tools that you run across are actually keyword-density analysis tools.

- ✔ The term also refers to the process of analyzing keywords in your Web site's access logs.

Starting Your Keyword Analysis

Perform a *keyword analysis* — a check of what keywords people use to search on the Web — or you're wasting your time. Imagine spending hundreds of hours optimizing your site for a keyword you think is good, only to discover that another keyword or phrase gets two or three times the traffic. How would you feel? Sick? Stupid? Mad? Don't risk your mental health — do it right the first time.

Identifying the obvious keywords

Begin by typing the obvious keywords into a text editor or word processor. Type the words you've already thought of, or, if you haven't started yet, the ones that immediately come to mind. Then study the list for a few minutes. What else can you add? What similar terms come to mind? Add them, too.

When you perform your analysis, you'll find that some of the initial terms you think of aren't searched very often, but that's okay. This list is just the start.

Looking at your Web site's access logs

Take a quick look at your Web site's access logs (often called *hit logs*). You may not realize it, but most logs show you the keywords that people used when they clicked a link to your site at a search engine. (If your logs don't contain this information, you probably need another program.) Write down the terms that are bringing people to your site.

Examining competitors' keyword tags

You probably know who your competitors are — you should, anyway. Go to their sites and open the source code of a few pages by following these steps:

1. **Choose View⇨Source from the browser's menu bar.**

2. **Look for the** `<META NAME="keywords">` **tag for any useful keywords.**

Often, the keywords are garbage, or simply not there; but, if you look at enough sites, you're likely to come up with some useful terms you hadn't thought of.

Brainstorming with colleagues

Talk to friends and colleagues to see whether they can come up with some possible keywords. Ask them something like, "If you were looking for a site where you could find the latest scores for rodent races around the world, what terms would you search for?" Give everyone a copy of your current keyword list and ask whether they can think of anything to add. Usually, reading the terms sparks an idea or two, and you end up with a few more terms.

Looking closely at your list

After you've put together your initial list, go through it looking for more obvious additions. Don't spend too much time on this; all you're doing here is creating a preliminary list to run through a keyword tool, which figures out some of these things for you.

Obvious spelling mistakes

Scan through your list and see if you can think of any obvious spelling mistakes. Some spelling mistakes are incredibly important, with 10, 15, or 20 percent (sometimes even more) of all searches containing the misspelled word. For example, about one-fifth of all Britney Spears–related searches are misspelled — spread out over a dozen misspellings. I'm not commenting on the intellect of Britney Spears fans . . . It's just a name that could be spelled several ways.

The word *calendar* is also frequently misspelled. Look at the following estimate of how often *calendar* is searched for each day in its various permutations:

calendar: 10,605 times

calender: 2,721

calander: 1,549

calandar: 256

Thirty percent of all searches on the word *calendar* are misspelled. (Where do I get these estimates, you're wondering? You find out later in this chapter in the "Using a Keyword Tool" section.)

If the traffic from a misspelling is significant, you may want to create a page on your site that uses that misspelling. Some sites contain what I call "Did You Mean" pages, such as the one shown in Figure 5-1. Some sites contain pages with misspellings in the `<TITLE>` tags, which can work very well. These don't have to be pages that many people see. After all, the only people who will see the misspelled titles in a search results page are those who misspelled the words in the first place.

One nice thing about misspellings is that competitors often miss them, so you can grab the traffic without much trouble.

Figure 5-1:
A page designed for the spelling challenged.

"But Google recognizes spelling mistakes, doesn't it?" I can hear you thinking. Yes, it does, and it handles them in a couple of ways. In some cases, when Google is pretty sure it that it was a spelling mistake, it goes ahead and searches for the assumed correct spelling and puts a line like this near the top of the page:

```
Showing results for free currency converter. Search
           instead for free currancy converter
```

On the other hand, sometimes Google isn't so sure, and it displays a couple of entries that have the assumed correct spelling, followed by another eight entries that are misspelled.

Synonyms

Sometimes similar words are easily missed. If your business is home related, for instance, have you thought about the term *house*? Americans may easily overlook this word, using *home* instead, but other English-speaking countries use the word *house* more often. Add it to the list because you may find quite a few searches related to it.

You might even use a thesaurus to find more synonyms. However, I show you some keyword tools that run these kinds of searches for you; see the section "Using a Keyword Tool," later in this chapter.

Split or merged words

You may find that although your product name is one word — *RodentRacing*, for instance — most people are searching for you by using two words, *rodent* and *racing*. Remember to consider your customer's point of view.

Also, some words are employed in two ways. Some people, for instance, use the term *knowledgebase,* while others use *knowledge base.* Which is more important? Both should be on your list, but *knowledge base* is used around four to five times more often than *knowledgebase.* If you optimize your pages for *knowledgebase* (I discuss page optimization in Chapter 6), you're missing out on around 80 percent of the traffic!

Singulars and plurals

Go through your list and add singulars and plurals. Search engines treat singulars and plurals differently. For example, searching on *rodent* and *rodents* provides different results; therefore, it's important to know which term is searched for most often. A great example is to do a search on *book* (1,635 searches per day, according to Wordtracker, which I discuss later in this chapter) and *books* (16,475 searches per day) in Google. A search on *book* returns Barnes and Noble as the number-one result, followed by Facebook and then Google Books, whereas *books* returns Google Books, Barnes and Noble, and then Amazon.com.

Don't worry about upper- versus lowercase letters. You can use *rodent* or *Rodent* or *RODENT*, for example. Most search engines aren't case sensitive. If you search for *rodent* (probably 90 percent of all searches are in lowercase), all the major search engines will find *Rodent* or *RODENT* — or *rODENT* or *ROdent,* for that matter.

Hyphens

Do you see any hyphenated words on your list that could be used without the hyphen, or vice versa? Some terms are commonly used both ways, so find out what your customers are using. Here are two examples:

- ✔ The terms *ecommerce* and *e-commerce* are fairly evenly split, with a little over 50 percent of searches using the latter term.

- ✔ The dash in *e-mail* is far less frequently used, with *email* being the most common term.

Find hyphenated words, add both forms to your list, and determine which is more common, because search engines treat them as different searches.

Search engines generally treat a hyphen as a space. So searching for *rodent-racing* is the same as searching for *rodent racing*. However, there is a real difference between *e-commerce* and *ecommerce*, or *rodentracing* and *rodent-racing*.

Geo-specific terms

Is geography important to your business? Are you selling shoes in Seattle or rodents in Rochester? Don't forget to include terms that include your city, state, other nearby cities, and so on. (See Chapter 10 for more on this topic.)

Your company name

If you have a well-known company name, add that to the list, in whatever permutations you can think of (for example, Microsoft, MS, MSFT, and so on).

Other companies' names and product names

If people are likely to search for companies and products similar to yours, add those companies and products to your list. That's not to say you should use these keywords in your pages (you can in some conditions, as I discuss in Chapter 6), but it's nice to know what people are looking for and how often they're looking.

Using a Keyword Tool

After you've put together a decent keyword list, the next step is to use a keyword tool. This tool enables you to discover additional terms you haven't thought of and helps you determine which terms are most important — which terms are used most often by people looking for your products and services.

Both free and paid versions of keyword tools are available. Both the major PPC (Pay Per Click) advertising systems provide keyword-analysis tools, though for MSN/Bing you have to sign up for a PPC account (or at least begin the process; Yahoo!'s PPC system is now run through the MSN/Bing system, *Microsoft adCenter*). For instance, go to `adcenter.microsoft.com` and begin the sign-up process for an MSN/Bing PPC account. (Don't worry, you won't have to pay anything until you get way past the keyword analysis tool.)

You tell Bing where you want to run your ads in the first step, create an ad in the second step, and then, in the third step, you pick your keywords. You see a page similar to that shown in Figure 5-2.

You enter some keywords and then click Next. A screen similar to Figure 5-3 appears.

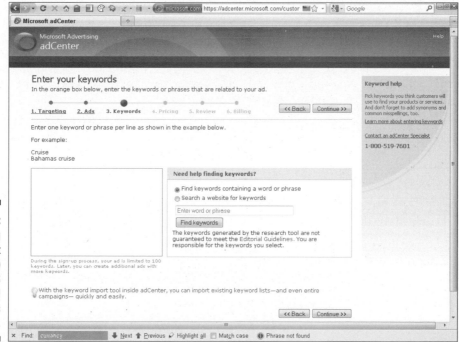

Figure 5-2:
The Bing (Microsoft AdCenter) PPC Keyword Analysis tool.

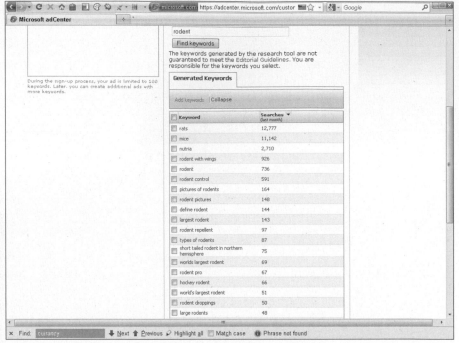

Figure 5-3:
Bing
(Microsoft
AdCenter)
Analysis
tool results.

This screen shows a list of suggested keywords with an estimate of the number of searches for that term in the previous month.

You can go down the list clicking the check boxes next to the keywords you want to use, then click the Add Keywords button at the top of the list to place those keywords into the keywords box top left; you can copy the keywords out of that box if you want.

Using the Free Google Keyword Tool

However, rather than use one of these half-hidden keyword tools from one of the smaller search engines, you can go directly to Google's keyword tool, here: `https://adwords.google.com/select/KeywordToolExternal`. This is a great keyword tool, as long as you understand a couple of things.

First, be aware that unless you sign up for a Google AdWords PPC account, Google doesn't show you all the results; you get only the first 100. You can sign up for an AdWords account (`www.adwords.com`) without running any ads (and thus without paying for anything).

The other thing to understand is exactly what Google is showing you; there's a lot of confusion among users here, so listen closely.

When you first view the Google Keyword tool, you see a page like that shown in Figure 5-4. You have three ways to get started:

✔ Type a keyword into the Word or Phrase box, or type multiple phrases if you like, each on a separate line.

✔ Type the domain name of a Web site into the Website box. Google pulls keywords from this site.

✔ Select a category from the left column.

In effect, you're telling Google to look through its database of searches — actual keywords typed in by real searchers on its Web site and partner sites — to find searches that it thinks may be related to your keyword phrase, the Web site you entered, or the category you picked. Note that you can also click the <u>Advanced options</u> link under the Word or Phrase box to specify criteria even more. You can

✔ Limit the keywords to searches within a particular country or language.

✔ Limit the information to only searches carried out on mobile devices (not including phones with full browsing capabilities — just those with simple Internet data access).

✔ Limit the information to just those keyword phrases that include the actual term you entered. Search for *rodent*, for instance, and Google returns *rodent removal*, *rodent repellant*, and (perhaps) *rodent racing*, but not *rat trap*.

✔ Filter results by using various criteria, such as "global monthly searches over 100,000" or "show low competition keywords only."

For the first two methods, click the Search button, and Google finds keywords related to your search term. (In the case of categories, as soon as you select a lower-level category, Google will provide keywords.)

In the case of the Web site search, Google looks at the words it finds in the Web site and then finds keywords related to those words. Whichever method you choose, you see something like Figure 5-5.

By the way, if the keyword tool seems to "stick," as it does sometimes, just reload the page to get it moving again.

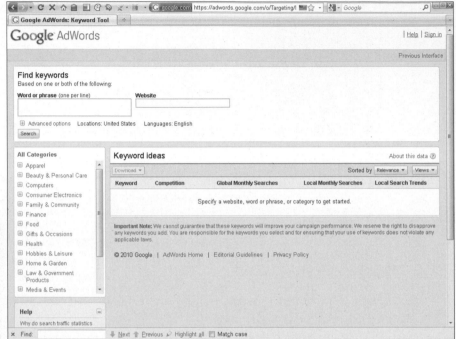

Figure 5-4:
Google's
free
keyword
analysis
tool.

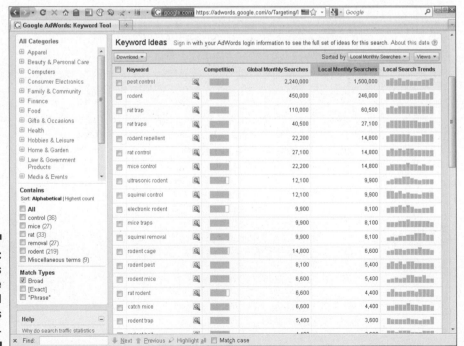

Figure 5-5:
Google's
free
keyword
analysis
tool.

So, Google has returned perhaps 100 keyword ideas — many more if you logged into your AdWords account first — and you can click the column headings to sort them. Figure 5-5 shows the keywords sorted by Local Monthly Searches. (You can add or remove columns, by the way, using the Views button on the right side of the table.)

Now, here's where people get confused. What does this table mean? In Figure 5-5, for instance, it shows the number 1,500,000 in the *pest control* row under Local Monthly Searches. I selected the United States, so does this mean that 1,500,000 searches occur for the term *pest control* in the United States every month?

No. Remember, this is really an AdWords tool, a service intended to help you work with your Google PPC ads. This number is actually the number of searches your ad would match every month if you chose to use the search term *pest control*.

Okay, bear with me; those of you who understand PPC probably already know what I'm getting at, but give me a moment and let me explain. First, a very quick explanation of PPC ads. When an advertiser places a PPC ad into one of the ad systems, such as AdWords, she has to say *when* the ad should run. So, for instance, the ad could be specified to run when someone searches for *rodent racing* or *rodent.* The ad is *matched* to a keyword or group of keywords. (Quick enough?)

Now, notice the Match Type check boxes on the left side of Figure 5-5. These determine how a PPC ad would be matched with a search term:

- **Broad:** This is the default match type. When someone searches for a phrase that Google believes is "similar" or a "relevant variation," the ad is triggered. Broad match keywords can have very unpredictable results because an ad may be triggered by many different searches. For instance, if an ad were triggered by a broad match of *rodent racing,* the ad may be triggered when someone searches for not just *rodent racing* but also *squirrels attic, mice trap,* and *kill rat.* That's pretty darn broad.

- **[Exact]:** Using an Exact match, the keyword phrase triggers the ad only if someone searches for that *exact* phrase. For instance, if an ad is triggered by the keyword phrase *rodent racing* using an Exact match, the ad appears only if someone searches for the exact phrase *rodent racing.*

- **"Phrase":** Using Phrase match, an ad appears when someone searches for the exact phrase, *or* for the exact phrase in combination with other words. For instance, if an ad is set to trigger on the phrase *rodent racing* set to Phrase match, the ad may be triggered when someone searches for *rodent racing scores* (though not for *racing rodent scores*).

Now you can understand what Google is showing you in the Local Monthly Searches column. Where it says 1,500,000 next to *pest control* (with Broad match selected), it means, "If you create an ad to be triggered by a broad match of the term *pest control*, the ad could be triggered as many as 1,500,000 times a month."

That's not the same, of course, as saying that each month there are 1,500,000 searches for the term *pest control*, because there really aren't. Here's how you can tell. Clear the Broad Match check box and select [Exact] match, and Google reloads the list of keywords. (Okay, okay, I know that you want to know why Exact is in square brackets like that; it's because in the AdWords console, when a entering a keyword, you can enclose it in brackets to tell Google it should be used for an Exact match.)

So what happens if you ask Google to give you Exact match numbers for the keywords it provides? You see the number 201,000 next to *pest control* (at least, I did when I tried it just now), which means, "If you use *pest control* as an Exact match to trigger your PPC ads, the ad could be triggered around 201,000 times a month." An Exact match means just that: The ad triggers only for that exact phrase. Google is, in effect, also telling you that 201,000 times a month, someone searches for the term *pest control*. (Someone should track him down and find out why he needs it so badly.)

Sorry, this concept takes a bit of explaining, but it's important. Google's keyword tool is incredibly popular; it's free, and it has the best data — Google data. But most users don't understand what they are looking at, and I don't want you to be included among that crowd.

The Google keyword tool is great. I keep a button on my browser toolbar to take me there whenever I feel a sudden urge for more keywords. Note that you can download the list of keywords, or selected keywords, into a spreadsheet (see the Download button, top left of the table), which is very handy for saving keyword analyses. However, it doesn't have some of the sophisticated keyword-analysis features that other, commercial keyword-analysis tools have . . . so I look at that subject next.

There's currently another, similar, version of the Google keyword tool, by the way, which you can find here: `www.google.com/sktool`.

Using Wordtracker

Wordtracker (`www.wordtracker.com`) is perhaps the most popular commercial keyword tool among SEO professionals.

Wordtracker, owned by a company in London, England, has access to data from a couple of large metacrawlers, and a large British ISP. A *metacrawler* is a system that searches multiple search engines for you. For example, type a word into Dogpile's search box (`www.dogpile.com`), and the system searches at Google, Yahoo!, MSN/Bing, and Ask.com.

Wordtracker's database has around 600 hundred million searches from the last 365 days.

Endorsement disclaimer

I generally don't like endorsing a product; else-where in this book, I mention products and even state that they're good. Wordtracker is a special case. It's been around a long time and is very popular among professionals. It's cheap to use, too, so I recommend that you do so. Disclaimer: I've done a little work for this firm. In fact, you may find some of my writing on the Wordtracker site. However, I mentioned Wordtracker in glowing terms in the first edition of this book, *before* I ever did business with the company.

Wordtracker allows its customers to search this database. Ask Wordtracker how often someone searched for the term *rodent,* and it tells you that it was searched for (at the time of writing) 76 times over the last year but that the term *rodents* is far more popular, with 454 searches over the last 365 days. (Those numbers don't sound like much, especially when compared to numbers that you'll find through Google. But Wordtracker is working with a much smaller database than Google is — 600M or so, compared with over 100 *billion* in Google's monthly dataset. In any case, what really counts are the relative numbers; you want to know which keywords are more popular than others.)

As I show you later, Wordtracker also allows queries using the Google keyword tool to get Google's information, too (though the data is modified slightly).

Remember that certain searches are seasonal: *pools* in the summer, *heaters* in the winter, and so on. In the past, Wordtracker had only the last 100 days of information, so it wasn't representative of a full year for some terms. Now, however, it has a full year, so some terms may be diluted; *christmas tree deco-ration*, over a full year, is less popular a term than it would be if you searched through data from just November and December.

Also, some searches may be influenced by the media. While searches for *paris hilton* were very high in November and December 2003, when I wrote the first edition of this book . . . oh, bad example, they're still absurdly high, unfortu-nately. Okay, here's another example. Early on in a catastrophe, such as an oil rig explosion and spill, searches are very high for a term relating to it (such as *oil spill,* — although nowhere near as high as for *paris hilton* . . . no, really!). But such searches drop off quickly when media coverage has waned.

Here's what information Wordtracker can provide:

- ✔ The number of times in the last year that the exact phrase you enter was searched for out of 600 million or so searches

- ✔ How often phrases *containing* the phrase you entered were searched for

- ✔ Similar terms and synonyms, and the search statistics about these terms

- ✔ Google's search statistics for the keywords
- ✔ Terms used in hundreds of competing sites' KEYWORDS meta tags, ranked according to frequency
- ✔ Common misspellings
- ✔ A comparison of how often a term is searched for with how many pages appear for that term — a nice way to find terms with relatively little competition

Do metacrawlers provide better results? Here's what Wordtracker claims:

- ✔ **Search results at the big search engines are skewed.** Many Web site owners use search engines to check their sites' rankings, sometimes several times a week. Thus, many searches are not true searches. Metacrawlers can't easily be used for this purpose, so they provide cleaner results.

- ✔ **Wordtracker analyzes searches to find what appear to be fake, automated searches.** Some companies carry out hundreds of searches an hour on particular keywords — company or product names, for instance — in an attempt to trick search engines into thinking these keywords generate a lot of interest.

Wordtracker is well worth the price: $59 for a month, or $329 for a year. Anyone heavily involved in the Web and search engines can easily get addicted to this tool.

By the way, here's another reason that some search numbers sound very low on Wordtracker; only 246 searches for *super nanny,* for example? *Primary* terms often are low because most searches are not for primary terms; many searches are for *the super nanny, super nanny show, super nanny on tv,* and other (sometimes bizarre) phrases. Although individual phrases may seem to have low numbers, these combined phrases often add up to a very large number.

Creating a Wordtracker project

Wordtracker allows you to create projects so you can store different groups of terms — perhaps one for each Web site or, if you're a consultant, one for each client. The first thing you do — after plunking down your money and setting up the standard username and password stuff — is create a project. Here's how:

1. **Log in and click the Create a New Project link in the Dashboard.**

2. **In the text box that appears, type a project name and click the Create button.**

You find your projects listed at the bottom of the Dashboard, the page that appears when you log in each time. Simply click a name to open that project (see Figure 5-6). From this page you can

- View the keyword lists currently held in the project.

- Rename the project.

- Delete the project.

- Delete selected keywords from the project.

- Move keywords to another project.

- Add an existing list of keywords to the project; for instance, you can copy a list of words you found through the Google Keywords tool and paste them into the project.

Note that a single project can contain multiple lists; when you save keywords in the Find Keywords tool (which I look at in a moment) or when you import a list of keywords, you have to select which list to place them in. In Figure 5-6, you can see two separate lists, one created from the Google Keywords tool and the other from Wordtracker's Find Keywords tool.

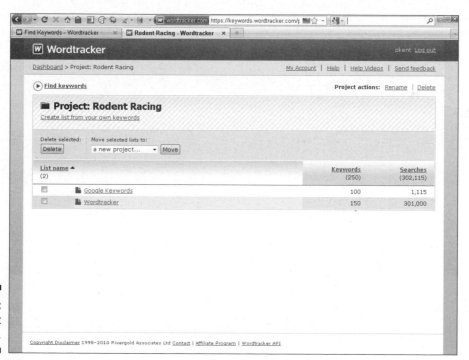

Figure 5-6:
The Project
page.

Most search systems are not case sensitive, so *Rodent* is the same as *rodent*.

Using the Find Keywords tool

To use Wordtracker to search for keywords, follow these steps:

1. **Click the <u>Dashboard</u> link in the "cookie crumb" navigation near the top left of any Wordtracker page.**

   You're taken to the Wordtracker Dashboard page.

2. **Click the <u>Start your keyword research</u> link.**

   You see the page shown in Figure 5-7.

   This page has two areas: the Find Keywords Related To box on the left and the Find Keywords That Include box on the right. (If you don't see the box on the left side, click the Show button on the Related Keywords Tool line.) You can go straight to the Find Keywords That Include box if you want — you don't have to use both — but I look at both methods.

3. **Type a keyword from your list into the search box on the left.**

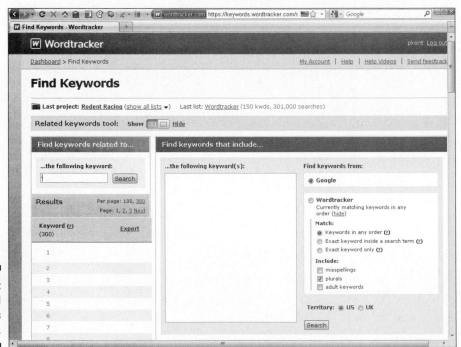

Figure 5-7: The Find Keywords page.

4. Click the Search button.

Wordtracker now looks for 100 Web sites that rank well for the term you entered and grabs keywords from those sites, sorting them by how often the words are found.

After clicking the Proceed button, wait a few minutes while Wordtracker builds a list. Scroll down the left frame to see the list.

5. When you see a keyword you want to work with, click the <u>search</u> link in the left frame next to that word.

You see a small pop-up box with a Search button and a Search & Save button.

6. Click the Search button.

Wordtracker begins searching its database for that keyword. When it finishes, scroll down the Web page, and you see something like what appears in Figure 5-8.

What just happened? Google took the word that you selected in the left box, entered it into the big text box on the right side — the . . . The Following Keyword(s) box — searched its database for that term, and retrieved search terms that *include* the one you selected. For instance, select *racing*, and Wordtracker comes back with *racing*, *racing games*, *summit racing*, *drag racing*, and so on. For each term, it provides a Searches number, which is the number of times the exact term appears in the Wordtracker database — with more than 600 million search terms collected over the last year.

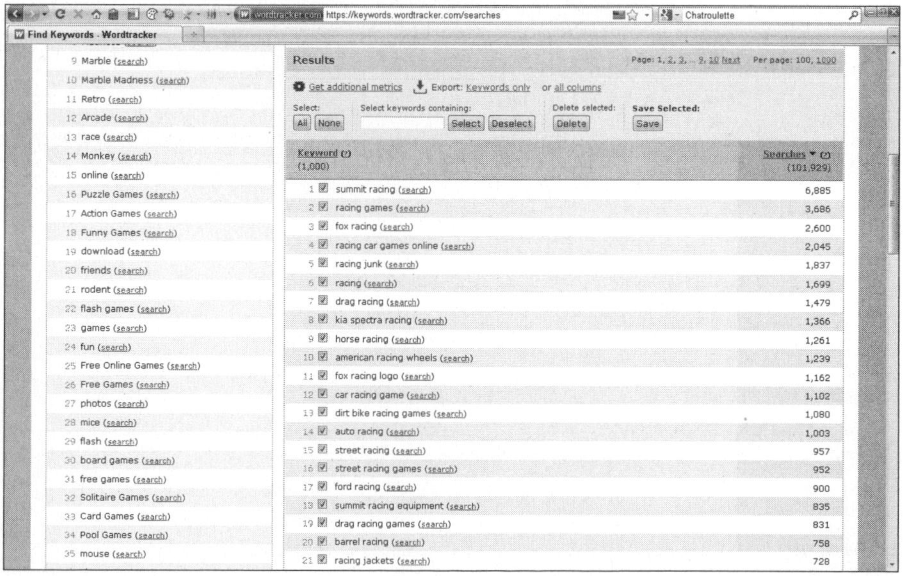

Figure 5-8: Word-tracker searched for phrases containing the keyword you clicked on.

Note that this is not the same as the Google Keyword tool; that tool searches for phrases related to the one you enter, whereas Wordtracker, at this point, searches for phrases that include the one you enter.

Using the Find Keyword search options

You don't have to use the Find Keywords Related To box; you can simply type one or more search terms (on separate lines) into the The Following Keyword(s) box and then click the Search box. But look closely at the right side of the Find Keywords That Include box, and you see a number of options:

- **Google option button:** Wordtracker lets you search the Google database if you prefer. Note, however, that it doesn't return quite the same results as you'd get from the Google Keywords tool directly. First, rather than provide you with keyword phrases related to the terms you provide, as Google does, Wordtracker provides phrases that *include* the terms you provide. Also, Google has different data centers providing these numbers, and each data center may have different data, so if Wordtracker queries a data center different from the one you do when using the Keyword tool, you see different numbers. Finally, note that the returned numbers are, at least at the time of writing, *broad match* numbers. Thus, they are *not* the actual number of searches (as explained earlier in this chapter). Wordtracker may change this technique, because this is clearly misleading. (I've discussed this with Wordtracker, and the company is aware of the issue.) Most Wordtracker users assume that the number returned is the number of searches for the phrase, not the number of searches an ad would match if the keyword phrase were set to broad match, a completely different animal!

- **Wordtracker option button:** Select this, and you get results from the Wordtracker database, which provides several more options.

  - **Keywords in any order option button:** Selected by default, this option button instructs Wordtracker to find search phrases that include the words you provide, in any order; search for *rodent racing,* and Wordtracker retrieves *rodent racing, racing for rodents, rodent racing scores,* and so on.

  - **Exact keywords inside a search term:** Select this, and Wordtracker retrieves only terms that include the exact search term.

  - **Exact keywords only:** With this selected, Wordtracker retrieves search data only for the keywords you entered, not for other search terms that include those keywords.

- • **Include misspellings:** With this box selected, Wordtracker searches for search terms that include misspelled versions of the keywords you provided.

- • **Include plurals:** With this selected, Wordtracker includes search terms that include plural versions of your terms; search for *rodent racing,* and Wordtracker will find *rodents racing worldwide.*

- • **Include adult keywords:** With this selected, Wordtracker includes the naughty search terms.

✔ **Territory — US or UK:** Whether searching the Google or Wordtracker database, you can specify which data to use, the United States or United Kingdom data.

Cleaning up the list

Now that you have your data, what do you do with it? Well, first you scroll through it to see whether the keywords look good to you.

Scroll through this list carefully and look for any keywords that aren't appropriate. Remove only those terms that are totally inappropriate. Don't worry about terms that aren't used much or terms that may be too general. I get to that topic in a moment.

You can use these features to work with your list:

✔ Select individual keywords using the check boxes next to them, or all of them using the Select All button at the top of the list; or remove check marks from all using the Select None button.

✔ Click the Delete button to delete selected keywords that are not useful to you.

✔ Click the <u>Search</u> link next to a keyword to begin a new search using that term. Click <u>Search</u> next to *pet rodents,* for example, to see a smaller list containing *list of pet rodents, best pet rodents, largest pet rodents,* and so on.

✔ Save selected terms into one of your project lists. Click the Save button, select a project, and then select a list within that project or type the name of a new list and click Save again.

Exporting the list

You can also export the keywords. Above the buttons at the top of the list, you see two Export links: <u>Keywords only</u> and <u>all columns</u>. Clicking either will download the keywords (not just the selected keywords, all that remain in the list) to a .csv file, which you can open in a spreadsheet program such as Microsoft Excel.

Performing competitive analysis

By doing a competitive analysis, you can identify terms that are searched for frequently but yield few results. If you then use these keywords on your pages, your pages are more likely to rank high in the search engines because you face little competition from other sites.

To look at competition metrics, click the Get additional metrics link and you see a page on which you can choose to see several more types of data related to each keyword in the report:

- **In Anchor and Title:** For every keyword returned by Wordtracker, you see another column of data that shows the number of Web pages Wordtracker found containing the keyword in the page's <TITLE> tag, *and* in link "anchor text" pointing to the page (see Chapter 14 for a discussion of anchor text). Selecting this option gives you an idea of how competitive the term is; that is, how many people are trying to rank highly for that keyword phrase.

- **KEI:** Wordtracker calculates the *KEI (Keyword Effectiveness Index),* which is a comparison of the number of people searching for a term and the number of Web pages that have links pointing to them that contain the keywords. The higher the KEI, the more powerful the term: There are relatively high searches for the keyword and relatively few matching pages. The formula works like this: KEI = (Searches ^ 2) / In Anchor.

- **KEI3:** A similar metric, KEI3 = Searches / In Anchor And Title. In other words, it divides the number of searches for the keyword by the number of pages containing the keyword in both incoming anchor text and page <TITLE>.

- **Google Count:** Select the Include Google Count check box, and Wordtracker tells you how many pages are returned by Google if you search for the keyword phrase.

- **Quote keywords when searching Google check box:** Wordtracker encloses the keywords in quotation marks when searching Google. As I discuss in Chapter 6, enclosing the term in quotation marks (*"rodent racing",* for instance) tells Google to find only pages containing the exact phrases, which provides a much more useful statistic than finding out how many pages might contain the words spread around in the page. Because searching Google without the quotation marks results in a meaningless number, I advise you to always select this box. When you click the Get Additional Metrics button in the metrics page, Wordtracker retrieves the additional data and places it into the current keyword list. In Figure 5-9, you can see an example of what this would look like; I sorted this data by the KEI3 column (just click a column heading to do that). Remember, a high KEI3 is good; it means relatively high

searches and low competing pages (pages with those keywords in the
<TITLE> tag and links pointing to the page. For instance, in Figure 5-9,
Wordtracker found a single page with the keywords *oma racing* (whatever that is) in the <TITLE> tag and links pointing to the page, and so,
because there were 393 searches, the keyword phrase gets a KEI3 of
393 (393/1).

KEI is not always useful. A term that has few competing pages and is
searched on infrequently can generate a high KEI. This term would
have little benefit to you because although the competition is low, the
number of searches is also low. What's really useful are very popular
keyword phrases with a high KEI.

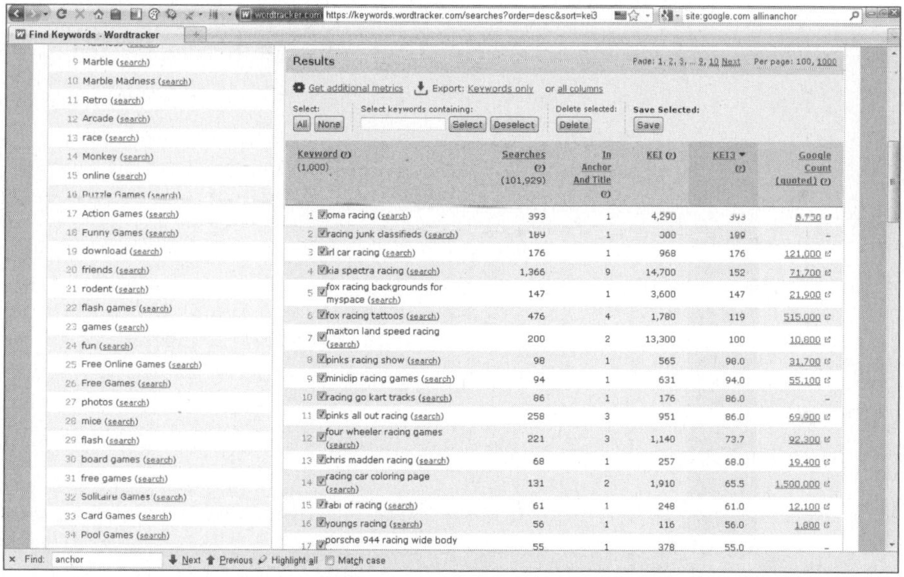

Figure 5-9:
The Find
Keywords
list with
Competition
data
included.

When you've finished working with a keyword tool, look at the final list to
determine how popular a keyword phrase actually is. You may find that many
of your original terms are not worth bothering with. My clients often have
terms on their preliminary lists — the lists they put together without the use
of a keyword tool — that are virtually never used. You also find other terms
near the top of the final list that you hadn't thought about.

Choosing Your Keywords

Cam again? You might be missing the target

Take a look at your list to determine whether you have any words that may have different meanings to different people. Sometimes, you can immediately spot such terms.

One of my clients thought he should use the term *cam* on his site. To him, the term referred to *Complementary and Alternative Medicine.* But to the vast majority of searchers, *cam* means something different. Search Wordtracker on the term *cam,* and you come up with phrases such as *web cams, web cam, free web cams, live web cams, cam, cams, live cams, live web cams,* and so on. To most searchers, the term *cam* refers to *Web cams* — cameras used to place pictures and videos online. The phrases from this example generate a tremendous amount of competition, but few of them would be useful to my client.

Ambiguous terms

A client of mine wanted to promote a product designed for controlling fires. One common term he came up with was *fire control system.* However, he discovered that when he searched on that term, most sites that turned up don't promote products relating to stopping fires. Rather, they're sites related to fire control in the military sense — weapons fire control.

This kind of ambiguity is something you really can't determine from a system that tells you how often people search on a term, such as Wordtracker. In fact, spotting such terms is hard even when you search to see what turns up when you use the phrase. If a particular type of Web site turns up when you search for the phrase, does that mean that people using the phrase are looking for that type of site? You can't say for sure. A detailed analysis of your Web site's access logs may give you an idea; see Chapter 23 for the details.

Very broad terms

Look at your list for terms that are incredibly broad. You may be tempted to go after high-ranking words, but make sure that people are really searching for your products when they type in the word.

Suppose that your site is promoting *degrees in information technology.* You discover that around 40 people search for this term each day, but approximately 1,500 people a day search on *information technology.* Do you think many people searching on *information technology* are really looking for a degree? Probably not. Although the term generates 40,000 to 50,000 searches a month, few of these returns will be your targets.

Here are a couple of reasons to forego a term that's too broad:

- ✔ **Tough to rank.** It's probably a very competitive term, which means ranking well on it would be difficult.

- ✔ **Relevance is elsewhere.** You may be better off spending the time and effort focusing on another, more relevant term.

Picking combinations

Sometimes it's a good idea to target terms lower on your list rather than the ones up top because the lower terms *include* the higher terms.

Suppose that you're selling an e-commerce system and find the following list in Wordtracker:

```
1828        ecommerce
1817        e-commerce
996         shopping cart
482         shopping carts
405         shopping cart software
285         ecommerce solutions
243         ecommerce software
21          ecommerce software solution
13          e-commerce solutions
7           e-commerce software
1           shopping carts and accessories
```

The term *e-commerce* is probably not a great term to target because it's very general and has a lot of competition. But lower on the list is the term *e-commerce solutions*. This term is a combination of two keyword phrases: *e-commerce* and *e-commerce solutions*. If you target *e-commerce solutions* and optimize your Web pages for that term, you're also optimizing for *e-commerce*.

Notice also the term *ecommerce* (which search engines regard as different from *e-commerce*) and the term a little lower on the list, *ecommerce software*. A term even lower encompasses both of these terms — *ecommerce software solution*. Optimize your pages for *ecommerce software solution,* and you've just optimized for three terms simultaneously.

The keyword analysis procedure I describe in this chapter provides you with a much better picture of your keyword landscape. In contrast to the majority of Web site owners, you'll have a good view of how people are searching for your products and services.

Yet More Keyword Tools

Though Wordtracker is probably the most popular keyword-analysis tool on the market, it's certainly not the only one.

Another one is KeywordSpy (http://www.keywordspy.com). This slick-looking system seems to focus primarily on keywords for pay-per-click campaigns, though some of its tools could be useful for organic campaigns, too. It's also a useful competitive-analysis tool, because by tracking PPC ads being run on Google, the system can see what keywords your competitors are bidding on. The data it holds related to organic searches comes from "publicly available information from various sources such as ISPs log files" (Web site traffic logs contain keywords that visitors at the site used to find the site). KeywordSpy also has historical data, so you can see how keyword use may have changed over time.

Yet another keyword-analysis tool is Trellian's Keyword Discovery (http://www.keyworddiscovery.com). This tool gathers data by monitoring searches carried out by 4 million Web users through the use of the Trellian toolbar (http://www.trellian.com/toolbar/) and some kind of "panel" that the site mentions without explaining what it is. One of the nice things about Keyword Discovery is that you can gather research keywords regionally; you can discover what keywords people are using in different areas of the world.

You may also want to check out Wordze (http://www.wordze.com/), an interesting service that provides historical keyword data, information on keywords in links pointing to many comparative sites, and so on.

If you are a real keyword junkie, just do a search for *keyword analysis*; you'll find plenty to keep you busy.

Chapter 6

Creating Pages That Search Engines Love

In This Chapter

▶ Getting your site read

▶ Knowing what search engines see

▶ Understanding keyword concepts

▶ Creating Web pages

▶ Blocking searchbots

*I*n this chapter, you find out how to create Web pages that search engines *really* like — pages that can be read and indexed and that put your best foot forward. Before you begin creating pages, I recommend that you read not only this chapter but also Chapter 7 to find out how to avoid things that search engines hate. There are a lot of ways to make a Web site work, and ways to break it, too. Before you get started creating your pages, you should be aware of the problems you may face and what you can do to avoid them.

I'm assuming that you or your Web designer understand HTML and can create Web pages. I focus on the most important search engine–related things you need to know while creating your pages. It's beyond the scope of this book to cover basic HTML and Cascading Style Sheets.

Preparing Your Site

When you're creating a Web site, the first thing to consider is *where* to put your site. By that, I mean the Web server and the domain name.

Finding a hosting company

Although many large companies place their Web sites on their own Web servers, most small companies don't. They shouldn't do this, in fact, because there's simply no way you can do it anywhere near as cheaply and reliably as a good hosting company can do it. Rather, a hosting company rents space on its servers to other businesses. Although you have to consider many factors when selecting a hosting company, I focus on the factors related to search engine optimization.

When looking for a hosting company, make sure that you can

- **Upload Web pages you created by yourself.** Some services provide simple tools you can use to create Web pages; it's fine if they provide these tools as long as you can also create pages yourself. You must have control over the HTML in your pages.

- **Use the company's traffic-analysis tool or, if you plan to use your own analysis tool, access the raw traffic logs.** A *log-analysis* tool shows you how many people visit your site and how they get there. See Chapter 23 for more information about traffic analysis. (These days many people use Google Analytics, Google's free stats program. As long as you can add a little piece of JavaScript to the bottom of every page, you can use Analytics; see `http://www.google.com/analytics/`.)

You need to consider many issues when selecting a hosting company, most of which aren't directly related to the search engine issue. If you want to find out more about what to look for in a hosting company, I've posted an article about selecting a host on my Web site; find it at `www.SearchEngineBulletin.com`.

Picking a domain name

Search engines read *uniform resource locators (URLs),* looking for keywords in them. For instance, if you have a Web site with the domain name `rodent-racing.com` and someone searches Google for *rodent racing,* Google sees *rodent-racing* as a match; because a dash appears between the two words, Google recognizes the words in the domain name. If, however, you run the words together (*rodentracing*), Google doesn't regard the individual words as individual words; it sees them as part of the same word. That's not to say that Google can't find text *within* words — it can, and you sometimes see words on the search results pages partially bolded when Google does just that — but when ranking the page, Google doesn't regard the word it found inside another word as the same as finding the word itself.

Read the fine print

Several years ago, I recommended that a non-profit client of mine register the *.com* version of its domain name. (The client had been using *.org* for years.) During the few hours that the *.com* domain was not yet pointing to its site, but instead was pointing to the domain registrar's site, the nonprofit received several calls from people trying to get to its Web site. These people wanted to let the company know that something was wrong with its server because its domain name was pointing to the wrong place. For years, the company printed all its materials using *.org*; it had never printed anything with *.com* because it didn't own that domain name; however, people were still trying to get to the *.com* version.

To see this concept in action, use the *allinurl:* search syntax at Google. Type *allinurl:rodent,* for example, and Google finds URLs that contain the word *rodent* (including the directory names and filenames).

So, putting keywords into the domain name and separating keywords with dashes provides a small benefit. Another advantage to adding dashes between words is that you can relatively easily come up with a domain name that's not already taken. Although it may seem as though most of the good names were taken long ago, you can often come up with some kind of keyword phrase, separated with dashes, that's still available. Furthermore, search engines don't care which first-level domain you use; you can use *.com*, *.net*, *.biz*, *.tv*, or whatever; it doesn't matter.

Now, having said all that, let me tell you my philosophy regarding domain names. In the search engine optimization field, it has become popular to use dashes and keywords in domain names, but in most cases the lift provided by keywords in domain names is relatively small, and you should consider other, more important factors when choosing a domain name:

- ✔ **A domain name should be short, easy to spell, and easy to remember.** It should also pass the "radio test." Imagine that you're being interviewed on the radio and want to tell listeners your URL. You want something that's instantly understandable without having to be spelled. You don't want to have to say "rodent dash racing dash events dot com"; it's better to say "rodent racing events dot com."

- ✔ **In almost all cases, you should get the *.com* version of a domain name.** If the *.com* version is taken, do *not* try to use the *.net* or *.org* version for branding purposes! People remember *.com,* even if you say *.org* or *.net* or whatever. So, if you're planning to promote your Web site in print, on the radio, on TV, on billboards, and so on, you need the *.com* version.

A classic example is a situation involving Rent.com and Rent.net. These two different Web sites were owned by two different companies. Rent.net spent millions of dollars on advertising; every time I saw a Rent.net ad on a bus, I had to wonder how much of the traffic generated by these ads actually went to Rent.com! (Rent.net is now out of business — it was bought by Homestore.com — and Rent.com isn't. I don't know whether that's a coincidence!)

Are keyworded domain names worth the trouble? Because the lift provided by keywords in the domain name may be rather small — and, in fact, putting too many keywords into a name can *hurt* your placement — you should probably focus on a single, brandable domain name (a *.com* version).

On the other hand, you might register both versions. For instance, register both Rodent-Racing-Events.com *and* RodentRacingEvents.com. Use Rodent-Racing-Events.com as the primary domain name, the one you want the search engines to see. Then do a 301 Redirect to point RodentRacingEvents.com to Rodent-Racing-Events.com. (See Chapter 23 for information on the 301 Redirect.) That way, you can tell people to go to "rodent racing events dot com" without having to mention the dashes, yet the search engine will regard all links to either domain as pointing to the same site and will see the keywords *rodent* and *racing* in the domain name.

Don't use a domain-forwarding service for Web sites that you want to turn up in search engines. Many registrars now allow you to simply forward browsers to a particular site: A user types *www.domain1.com*, and the registrar forwards the browser to *www.domain2.com*, for instance. Such forwarding systems often use frames (discussed in Chapter 7), which means that search engines don't index the site properly. Your site should be properly configured by using the name server settings, not a simple forward.

Seeing Through a Search Engine's Eyes

What a search engine sees when it loads one of your pages isn't the same as what your browser sees. To understand why, you need to understand how a Web page is created. See Figure 6-1 and read this quick explanation:

1. A user types a URL into his browser or clicks a link, causing the browser to send a message to the Web server asking for a particular page.

2. The Web server grabs the page and quickly reads it to see whether it needs to do anything to the page before sending it.

3. The Web server compiles the page, if necessary.

In some cases, the Web server may have to run ASP or PHP scripts, for instance, or it may have to find an *SSI (server-side include),* an instruction telling it to grab something from another page and insert it into the one it's about to send.

4. After the server has completed any instructions, it sends the page to the browser.

5. When the browser receives the page, it reads through the page looking for instructions and then, if necessary, further compiles the page.

6. When the browser is finished, it displays the page for the user to read.

Here are a few examples of instructions the browser may find inside the file:

- `<SCRIPT>` **tags containing JavaScript scripts or references to scripts stored in other files:** The browser then runs those scripts.

- **Cascading Style Sheets (CSS):** These instructions tell the browser how the page — in particular, the text on the page — should be formatted.

- **References to images or other forms of media:** After the browser finds these references, it pulls them into the page.

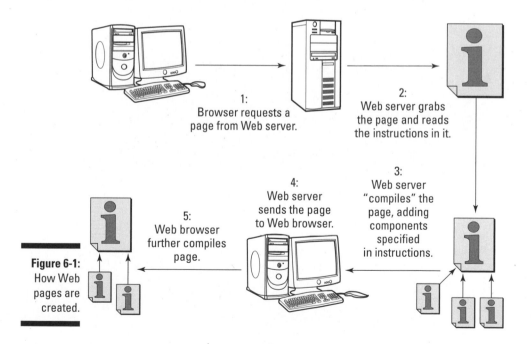

1:
Browser requests a
page from Web server.

2:
Web server grabs
the page and reads
the instructions in it.

3:
Web server
"compiles" the
page, adding
components
specified
in instructions.

4:
Web server
sends the page
to Web browser.

5:
Web browser
further compiles
page.

Figure 6-1:
How Web
pages are
created.

Scripting

ASP and *PHP* scripts are little programs that are written into Web pages. The scripts are read by a program working in association with the Web server when a page is requested. The search-bots see the results of the scripts because the scripts have been run by the time the Web server sends the page. *Server-side includes* *(SSIs)* are simple statements placed into the HTML pages that name another file and, in effect, say to the Web server, "Grab the information in this file and drop it into the Web page here." Again, the searchbots see the information in the SSI because the Web server inserts the information before sending the Web page.

So that's what happens normally when Web pages are created. But *search-bots,* used by search engines to index pages, work differently. When a search-bot requests a page, the server does what it normally does — constructs the page according to instructions and sends it to the searchbot. But the searchbot doesn't follow all the instructions in the page — it just reads the page. For example, it doesn't run scripts in the page, and it doesn't use the Cascading Style Sheet information to format the page.

Thus, you can use two kinds of instructions to build Web pages:

✔ **Server-side instructions:** These instructions, such as ASP and PHP scripts and SSI instructions, are carried out by the server before sending the information to the searchbots.

✔ **Browser-side (or *client-side*) instructions:** These instructions are embedded into the Web page and generally ignored by searchbots. For instance, if you create a page with a navigation system built with JavaScript, the search engines may not be able to read it. (Google may, in some circumstances, read some simple JavaScript; it may, for example, pick up links inside JavaScript. However, if you want to make sure that search engines find content, keep it *outside* JavaScript.) Some people even use browser-side instructions to *intentionally* hide things from search engines.

Of course, an SSI can place browser-side instructions into a page. In this case, although the searchbot sees the instructions — because the server has placed them there — the searchbot ignores the instructions.

These concepts are very important:

Server side = visible to searchbots

Browser side = often not visible to searchbots

Understanding Keyword Concepts

Here's the basic concept of using keywords: You put keywords into your Web pages in such a manner that search engines can find them, read them, and regard them as significant.

Your keyword list is probably very long, perhaps hundreds of keywords, so you need to pick a few to work with. (If you haven't yet developed a keyword list, refer to Chapter 5 for details.) The keywords you pick should be either

✔ Words near the top of the list that have many searches.

✔ Words lower on the list that may be worth targeting because you have relatively few competitors. That is, when someone searches for a keyword phrase by using an exact search in quotation marks (*"rodent racing"* rather than *rodent racing*), the search engine finds relatively few matches.

It's often easy to create pages that rank well for the keywords at the bottom of your list because they're unusual terms that don't appear in many Web pages. However, they're at the bottom of your list because *people don't often search for them!* Therefore, you have to decide whether it's worthwhile to rank well on a search term that's searched for only once or twice a month.

Picking one or two phrases per page

You optimize each page for one or two keyword phrases. By *optimize,* I mean that you create the page in such a manner that it has a good chance of ranking well for the chosen keyword phrase or phrases when someone uses them in a search engine.

You can't optimize a page well for more than one keyword phrase at a time. The <TITLE> tag is one of the most important components on a Web page, and the best position for a keyword is at the beginning of that tag. Remember that you can place only one phrase at the beginning of the tag. (However, sometimes, as you find out in Chapter 5, you can combine keyword phrases — for example, optimizing for *rodent racing scores* also, in effect, optimizes for *rodent racing.*)

Have primary and secondary keyword phrases in mind for each page you're creating, but also consider all the keywords you're interested in working into the pages. For instance, you might create a page that you plan to optimize for the phrase *rodent racing,* but you also have several other keywords that you want to scatter around your site: *rodent racing scores, handicap, gerbil, rodentia, furry friend events,* and so on. Typically, you pick one main phrase for each page and incorporate the other keyword phrases throughout the page, where appropriate.

Place your keyword list into a word processor, enlarge the font, and then print the list and tape it to the wall. Occasionally, while creating your pages, glance at the list to remind yourself which words you need to weave into your pages.

Checking prominence

The term *prominence* refers to where the keyword appears — how prominent it is within a page component (the body text, the <TITLE> tag, and so on). A word near the top of the page is more prominent than one near the bottom; a word at the beginning of a <TITLE> tag is more prominent than one at the end; a word at the beginning of the DESCRIPTION meta tag is more prominent than one at the end; and so on.

Prominence is good. If you're creating a page with a particular keyword or keyword phrase in mind, make that term prominent — in the body text, in the <TITLE> tag, in the DESCRIPTION meta tag, and elsewhere — to convey to search engines that the keyword phrase is important in this particular page. Consider this title tag:

```
<TITLE>Everything about Rodents - Looking after Them,
        Feeding Them, Rodent Racing, and More.</TITLE>
```

When you read this tag, you can see that *Rodent Racing* is just one of several terms the page is related to. The search engine comes to the same conclusion because the term is near the end of the title, meaning that it's probably not the predominant term. But what about the following tag?

```
<TITLE>Rodent Racing - Looking after Your Rodents, Feeding
        Them, Everything You Need to Know</TITLE>
```

Placing *Rodent Racing* at the beginning of the tag places the stress on that concept; search engines are likely to conclude that the page is mainly about rodent racing.

Watching density

Another important concept is *keyword density*. When a user searches for a keyword phrase, the search engine looks at all pages that contain the phrase and checks the *density* — the ratio of the search phrase to the total number of words in the page.

Suppose that you search for *rodent racing* and the search engine finds a page that contains 400 words, with the phrase *rodent racing* appearing 10 times — that's a total of 20 words. Because 20 is 5 percent of 400, the keyword density is 5 percent.

Keyword density is important, but you can overdo it. If the search engine finds that the search phrase makes up 50 percent of the words in the page, it may decide that the page was created purely to grab the search engine's attention for that phrase and thus decide to ignore it. On the other hand, if the density is too low, you risk having the search engines regard other pages as more relevant for the search.

You can get hung up on keyword density, and some people use special tools to check the density on every page. This strategy can be very time consuming, especially for large sites. You're probably better off "eyeballing" the density in most cases.

Here's my rule of thumb: If the phrase for which you're optimizing appears an awful lot, you've overdone it. If the text sounds clumsy because of the repetition, you've overdone it.

Placing keywords throughout your site

Suppose that someone searches for *rodent racing* and the search engine finds two sites that use the term. One site has a single page in which the term occurs; the other site has dozens of pages containing the term. Which site does the search engine think is most relevant? The one that has many pages related to the subject, of course.

Some search engines — such as Google — often provide two results from a site, one indented below the other; which is great, of course, because you are in effect grabbing more search-results "real estate." So if your site has only one page related to the subject, having an indented result can't happen.

To see how this practice works in the real world of search engines, refer to Figure 6-2, which appears a little later in this chapter. You notice that Google provides two pages from the Britney Spears Guide to Semiconductor Physics. (Britney Spears's lectures — on semiconductor physics, radiative and non-radiative transitions, edge-emitting lasers, and VCSELs — are not what she is best known for and are probably of little interest to most of her fans, yet interesting nonetheless.)

In most cases, you're not likely to grab a top position by simply creating a single page optimized for the keyword phrase. You may need dozens, perhaps hundreds, of pages to grab the search engines' attention (with plenty of links between pages and from other sites back to yours — which you find out about in Chapters 14 through 16).

Creating Your Web Pages

When you're creating your Web pages, you need to focus on two essential elements:

- ✔ The underlying structure of the pages
- ✔ The text you plunk down on the pages

The next sections fill you in on what you need to look out for.

Naming files

Search engines get clues about the nature of a site from its domain name as well as from the site's directory and file structure. The added lift is probably not large, but every little bit counts, right? You might as well name directories, Web pages, and images by using keywords.

For example, rather than create a directory named /events/, you could name it /rodent-racing-events/. Rather than have a file named gb123. jpg, you can use a more descriptive name, such as rodent-racing-scores.jpg. Don't have too many dashes in the file and directory names, though, because overdoing it may cause search engines to ignore the name.

You should separate keywords in a name with dashes, but *not* with underscores, despite what your Web designer may tell you. Try this test: Search Google for *rodent-racing* and then for *rodent racing,* and you'll notice that the results are almost the same (with perhaps just a very slight difference). Now try searching for *rodent_racing.* When I tried, Google returned 8 results, compared with 214,000 results for *rodent-racing.* Clearly, Google regards *rodent_racing* as a single word. Don't let anyone tell you that you should be using underscores rather than dashes in file and directory names — it's simply not true!

Creating directory structure

First, let me explain a common belief in the SEO business: It may be a good idea to keep a *flat* directory structure in your Web site. That is, keep your pages as close to the root domain as possible, rather than have a complicated multilevel directory tree. Create a directory for each navigation tab and keep all the files in that directory.

Many observers believe that search engines downgrade pages that are lower in the directory structure. This effect is probably small, but the theory is that you're better off using a structure with fewer sublevels than with more. For instance, the first page that follows, according to this theory, would be weighted more highly than the second page:

```
http://www.domainname.com/page.html
```

```
http://www.domainname.com/dir1/dir2/dir3/dir4/page.html
```

However, a flat directory structure is probably not terribly important. Matt Cutts of Google (see Chapter 22) claims that the directory structure doesn't matter to Google, the single most important search engine, of course. And sometimes it's nice to use a directory structure to add a few keywords to the URL to tell the search engines what the page is about. For instance, you might have the following in a real estate site:

```
http://www.domain.com/real-estate/colorado-homes-for-sale/
           denver-county/lakewood.html
```

Don't use too may hyphens, though; a few here and there are okay (I have three in the second directory name), but overdoing it might cause problems.

Viewing <TITLE> tags

Most search engines use the site's <TITLE> tag as the link and main title of the site's listing on the search results page, as shown in Figure 6-2.

<TITLE> tags tell a browser what text to display in the browser's title bar and are very important for search engines as well. Searchbots read page titles and use that information to determine what the pages are about. If your <TITLE> tags have a keyword between them that competing pages don't have, you have a good chance of getting at or near the top of the search results.

The <TITLE> tag is one of the most important components as far as search engines are concerned. However, these tags are usually wasted because few sites bother placing useful keywords in them. Titles are often generic: *Welcome to Acme, Inc.,* or *Acme Inc. – Home Page.* Such titles are not beneficial for search engine optimization.

I searched at Google for *intitle:welcome* to find out how many pages have the word *welcome* in their <TITLE> tags. The result? Around 40 million! Around 2 million have *welcome to* in the title (*allintitle:"welcome to"*). Having *Welcome to* as the first words in your title is a waste of space — only slightly more wasteful than your company name! Give the search engines a really strong clue about your site's content by using a keyword phrase in the <TITLE> tags. Here's how:

This text comes from between the page's <TITLE></TITLE> tags

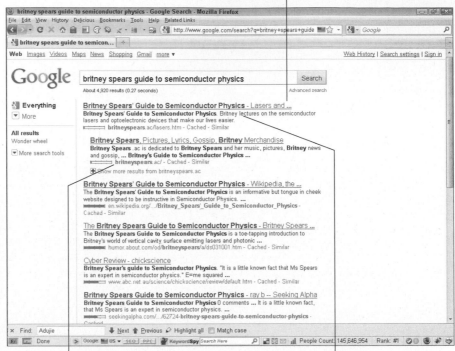

Figure 6-2:
Search
results from
Google,
showing
where
components
come from.

This is the page's URL

This text is often the meta description text

1. **Place your** <TITLE> **tags immediately below the** <HEAD> **tag.**

2. **Place 40 to 60 characters between the** <TITLE> **and** </TITLE> **tags, including spaces.**

3. **Put the keyword phrase you want to focus on for this page at the beginning of the** <TITLE> **tag.**

   If you want, you can repeat the primary keywords once. Limit the number of two-letter words and very common words (known as *stop words*), such as *as, the,* and *a,* because search engines ignore them.

Here's a sample <TITLE> tag:

```
<TITLE>Rodent Racing Info. Rats, Mice, Gerbils, Stoats,
        All Kinds of Rodent Racing</TITLE>
```

(By the way, I am aware that a stoat is not, strictly speaking, a rodent, but it looks quite rodenty to me, and I'm sure someone races them.)

Although the title tag is used as the link on the search-results page, it will be truncated if it's too long. On Google, for instance, depending on spacing between words, the title may be truncated to around 55–65 characters, and have an ellipsis (. . .) displayed at the end of the line; that is, *Rodent Racing Info. Rats, Mice, Gerbils, Stoats, All Kinds of Rodent Racing* may be displayed as *Rodent Racing Info. Rats, Mice, Gerbils, Stoats, All Kinds of Rodent. . .*, so make sure you get the important words that you want to be visible on the search-results page into those first 55 or so characters.

Also, use title case (capitalizing the initial letter of each word, as in Rodent Racing Info. Rats, Mice, Gerbils, Stoats, All Kinds of Rodent Racing, not Rodent racing info. rats, mice, gerbils, stoats, all kinds of rodent racing). Title case is much easier for people to read as they scan down the page.

The <TITLE> tag and often the DESCRIPTION tag (explained in the next section) appear on the search results page, so both these tags should encourage people to visit your site.

Using the DESCRIPTION meta tag

Meta tags are special HTML tags that you can use to carry information, which browsers or other programs can then read. When Internet search engines were first created, Webmasters included meta tags in their pages to make it easy for search engines to determine what the pages were about. Search engines also used these meta tags when deciding how to rank the page for different keywords.

The DESCRIPTION meta tag describes the Web page to the search engines. Search engines use this meta tag in two ways:

✔ They read and index the text in the tag and, in some circumstances, use it to figure out a page's relevance to a search term. (Google claims it *doesn't* use the tag for page ranking, but other search engines may.)

✔ In many cases, they use the text verbatim in the search results page. That is, if your Web page is returned in the search results page, the search engine may grab the text from the DESCRIPTION tag and place it under the text from the <TITLE> tag so that the searcher can read your description.

Now, this process can vary between search engines, and over time for the same search engine. Until sometime in 2007, in most cases Google *didn't* use the text from the DESCRIPTION meta tag in its search results page. Rather, Google grabbed a *snippet* (a block) of text near where it found the search keywords on the page and then used that text in the results page. However, Google changed the manner in which it gathers the search-results description text. At the time of this writing, here's how it works:

✔ If, in the DESCRIPTION tag, Google finds all keywords you entered in the search query, it uses the DESCRIPTION tag text.

✔ If Google finds some of the keywords in the DESCRIPTION tag and some in the body of the Web page, it uses part of the DESCRIPTION tag text and part of the body text.

✔ If Google finds none of the words in the DESCRIPTION tag, it grabs a snippet or two of text from the body of the page.

The DESCRIPTION meta tag is pretty important, so you should definitely use it. Think of it as serving two purposes:

✔ It's a page-ranking tool, helping, in some search engines, the page to rank higher on the search-results page.

✔ It's a "sales pitch," seen by people viewing the search engine's search-results page; it should encourage people to click the link.

As is the <TITLE> tag, the DESCRIPTION is truncated; in Google search results, the text will be truncated to around 140 or 150 characters. For instance, here's the description tag from Payless.com:

```
Find New Styles at Great Prices. Shop DSW Shoes Online
       with Free Shipping for DSW Rewards members.
       1000s of Women's Shoes, Men's Shoes, Boots,
       Sandals and more.
```

And here's how it appears in the Google search results:

Find New Styles at Great Prices. Shop DSW *Shoes* Online with Free Shipping for DSW Rewards members. 1000s of Women's *Shoes*, Men's *Shoes*, Boots, ...

So if you want part of the text to be seen, make sure it appears before that 140th-or-so character. You can have a longer description and get a few more keywords in there, but don't make it too long; perhaps 170–200 characters maximum (including spaces). Place the DESCRIPTION tag immediately below the <TITLE> (opening and closing) tags. Here's an example:

```
<META NAME="description" CONTENT="Rodent Racing - Scores,
       Schedules, Everything Rodent Racing. Mouse
       Racing, Stoat Racing, Rat Racing, Gerbil
       Racing. The Web's Top Rodent Racing Systems and
       Racing News">
```

As with the <TITLE> tag, title case is also a good thing; title case makes the DESCRIPTION text easier to read. Duplicating your most important keywords once is okay, but don't overdo it or you'll upset the search engines. Don't, for instance, do this:

```
<META NAME="description" CONTENT="Rodent Racing, Rodent
        Racing, Rodent Racing, Rodent Racing, Rodent
        Racing, Rodent Racing, Rodent Racing, Rodent
        Racing, Rodent Racing, Rodent Racing">
```

Overloading your `DESCRIPTION` (or any other page component) with the same keyword or keyword phrase is known as *spamming* (a term I hate, but hey, I don't make the rules), and trying such tricks may get your page penalized; rather than *help* your page's search engine position, it may cause search engines to omit it from their indexes.

Sometimes Web developers switch the attributes in the tag: `<META CONTENT="your description goes here" NAME="description">` for instance, rather than `<META NAME="description" CONTENT="your description goes here">`. Make sure that your tags don't do the former because some search engines choke on such tags.

By the way, you should consider your `DESCRIPTION` tag to be not only a search engine component but also a sales tool. Remember that much of the tag — perhaps the first 150 to 160 characters — will quite likely be seen in the search results (especially the Google search results), so you want to use text that encourages people to click the link — text that helps your links stand apart from the others on the page. An example is a compelling sales message or your phone number, which helps build credibility by ensuring that people recognize that it's a real site and not some search engine spam result! (Using a phone number also has the effect of making your listing stand out a little; the eye "trips" over changes in the pattern, such as numbers and capitalized words.) You might also want to think about your site's Unique Selling Proposition (USP). What makes your site special compared to others — a huge selection? Free shipping? Remember, this is a sales pitch to get people to click, so think about how you can do that.

Tapping into the KEYWORDS meta tag

The `KEYWORDS` meta tag was originally created as an indexing tool; that is, a way for the page author to tell search engines what the page is about by listing (yep) keywords. Although quite important many years past, this meta tag isn't so important these days. Some search engines may use it, but many don't, and even those that do use it don't give it much value. (Google and MSN/Bing almost certainly don't use it. Ask.com probably does, but again, it doesn't give it much weight.) Still, you might as well include the `KEYWORDS` meta tag. You do have a list of keywords, after all.

Don't worry too much about the tag — it's not worth spending a lot of time over. Here are a few points to consider, though:

- ✔ **Limit the tag to 10 to 12 words.** Originally, the KEYWORDS tag could be very large, up to 1,000 characters. These days, many search engine observers are wary of appearing to be spamming search engines by stuffing keywords into any page component, so these observers recommend that you use short KEYWORDS tags.

- ✔ **You can separate each keyword with a comma and a space.** However, you don't have to use both — you can have a comma and no space, or a space and no comma.

- ✔ **Make sure that most of the keywords in the tag are also in the body text.** If they aren't, the tag probably won't do you any good. Many people also use the KEYWORDS tag as a good place to stuff spelling mistakes that are commonly searched.

- ✔ **Don't use a lot of repetition.** You shouldn't do this, for instance: *Rodent Racing, Rodent Racing, Rodent Racing, Rodent Racing, Rodent Racing, Rodent Racing,* or even *Rodent Racing, Rodent Racing Scores, Rodent Racing, Gerbils, Rodent Racing Scores, Rodent Racing. . . .*

- ✔ **Don't use the same** KEYWORD **tag in all your pages.** You can create a primary tag to use in your first page and then copy it to other pages and move terms around in the tag.

Here's an example of a well-constructed KEYWORD tag:

```
<META NAME="keywords" CONTENT="rodent racing, racing
            rodents, gerbils, mice, mouse, raceing, mouse,
            rodent races, rat races, mouse races, stoat,
            stoat racing">
```

Using other meta tags

What about other meta tags? Sometimes if you look at the source of a page, you see all sorts of meta tags, as shown in Figure 6-3 (in bold to make seeing them easier). Meta tags are useful for various reasons, but from a search engine perspective, you can forget most of them. (And most meta tags really aren't of much use for any purpose.)

```
<meta name="resource-type" content="document">
<meta http-equiv="pragma" content="no-cache">
<meta name="revisit-after" content="1">
<meta name="classification" content="Arts and Crafts">
<meta name="description"
content="New York Alive! Photographs is an online gallery containing dozens of signed, original, custom-
printed black and white photographs of New York City, its landmarks, buildings, neighborhoods, people,
and places.  Buy original images for home or office direct from the photographers.">
<meta name="keywords"
content=" New York City, New York, New York NY, NYC, skyline, landmarks, buildings, Manhattan,
Brooklyn, neighborhood, neighbourhood, neighborhoods, neighbourhoods, photography, fine, fine art, art,
artist, artists, artistic, arts, photo, photographic, photographs, photograph, photographer, photographers,
pictures, black, black and white, white, images, imagery, image, gallery, galleries, virtual, online, on-line,
exhibits, exibits, exhibition, exhibitions, exhibit, contemporary, Central Park, Greenwich Village, Soho,
Wall Street, Statue of Liberty, Harlem, Washington Heights, Lower East Side, Ethnic, Empire State
Building, Flatiron, Flat Iron, Building, Chrysler, Brooklyn Bridge, Wall Street, New York Stock Exchange,
Chinatown, Little Italy, Yankees, people">
<meta name="robots" content="ALL">
<meta name="distribution" content="Global">
<meta name="rating" content="General">
<meta name="copyright" content="(c) Naomi Diamant, 2000. All rights reserved.">
<meta name="author" content="Abacus Consultants">
<meta http-equiv="reply-to" content="abacusconsultants@yahoo.com">
<meta name="language" content="English">
<meta name="doc-type" content="Public" ">
<meta name="doc-class" content="Completed">
<meta name="doc-rights" content="Copywritton Work">
```

Figure 6-3:
Examples of
meta tags
you gener-
ally don't
need.

You've heard about DESCRIPTION and KEYWORDS meta tags, but also of relevance to search engine optimization — though not always useful — are the REVISIT-AFTER and ROBOTS meta tags:

✔ REVISIT-AFTER tells search engines how often to reindex the page. Save the electrons; don't expect search engines to follow your instructions. Search engines re-index pages on their own schedules.

✔ ROBOTS blocks search engines from indexing pages. (I discuss this topic in detail later in this chapter.) But many Web authors use it to *tell* search engines to index a page. Here's an example:

```
<META NAME="robots" CONTENT="ALL">
```

This tag is a waste of time. If a search engine finds your page and wants to index it, and hasn't been blocked from doing so, it will. And if the search engine doesn't want to index the page, it doesn't. Telling the search engine to do so doesn't make a difference.

Here's a special Google meta tag that you can use in a couple of ways:

```
<META NAME="googlebot" CONTENT="nosnippet">
```

This meta tag tells Google not to use the description *snippet,* the piece of information it grabs from within a Web page to use as the description; instead, it uses the DESCRIPTION meta tag. However, this tag, at least at the time of writing, may be rather redundant because Google isn't usually using a snippet (as explained earlier in this chapter); also, this tag has the effect of removing the page from Google's cache (the saved version of an indexed Web page; you'll see <u>cached</u> links under entries in the search-results page).

Here's another example:

```
<META NAME="googlebot" CONTENT="noarchive">
```

This meta tag tells Google not to place a copy of the page into the cache. If you have an average corporate attorney on staff who doesn't like the idea of Google storing a copy of your company's information on its servers, you can tell Google not to.

These Google meta tags may work, but many users report that sometimes they don't.

Including image ALT text

You use the <IMG> tag to insert images into Web pages. This tag can include the ALT= attribute, which means *alt*ernative text. ALT text was originally displayed if the browser viewing the page couldn't display images. ALT text is also used by programs that "speak" the page (for individuals without sight). In many browsers, ALT text also appears in a little pop-up box when you hold your mouse over an image for a few moments. (If you use Firefox, you can install an add-on called Popup ALT Attribute to make it happen.)

ALT attributes are also read by search engines. Why? Because these tag "attributes" offer another clue about the content of the Web page. How much do ALT tags help? Perhaps not so much these days, because some Web designers have abused the technique by stuffing ALT attributes with tons of keywords. But using ALT attributes can't hurt (assuming that you *don't* stuff them with tons of keywords, but rather simply drop in a few here and there) and may even help push your page up a little in the search engine rankings.

You can place keywords in your ALT attributes like this:

```
<IMG SRC="rodent-racing-1.jpg" ALT="Rodent Racing - Ratty
          Winners of our Latest Rodent Racing Event">
```

It's definitely a good idea to use ALT attributes on image links, by the way. Doing so gives Google an idea of what the page referenced by the link is about.

Adding body text

You need text in your page. How much? More than a little, but not too much. Maybe 200 to 400 words is a good range. Don't get hung up on these numbers, though. If you put an article in a page and the article is 1,000 words, that's fine, and some pages may not have much text at all. But in general, when building a page that you want people to find in the search engines, a number in the 200–400 word range is good. That amount of content allows you to really define what the page is about and helps the search engine understand what the page is about.

Keep in mind that a Web site needs content in order to be noticed by search engines. (For more on this topic, see Chapter 9.) If the site doesn't have much content for the search engine to read, the search engine will have trouble determining what the page is about and may not properly rank it. In effect, the page loses points in the contest for search engine ranking. Certainly, placing keywords in content is not all there is to being ranked in search engines; as you find out in Chapters 14 through 16, for instance, linking to the pages is also very important. But keywords in content are very significant, so search engines have a natural bias toward Web sites with a large amount of content.

This bias toward content could be considered very unfair. After all, your site may be the perfect fit for a particular keyword search, even if you don't have much content in your site. In fact, inappropriate sites often appear in searches simply because they have a lot of pages, some of which have the right keywords.

Suppose that your rodent-racing Web site is the only site in the world at which you can buy tickets for rodent-racing events. Your site doesn't provide a lot of content because rodent-racing fans simply want to be able to buy tickets and nothing more. However, because your site has less content than other sites, it is at a disadvantage to sites that have lots of content related to rodent racing, even if these other sites aren't directly related to the subject. (On the other hand, if rodent-racing fans throughout the world decide that your site is *the* one on which to buy tickets, and enough of them link to you, you can still rank well regardless of how much page content you have.)

You can't do much to confront this problem, except to add more content (or create a lot of links)! You can find some ideas on where to get content in Chapter 9, and read all about links in Chapters 14 through 16.

Creating headers: CSS versus <H> tags

Back when the Web began, browsers defined what pages looked like. A designer could say, "I want body text here and a heading there and an address over there," but the designer had no way to define what the page actually looked like. The browser decided. The browser defined what a header looked like, what body text looked like, and so on. The page might appear one way in one browser program and another way in a different program.

These days, designers have a useful tool available to them: *Cascading Style Sheets (CSS)*. With CSS, designers can define exactly what each element should look like on a page.

Now, here's the problem. HTML has several tags that define headers: <H1>, <H2>, <H3>, and so on. These headers are useful in search engine optimization because when you put keywords into a heading, you're saying to a search engine, "These keywords are so important that they appear in my heading text." Search engines pay more attention to them, weighing them more heavily than keywords in body text.

But many designers have given up on using the <H> tags and rely solely on CSS to make headers look the way they want them to. The plain <H> tags are often rather ugly when displayed in browsers, so designers don't like to use them. <H> tags also cause spacing issues; for example, an <H1> tag always includes a space above and below the text contained in the tag.

However, there's no reason you can't use both <H> tags *and* CSS. You can use style sheets in two basic ways:

✔ Create a style class and then assign that class to the text you want to format.

✔ Define the style for a particular HTML tag.

Many designers do the former; they create a style class in the style sheet, as in the following example:

```
.headtext { font-family: Verdana, Arial, Helvetica, sans-
        serif; font-size: 16px; font-weight: bold;
        color: #3D3D3D }
```

Then they assign the style class to a piece of text, like this:

```
<DIV CLASS="headtext">Rodent Racing for the New
        Millennium!</div>
```

In this example, the headtext class makes the text appear the way the designer wants the headings to appear. But, as far as search engines are concerned, this is just normal body text.

A better way is to define the <H> tags in the style sheets, as in the following example:

```
H1 {
font-family: Verdana, Arial, Helvetica, sans-serif;
font-size: 16px;
font-weight: bold;
color: #3D3D3D
}
```

Now, whenever you add an <H1> tag to your pages, the browser reads the style sheet and knows exactly which font family, size, weight, and color you want. It's the best of both worlds — you get the appearance you want, and search engines know it's an <H1> tag. (Note to Web designers who don't want to listen: Don't take my word for it . . . even Google recommends that you use <H> tags.)

Formatting text

You can also tell search engines that a particular word might be significant in several other ways. If the text is in some way different from most of the other text in the page, search engines may assume that it has been set off for some reason, that the Web designer has treated it differently because it *is* in some way different and more significant than the other words.

Here are a few things you can do to set your keywords apart from the other words on the page:

- Make the text **bold.**
- Make the text *italic.*
- Use title case (uppercase the First Letter in Each Word and lowercase the other letters in the word).
- Put the keywords in bullet lists.

For each page, you have a particular keyword phrase in mind; this is the phrase for which you use the preceding techniques.

Another way to emphasize the text is to make a piece of text larger than the surrounding text. (Just make sure that you do this in a way that doesn't look tacky.) For example, you can use <H> tags for headers but also use slightly larger text at the beginning of a paragraph or for subheaders.

Creating links

Links in your pages serve several purposes:

- ✔ They help searchbots find other pages in your site.
- ✔ Keywords in links tell search engines about the pages that the links are pointing at.
- ✔ Keywords in links also tell search engines about the page containing the links.

You need links into — and out of — your pages. You don't want *dangling* or *orphan* pages — pages with links into them but no links out. All your pages should be part of the navigation structure. It's also a good idea to have links within the body text, too.

Search engines read link text for not only clues about the page being referred to but also hints about the page containing the link. I've seen situations in which links convinced a search engine that the page the links pointed to were relevant for the keywords used in the links, even though the page didn't contain those words. The classic example was an intentional manipulation of Google, late in 2003, to get it to display George Bush's bio (`www.white house.gov/president/gwbbio.html`) when people searched for the term *miserable failure*. This was done by a small group of people using links in blog pages. Despite the fact that this page contained neither the word *miserable* nor the word *failure,* and certainly not the term *miserable failure,* a few dozen links with the words *miserable failure* in the link text were enough to trick Google. (After several years, Google put a stop to the *miserable failure* situation, but the principle still works. I discuss this Googlebomb in Chapter 14.)

So when you're creating pages, create links on the page to other pages, and make sure that other pages within your site link back to the page you're creating, using the keywords you placed in your `<TITLE>` tag.

Don't create simple Click Here links or You'll Find More Information Here links. These words don't help you. Instead, create links like these:

> For more information, see our *rodent-racing scores page*.
>
> Our *rodent-racing background page* provides you with the information you're looking for.
>
> Visit our *rat events* and *mouse events* pages for more info.

Links are critical. Web developers have played all sorts of tricks with keywords — overloading `<TITLE>` tags, `DESCRIPTION` tags, `ALT` attributes, and so on — and all these tricks are well known to search engines and don't do much good any more. Search engines constantly look for new ways to analyze and index pages, and link text is a good way for them to do that.

In Chapters 15 through17, you find out about another aspect of links: getting links from other sites to point back to yours.

Using other company and product names

Here's a common scenario: Many of your prospective visitors and customers are searching online for other companies' names or for the names of products produced or sold by other companies. Can you use these names in your pages? Yes, but be careful *how* you use them.

Many large companies are aware of this practice, and a number of lawsuits have been filed that relate to the use of keywords by companies other than the trademark owners. Here are a few examples:

- A law firm that deals with Internet domain disputes sued Web-design and Web-hosting firms for using its name, Oppedahl & Larson, in their KEYWORDS meta tags. These firms thought that merely having the words in the tags could bring traffic to their sites. The law firm won. Duh! (Didn't anyone ever tell you not to upset large law firms?)

- Playboy Enterprises sued Web sites that were using the terms *playboy* and *playmates* throughout their pages, site names, domain names, and meta tags to successfully boost their positions. Not surprisingly, Playboy won.

- Insituform Technologies, Inc. sued National Envirotech Group after discovering that Envirotech was using its name in its meta tags. Envirotech lost. The judge felt that using the name in the meta tag without having any relevant information in the body of the pages was clearly a strategy for misdirecting people to the Envirotech site.

So, yes, you can get sued. But then again, you can get sued for anything. In some instances, the plaintiff loses. Playboy won against a number of sites, but lost against former playmate Terri Welles. Playboy didn't want her to use the terms *playboy* and *playmate* on her Web site, but she believed she had the right to, as a former Playboy Playmate. A judge agreed with her. The real point of the Terri Welles case is that nobody owns a word, a product name, or a company name. They merely own the right to use it in certain contexts. Thus, Playboy doesn't own the word *playboy* — you can say "playboy," and you can use it in print. But Playboy owns the right to use the word in certain contexts and to stop other people from using it in those same contexts.

If you use product and company names to mislead or misrepresent, you could be in trouble. But you can use the terms in a valid, nonfraudulent manner. For instance, you can have a product page in which you compare your products to another, named competitor. That's perfectly legal. No, I'm not a lawyer, but I'm perfectly willing to play one on TV, given the opportunity. And I would bet that you won't be seeing the courts banning product comparisons on Web sites.

If you have information about competing products and companies on your pages, used in a valid manner, you can also include the keywords in the <TITLE>, DESCRIPTION, and KEYWORDS tags, as Terri Welles did:

```
<META NAME="keywords" CONTENT=" terri, welles, playmate,
         playboy, model, models, semi-nudity, naked,
         censored by editors, censored by editors,
         censored by editors, censored by editors,
         censored by editors, censored by editors,
         censored by editors, censored by editors">
```

And there's nuthin' Playboy can do about it.

What's ironic is that firms are being sued for putting other companies' names and brand names in their KEYWORDS tags, when it has very little influence on search engine rank these days.

Creating navigation structures that search engines can read

Your navigation structure needs to be visible to search engines. As I explain earlier in this chapter, some page components are simply invisible to search engines. For instance, a navigation structure created with JavaScript doesn't work for search engines. If the only way to navigate your Web site is with the JavaScript navigation, you have a problem. The only pages search engines will find are the ones with links pointing to them from other Web sites; search engines can't find their way around your site.

Here are a few tips for search engine–friendly navigation:

- ✔ If you use JavaScript navigation or another technique that's invisible (which is covered in more detail in Chapter 7), make sure that you have a plain HTML navigation system, too, such as basic text links at the bottom of your pages.

- ✔ Even if your navigation structure is visible to the search engines, you may want to have these bottom-of-page links as well. They're convenient for site visitors and provide another chance for the search engines to find your other pages.

  Yet another reason for bottom-of-page, basic text navigation: If you have some kind of image-button navigation, you don't have any keywords in the navigation for the search engines to read.

✔ Add a sitemap page and link to it from your main navigation. It provides another way for search engines to find all your pages.

✔ Whenever possible, provide keywords in text links as part of the navigation structure.

Blocking searchbots

You may want to block particular pages, or even entire areas of your Web site, from being indexed. Here are a few examples of pages or areas you may want to block:

✔ Pages that are under construction

✔ Pages with information intended for internal use (You should probably password-protect that area of the site, too.)

✔ Directories in which you store scripts and CSS style sheets

Using the ROBOTS meta tag or the robots.txt file, you can tell search engines to stay away. The meta tag looks like this:

```
<META NAME="robots" CONTENT="noindex, nofollow">
```

This tag does two things: *noindex* means "Don't index this page" and *nofollow* means "Don't follow the links from this page."

To block entire directories on your Web site, create a text file called robots.txt and place it in your site's root directory — which is the same directory as your home page. When a search engine looks at a site, it generally requests the robots.txt file first; that is, it requests http://www.domainname.com/robots.txt.

The robots.txt file allows you to block specific search engines and allow others, but Webmasters rarely do so. In the file, you specify which search engine (user agent) you want to block and from which directories or files. Here's how:

```
User-agent: *
Disallow: /includes/
Disallow: /scripts/
Disallow: /info/scripts/
Disallow: /staff.html
```

Because User-agent is set to *, all searchbots are blocked from www.domainname.com/includes/, www.domainname.com/scripts/, www.domainname.com/info/scripts/ directories, and the www.domainname.com/staff.html file. (If you know the name of a particular searchbot that you want to block, replace the asterisk with that name.)

Be careful with your `robots.txt` file. If you make incomplete changes and end up with the following code, you've just blocked all search engines from your entire site:

```
User-agent: *
Disallow: /
```

In fact, this technique is sometimes used nefariously; I know of one case in which someone hacked into a site and placed the `Disallow: /` command into the `robots.txt` file — and Google dropped the site from its index!

Google now has a nice little `robots.txt` test tool in its Webmasters Console; see Chapter 11 for more information.

Chapter 7

Avoiding Things That Search Engines Hate

In This Chapter

▶ Working with frames and iframes

▶ Creating a readable navigation system

▶ Avoiding problems with Flash and images

▶ Reducing page clutter

▶ Dealing with dynamic Web pages

*I*t is possible to look at your Web site in terms of its search engine friendliness. (Chapter 6 of this book does just that.) It is equally possible, however, to look at the flip side of the coin — the things people often do that hurt their Web site's chances with search engines, and in some cases even making their Web sites invisible to search engines.

This tendency on the part of Web site owners to shoot themselves in the foot is very common. In fact, as you read through this chapter, you're quite likely to find things you're doing that are hurting you. Paradoxically, serious problems are especially likely for sites created by mid- to large-size companies using sophisticated Web technologies.

Steering you clear of major design potholes is what this chapter is all about. Guided by the principle *First Do No Harm*, the following sections show you the major mistakes to avoid when setting up your Web site.

Dealing with Frames

Frames were very popular a few years ago, but they're much less so these days, I'm glad to say. A *framed* site is one in which the browser window is broken into two or more parts, each of which holds a Web page (as shown in Figure 7-1).

Figure 7-1:
A framed
Web site;
each frame
has an indi-
vidual page.
The scroll
bar moves
only the
right frame.

Frame 1 contains
navigational links.

Frame 2 contains
content pages.

Frames cause a number of problems. One problem is that many designers create framed sites without properly testing them. They build the sites on large, high-resolution screens, so they don't realize that the sites would be almost unusable on smaller, low-resolution screens. That's less of a problem these days, but there are still significant search engine problems.

From a search engine perspective, frames create the following problems:

✔ **Search engines index individual pages, not framesets.** Each page is indexed separately, so pages that make sense only as part of the frame-set end up in the search engines as independent pages — *orphaned* pages, as I like to call them. (Jump ahead to Figure 7-2 to see an example of a page, indexed by Google, that belongs inside a frameset.)

✔ **You can't point to a particular page in your site.** This problem may occur in the following situations:

• *Linking campaigns (see Chapters 14 through 16):* Other sites can link only to the front of your site; they can't link to specific pages.

• *Pay-per-click campaigns:* If you're running a *pay-per-click (PPC)* campaign, you can't link directly to a page related to a particular product.

• *Indexing products by shopping directories (see Chapter 13):* In this case, you need to link to a particular product page.

Refraining

Here's how Google responded to a question about frames from the technical editor of the first edition of this book, Micah Baldwin, of the blog Current Wisdom:

"Google does support frames to the extent that it can. Frames can cause problems for search engines because frames don't correspond to the conceptual model of the Web. In this model, one page displays only one URL. Pages that use frames display several URLs (one for each frame) within a single page. If Google determines that a user's query matches the page as a whole, it will return the entire frameset. However, if the user's query matches an individual frame within the larger frameset, Google returns only the relevant frame. In this case, the entire frameset of the page will not appear."

Google often does just that — return a page pulled out of its frame; the page is, in effect, "orphaned."

Search engines index URLs — single pages, in other words. By definition, a framed site is a collection of URLs, and search engines therefore can't properly index the pages.

The HTML Nitty-Gritty of Frames

Here's an example of a *frame-definition*, or *frameset*, document:

```
<HTML>
<HEAD>
</HEAD>
<FRAMESET ROWS="110,*">
<FRAME SRC="navbar.htm">
<FRAME SRC="main.htm">
</FRAMESET>
</HTML>
```

This document describes how the frames should be created. It tells the browser to create two rows, one 110 pixels high and the other * high — that is, it occupies whatever room is left over. The document also tells the browser to grab the navbar.htm document and place it in the first frame — the top row — and place main.htm into the bottom frame.

Most search engines these days can find their way through the frameset to the navbar.htm and main.htm documents, so Google, for instance, indexes those documents.

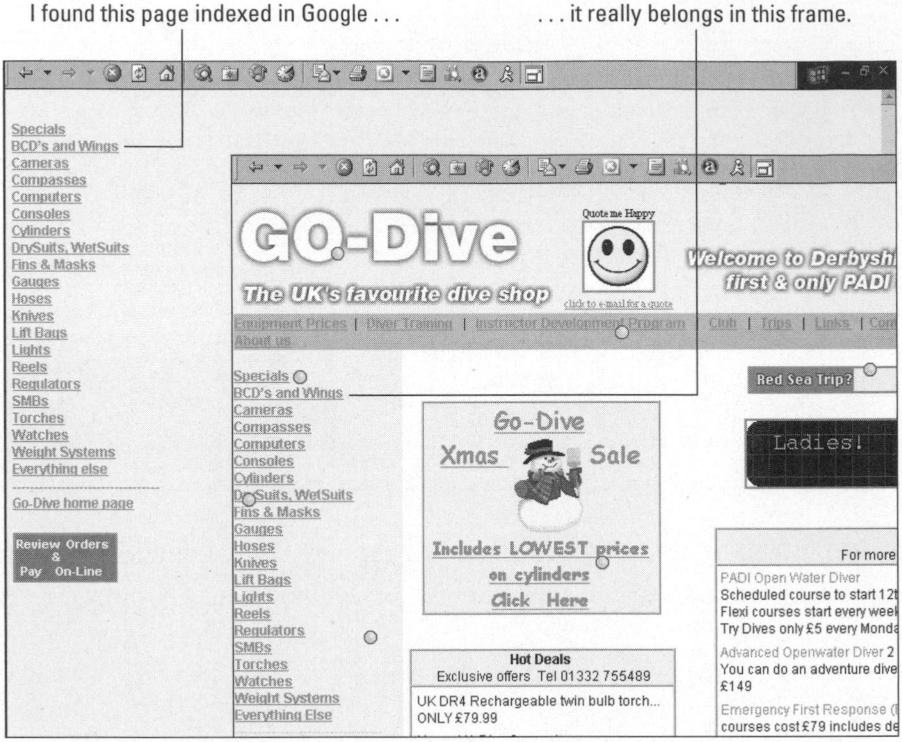

I found this page indexed in Google . . .   . . . it really belongs in this frame.

Figure 7-2:
The document on the left, which I found through Google, belongs in the frameset shown on the right.

But suppose the pages *are* indexed. Pages intended for use inside a frameset are individually indexed in the search engine. In Figure 7-2, you can see a page that I reached from Google — first (on the left) in the condition that I found it and then (on the right) in the frameset it was designed for.

This is not a pretty sight — or site, as it were. But you can work around this mess by doing the following:

- ✔ Provide information in the frame-definition document to help search engines index it.
- ✔ Ensure that all search engines can find their way through this page into the main site.
- ✔ Make sure that pages are opened in the correct frameset (perhaps).

The next few sections give you the details for following these strategies.

Providing search engines with the necessary information

The first thing you can do is provide information in the frame-definition document for the search engines to index. First, add a <TITLE> and your meta tags, like this:

```
<HTML>
<HEAD>
<TITLE> Rodent Racing Info. Rats, Mice, Gerbils, Stoats,
        All Kinds of Rodent Racing</TITLE>
<meta name="description" content=" Rodent Racing -
        Scores, Schedules, Everything Rodent Racing.
        Mouse Racing, Stoat Racing, Rat Racing, Gerbil
        Racing. The Web's Top Rodent Racing Systems and
        Racing News">
<META NAME="keywords" CONTENT="Rodent Racing, Racing
        Rodents, Gerbils, Mice, Mouse, Rodent Races,
        Rat Races, Mouse Races, Stoat, Stoat Racing,
        Rats, Gerbils">
</HEAD>
<FRAMESET ROWS="110,*">
<FRAME SRC="navbar.htm">
<FRAME SRC="main.htm">
</FRAMESET>
</HTML>
```

Then at the bottom of the <FRAMESET>, add <NOFRAMES> tags —
<NOFRAMES> tags were originally designed to enclose text that would be displayed by a browser that couldn't handle frames — with <BODY> tags and information inside, like this:

```
<FRAMESET ROWS="110,*">
<FRAME SRC="navbar.htm">
<FRAME SRC="main.htm">
<NOFRAMES>
<BODY>
<H1>Rodent Racing - Everything You Ever Wanted to Know
        about Rodent Racing Events and the Rodent
        Racing Lifestyle</H1>
<P>[This site uses frames, so if you are reading this,
        your browser doesn't handle frames]</P>
<P>This is the world's top rodent-racing Web site. You
        won't find more information about the world's
        top rodent-racing events anywhere else …[more
        info]
</BODY>
</NOFRAMES>
</FRAMESET>
</HTML>
```

Although few people use browsers that can't work with frames, you can use the <NOFRAMES> tags to provide search engines with information that they can index. For example, you can place the information from main.htm into the NOFRAMES area. Provide 200 to 400 words of keyword-rich text to give the search engines something to work with. Make sure that the content between the <NOFRAMES> tags is about your site and is descriptive and useful to visitors.

Google suggests that the NOFRAMES area should be for alternate content (though, as every good editor knows, it probably means *alternative* content) and says:

> If you use wording such as 'This site requires the use of frames,' or 'Upgrade your browser,' instead of providing alternate content on your site, then you will exclude both search engines and people who have disabled frames on their browsers. For example, audio Web browsers, such as those used in automobiles and by the visually impaired, typically do not deal with such frames. You read more about the <NOFRAMES> tag in the HTML standard here at the following URL: www.w3.org/TR/REC-html40/present/ frames.html#h-16.4....

Unfortunately, many Web designers use the <NOFRAMES> tags as a convenient place to add keywords, even if the page isn't a frame-definition document. For this reason, search engines may treat the text within the tags in one of three ways: Ignore it if it's not within <FRAMESET> tags; downgrade it, awarding less weight to text in a FRAMESET; or ignore it altogether. I believe that although in years past putting keywords within the <NOFRAMES> tags *was* effective, text placed here is no longer given much weight by the search engines.

Providing a navigation path

You can easily provide a navigation path in the NOFRAMES area: Simply add links in your text to other pages in the site. Include a simple text-link navigation system on the page and remember to link to your sitemap.

Remember also to do the following:

- Give *all* your pages unique <TITLE> tags and meta tags, as shown in Figure 7-3. Many designers don't bother to do this for pages in frames because browsers read only the TITLE in the frame-definition document. But search engines index these pages individually, not as part of a frameset, so they should all have this information.

- Give *all* your pages simple text-navigation systems so that a search engine can find its way through your site.

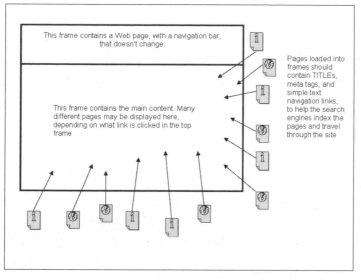

Figure 7-3:
All pages that are loaded into frames should contain TITLE tags, meta tags, and navigation links.

You'll run into one problem with these links inside the pages. The links work fine for people who arrive at the page directly through the search engines; and any link that points at another page works fine in that situation or for someone who arrives at your home page and sees the pages in the frames. However, any link that points at a frame-definition document instead of at another page doesn't work properly (unless you use the fix I'm about to describe) if someone is viewing the page in a frame.

Suppose that you have a link back to the frame-definition document for your home page. If someone is viewing one of your pages inside a frame, as you intended it to be viewed, and clicks the link, the frame definition loads the new frameset into the existing frameset. Now, rather than see, say, two frames, the visitor sees three frames — the two new frames are loaded into the current frame. To get around this problem, use the _top target, like this:

```
<a href="index.html" TARGET = "_top">Home</a>
```

This line "breaks" the frames, opening the index.html document alone in the browser window.

Opening pages in a frameset

Given the way search engines work, pages in a Web site are indexed individually. (Refer to Figure 7-3.) If you create a site by using frames (hey, it takes all kinds!), presumably you want the site displayed in frames. You don't want individual pages pulled out of the frames and displayed, well, individually.

You can use JavaScript to force the browser to load the frameset. Of course, this technique won't work for the small percentage of users working with browsers that don't handle JavaScript — but those browsers probably don't handle frames, either. This technique also won't work for the small percentage of people who turn off JavaScript; but, hey, you can't have everything.

You have to place a small piece of JavaScript into each page so that when the browser loads the page, it reads the JavaScript and loads the frame-definition document. It's a simple little JavaScript that goes something like this:

```
<script language="javascript">
<!--
if (top == self) self.location.href = "index.html";
// -->
</script>
```

Admittedly, this JavaScript example causes two problems:

✔ The browser loads the frameset defined in `index.html`, which may not include the page that was indexed in the search engine. Visitors may have to dig around in the Web site to find the page that, presumably, had the content they were looking for.

✔ The Back button doesn't work correctly because each time the browser sees the JavaScript, it loads the `index.html` file again.

Another option is to have a programmer create a customized script that loads the frame-definition document and drops the specific page into the correct frame.

There's a *much* better fix, though: Don't use frames in the first place! I've spent a lot of time on frames, for one purpose, really: so that you can quickly fix a site that's using frames. But you shouldn't build Web sites with frames. You may need to fix what someone else did or what you did in earlier, less knowledgeable, days. In general, though, frames are used far less today than they were used a few years ago, for good reason: They're an unnecessary nuisance. Sure, frames may be appropriate in a few instances, but the general rule is this:

> If you think it's a good idea to build a Web site by using frames, you're almost certainly wrong!

Handling iframes

An *iframe* is an inline floating frame. This feature may now be more common than regular frames, as regular framing has fallen out of favor. You can use an iframe to grab content from one page and drop it into another, in the same way that you can grab an image and drop it into the page. The tag looks like this:

```
<iframe src ="page.html">
</iframe>
```

I think iframes can be very useful now and then, but you should be aware of the problems they can cause. In particular, search engines index the main page and the content in an iframe separately, even though to a user they appear to be part of the same page.

First, you can add a link within the `<IFRAME>` tag so that older searchbots find the document (some may not), like this:

```
<iframe src="page.html"><a href="page.html" target="_
        blank">Click here for more Rodent Racing
        information if your browser doesn't display
        content in this internal frame.</a></iframe>
```

You can also use the JavaScript discussed in the preceding section to load your home page and to provide a link at the bottom of the iframe content that people can use to load your home page. And you may want to add links at the bottom of the iframe content, in case someone stumbles across it, orphaned, in a search result.

Here's another reason not to use frames and iframes; because you can achieve a similar effect using CSS (Cascading Style Sheets).

Fixing Invisible Navigation Systems

Navigation systems that never show up on search engine radar screens are a common problem, probably even more common than the frames problem I cover in the previous section. Fortunately, you can deal with a navigation-system problem very easily.

Many Web sites use navigation systems that are invisible to search engines. In Chapter 6, I explain the difference between *browser-side* and *server-side* processes, and this issue is related. A Web page is compiled in two places — on the server and in the browser. If the navigation system is created in the browser, it may not be visible to a search engine.

Examples of such systems include those created by using

- Java applets
- JavaScripts
- Macromedia Flash

How can you tell whether your navigation is invisible to search engines? If you created the pages yourself, you probably know how you built the navigation system (although you may be using an authoring tool that did it all for you). If that's the case, or if you're examining a site built by someone else, here are a few ways to figure out how the navigation system is built:

- ✔ If navigation is created with a Java applet, when the page loads, you probably see a gray box where the navigation sits for a moment, with a message such as `Loading Java Applet`.
- ✔ Look in the page's source code.
- ✔ Turn off the display of JavaScript and other active scripting, and then reload the page to see whether the navigation is still there. (I explain how to do this in the section "Turning off scripting and Java," a little later in this chapter.)

Looking at the source code

Take a look at the source code of the document to see how it's created. Open the raw HTML file or choose View➪Source from the browser's main menu, and then look through the file for the navigation.

If the page is large and complex, or if your HTML skills are correspondingly small and simple, you may want to try the technique in the later section "Turning off scripting and Java."

Suppose that you find the following code where the navigation should be:

```
<applet code="MenuApplet" width="160" height="400"
        archive="http://www.yourdomain.com/menu.jar">
```

This navigation system was created with a Java applet. Search engines don't read applet files, so they won't see the navigation system.

Here's another example:

```
<script type="javascript" src="/menu/menu.js"></script>
```

This one is a navigation tool created with JavaScript. Search engines have difficulty reading JavaScript, so they may not see this navigation system either.

Here's an example of a Flash-based navigation system. Links in Flash navigation systems may be read by Google, though probably not by other search engines:

```
<embed src="flash/rcbank_nav02.swf" quality=high
       pluginspage="http://www.macromedia.
       com/shockwave/download/index.
       cgi?P1_Prod_Version=ShockwaveFlash"
       type="application/x-shockwave-flash"
       width="750" height="84"></embed>
```

The preceding examples are easy to identify. The script calls a Java applet or JavaScript, and you know that the searchbots don't read these, so they don't see the navigation.

Here's another form that can create a problem:

```
<a href="javascript:void(0)" onclick="Javascript:window.
       open('http://yourdomain.com/rat-race/','Rat
       Race','width=550,height=600,left=20,top=20,
       screenX=0,screenY=100,resizable=yes,scrollbars=
       yes')" onMouseOut="MM_swapImgRestore()"on
       MouseOver="MM_swapImage('rat_race','','images/
       rat_race2.gif',1)"> <img src="images/rat_race1.
       gif" alt="Living and Shopping" name="rat_
       race"></a>
```

This link uses JavaScript *event handlers* to do several things when triggered by particular events:

- ✔ onclick runs when someone (guess!) clicks the link. This action opens a new window and places the referenced document in that window.

- ✔ onMouseOver runs when someone points at the link. In this case, it runs the MM_swapImage function, which changes the image file used for this navigation button.

- ✔ onMouseOut runs when the mouse is moved away from the link. In this case, it runs the MM_swapImgRestore function, presumably to display the original image.

The link in this example is real, but it doesn't work if JavaScript is turned off, because the URL normally goes in the href= attribute of the anchor tag (the <A> tag); href= is disabled in this link because it uses JavaScript to do all the work. Search engines probably won't follow a link like this.

Turning off scripting and Java

You can also turn off scripting and Java in the browser and then look at the pages. If the navigation system has simply disappeared or if it's there but doesn't work any more, you've got a problem.

How do you disable JavaScript and Java? Every browser's a little different, so I don't go into details here; check your browser's Help information.

Reload a page that you want to check after disabling JavaScript — use the Reload or Refresh button — and see whether the navigation system is still there. If it is, try to use it. Does it still work? If the navigation system has gone or if it's broken, the search engines will have a problem. (Figures 7-4 and 7-5 show you how effective this little trick can be. Navigation bar? Now you see it, now you don't.)

Disabling scripting and Java doesn't stop Flash from working; to stop Flash from working in a browser, you'll probably have to install an add-on.

Unfortunately, you have no simple, quick, and temporary way to stop Flash from working in Internet Explorer. Some other browsers have such a tool, though. Your best option for Internet Explorer is to install other blocking software, such as Toggle Flash (`http://flash.melameth.com/`) or PopUpCop (`www.popupcop.com`). Here's another way to figure out whether a component is Flash, though: Right-click it, and if it *is* Flash, you'll see a menu such as the one shown in Figure 7-6.

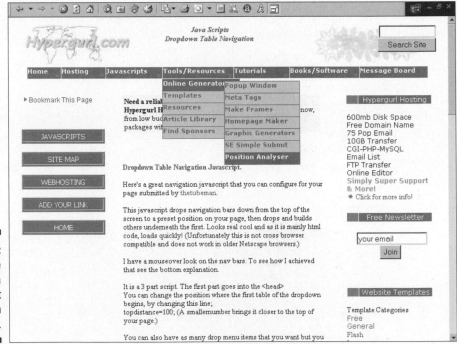

Figure 7-4:
This page has a JavaScript navigation menu bar.

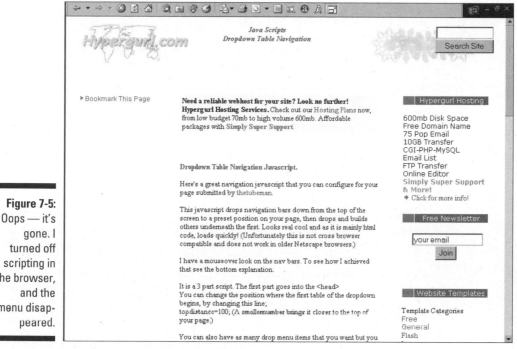

Figure 7-5:
Oops — it's
gone. I
turned off
scripting in
the browser,
and the
menu disap-
peared.

Figure 7-6:
Right-click a
Flash com-
ponent, and
you'll see
this menu.

Fixing the problem

If you want, you can continue to use invisible menus and navigation tools; they can be attractive and effective. Search engines may not see them, but that's okay because you can add a secondary form of navigation that dupli-cates the top navigation.

You can duplicate the navigation structure by using simple text links at the bottom of the page, for instance, or perhaps in a navigation bar on the side of the page. If you have long pages or extremely cluttered HTML, you may want to place small text links near the top of the page, perhaps in the leftmost table column, to make sure that search engines get to them. (Table columns on the right are lower on the page, as far as the HTML is concerned, and search engines read the text in the HTML rather than view the page as people do.)

Flush the Flash Animation

An Adobe Flash animation is a very useful tool. But you should be aware of the SEO problems related to using it.

Many Web designers place fancy Flash animations on their home pages just to make them look cool. But rarely do these animations serve any purpose beyond making site visitors wait a little longer to see the site. Some search engines can now read and index Flash content (albeit not well), but Flash animations often don't contain any useful text for indexing. So, if you built your entire home page — the most important page on your site — by using Flash, the page is worthless from a search engine perspective.

Some designers even create entire Web sites using Adobe Flash (generally because they are Flash designers, not Web designers). Do this, and your site will almost certainly *not* do well in search results.

Even if a page with Flash animation *does* appear in the search results — perhaps because you used the perfect <TITLE> tag — the search engine doesn't have much to work with. For example, in Figure 7-7, the search engine will find the following text:

> Skip Intro. The Celtic Bard is optimized for a 56k modem and above. If you are running a 28.8 modem please be advised you will have to wait for the Flash elements to download.

This bit of text is probably not what you want the search engine to index.

(By the way, many home-page Flash animations automatically forward the browser to the next page — the *real* home page — after they finish running. If you really have to have a Flash intro, make sure that you include a clearly visible Skip Intro link somewhere on the page.)

If you create a page based on Flash, you can do a few things to help with indexing:

- ✔ Make sure to use your <TITLE> tags and DESCRIPTION and KEYWORDS meta tags.
- ✔ Put text between <NOSCRIPT> and </NOSCRIPT> tags. You can use the text displayed in the Flash within these tags, or if you're using audio, use a transcription of the text audio.

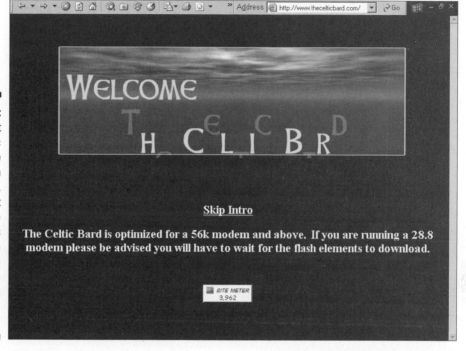

Figure 7-7:
Check out
this classic
example
of a Flash
animation.
At least
the site
designer is
honest in
explaining
that some
site visitors
will have to
wait.

Flash has many good uses, and search engines *can* index Adobe Flash files . . . but generally not well. And here's the proof. Ask yourself how often you find Flash files, or pages that are mostly Flash components, at the top of the search results. The answer is virtually *never*. I've received a lot of criticism of the years from fans of Flash, and they sometimes point me to documents (generally on the Adobe Web site), talking about how well Flash files work with the search engines. Sure, those files can be indexed, but they almost certainly will not rank well. Furthermore, they may on occasion be "orphaned"; that is, the search engine may provide a link in the search results to the Flash file itself, rather than the page containing the file.

So use Flash when necessary, but *don't* rely on it for search engine indexing.

Avoiding Embedded Text in Images

Many sites use images heavily. The overuse of images is often the sign of an inexperienced Web designer — in particular, one who's quite familiar with graphic design tools — perhaps a graphic artist who has accidentally encountered a Web project. Such designers often create entire pages, including the text, in a graphical design program and then save images and insert them into the Web page.

The advantage of this approach is that it gives the designer much more control over the appearance of the page — and is often much faster than using HTML to lay out a few images and real text.

Putting text into graphics has significant drawbacks, though. Such pages transfer across the Internet much more slowly, and because the pages contain no real text, search engines don't have anything to index. And don't believe the "Google is magic" hype; Google does *not* read text in the images it finds online, and is unlikely to do so for a number of years yet.

For example, the text shown in Figure 7-8 isn't real text; the text is part of one large image. This example may be the perfect text to get you ranked highly for your most important keyword phrase, but because it's a picture, it doesn't do you any good.

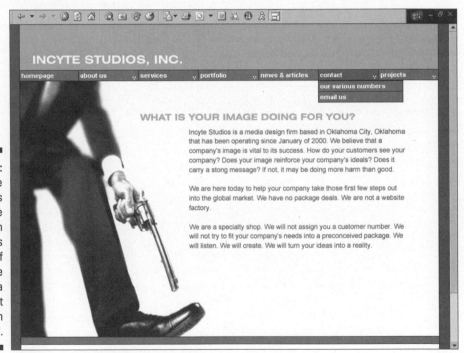

Figure 7-8: This entire page is invisible to search engines. It's made up of one large image and a JavaScript navigation tool.

Reducing the Clutter in Your Web Pages

Simple is good; cluttered is bad. The more cluttered your pages, the more work it is for search engines to dig through them. What do I mean by *clutter?* I'm referring to everything in a Web page that is used to create the page but that is not actual page content.

For instance, one of my clients had a very cluttered site. The HTML source document for the home page had 21,414 characters, of which 19,418 were characters other than spaces. However, the home page didn't contain a lot of text: 1,196 characters, not including the spaces between the words.

So, if 1,196 characters were used to create the words on the page, what were the other 18,222 characters used for? They were used for elements such as these:

- ✔ **JavaScripts:** 4,251 characters

- ✔ **JavaScript event handlers on links:** 1,822 characters

- ✔ **The top navigation bar:** 6,018 characters

- ✔ **Text used to embed a Flash animation near the top of the page:** 808 characters

The rest is the normal clutter that you always have in HTML: tags used to format text, create tables, and so on. The problem with this page was that a search engine had to read 18,701 characters (including spaces) *before it ever reached the page content.* Of course, the page didn't have much content, and what was there was hidden away below all that HTML.

This clutter above the page content means that some search engines may not reach it. Fortunately, you can use some simple methods to unclutter cluttered pages. (In my client's pages, we were able to remove around 11,000 characters without much effort.)

Use external JavaScripts

You don't need to put JavaScripts inside a page. JavaScripts generally should be placed in an *external file* — a tag in the Web page "calls" a script that is pulled from another file on the Web server — for various reasons:

- ✔ **They're safer outside the HTML file.** That is, they're less likely to be damaged while making changes to the HTML.

- ✔ **They're easier to manage externally.** Why not have a nice library of all the scripts in your site in one directory?

✔ **The download time is slightly shorter.** If you use the same script in multiple pages, the browser downloads the script once and caches it.

✔ **They're easier to reuse.** You don't need to copy scripts from one page to another and fix all the pages when you have to make a change to the script. Just store the script externally and change the external file to automatically change the script in any number of pages.

✔ **Doing so removes clutter from your pages!**

Creating external JavaScript files is easy: Simply save the text between the `<SCRIPT></SCRIPT>` tags in a text editor, and copy that file to your Web server (as a `.js` file — `mouseover_script.js`, for instance).

Then add an `src=` attribute to your `<SCRIPT>` tag to refer to the external file, like this:

```
<script language="JavaScript" type="text/javascript"
        src="/scripts/mouseover_script.js"></script>
```

Use document.write to remove problem code

If you have a complicated top navigation bar — perhaps a navbar with text colors in the main bar that change when you point at options, or menus with drop-down lists — your code character counts can easily be up to 6,000 characters or so. That's a lot of characters, which can easily end up being a significant portion of the overall code for the page. You can easily remove all this clutter by using JavaScript to write the text into the page. Here's how:

1. **In an external text file, type this text:**

```
<!--
document.write("")
//-->
```

2. **Grab the entire chunk of code that you want to remove from the HTML page, and then paste it between the following quotation marks:**

```
document.write("place code here")
```

3. **Save this file and place it on your Web server.**

4. **Call the file from the HTML page by adding an** `src=` **attribute to your** `<SCRIPT>` **tag to refer to the external file, like this:**

```
<script language="JavaScript" src="/scripts/navbar.js"
        type="text/javascript"></script>
```

Of course, if you remove the navigation from the page — remember that the searchbots often don't read these JavaScripts, so they don't see the navigation — you don't have navigation that the search engines can follow. Remember to add simple text navigation somewhere else on the page (maybe at the bottom, now that the page is much smaller). Simple text navigation takes up much less room than a complex navigation bar.

Use external CSS files

If you can stick JavaScript stuff into an external file, it shouldn't surprise you that you can do the same thing — drop stuff into a file that's then referred to in the HTML file proper — with Cascading Style Sheet (CSS) information. For reasons that are unclear to me, many designers place CSS information directly into the page, despite the fact that the ideal use of a style sheet is generally *external*. One of the original ideas behind style sheets is to allow you to make formatting changes to an entire site very quickly. If you want to change the size of the body text or the color of the heading text, for example, you make one small change in the CSS file and it affects the whole site immediately. If you have CSS information in each page, though, you have to change each and every page. (Rather defeats the object of CSS, doesn't it?)

Here's how to remove CSS information from the main block of HTML code. Simply place the targeted text in an external file — everything between and including the <STYLE></STYLE> tags — and then call the file in your HTML pages by using the <LINK> tag, like this:

```
<link rel="stylesheet" href="site.css" type="text/css">
```

Move image maps to the bottom of the page

An image map (described in detail later in this chapter) is an image that contains multiple links. One way to clean up clutter in a page is to move the code that defines the links to the bottom of the Web page, right before the </BODY> tag. Doing so doesn't remove the clutter from the page — it moves the clutter to the end of the page, where it doesn't get placed between the top of the page and the page content. That makes it more likely that the search engines will reach the content.

Avoid the urge to copy and paste from MS Word

That's right. Don't copy text directly from Microsoft Word and drop it into a Web page. You'll end up with *all sorts* of formatting clutter in your page!

Here's one way to get around this problem:

1. **Save the file as an HTML file.**

   Word provides various options to do this, but you want to use the simplest: Web Page (Filtered).

2. **In your HTML-authoring program, look for a Word-cleaning tool.**

   Word has such a bad reputation that HTML programs are now starting to add tools to help you clean the text before you use it. Dreamweaver has such a tool, for instance (Commands➪Clean Up Word HTML).

Managing Dynamic Web Pages

Chapter 6 explains how your standard, meat-and-potatoes Web page gets assembled in your browser so that you, the surfer, can see it. But you can assemble a Web page in more than one way. For example, the process can go like this:

1. The Web browser requests a Web page.

2. The Web server sends a message to a database program requesting the page.

3. The database program reads the URL to see exactly what is requested, compiles the page, and sends it to the server.

4. The server reads any instructions inside the page.

5. The server compiles the page, adding information specified in server-side includes (SSIs) or scripts.

6. The server sends the file to the browser.

Pages pulled from databases are known as *dynamic pages,* as opposed to normal *static pages*, which are individual files saved on the hard drive. The pages are dynamic because they're created on the fly, when requested. The page doesn't exist until a browser requests it, at which point the data is grabbed from a database by some kind of program — a CGI, ASP, or PHP script, for instance, or from some kind of content-management system — and dropped into a Web page template and then sent to the browser requesting the file.

Unfortunately, dynamic pages can create problems. Even the best search engines sometimes don't read them. Of course, a Web page is a Web page, whether it was created on the fly or days earlier. After the searchbot receives the page, the page is already complete, so the searchbots *can* read them if they want to, but sometimes, based on what the page URL looks like (I look at this in the next section), they choose not to. So why don't search engines always read dynamic pages? Because in some cases search engines don't want to read them (or their programmers don't want them to).

Search engine programmers have discovered that dynamic pages are often problem pages. Here are a few of the problems that searchbots can run into while reading dynamic pages:

- ✔ Dynamic pages often have only minor changes in them. A searchbot reading these pages may end up with hundreds of pages that are almost exactly the same, with nothing more than minor differences to distinguish one from each other.

- ✔ Search engines are concerned that databased pages might change frequently, making search results inaccurate.

- ✔ Searchbots sometimes get stuck in the dynamic system, going from page to page to page among tens of thousands of pages. On occasion, this happens when a Web programmer hasn't properly written the link code and the database continually feeds data to the search engine, even crashing your server.

- ✔ Hitting a database for thousands of pages can slow down the server, so searchbots often avoid getting into situations in which that is likely to happen.

- ✔ Sometimes URLs can change (I talk about session IDs a little later in this chapter), so even if the search engine indexes the page, the next time someone tries to get there, it's gone; and search engines don't want to index dead links.

All these problems were more common a few years ago, and in fact the major search engines are now far more likely to index databased pages than they were a few years ago. However, databased pages can still cause problems for search engines, and in any case they have another serious problem: The filenames are often complicated database queries instead of simple filenames containing useful keywords, as you see in the following section.

Determining whether your dynamic pages are scaring off search engines

You can often tell whether search engines are likely to omit your pages just by looking at the URL. Go deep into the site; if it's a product catalog, for instance, go to the farthest subcategory you can find. Then look at the URL. Suppose that you have a URL like this:

```
http://www.yourdomain.edu/march/rodent-racing-scores.php
```

This URL is a normal one that should have few problems. It's a static page — or at least it looks like a static page, which is what counts. (It *might* be a dynamic, or databased, page, but there's no way to tell from the URL.) Compare this URL with the next one:

```
http://www.yourdomain.edu/march/scores.php?prg=1
```

This filename ends with ?prg=1. This page is almost certainly a databased dynamic page; ?prg=1 is a *parameter* that's being sent to the server to let it know which piece of information is needed from the database. This URL is okay, especially for the major search engines, although a few smaller search engines may not like it; it almost certainly won't stop a searchbot from indexing it. It's still not very good from a search engine perspective, though, because it doesn't contain good keywords.

Now look at the following URL:

```
http://yourdomain.com/march/index.html?&DID=18&CATID=13&Ob
          jectGroup_ID=79
```

This URL is worse. It contains three parameters: DID=18, CATID=13, and ObjectGroup_ID=79. Three parameters may be too much. These days, Google may index this page; at one point it probably wouldn't have. Still, the more parameters, the less likely the pages are to be indexed, and even as late as 2009, Google was claiming that complicated URLs were still a problem.

If you have a *clean* URL with no parameters, search engines should be able to find it. If you have a single parameter, it's okay for the major search engines, though not necessarily for older systems. If you have two parameters, it's still probably okay for major search engines. If you have three parameters, you start to risk limiting your page indexing. And, it doesn't matter how many parameters you have, using good, clean URLs with nice keywords are always better than long, complicated URLs with no keywords.

You can find out whether a page in your site is indexed by using the following techniques:

✔ If you have the Google Toolbar, open the page you want to check, click the i button, and select Cached Snapshot of Page. Or, go to Google and type **cache:** *YourURL*, where *YourURL* is the site you're interested in. If Google displays a cached page, it's there, of course. If Google doesn't display it, move to the next technique. (For more information on the Google Toolbar — including where to download it — see Chapter 1.)

✔ Go to Google and type the URL of the page into the text box, and then click Search. If the page is in the index, Google displays some information about it.

✔ Use similar techniques with other search engines if you want to check them for your page. Take a look at their Help pages for more information.

Fixing your dynamic Web page problem

So how do you make search engines take a look at your state-of-the-art dynamic Web site? Here are a few ideas:

✔ **Find out whether the database program has a built-in way to create static HTML.** Some e-commerce systems, for instance, spit out a static copy of their catalog pages, which is intended for search engines. When visitors click the Buy button, they're taken back into the dynamic system.

✔ **Modify URLs so that they don't look like they're pointing to dynamic pages.** You can often help fix the problem by removing characters such as ?, #, !, *, %, and & and reducing the number of parameters to one. For the specifics, talk with the programmer responsible for the database system.

✔ **Use a URL rewrite trick — a technique for changing the way URLs look.** Different servers have different tools available; the mod_rewrite tool, for instance, is used by the Apache Web server (a very popular system), and ISAPI Rewrite can be used on Windows servers. *Rewriting* is a process whereby the server can convert fake URLs into real URLs. The server might see, for instance, a request for a page at

```
http://yourdomain.com/march/rodent-racing-scores.html
```

The server knows that this page doesn't exist and that it really refers to, perhaps, the following URL:

```
http://yourdomain.com/ showprod.cfm?&DID=7&User_ID=
        2382175&st=6642&st2=45931500&st3=-
        43564544&topcat_id=20018&catid=20071&objectgro
        up_id=20121.
```

In other words, this technique allows you to use what appear to be static URLs yet still grab pages from a database. This topic is complicated, so if your server administrator doesn't understand it, it may take him or her a few days to figure it all out; for someone who understands URL rewriting, however, it's fairly easy and can take just a few hours to set up.

✔ **Find out whether the programmer can create static pages from the database.** Rather than create a single Web page each time it's requested, the database could "spit out" the entire site periodically — each night for instance, or when the database is updated — creating static pages with normal URLs.

If you want to find out more about URL rewriting, here are a couple of places to look:

✔ www.asp101.com/articles/wayne/extendingnames

✔ httpd.apache.org/docs/mod/mod_rewrite.html

Or simply search for *url rewrite* and you'll find tons of information.

Using Session IDs in URLs

Just as dynamic Web pages can throw a monkey wrench into the search engine machinery, session IDs can make search engine life equally interesting. A *session ID* identifies a particular person visiting the site at a particular time, which enables the server to track which pages the visitor looks at and which actions the visitor takes during the session.

If you request a page from a Web site — by clicking a link on a Web page, for instance — the Web server that has the page sends it to your browser. Then if you request another page, the server sends that page too, but the server doesn't know that you're the same person. If the server needs to know who you are, it needs a way to identify you each time you request a page. It does that by using session IDs.

Session IDs are used for a variety of reasons, but their main purpose is to allow Web developers to create various types of interactive sites. For instance, if developers have created a secure environment, they may want to force visitors to go through the home page first. Or, the developers may want a way to resume an unfinished session. By setting cookies containing the session ID on the visitor's computer, developers can see where the visitor was in the site at the end of the visitor's last session. (A *cookie* is a text file containing information that can be read only by the server that set the cookie.)

Session IDs are common when running software applications that have any kind of security procedure (such as requiring a login) or that need to store variables or that want to defeat the browser cache — that is, ensure that the browser always displays information from the server, never from its own cache. Shopping cart systems typically use session IDs — that's how the system can allow you to place an item in the shopping cart and then go away and continue shopping. It *recognizes* you based on your session ID.

A session ID can be created in two ways:

✔ Store it in a cookie.

✔ Display it in the URL itself.

Some systems are set up to store the session ID in a cookie but then use a URL session ID if the user's browser is set to not accept cookies. (Relatively few browsers, perhaps 1 or 2 percent, don't accept cookies.) Here's an example of a URL containing a session ID:

```
http://yourdomain.com/index.jsp;jsessionid=07D3CCD4D9A6A9F
       3CF9CAD4F9A728F44
```

The `07D3CCD4D9A6A9F3CF9CAD4F9A728F44` piece of the URL is the unique identifier assigned to the session.

If a search engine recognizes a URL as including a session ID, it probably doesn't read the referenced page because the server can handle a session ID in two different ways when the searchbot returns. Each time the searchbot returns to your site, the session ID will have expired, so the server can do either of the following:

✔ **Display an error page rather than the indexed page or perhaps display the site's default page (generally the home page).** In other words, the search engine has indexed a page that isn't there if someone clicks the link in the search results page. This behavior is admittedly less common than the one described in the following bullet.

✔ **Assign a new session ID.** The URL that the searchbot originally used has expired, so the server replaces the ID with another one and changes the URL. So, the spider could be fed multiple URLs for the same page.

Even if the searchbot reads the referenced page (and sometimes it does), it probably doesn't index it or doesn't index much of your site. Webmasters sometimes complain that a search engine entered their site, requested the same page over and over, and left without indexing most of the site. The searchbot simply got confused and left. Or, sometimes the search engine doesn't recognize a session ID in a URL. One of my clients had hundreds of URLs indexed by Google, but because they were all long-expired session IDs, they all pointed to the site's main page.

Fixing the session ID problem is like performing magic: Sites that were invisible to search engines suddenly become visible! One site owner in a search engine discussion group described how his site had never had more than 6 pages indexed by Google, yet within a week of removing session IDs, Google had indexed over 600 pages.

If your site has a session ID problem, you can do various things:

- **Rather than use session IDs in the URL, store session information in a cookie on the user's computer.** Each time a page is requested, the server can check the cookie to see whether session information is stored there. (Few people change their browser settings to block cookies.) However, the server shouldn't *require* cookies, or you may run into further problems (as you find out in a moment).

- **Get your programmer to omit session IDs if the device requesting a Web page from the server is a searchbot.** The server delivers the same page to the searchbot but doesn't assign a session ID, so the searchbot can travel throughout the site without using session IDs. (Every device requesting a page from a Web server identifies itself, so it's possible for a programmer to send different pages according to the requestor — a topic I talk more about in Chapter 8.) This process is known as *user agent delivery,* in which user agent refers to the device — browser, searchbot, or other program — that is requesting a page.

The user agent method has one potential problem: In the technique sometimes known as *cloaking,* a server sends one page to the search engines and another to real site visitors. Search engines generally don't like cloaking because some Web sites try to trick them by providing different content from the content that site visitors see. Of course, in the context of using this technique to avoid the session-ID problem, that's not the intent; it's a way to show the *same* content that the site visitor sees, so it isn't true cloaking. However, the (very slight) danger is that the search engines may view it as cloaking if they discover what is happening. (I don't believe that the risk is big, though some people in the SEO business will tell you that it is.) For more on cloaking, see Chapter 8.

Examining Cookie-Based Navigation

Cookies — the small text files that a Web server can store on a site visitor's hard drive — can often prove as indigestible to search engines as dynamic Web pages and session IDs. Imagine this scenario: You visit a site that's using cookies, and at some point the server decides to store a cookie. The server sends the information to your browser, and the browser duly creates a text file, which it then stores on your computer's hard drive. This text file might contain a session ID (as discussed in the preceding section) or something else. Cookies enable systems to remember who you are so that you don't have to log in each time you visit.

Cookies are sometimes used for navigation purposes. For instance, you may have seen *crumb trails,* a series of links showing where you have been as you travel through the site. Crumb trails look something like this:

```
Home->Rodents->Rats->Racing
```

This information is generally stored in a cookie and is read each time you load a new page.

Or, the server may read the cookie to determine how many times you visited the site or what you did the last time you were on the site, and then direct you to a particular page based on that information.

If you're using Internet Explorer 8 in Microsoft Windows, follow these steps to see what these cookie files look like:

1. **Choose Tools➪Internet Options from the main menu.**

   The Internet Options dialog box appears.

2. **In the Internet Options dialog box, make sure that the General tab is selected.**

3. **Click the Settings button in the Browsing History area.**

   The Temporary Internet Files and History Settings dialog box appears.

4. **In the Settings dialog box, click the View Files button.**

   A Windows Explorer window opens, displaying the directory containing your temporary files, including cookies. The files are named *cookie:username@domainname.com.* For instance, when I visited the www.nokiausa.com Web site, the server created a cookie named *cookie:peter kent@nokiausa.com.*

5. **Double-click any of these cookie files.**

The file will open in a text editor. Here are the contents of a cookie that was set by a www.vistaprint.com ad server:

```
v1st92B987F91B8D5DEFvistaprint.com/10243378255872307955684
        22644433630078134*
```

There's nothing wrong with using cookies, *unless* they're *required* in order to navigate through your site. A server can be set up to simply refuse to send a Web page to a site visitor if the visitor's browser doesn't accept cookies. That's a problem for several reasons:

✔ A few browsers simply don't accept cookies.

✔ A small number of people have changed their browser settings to refuse to accept cookies.

✔ Searchbots can't accept cookies.

If your Web site *demands* the use of cookies, it doesn't get indexed. That's all there is to it! The searchbot requests a page, your server tries to set a cookie, and the searchbot can't accept it. The server doesn't send the page, so the searchbot doesn't index it.

How can you check to see whether your site has this problem? Turn off cookies in your browser (see your browser's Help information), and then try navigating your site. (In Internet Explorer 8, choose Tools⇨Options, click the Privacy Tab, click the Advanced button, click the Override Automatic Cookie Handling check box, and select the Prompt option buttons.)

I recommend that you select Prompt rather than Block to make testing your site easier. Now each time a server tries to set a cookie, you see a warning box and you can accept or block the cookie at will.

Clear your cookies, too, so that you can start fresh, and then go to your Web site and see what happens. (In IE 8, click the Safety menu on the Command bar at the top of the Web page, click Delete Browsing History, and then, with the Cookies check box selected, click the Delete button.) Each time the site tries to set a cookie, you see a message box, similar to the one shown in Figure 7-9. Block the cookie and then see whether you can still travel around the site. If you can't, the searchbots can't navigate it either.

Figure 7-9:
The Privacy
Alert dialog
box.

Follow these suggestions to fix this problem:

✔ **Don't require cookies.** Ask your site programmers to find some other way to handle what you're doing with cookies, or just do without the fancy navigation trick.

✔ **Use a user agent script (as you can with session IDs) that treats search-bots differently.** If the server sees a normal visitor, it requires cookies; if it's a searchbot, it doesn't.

Fixing Bits and Pieces

Forwarded pages, image maps, and special characters can also cause problems for search engines.

Forwarded pages

Search engines don't want to index pages that automatically forward to other pages. You've undoubtedly seen pages telling you that a page has moved to another location and that you can click a link or wait a few seconds for the page to automatically forward the browser to another page. This is often done with a REFRESH meta tag, like this:

```
<meta http-equiv="refresh" content="0; url=http://
         yourdomain.com">
```

This meta tag forwards the browser immediately to *yourdomain*.com. Quite reasonably, search engines don't like these pages. Why index a page that doesn't contain information but instead forwards visitors to the page *with* the information? Why not index the target page? That's just what search engines do.

If you use the REFRESH meta tag, you can expect search engines to ignore the page (unless it's a very slow refresh rate of over ten seconds, which is specified by the number immediately after content=). But don't listen to the nonsense that you'll hear about your site being penalized for using refresh pages: Search engines don't index the page, but there's no reason for them to penalize your entire site.

Image maps

An *image map* is an image that has multiple links. You might create the image like this:

```
<img name="main" src="images/main.gif" usemap="#m_main">
```

The usemap= parameter refers to the map instructions. You can create the information defining the *hotspots* on the image — the individual links — by using a <MAP> tag, like this:

```
<map name="m_main">
<area shape="rect" coords="238,159,350,183" href="page1.
        html">
<area shape="rect" coords="204,189,387,214" href=" page2.
        html">
<area shape="rect" coords="207,245,387,343" href=" page3.
        html">
<area shape="rect" coords="41,331,155,345" href=" page4.
        html">
<area shape="rect" coords="40,190,115,202" href=" page5.
        html">
<area shape="rect" coords="42,174,148,186" href=" page6.
        html">
<area shape="rect" coords="40,154,172,169" href=" page7.
        html">
<area shape="rect" coords="43,137,142,148" href=" page8.
        html">
<area shape="rect" coords="45,122,165,131" href=" page9.
        html">
<area shape="rect" coords="4,481,389,493" href=" page10.
        html">
<area shape="rect" coords="408,329,588,342" href=" page11.
        html">
    <area shape="rect" coords="410,354,584,391" href="
        page12.html">
    </map>
```

There was a time when search engines wouldn't read the links, but that time is long gone; major search engines now read image maps, though some smaller ones may not. A more important problem these days is that links in images don't provide the benefit of keywords that search engines can read. The solution is simple: Use additional simple text links in the document.

Special characters

The issue of using special characters is a little complicated. Currently Google seems to handle special-character searches well. Search for *rôle* and for *role*, and you'll get different results. Try the test at MSN/Bing, and you'll get the same result both times.

Consider, then, that when people search, they don't use special characters. They simply type the search term with the keyboard characters in front of them. Almost nobody would search for *shakespearean rôles*; people would search for *shakespearean roles* (even if they realized that the word role has an accented *o*). Thus if you use the word rôle, your page won't match searches for *role*.

My general advice is to avoid special characters when possible, particularly in really SEO-valuable fields such as the <Title> tag and DESCRIPTION meta tag.

Chapter 8

Dirty Deeds, Done Dirt Cheap

· ·

· ·

*E*veryone wants to fool the search engines — and the search engines know it. That's why search engine optimization is such a strange business — a hybrid of technology and, oh, I dunno . . . industrial espionage, perhaps? Search engines don't want you to know exactly how they rank pages because if you did, you would know exactly how to trick them into giving you top positions.

Now for a bit of history. When this whole search engine business started out, search engines just wanted people to follow some basic guidelines — make the Web site readable, provide a `<TITLE>` tag, provide a few keywords related to the page's subject matter, and so on — and then the search engines would take it from there.

What happened, though, is that Web sites started jostling for position. For example, although the `KEYWORDS` meta tag seemed like a great idea, so many people misused it (by repeating words and using words that *weren't* related to the subject matter) that it eventually became irrelevant to search engines. Eventually, the major search engines stopped giving much weight to the tag or just ignored it altogether.

Search engines try to hide their methods as much as they can, but it sometimes becomes apparent what the search engines want, and at that point, people start trying to give it to them in a manner the search engines regard as manipulative. This chapter discusses which things you should avoid doing because you risk upsetting the search engines and getting penalized — potentially even getting booted from a search engine for life!

Tricking Search Engines

Before getting down to the nitty-gritty details about tricking search engines, I focus on two topics: why you need to understand the dangers of using dirty tricks and what the overriding principles behind tricking the search engines are based on.

Deciding whether to trick

Should you use the tricks in this chapter, and if not, why not? You'll hear several reasons for not using tricks. The first, ethics, is one I don't belabor, because I'm not sure that the argument behind this reason is very strong. You'll hear from many people that the tricks in this chapter are unethical, that those who use them are cheating and are one step on the evolutionary ladder above pond scum (or one step below pond scum, depending on the commentator).

Self-righteousness is in ample supply on the Internet. Maybe these people are right, maybe not. I do know that many people who try such tricks also have great reasons for doing so and are not the Internet's equivalent of Pol Pot or Attila the Hun. They're simply trying to put their best foot forward in a difficult technical environment.

Many people have tried search engine tricks because they invested a lot of money in Web sites that turn out to be invisible to search engines. These folks can't afford to abandon their sites and start again. (See Chapter 7 for a discussion of why search engines sometimes can't read Web pages.) You can, and rightly so, point out that these folks can deal with the problem in other ways, but that just means the people involved are misinformed, not evil. The argument made by these tricksters might go something like this: *Who gave search engines the right to set the rules, anyway?*

One could argue that doing pretty much anything beyond the basics is cheating. Over the past few years, I've heard from hundreds of people who have put into action many of the ideas in this book, with great results. So if smart Webmasters armed with a little knowledge can push their Web sites up in the ranks above sites that may be more appropriate for a particular keyword phrase, yet are owned by folks with less knowledge . . . is that fair?

Ethics aside, the really good reason for avoiding egregious trickery is that it may have the opposite effect and *harm* your search engine position. A corollary to that reason is that other, legitimate ways exist to get a good search engine ranking. (Unfortunately, they're often more complicated and time consuming.)

Figuring out the tricks

The idea behind most search engine tricks is simple: to confuse the search engines into thinking that your site is more appropriate for certain keyword phrases than they would otherwise believe, and you do this generally by showing the search engine something that the site visitor doesn't see.

Search engines want to see what site visitors see, yet they know they can't. It will be a long, long time before search engines will be able to see and understand the images in a Web page, for instance. Right now, they can't even read text in the images, although that could be possible at some point. (Recent patents suggest that this is something Google is working on now — but I bet it will still be years before Google tries to read all the text it finds in the average Web site's images, if it ever does.) But to view and understand the images as a real person sees them? Britney Spears could well be president of the United States before that happens.

The search engine designers have started with this basic principle:

> *What the search engine sees should be what the user sees* (except for certain things it's not interested in — images, JavaScript navigation systems, and so on) and of certain technical issues that are not important to the visitor (such as the DESCRIPTION meta tag, which <H> tag has been applied to a heading, and so on).

For various reasons, searchbots aren't terribly sophisticated. They generally don't read JavaScript, Cascading Style Sheets (CSS), and so on because of the complexity of doing so. In theory, they could read these things, but it would greatly increase the time and hardware required. So by necessity, they ignore certain components.

Here's one other important principle: *The text on the page should be there for the benefit of the site visitor, not the search engines.*

Ideally, search engine designers want Web designers to act as though search engines don't exist. (Of course, this is *exactly* what many Web designers have done and the reason that so many sites rank poorly in search engines!) Search engine designers want their programs to determine which pages are the most relevant for a particular search query. They want you — the Web designer — to focus on creating a site that serves your visitors' needs and let search engines determine which site is most appropriate for which searcher.

What search engines definitely don't want is for you to show one version of a page to visitors and another version to search engines because you feel that version is what the search engine will like most.

Do these tricks work?

Tricks do work, at least in some circumstances for some search engines. Even some tricks that are very crude and have been known to search engines for a long time still work. On the other hand, over time, search engines get better and better at dropping the more obvious tricks; you don't find crudely keyword-stuffed pages and pages with hidden text ranking well very often these days, for instance, though only a few years ago, you did.

Could you use sophisticated tricks and rank first for your keywords? Perhaps, but your rank may not last long, and the penalty it could incur can last for a long time. (Although in most cases, the pages will simply drop in rank as the search engines apply an algorithm that recognizes the trick, in some cases a search engine could decide to remove all pages from a particular site from the index, permanently.)

These tricks can be dangerous. You may get caught in one of several ways:

- A search engine algorithm may discover your trickery, and your page or your entire site could be dropped from the search engine.

- A competitor might discover what you're doing and report you to the search engines. Google has stated that it prefers to let its algorithms track down cheaters and uses reports of search engine spamming to tune these algorithms, but Google will take direct action in some cases; in fact, it does employ a team of people to examine suspected "spam" sites.

- Your trick may work well for a while, until a major search engine changes its algorithm to block the trickery — at which point your site's ranking will drop like a rock.

If you follow the advice from the rest of this book, you'll surpass 80 percent of your competitors. You don't *need* tricks.

Concrete Shoes, Cyanide, TNT — An Arsenal for Dirty Deeds

The next few sections take a look at some search engine tricks employed on the Web.

Keyword stacking and stuffing

You may run across pages that contain the same word or term, or maybe several words or terms, repeated again and again, often in hidden areas of the page (such as the KEYWORDS tag), though also sometimes visible to visitors. This is one of the earliest and crudest forms of a dirty deed, one that search engines have been aware of for years and are pretty good at finding these days. You'd think keyword stacking wouldn't work, but search engines aren't perfect, and sometimes keyword-stacked pages slip through.

Take a look at Figure 8-1. The Web designer has repeated the word *glucosamine* numerous times, each one in a hyperlink to give it a little extra oomph. I found this page in Google a few years ago by searching for the term *glucosamine glucosamine glucosamine*; more recently, the same search phrase didn't pull up anything nearly as crude as this page.

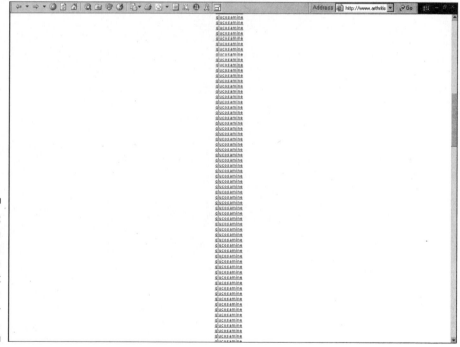

Figure 8-1:
The person creating this page stacked it with the word *glucosamine.*

Look at this tactic from the search engine's perspective. Repeating the word *glucosamine* over and over isn't of any use to a site visitor, so it's understandable why search engine designers don't appreciate this kind of thing. This sort of trick rarely works these days, so sites doing this are also becoming less abundant.

The terms *keyword stacking* and *keyword stuffing* are often used interchangeably, though some people regard keyword stuffing as something a little different — placing inappropriate keywords inside image ALT attributes and in hidden layers.

Hiding (and shrinking) keywords

Another old (and very crude) trick is to hide text; that is, to hide it from the site visitor but make it visible to the search engine, allowing you to fill a simple page with keywords for the sake of search engine optimization. (Remember that search engines don't want you to show them content that isn't also visible to the site visitor.)

This trick, often combined with keyword stuffing, involves placing large amounts of text into a page and hiding it from view. For instance, take a look at Figure 8-2. I found this page in Google some time ago. It has hidden text at the bottom of the page.

If you suspect that someone has hidden text on a page, you can often make it visible by clicking inside text at the top of the page and dragging the mouse to the bottom of the page to highlight everything in between. You can also look in the page's source code.

How did this designer make the text disappear? At the bottom of the source code (choose View⇨Source), I found this:

```
<FONT SIZE=7 COLOR="#ffffff"><H6>glucosamine glucosamine
        glucosamine glucosamine glucosamine emu oil
        emu oil emu oil kyolic kyolic kyolic wakunaga
        wakunaga wakunaga</H6></FONT>
```

Notice the COLOR="#ffffff" piece; #ffffff is hexadecimal color code for the color white. The page background is white, so — abracadabra — the text disappears.

There's a big space at the bottom of this page . . .

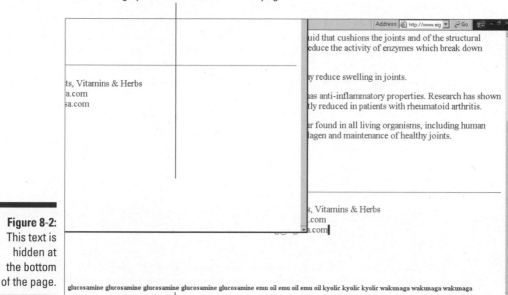

Figure 8-2:
This text is
hidden at
the bottom
of the page.

. . . but if you drag the cursor down from the end of the text, you'll see the hidden text.

Surprisingly, I still see this trick employed now and then. In fact, I sometimes get clients who have a sudden inspiration — "Hey, couldn't we just put a bunch of keywords into the site and make it the same color as the background?" they ask, as if they have discovered something really clever. I have to explain that it's the oldest trick in the book.

My opinion of this crude trick goes like this:

- ✔ **It may help.** The trick actually *can* work.
- ✔ **It might not hurt.** You still find pages using this trick, so clearly the search engines don't always find it.
- ✔ **. . . but it might.** But search engines *do* discover the trick, frequently, and may penalize your site for doing it. The page may get dropped from the index, or you may have your entire site dropped.
- ✔ **So why do it?** It's just way too risky . . . and unnecessary, too.

Here are some other tricks used for hiding text from the visitor while still making it visible to the search engine:

- ✔ **Placing text inside** `<NOFRAMES>` **tags:** Some designers do this even if the page isn't a frame-definition document. I've seen this method work, too, but not in recent years.

- ✔ **Placing text inside** `<NOSCRIPT>` **tags:** `<NOSCRIPT></NOSCRIPT>` tags are used to put text on a page that can be read by browsers that don't work with JavaScript. Some site owners use them to give more text to the search engines to read, and from what I've seen, the major search engines often do read this text, or at least they did a few years ago. However, the text inside these tags probably isn't given as much weight as other text on a page, and over time will probably be given less and less weight.

- ✔ **Using hidden fields:** Sometimes designers hide words in a form's hidden field (`<INPUT TYPE="HIDDEN">`). I doubt whether this does anything to help, anyway.

- ✔ **Using hidden layers:** Style sheets can be used to position a text layer underneath the visible layer or outside the browser. This trick is quite common and probably hard for search engines to figure out.

Some Web designers still stuff keywords into page by using a very small font size. This trick is another one that search engines may look for and penalize.

Here's another variation: Some Web designers make the text color just a little different from the background color to make it hard for the browser to catch. However, the text remains invisible, especially if it's at the bottom of the page preceded by several blank lines. Search engines can look for ranges of colors to determine whether this trick is being employed.

And remember, it's not just the search engines looking, it's your competitors, too. They might just report you. (See the section "Paying the Ultimate Penalty," later in this chapter.)

Hiding links

A variation on the old hidden-text trick is to hide links. As you discover in Chapters 14 through 16, links provide important clues to search engines about the site's purpose. They also provide a way for search engines to discover pages. Thus, some Web designers create links that are specifically for search engines to find but are not intended for site visitors. Links can be made to look exactly like all the other text on a page or may even be hidden on punctuation marks — visitors are unlikely to click a link on a period, so the link can be made "invisible," allowing a search engine to discover a page that the site visitor will never see. Links may be placed in transparent images or invisible layers, in small images, or in `<NOFRAMES><NOSCRIPT>` tags or may be hidden in any of the ways discussed previously for hiding ordinary text.

Duplicating pages and sites

If content with keywords is good, then twice as much content is better, and three times as much is better still, right? Some site developers have duplicated pages and even entire sites, making virtual photocopies and adding the pages to the site or placing duplicated sites at different domain names.

Sometimes called *mirror pages* or *mirror sites,* these duplicate pages are intended to help a site gain more than one or two entries in the top positions. If you can create three or four Web sites that rank well, you can dominate the first page of the search results, with from four to eight entries out of the first ten. (Google, for instance, displays one or two pages from a site.)

Some people who use this trick try to modify each page just a little to make it harder for search engines to recognize duplicates. But search engines have designed tools to find duplication and often drop a page from their indexes if they find it's a duplicate of another page at the same site. Duplicate pages found across different sites are often okay, which is why content syndication can work well if done right (see the discussion of duplicate content in Chapter 9), but entire duplicate sites are something that search engines frown on.

Page swapping and page jacking

Here are a couple of variations on the duplication theme:

- **Page swapping:** In this now little-used technique, one page is placed at a site and then, after the page has attained a good position, it's removed and replaced with a less-optimized page. One serious problem with this technique is that major search engines often reindex pages very quickly, and it's impossible to know *when* the search engines will return.

- **Page jacking:** Some truly unethical search engine marketers have employed the technique of using other peoples' high-ranking Web pages, in effect stealing pages that perform well for a while. This is known as *page jacking.*

Doorway and Information Pages

A *doorway page* is created solely as an entrance from a search engine to your Web site. Doorway pages are sometimes known as *gateway pages* and *ghost pages.* The idea is to create highly optimized pages that are picked up and indexed by search engines and that, with luck, rank well and thus channel traffic to the site.

Search engines hate doorway pages because they break one of the cardinal rules: They're intended for search engines, not for visitors. The sole purpose of a doorway page is to channel people from search engines to the real Web site.

One man's doorway page is another man's *information page* — or what some people call *affiliate pages, advertising pages,* or *marketing pages.* The difference between a doorway page and an information page is that the information page is designed for use by the visitor in such a manner that search engines will rank it well, whereas the doorway page is designed in such a manner that it's utterly useless to the visitor because it's intended purely for the search engine; in fact, originally doorway pages were stuffed full of keywords and duplicated hundreds of times.

Doorway pages typically don't look like the rest of the site, having been created very quickly or even by some kind of program. Doorway pages are part of other strategies. The pages used in redirects and cloaking (discussed in the next section) are, in effect, doorway pages.

Where do you draw the line between a doorway page and an information page? That's a question I can't answer here; it's for you to ponder and remains a matter of debate in the search engine optimization field. If a client asks me to help him in the search engine race and I create pages designed to rank well in search engines but in such a manner that they're still useful to the visitor, have I created information pages or doorway pages? Most people would say that I created legitimate information pages.

Suppose, however, that I create lots of pages designed for use by the site visitor — pages that, until my client started thinking about search engine optimization, would have been deemed unnecessary. Surely these pages are, by *intent,* doorway pages, aren't they, even if one could argue that they're useful in some way?

Varying degrees of utility exist, and I know people in the business of creating "information" pages that are useful to the visitor in the author's opinion only! Also, a number of search engine optimization companies create doorway pages that they simply *call* information pages.

Still, an important distinction exists between the two types of pages, and creating information pages is a widely used strategy. Search engines don't know your intent, so if you create pages that appear to be useful, are not duplicated dozens or hundreds of times, and don't break any other rules, they'll be fine.

Here's a good reality check. Be honest: Are the pages you just created truly of use to your site visitors? If you submitted these pages to Yahoo! Directory or the Open Directory Project for review by a human, would the site be accepted? If the answer is no, the pages probably aren't informational. The "trick," then, is to find a way to convert the pages you created for search engine purposes into pages that are useful in their own right — or for which a valid argument, at least, for utility can be made.

Using Redirects and Cloaking

Redirecting and cloaking serve the same purpose. The intention is to show one page to the search engines but a completely different page to the site visitor. Why do people want to do this? Here are a few reasons:

- If a site has been built in a manner that makes it invisible to search engines, cloaking allows the site owner to deliver indexable pages to search engines while retaining the original site.

- The site may not have much textual content, making it a poor fit for the search engine algorithms. Although search engine designers might argue that this fact means that the site isn't a good fit for a search, this argument clearly doesn't stand up to analysis and debate.

- Each search engine prefers something slightly different. As long as search engines can't agree on what makes a good search match, why should they expect site owners and developers to accept good results in some search engines and bad results in others?

I've heard comments such as the following from site owners, and I can understand their frustration: "Search engines are defining how my site should work and what it should look like, and if the manner in which I want to design my site isn't what they like to see, that's not my fault! Who gave them the right to set the rules of commerce on the Internet?!"

What might frustrate and anger site owners more is if they realized that one major search engine *does* accept cloaking, as long as you pay for it. (See the information on trusted feeds in Chapter 11; a trusted feed is, in effect, a form of cloaking.) So cloaking is a crime, but one search engine says, "Pay us, and we'll help you do it." (Is that a fee, a bribe, or a protection-racket payment?)

Understanding redirects

A *redirect* is the automatic loading of a page without user intervention. You click a link to load a Web page into your browser, and within seconds, the page you loaded disappears and a new one appears. Designers often create pages designed for search engines — optimized, keyword-rich pages — that redirect visitors to the real Web site, which is not so well optimized. Search engines read the page, but visitors never really see it.

Redirects can be carried out in various ways:

✔ By using the REFRESH meta tag. This is an old trick that search engines discovered long ago; most search engines don't index a page that has a REFRESH tag that quickly bounces the visitor to another page.

✔ By using JavaScript to automatically load another page within a split second.

✔ By using JavaScript that's tripped by a user action that is almost certain to occur. You can see an example of this method at work in Figure 8-3. The large button on this page has a JavaScript mouseover event associated with it; when users move their mice over the image — as they're almost certain to do — the mouseover event triggers, loading the next page.

You're unlikely to be penalized for using a redirect. But a search engine may ignore the redirect page. That is, if the search engine discovers that a page is redirecting to another page, it simply ignores the redirect page and indexes the destination page. Search engines reasonably assume that redirect pages are merely way stations on the route to the real content.

Examining cloaking

Cloaking is a more sophisticated trick than using a redirect, and harder for search engines to uncover than a basic REFRESH meta tag redirect. When browsers or searchbots request a Web page, they send information about themselves to the site hosting the page — for example, "I'm Version 6.1 of Internet Explorer," or "I'm Googlebot." The cloaking program quickly looks in its list of searchbots for the device requesting the page. In addition, a cloaking program also has a list of IP numbers that it knows are used by searchbots; if the request comes from a matching IP number, it knows it's a searchbot.

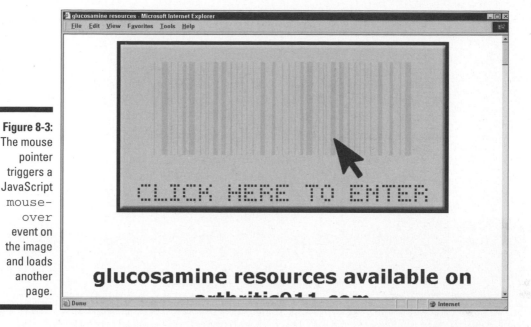

Figure 8-3:
The mouse pointer triggers a JavaScript mouse-over event on the image and loads another page.

So, if the device or IP number isn't found in the list of searchbots, the cloaking program tells the Web server to send the regular Web page, the one intended for site visitors. But if the device name or IP number *is* listed in the searchbot list — as it would be for Googlebot, for instance — the cloaking program sends a *different* page, one that the designer feels is better optimized for that particular search engine. (The cloaking program may have a library of pages, each designed for a particular search engine or group of engines.)

Here's how the two page versions differ:

- **Pages provided to the search engine:** Often much simpler; created in a way to make them easy for search engines to read; have lots of heavily keyword-laden text that would sound clumsy to a real person.

- **Pages presented to visitors:** Often much more attractive, graphics-heavy pages, with less text and more complicated structures and navigation systems.

Search engines don't like cloaking. Conservative search engine marketers steer well clear of this technique. Here's how Google defines cloaking:

> *The term "cloaking" is used to describe a Web site that returns altered Web pages to search engines crawling the site.*

Well, that's pretty clear — cloaking is cloaking is cloaking. But, wait a minute:

> *In other words, the Web server is programmed to return different content to Google than it returns to regular users, usually in an attempt to distort search engine rankings.*

Hang on: These two definitions aren't describing the same concept. The phrase "in an attempt to distort" is critical. If I "return altered pages" without intending to distort rankings, am I cloaking? Here's more from Google:

> *This can mislead users about what they'll find when they click on a search result. To preserve the accuracy and quality of our search results, Google may permanently ban from our index any sites or site authors that engage in cloaking to distort their search rankings.*

Notice a few important qualifications: *altered pages . . . usually in an attempt to distort search engine rankings . . . cloaking to distort their search engine rankings.*

This verbiage is ambiguous and seems to indicate that Google doesn't totally outlaw the use of cloaking; it just doesn't like you to use cloaking to cheat. Some would say that using cloaking to present to Google dynamic pages that are otherwise invisible, for instance, or that are blocked from indexing perhaps by the use of session IDs (see Chapter 7), would be an acceptable practice. And here's another very common use for "cloaking"; many, many sites display different content depending on the location of the person viewing the page (they use IP location to do this; see Chapter 10). Thus, they show different content to different people, including "searchbots." So there are many legitimate uses for cloaking. However, as I've pointed out, many in the business advise that you never use cloaking in any circumstance, just in case Google *thinks* your purpose is to "distort search engine rankings."

Tricks versus Strategies

When is a trick not a trick but merely a legitimate strategy? I don't know, but I'll tell you that there are many ways to play the SEO game, and what to one man is a trick might to another be the obvious thing to do.

Here's an example: creating multiple Web sites. One client has *two* Web sites ranking in the top five on Google for his most important keyword. (No, I can't tell you what the keyword is!) Another client at one point had around seven of the top ten results for one of his critical keywords; several of the links pointed to his own Web sites, and several pointed to his products positioned on other people's Web sites.

Now, this is definitely a trick: Build a bunch of small Web sites that point links back to your "core" site and then link all those sites from various places. The aim (and it can sometimes work if it's done correctly) is to boost the core site by creating many incoming links, but in many cases the "satellite" sites may also rank well. I've seen this technique work; I've also seen it fail miserably.

Is this a trick, though — building standalone sites with the intention of seeing which ones will rank best? And doing so not merely as a way to create links to a core site but as a way to see what works best for search engines? I don't know. I'll leave it for you to decide.

Paying the Ultimate Penalty

Just how much trouble can you get into by breaking the rules? The most likely penalty isn't really a penalty. It's just that your pages won't work well with a search engine's algorithm, so they won't rank well.

You can receive the ultimate penalty, though: having your entire site booted from the index. Here's what Google has to say about it:

> *We investigate each report of deceptive practices thoroughly and take appropriate action when abuse is uncovered. At minimum, we will use the data from each spam report to improve our site ranking and filtering algorithms. The result of this should be visible over time as the quality of our searches gets even better.*

Google is describing what I just explained — that it tweaks its algorithm to downgrade pages that use certain techniques. But:

> *In especially egregious cases, we will remove spammers from our index immediately so they don't show up in search results at all. Other steps will be taken as necessary.*

One of the dangers of using tricks, then, is that someone — perhaps your competitors — might report you, and if the trick is bad enough, you get the boot. Where do they report you?

- ✔ Google: In your Webmaster account (see Chapter 11), on `https://www.google.com/webmasters/tools/spamreport`.

- ✔ MSN/Bing makes it very difficult to report spam. If you want to try, search the Bing Help system. However, for the moment at least, the Yahoo! "Report Abuse Form" is still available, so you may want to submit there (remember, Bing provides search results to Yahoo!). See `http://help.yahoo.com/l/us/yahoo/search/abuse.html`.

- ✔ Ask.com at `http://asksupport.custhelp.com/app/ask/sno/0`.

People reporting spam may also be investigated, so don't throw stones in a glass house.

What do you do if you think you've been penalized? You see Chapter 19.

Chapter 9

Bulking Up Your Site — Competing with Content

· ·

In This Chapter

▶ Creating content yourself

▶ Understanding copyright

▶ Finding free material

▶ Paying for content

· ·

Content is an extremely important factor in getting a high ranking in the search engines. *Content* is a geeky Web term that means, in the broadest sense, "stuff on your Web site." A *content-rich* Web site is one that contains lots and lots of information for people to see, read, and use.

For search engines, content has a more narrow definition: words, and lots of 'em. So if you're interested in search engine optimization, you should concentrate on the *text* part of your Web site's content (the right text, of course, using the keywords you find out about in Chapter 5). You don't need to worry about pictures, video, or sound — at least as far as the search engines are concerned — because those forms of content generally don't help you get higher rankings. You don't need Flash animations, either, because although some search engines index them, they don't index well; how often do you find a Flash page ranking highly in the search results?

What you should be concerned about is text — words that the search engines can read. Now, it's not *always* necessary to bulk up your site by adding textual content — in some cases, it's possible to get high search engine rankings with a small number of keyword-laden pages. If that's your situation, congratulations. Sit back and enjoy the fruits of your rather minimal labors and skip this chapter. But if you don't find yourself in that happy situation, you need this chapter.

You may find that your competitors have Web sites stacked full of content. They have scores of pages, perhaps even hundreds of pages — or hundreds of thousands — full of text that is nicely laden with all the juicy keywords you're interested in. That's tough to compete with.

Content is not a subject that's covered in many books, newsletters, or Web sites related to search engine optimization and ranking. Most publications say, "You need content, so create some." But I believe that this issue is critical and shouldn't be glossed over with such trite comments, especially when several simple ways exist to *find* content. If you know the shortcuts, creating content doesn't have to be difficult. This chapter describes a slew of shortcuts to free and low-cost content, such as government materials, marketing and technical documents from manufacturers, and even something called *copyleft.*

Creating Content Three Ways

You can compete in the search engines in several different ways: Create a few well-optimized pages, get lots of links into your site, target keywords that competitors have missed, and put masses of content on your site. (Chapter 3 has more on these "basic" strategies.) In some cases, when going up against a well-entrenched competitor, you may have no choice but to fight on several fronts. You may find that you *must* do something to stack your site with content.

Evaluate competing sites to help you determine at what point you should stop adding content. Compare your site to competitors that rank well in search engines. All major search engines now use some kind of link popularity to rate Web pages. If you're sure that your site has more well-optimized pages than those competing sites, it may be time to stop adding content. You may want to focus instead on getting links to your site. (For more on that subject, check out Chapters 14 to 16.)

I've got some bad news and some good news about creating content:

 ✔ **The bad news:** The obvious way to create content — writing it yourself or getting someone else to write it for you — is a huge problem for many people. Most people find writing difficult, and even if they find it easy, the results are often less than appealing. Perhaps you know someone who can write well and you can convince this person to write a few paragraphs for you. But are your powers of persuasion sufficient to get you 10, 20, or 50 pages? What about 500 or 5,000? You can always pay someone for content, but the problem with paying is that it costs money.

✔ **The good news:** You can use some shortcuts to create content. Tricks of the trade can help you quickly bulk up your Web site (even if your writing skills match those of a dyslexic gerbil and your funds make the Queen of England's bikini budget look large in comparison). Note, though, that these tricks involve using *someone else's content.*

Here are three different ways to get content for your site:

✔ Write your own content

✔ Convince (force, bribe) someone else to create your content

✔ Find existing content from somewhere else

Writing Your Own Stuff

The obvious way to create content, for many small-site owners anyway, is to start writing articles. That's not a terrible idea in many cases. Thousands of sites rank well using content from the sites' owners.

If you use the write-it-yourself approach, keep the following points in mind:

✔ **Writing content is time consuming, even for good writers.** You may want to evaluate whether you can devote the time to writing and maintaining your own content and then allocate time in your schedule to do so.

✔ **Many people are *not* good writers.** Not only is the writing process time consuming but the results are also often sad.

✔ **If you *do* write your own stuff, pleeze spill chuck it.** Then have it edited by someone who has more than a third-grade education, and then spill chuck it again.

Do *not* rely on a word processor's grammar checker. This tool is worse than useless for most writers. Grammar checkers are of benefit only to those what already has a good grasp of grammar.

What will you write about? The obvious topic, of course, is your product or service (assuming that your site is selling something). The more you can say about each item you sell, the better. That should keep you busy for a while, but eventually most businesses find that they have written all they can about their products, and they still don't have a large site, so the next few sections present a few other ideas.

Summarizing online articles

Here's a quick way to get keywords onto your page:

1. **Use the search engines to track down articles related to your subject area.**

2. **Create a library area on your Web site in which you link to these articles.**

3. **For each link, write a short, keyword-laden summary of what the article is all about.**

The advantage to this kind of writing is that it's fairly quick and easy.

You may want to include the first few sentences of the article. This strategy comes under the gray area of copyright *fair use* (which you find out about in the appendix for this book). What really counts is what the article's owner thinks. In most cases, if you contact the article's owner (and you don't *have* to contact that person), the owner is happy to have you summarize the article, excerpt a small portion of it, and link to his or her site. Most people recognize that *this process is good for them!* However, occasionally you find someone who just doesn't get it and creates a fuss. Just remove the link and move on.

By the way, there are a number of highly popular and successful blogs — in particular celebrity and news blogs — that are based on this very concept — that is, summarizing other people's work.

You may want to approach the owners of the sites you're linking to and ask them to add a link back to your site. See Chapter 15 for more information.

Reviewing Web sites

Similarly to how you summarize, you can link to useful Web sites and write short (yes, keyword-laden) reviews of each one.

Reviewing products

Write short (um, keyword-laden) reviews of products related to the subject matter covered by your site. An additional benefit of such a program is that eventually people may start sending you free stuff to review. There are many successful sites — earning money mainly from advertising — based solely on this concept, such as PopGadget.net and Engadget.com.

Convincing Someone Else to Write It

You may find that having articles written (by others) specifically for your site is rather appealing, for two reasons. First, someone else does the work, not you. Second, if it doesn't turn out well, someone else (not you) gets blamed.

One approach, assuming that you can't force someone to write for you, is to pay someone. Luckily (for you), writers are cheap. For some reason, people often have a bizarre vision of a glamorous writing life that's awaiting them. (It has been 17 years since I wrote my first bestseller, and I'm still waiting for the groupies to turn up.) So you may be able to find someone to write for you for $10 or $12 an hour, depending on where you live and how well you lie. Or, maybe you can find a high school kid who can string together a few coherent words and is willing to work for less.

If you work for a large corporation, you may be able to convince a variety of people to write for you — people who may assume that it's actually part of their jobs (again, depending on how well you lie). Spread the work throughout various departments — marketing, technical support, sales, and so on — and it may turn into a decent amount of content. Still, you can use quicker and easier ways to get content, as described in the next section.

If you pay someone to write for you, draw up a simple contract saying that the work is a work for hire and that you're buying all rights to it. Otherwise, you don't own it and can use it for only limited purposes that are either stated in the contract or are more or less obvious. If you ask someone to write an article for your Web site and you don't get a contract giving you full rights, you can't later decide to syndicate the article on other sites or in newsletters. (Chapter 15 has more information on this syndication stuff.) If an employee writes the material for you on company time, the work is generally considered a work for hire and company property. However, if you have a very small company with an informal employment relationship and the writing is outside the scope of the employee's normal work duties, you should request that the employee sign a contract.

A huge (politically incorrect) business has grown up over the past few years: overseas outsourced SEO work, specifically (regarding this chapter's subject) the outsourcing of articles written for SEO purposes. If you hire an Indian writer or a Chinese writer, for example, you may find that the writing, um, doesn't sound quite *right*. In fact some of this work is truly dreadful. On the other hand, you can find people in these countries (and in other, less obvious nations, such as South Africa), who can write very well and can produce articles for your site for around $10 to $20 apiece. If you want to try this method, you can find writers on sites such as Elance.com, Naukri.com, Guru.com, and oDesk.com.

There are also companies that will manage content for you. They'll work with you to develop a content plan and write the content. For instance:

✔ **Brafton:** www.brafton.com

✔ **IdeaLaunch:** www.idealaunch.com

Using OPC — Other People's Content

Writing or hiring is the slow way to create content. Using someone else's content — that's the quick way. See the following list of quick content sources for your site (I explain the details later in this chapter):

✔ **Product information:** Contact the manufacturer or distributor of the products you sell on your site for marketing and sales materials, technical documentation, and so on.

✔ **Web sites and e-mail newsletters:** Contact the owners of other sites and e-mail newsletters and ask whether you can use their work.

✔ **Government sources:** Check U.S. government Web sites for free materials.

✔ **Content-syndication sites:** A number of sites provide free content for the asking.

✔ **Traditional syndication services:** Numerous companies sell materials you can use on your site.

✔ **RSS syndication feeds:** Check out this new, geeky technique for feeding syndicated content into Web sites.

✔ **Open content and copyleft:** This unusual new movement is probably based on the old Internet maxim "Information wants to be free."

✔ **Search pages:** You can search at a site to generate a search results page with your favorite keywords.

✔ **Press releases:** You may be able to find press releases related to your area of business. They're copyright free, and you can use them as you want. (Of course, you should make sure that they're not from competitors.)

✔ **A Q&A area on your site:** This is a way to serve your site visitors *and* get keywords onto the site.

✔ **Forums or message boards:** With forums and message boards on your site, your visitors create the keywords for you.

✔ **Blogs:** From the term *Weblogs,* these journals provide another way to let people create content for you.

This list gives you a good idea of the sources of content, and the "Hunting for Other People's Content" section, later in this chapter, explores how you find, evaluate, and procure content from these sources.

Before I show you how to help yourself to someone else's content, I need to warn you about a critical legal issue: copyright law. You must have a working knowledge of copyright restrictions so that you can properly evaluate whether (and how) it's appropriate to use the content you find. The next section gives you an overview of what you need to know, and the additional free chapter at `http://SearchEngineBulletin.com` goes into excruciating detail, in case you're curious.

Understanding Copyright —
It's Not Yours!

I'm continually amazed at how few people understand copyright — even people who should know better.

When I speak to clients about adding content to a Web site, I sometimes hear something like this: "How about that magazine article I read last week? Let's put that up there!" Or maybe, "Such and such a site has some great information — let's use some of that." That's called *copyright infringement*. It's against the law, and although serious harm is unlikely to befall you in most cases, you *can* get sued or prosecuted. Plus, it's just, well, not very nice. (That's the perspective of a writer who has found his work stolen on a number of occasions.)

Let me quickly summarize copyright law so that you have a better idea of what you can and can't use on your site:

✔ As soon as someone creates a work — writes an article, writes a song, composes a tune, or whatever — copyright is automatic. There's no need to register copyright; the creator owns the copyright whether or not it has been registered. Most copyright works, in fact, aren't registered, which is a good thing. If they were, the Library of Congress, which houses the Copyright Office and stores copyright registrations, would be the size of Alabama.

✔ If you don't see a copyright notice attached, it doesn't mean that the work's copyright isn't owned by someone. Current copyright law doesn't require such notices.

✔ If someone owns the copyright, that person has the right to say what can be done with, um, copies. Therefore, you generally can't take an article you find in a newspaper, magazine, or Web site and use it without permission. (There are exceptions, which you find out about in a moment.)

✔ In the United States, certain kinds of copyright infringement are felonies. You may not only get sued but also prosecuted.

✔ If you don't know whether you have the right to use something, assume that you *don't*.

✔ You can't just rewrite an article. *Derivative works* are also protected. If the result is clearly derived from the original, you could be in trouble.

✔ Copyright has to be expressly assigned. If you hire me to write an article for your Web site and don't sign a contract saying that you own all rights or that the work was a work for hire, you only have the right to place it on your Web site. I still have the right to use the article elsewhere.

A number of exceptions can prove *very* important when you're gathering content, so listen closely:

✔ **If it's really old, you can use it.** Copyright eventually expires. Anything published before 1923, for instance, is free for the taking.

✔ **If the "guvmint" created it, you can use it.** The U.S. government spends millions of dollars creating *content*. This content is *almost* never copyright-protected.

✔ **If it's donated, you can use it.** Authors often *want* you to use their materials. If they have given the public permission to use it, you can use it.

✔ **It's only fair.** Copyright law has a *fair use* exception that allows you to use small parts of a work, without permission, under particular conditions.

I strongly suggest that you read the free chapter, *Staying Out of Copyright Jail,* to get the details on copyright, and make sure that you beg or borrow, but not steal, other people's work. You can find that chapter here: `http://SearchEngineBulletin.com`.

Hunting for Other People's Content

In this chapter, I list different types of other people's content and warn you about copyright. Now it's time to get out there and grab tons of content. You're about to find some great places to look.

Keywords

When you're out on your content hunt, remember that the purpose is to find *keywords* to add keywords to your site. You can do that in several ways:

- **Find content with the keywords already in it.** You want content that has at least *some* of your keywords, though you'll often find that it's not enough.

- **Add keywords to the content you get.** In some cases, you shouldn't edit the content because you're expected to use the content without changes. In other cases, you may be allowed to modify the content. You can, for instance, modify *open content* (described later in this chapter), and some syndicators allow it. As syndicator Featurewell says, "Clients can make minor edits to stories and photos, provided they do not modify or change the meaning, tone or general context of the articles. . . ." Thus, you can replace a few words here and there with your keywords, as long as the article still makes sense and retains the same tone and context.

- **"Chunk up" the article.** Break it into smaller, Web-friendly pieces and separate each piece with a heading (containing keywords, of course).

Newspapers often modify content they buy. A syndicated column you read in New York may be different from the same column run in a paper in Los Angeles, because newspapers cut and modify for space reasons or because they don't like the way something is worded.

When adding content, you're generally interested in adding pages with a variety of keywords sprinkled throughout. Remember, if you have a rodent-racing site, you want lots of pages with the words *rodent, racing, race, event, mouse, rat,* and so on.

Product information

Does your Web site sell products that you buy from a wholesaler or manufacturer? If so, contact your source and find out what materials are available: brochures, spec sheets, technical documentation, or user manuals. Take a look at anything the manufacturer has available. (I have one client who built an entire retail Web site around the idea of scanning and posting brochure content from wholesalers. It's a multimillion dollar business now.)

In many cases, the material may be available in Adobe Acrobat PDF files. You can post these files on your site within seconds, and they will be indexed by the major search engines, including Google. However, such files generally don't rank well in the search engines, so the ideal approach is to also convert the work to HTML files.

In fact, you may want to convert PDF files to Web pages for several reasons:

✔ Web pages load more quickly than PDF files.

✔ After a file is converted, you can link from the document into your site, whereas a PDF file itself becomes *orphaned* in the search result — a file with no indication of, or link to, the site it comes from.

✔ You can insert keywords into the `<TITLE>`, `DESCRIPTION`, and `KEYWORDS` tags, and stress keywords by putting them in bold, italic, and `<H>` tags.

✔ You can add links to other pages within your site.

✔ You can do more keywording in Web pages, adding headers, side navigation, footer links, and so on.

Just *how* do you convert PDF files? If you own Adobe Acrobat, you can try to use that program, though you may not like the results. Various other programs do it for you, such as PDF-to-HTML, at `http://convert-in.com/pdf2html.htm`, and PDF Online, a free system at `www.pdfonline.com`. Adobe even has its own online conversion tool (`www.adobe.com/products/acrobat/access_onlinetools.html`). Or, search for *pdf converter*. None of these tools is perfect, so you may have some "clean-up" work to do on the PDF files.

Web sites and e-mail newsletters

The Web is so full of content that it's about to sink (well, not your site, obviously, or you wouldn't be reading this chapter). Why not grab a few articles you like from other sites or from the e-mail newsletters you subscribe to? In fact, you may want to go hunting to find articles for this very purpose.

If you ask nicely, many people are happy to let you use their content. In fact, as I explain in Chapter 15, many people use content-syndication as a strategy for site promotion. They *want* people to use their stuff, as long as the sites that are using the material provide *attribution* (clearly state where the material is from and who wrote it) and then provide a link back to the site of origin.

Asking for permission is quite easy: Simply contact the owner of the article you saw on a site or in a newsletter and ask whether you can use the article. I did this recently and, within *10 minutes,* received a positive response. Within 16 minutes, I had an article on my site that was loaded with keywords and that ranked very highly in the search engines in its own right. (I later realized that the author's page ranked number three for one of my critical keywords. Thus, within minutes, I had a page that had the potential to rank very highly for some important keywords.)

When you talk to the article's owner, make sure that you praise the article. (After all, you do like it, or you wouldn't be asking. Too much good content is out there to be using garbage.) Also, clearly state that you will provide the owner's bio at the bottom of the article and a link back to the owner's site.

If you own your own site, you have it easy: You can simply save the e-mail response from the article's author as evidence of permission to use the article. If you're working for a large corporation with a legal department, however, you have a bigger problem: Your lawyers, working under the principle of "common sense is dead," will expect you to have the article's author sign a 32-page document providing permission, declaring that he or she has the right to give permission, and signing over exclusive and lifetime rights to the article and any spin-off toys or clothing derived from it, in this or any other universe. (I didn't make up that universe bit, by the way; I took it from a very real publishing contract.) Sorry, I don't know how to help you here. (I would tell you to just remember what Shakespeare said — "First thing we do, let's kill all the lawyers" — except that I'm sure my publisher's legal department would complain.)

Where can you find these articles? For Web site articles, search for sites that are likely to have the type of information you need. I suggest that you avoid sites that are directly competing. Also keep your eyes open for newsletters while you're doing your Web search, or look for appropriate newsletters at some of these sites:

- ✔ **Ezine Locator:** www.ezinelocater.com
- ✔ **EzineHub:** www.ezinehub.com
- ✔ **Ezine-Universe:** http://new-list.com/

Try searching for a combination of one of your keyword phrases and the words *article* and *newsletter* — for instance, *rodent racing article* and *rodent racing newsletter.*

How do you know who owns the copyright to the article? Here's a quick rule of thumb: If the article has an attribution attached to it, contact that person. For instance, many e-mail newsletters are either written by a single person (in which case you contact him or her) or have a variety of articles, each one with an author bio and an e-mail address (in which case you contact the author, not the newsletter itself). In the majority of cases, the author has given the newsletter one-time rights and still owns the copyright.

Some mechanisms used for syndicating content ensure that search engines don't read the syndicated content! So, you need to make sure that you use the right technique. See "Content-syndication sites," later in this chapter, for more information.

Government sources

I love government sources because they're *huge,* with a surprising range of information. In general, documents created by the U.S. federal government are in the public domain. Under the terms of Title 17 United States Code section 105, works created by U.S. government departments do not have copyright protection.

However, you should be aware of some important exceptions:

- ✔ The government may still hold copyrights on works that have been given to the government — bequests or assignments of some kind.

- ✔ The law is a U.S. law, making U.S. government works copyright free. Most other governments hold copyrights on their works.

- ✔ In some cases, works that nongovernment agencies create on behalf of the government may or may not be protected by copyright — the law isn't clear.

- ✔ Works created by the National Technical Information Service (NTIS; www.ntis.gov) may have a limited, five-year copyright protection.

- ✔ The United States Postal Service is exempt from these regulations. The Postal Service can have copyright protection for its works. (It doesn't want people printing their own stamps!)

- ✔ In some cases, the government may publish works that were originally privately created works. Such documents are copyright protected.

Even with these exceptions, vast quantities of juicy government content are available. Now, don't think, "Oh, there probably aren't any government documents related to *my* area!" Maybe; maybe not. Where do you think all our tax billions go? The money can't *all* go to defense and schools. It has to be spent somehow, so some of it goes to creating vast amounts of Web content!

You can place this content directly on your Web site. You'll find the content in Web pages or Adobe Acrobat PDF files; as discussed earlier in this chapter, you'll probably want to convert PDF files to HTML.

You will find not only useful documents for your purposes (text-heavy documents that search engines can read) but also other materials that may be useful for your site, such as videos.

Here are a few good places to find government materials:

- **FedWorld:** `www.fedworld.gov`
- **Government Printing Office:**
  - *Catalog of U.S. Government Publications:* `http://catalog.gpo.gov/F`
  - *New Electronic Titles:* `www.access.gpo.gov/su_docs/locators/net`
- **Library of Congress — Government Web Resources:** `lcweb.loc.gov/rr/news/extgovd.html`
- **CIA's Electronic Reading Room:** `www.foia.cia.gov`
- **U.S. Department of State's Electronic Reading Room:** `http://www.state.gov/m/a/ips/`
- **FBI's Freedom of Information Web Site:** `foia.fbi.gov`

Or, just try this search syntax: *site:.gov your keywords*. For instance, typing *site:.gov rodent racing* tells the search engine to search within `.gov` domains only for *rodent racing*. (A lot of search results are returned for that search, though, surprisingly, nothing is returned when you search for *site:.gov "rodent racing"*.)

Content-syndication sites

In the "Web sites and e-mail newsletters" section, earlier in this chapter, I discuss the idea of finding Web pages or e-mail newsletter articles you like and asking the owners for permission to use them. Well, here's a shortcut: Go to content-syndication sites.

Content-syndication sites are places where authors post their information so that site owners or newsletter editors can pick it up and use it for free. Why? Because you agree to place, in return, a short blurb at the bottom of the article, including a link back to the author's Web site.

Here are a few places to get you started in the wonderful world of content-syndication:

- **Article Dashboard:** www.articledashboard.com

- **EZineArticles.com:** ezinearticles.com

- **FreeSticky.com:** www.freesticky.com

- **GoArticles.com:** www.goarticles.com

- **IdeaMarketers.com:** www.ideamarketers.com

- **World Wide Information Outlet:** certificate.net

- **The Open Directory Project's List of Content Providers:** www.dmoz.org/Business/Publishing_and_Printing/Publishing/Services/Free_Content

There are scores of these syndication libraries, so you'll have plenty of choice. (You'll find a lot of duplicates, though.)

Some Web sites have their own *syndication areas* — libraries from which you can pick articles you want to use. Also, see Chapter 15, where I talk about syndicating your own content and point you to other syndication sites.

Make sure that when you grab articles from a content-syndication site you're not using a competitor's article! All these articles have links back to the author's site, so you don't want to be sending traffic to the enemy.

Geeky stuff you must understand

I have to get into a little technogeeky information now, I'm afraid. I hate to do it, but if you don't understand this topic, you're just wasting your time with content-syndication.

Many syndication systems use a simple piece of JavaScript to allow you to pull articles from their sites onto yours. For instance, take a look at this code I pulled from a site that syndicates news articles:

```
<script src="http://farmcentre.com/synd/synd.jsp?id=cfbmc"> </script>
```

This piece of code tells the Web browser to grab the synd.jsp file from the farmcentre.com Web site. That file uses JavaScript to insert the article into the Web page. Articles or other forms of content are automatically embedded in other ways, too. They may be inserted using Java applets, and sometimes with <iframe> tags.

None of these ways of embedding an article into your site does you any good with search engines. As I explain in Chapter 7, the search engine bots generally *don't read JavaScript!* And even if they do read it, you probably won't get credit for content inserted into your pages using JavaScript.

Nor do search engines read Java applets. And, if they do read inside the `<iframe>` tags, it doesn't help, because they follow the link that's used to pull the page into the frame and view that content as though it were on the origin Web site.

The `<iframe>` tag is used by Internet Explorer to place an internal frame inside a Web page. That frame contains information from another Web page — in this case, a page on another Web site. Depending on how the iframe is set up, it can appear as though the information inside the frame is part of the original page — readers can't tell the difference.

So the searchbot grabs the page and reads the source code. The searchbot sees the JavaScript (such as the preceding sample code) but ignores it, moving on to the next line. The syndicated article you wanted to place into the Web page *never gets placed into the page that the searchbot reads!* All the time and energy you spent placing content is wasted.

This whole geeky topic strikes me as quite humorous, really. Thousands of people are syndicating content or using syndicated content, mostly for search engine reasons. People syndicating the content want to place their links on as many Web pages as possible, for two reasons:

- ✔ Readers will see the links and click them.
- ✔ The search engines will see the links and rank the referenced site higher.

Also, people using the syndicated content are doing so because they want content, stuffed with good keywords, for search engines to read.

In many cases, both the syndicators and the people using syndicated content are wasting their time because search engines aren't placing the content, seeing the keywords, or reading the links!

To make sure the content you use works for you, follow the suggestions in this list:

- ✔ **Don't use browser-side inclusion techniques.** That includes JavaScript, Java, and iframes.
- ✔ **Use server-side inclusion techniques**. That includes server includes, PHP, and ASP. If you're not sure whether a technique is server side or browser side, ask a knowledgeable geek — you want an inclusion technique

that loads the content into the page *before* it's sent to the browser or searchbot.

✔ **Use manual inclusion techniques.** That is, copy and paste the content into your pages directly. Plenty of content relies on manual inclusion, and you may even get content owners who are using automatic-inclusion techniques to agree to let you manually copy their content.

As long as you're aware of syndicated content's pitfalls and how to avoid them, it's quite possible to find syndicated content and make it work so that you reap the search engine benefits of having that content on your site.

A *hosted-content service* hosts the content on its site along with a copy of your Web site template so that the content appears to be on your site (unless you look in the browser's Location or Address bar, where you see the company's URL). The problem with these services is that search engines are unlikely to pick up the content because they see the same articles duplicated repeatedly on the same domain. Google, for instance, will probably keep one set and ignore duplicates. (Also, see the section "A Word about Duplicated Content," later in this chapter.)

The problem with automatic updates

Another problem with content-syndication sites involves *automatic updates,* which allow a content owner to change the content immediately. For example, sites that provide weekly or monthly newsletters use automatic updates. The content provider can use this technique to update the content on dozens or hundreds of sites by simply changing the source file. The next time a page is loaded on one of the sites with the syndicated content, the new information appears.

But if you're adding content for keyword purposes, automatic updating may not be such a good thing. If you find an article with lots of nice keywords, it could be gone tomorrow. Manual inclusion techniques ensure that the article you placed remains in place and also allow you to, for instance, break the article into chunks by adding keyword-laden headings. (Although it's hard to say whether a site owner who uses automatic updating is likely to let you use manual inclusion, plenty of content is out there.)

Traditional syndication services

Content-syndication is nothing new — it has been around for a hundred years. (I just made up that statement, but it's probably true.) Much of what you read in your local newspaper isn't written by the paper's staff; it comes from a syndication service.

Some syndication services sell content for your site. In general, this material should be better than free syndicated content. However, much of the free stuff is pretty good, too, so you may not want to pay for syndicated material until you exhaust your search for free content. (This content is often fed to Web sites using RSS feeds, so see the upcoming section "RSS syndication feeds.")

Here are a few places you can find commercial syndicated material:

- **Featurewell:** www.featurewell.com (Articles from $70)
- **Brafton:** http://www.brafton.com/
- **Moreover:** www.moreover.com
- **StudioOne:** www.studioonenetworks.com/
- **uclick:** www.uclick.com
- **YellowBrix:** www.yellowbrix.com
- **The Open Directory Project list of content providers:** www.dmoz.org/News/Media/Services/Syndicates
- **Yahoo! News and Media Syndicates page:** dir.yahoo.com/Business_and_Economy/Business_to_Business/News_and_Media/Syndicates

Specialty syndication services provide content for particular industries. For example, Inman (www.inman.com) provides content for the real estate industry.

RSS syndication feeds

RSS is one of those geeky acronyms that nobody can define for certain. Some say it means *really simple syndication*; others believe that it means *rich site summary* or *RDF site summary*. What it stands for doesn't really matter. All you need to know is that RSS is an important content-syndication tool.

RSS systems comprise two components:

- An RSS *feed,* or a source of content of some kind
- An RSS *aggregator* or *news reader,* or a system that drops the information from the feed into a Web page

For example, all top search engines provide RSS feeds of their news headlines, at least for personal or noncommercial use. You can install an RSS aggregator on your site and point it to an RSS news feed. The page will then contain recent searches on news headlines.

The big advantage of RSS feeds is that you define the keywords you want to have sent to your site. Tell the feed that you want feeds related to rodent racing and, naturally, content is fed back to you with the keywords `rodent racing` in it, along with lots of other, related keywords.

What you need, then, is an aggregator that you can install into your Web site. Aggregators range from fairly simple to quite complicated — and that's assuming you have some technical abilities in the first place. (If you don't, there's no range; they're all complicated!)

Before you go to the trouble of getting an aggregator, decide whether you will receive enough suitable content to make it worthwhile. Technical subjects predominate, so if your subject area is *macramé and knitting,* you *may* find a dearth of material. (On the other hand, search and you may be surprised). Also, often RSS feeds merely pass a link to material on another site, in which case you don't benefit much. Make sure that you're getting useful content passed to your site.

To find RSS feeds, keep your eyes open for RSS or XML symbols and other indicators showing that an RSS feed is available — many blogs, for instance, provide RSS feeds. You can see examples of these icons in Figure 9-1.

Figure 9-1:
Look for these sorts of icons and links to indi-cate that an RSS feed is available.

Check out these RSS feed sites:

- ✔ **NewsKnowledge:** `www.newsknowledge.com`
- ✔ **Syndic8:** `syndic8.com`
- ✔ **Feedzilla:** `www.feedzilla.com`

You can also find RSS feeds by searching for blogs. Google has a blog-search function at `blogsearch.google.com`.

However, you must remember that just because you find an RSS feed available doesn't mean that you can put it into your site without permission. In fact, many blog owners provide feeds so that their readers can view the blogs in a personal RSS reader; you can, for instance, subscribe to RSS feeds within Microsoft Outlook, Internet Explorer, and a Yahoo! or Google account. Before you use a feed, read the feed license agreement or, if you can't find it, contact the owner.

In contrast to the automated syndication techniques I mention earlier in this chapter, which use JavaScript and other browser-side systems for inserting content, RSS aggregators for Web pages often use *server-side* techniques, so the content is inserted into the Web page *before* the search engines see it. That's what they call in the search engine business *A Good Thing.*

If you decide that you want to go ahead with RSS, you need an aggregator. Try searching for *news aggregator* or *rss aggregator,* and either check out the following software directories or ask your favorite geek to do so for you:

- **freshmeat:** `freshmeat.net`
- **SourceForge.net:** `sourceforge.net`

If your geek has never heard of freshmeat or SourceForge, it's just possible that he or she isn't quite geeky enough.

Open content and copyleft

Have you heard of *open-source software?* This type of software is created through the contributions of multiple individuals who agree to allow pretty much anyone to use the software, at no charge. Another movement that doesn't get quite the same attention as open-source software is the open-content movement. *Open content i*s, as explained on the Open Content List Web site, free and available for your use.

Open content relies on the concept known as *copyleft.* Under copyleft, the owner of a copyrighted work doesn't release it into the public domain. Instead, he or she releases the work for public modification, with the understanding that anyone using the work must agree to not claim original authorship and to release all derivative works under the same conditions.

Stacks of information are released under copyleft. Start at these sites:

> ✔ **Creative Commons:** www.creativecommons.org
>
> ✔ **The Open Directory Project's open content page:** dmoz.org/
> Computers/Open_Source/Open_Content

You should check out open content — in particular, the open-content wikis, the best known of which as Wikipedia.org, which has information on just about anything. (You can find a list of them here: http://en.wikipedia.org/wiki/List_of_wikis).

Watch for competitors' information. Some companies use open content as a way to get their links onto the Web.

Search results pages

The great thing about search results pages is that they have the exact keywords you define, liberally scattered throughout. When you conduct a search in a search engine — whether you're searching Web sites, a directory of magazine articles, or news headlines — what does the search engine return? Matches for your keywords.

RSS provides one way to insert searches — in particular, searches of news headlines — into your pages. Even though the page's content changes continually, you don't have to worry about the content changing to a page that doesn't contain your keywords, because the content is a reflection of the keywords you provide. You may also be able to find search pages that you can manually copy and paste. Sites that contain large numbers of articles and a search function may be good candidates. Run a search; then, copy the results and paste them into a Web page.

Make sure that the links in the search results still work and that they open the results in a new window. (You don't want to push people away from your site.) Also check with the site owner to make sure that this strategy is okay. In many cases, site owners are fine with it; again, it means more links to their sites!

Press releases

The nice thing about press releases is that you can use them without permission. The purpose of a press release is to send it out and see who picks it up. You don't need to contact the owner of the press release, because you already have an implied agreement that you can simply post the release wherever you want (unchanged and in its entirety, of course).

You may be able to find press releases that have the keywords you want, are relevant to your site in some way, and are not released by competitors. For instance, if you're in the business of running rodent-racing events, companies selling rodent-racing harnesses and other gear aren't direct competitors and may well have press releases you can use.

Where do you find these press releases? Try searching for *press releases* at a search engine. Combine the search term with some keywords, such as *rodent racing press release.* You can also find them at press release sites, such as these:

- ✓ **EmailWire:** www.emailwire.com
- ✓ **Free-Press-Release.com:** www.free-press-release.com
- ✓ **Hot Product News:** www.hotproductnews.com
- ✓ **I-Newswire.com:** i-newswire.com
- ✓ **M2PressWIRE:** www.presswire.net
- ✓ **Online Press Releases:** www.onlinepressreleases.com
- ✓ **OpenPR.com:** www.openpr.com
- ✓ **PR Newswire:** www.prnewswire.com
- ✓ **PR Web:** www.prweb.com
- ✓ **PR.com:** www.pr.com
- ✓ **PR9.net:** www.pr9.net
- ✓ **PressBox.co.uk:** www.pressbox.co.uk
- ✓ **PR-GB.com:** www.pr-gb.com
- ✓ **PRLeap:** www.prleap.com
- ✓ **PRLog.org:** www.prlog.org
- ✓ **TransWorldNews.com:** www.transworldnews.com

You can even subscribe to some of these press release services so that you get relevant press releases sent to you as soon as they're published.

Q&A areas

After you attract sufficient traffic to your site, you may want to set up a question-and-answer (Q&A) or Frequently Asked Questions (FAQ) area on your site. Visitors to your site can ask questions — providing you with keyword-laden questions in many cases — and you can answer them.

A number of free and low-cost software tools automate the creation and management of these Q&A areas. Search the utility sites, such as www.resource index.com, for these tools, and find a friendly geek if you need help installing a tool.

Make sure that search engines can read pages created by any tool you install on your site, such as the FAQ tool or the BBS and blog tools I tell you about next. Find a tool you like and then find out whether Google indexes the pages in the demo or sample sites. If not, ask the software author to point you to a demo that *does* have indexed pages.

Message boards

Message board areas can be quite powerful, in more than one way. Setting up a message board — also known as a forum or bulletin board system (BBS) — allows site visitors to place keywords in your site for you! A message board often draws traffic, bringing people in purely for the conversation.

Do you own a site about kayaks? As you sleep, visitors can leave messages with the word *kayak* in them over and over. Does your site sell rodent supplies? While you go about your daily business, your visitors can leave messages containing words such as *rodent, mouse,* and *rat.* Over time, this process can build up to hundreds of pages with many thousands of keywords.

BBS systems — even cool ones with lots of features, such as the ability to post photos — are cheap — or, often, free. They're relatively easy to set up, even for low-level geeks. Don't underestimate this technique: If you have a lot of traffic on your Web site, a BBS can be a great way to build huge amounts of content. Search for terms such as *bbs software* and *forum software.*

Blogs

Blogs are sort of like diaries. (The term is a derivation of We*blog.*) These systems allow people to write any kind of twaddle — er, musings — they want and then publish this nonsense — um, literature — directly to their Web sites. My cynicism aside, you *can* find some extremely interesting blogs out there.

In fact, over the past few years, blogs have become important SEO tools — search engines seem to like them and to visit frequently to index them. In fact, Google even owns one of the top blogging-tools companies, Blogger (`blogger.com`). (Would you bet that blogs hosted by Blogger are indexed by Google?!) In fact, there are plenty of blog-hosting sites, such as Blog.com, Blogster.com, and many more. Search for *blog hosting.*

There are also free and low-cost blog programs that you can install directly onto your Web site. WordPress, for instance (www.wordpress.com), is a very sophisticated blog system that's free and relatively easy to install. (For everything you need to know about using WordPress, check out the latest edition of *WordPress For Dummies,* by Lisa Sabin-Wilson.) In addition, many blog-hosting services, such as Blogger, provide a way to integrate pages into your Web site, and blogs can be effective SEO tools, if you can find a way to create enough content. Although many people set up blogs, the number that *maintain* them is far lower!

If you use any tool that allows visitors to post messages on your site, you should monitor and delete inappropriate messages. Many search engine marketers use such tools to post messages (known as *blog spam*) with links pointing back to their sites.

Blogs can be quite useful for search engine optimization, but I don't think blogs are an SEO magic bullet, as some people have suggested. Blogs are a way to get more content onto your site, and they typically get reindexed frequently. They also have tools that interlink blogs, so if you run an active blog, you can get links back to your site. However, the big problem with blogs is that someone must have the time to write frequently, the inclination to write frequently, and the ability to write well and to write what people want to read. This is often a tall order!

A Word about Duplicated Content

Before you move on, a quick discussion about *duplicated content.* The idea is that search engines don't like the same content appearing in different places; after all, why would they want to provide people with lots of different ways to get to the same information? As a Google employee stated on the Google Webmaster Central blog (http://googlewebmastercentral.blogspot.com):

> *Our users typically want to see a diverse cross-section of unique content when they do searches. In contrast, they're understandably annoyed when they see substantially the same content within a set of search results.*

What does Google do about duplicated content? In general, it tries to eliminate copies. For instance:

> *. . . if your site has articles in "regular" and "printer" versions and neither set is blocked in robots.txt or via a noindex meta tag, we'll choose one version to list.*

A lot of paranoia exists about duplicated content; people talk about how sites can get themselves banned for using duplicated content. Most of this talk is gross exaggeration because sites often have good reasons to have duplicated content. Perhaps you're running news feeds from a popular central source or using press releases about events in your industry. It wouldn't make sense for search engines to penalize people for such innocent uses. Thus, as this Google employee stated,

> *In the rare cases in which we perceive that duplicate content may be shown with intent to manipulate our rankings and deceive our users, we'll also make appropriate adjustments in the indexing and ranking of the sites involved. However, we prefer to focus on filtering rather than ranking adjustments . . . so in the vast majority of cases, the worst thing that'll befall webmasters is to see the "less desired" version of a page shown in our index.*

(For more from this blog entry, search the blog for `deftly dealing with duplicate content`.)

In fact, there are various reasons why search engines can't penalize sites for republishing content. Whom will they punish — every site holding the content or all but the first one to publish it? Also, how would they know who was first?

Here's another reason that the search engines can't "punish" sites for duplicated content. Say that I've noticed that your rodent-racing site is coming up quickly in the search ranks and you've got a lot of excellent, unique content related to the exciting world of racing very small animals. If I were of a nefarious bent (which I'm not, but if I were . . .), here's what I'd do: Build a bunch of Web sites on different servers, but build them anonymously. I'd then "scrape" data from your rodent site and republish it on these other sites, forcing the search engines to penalize you.

In general, then, the dire warnings about duplicated content are wrong. However, if Google *does* figure out that you have duplicated content, it may drop the duplicate pages.

So what can you do about duplicated content, with articles you get from syndication sites, for instance, or press releases you drop into your site? If you want to make it more likely that the content isn't ignored, mix it up a little: Add headings within the pieces, change a few words here and there, surround it with other information that's unique to your site, and so on. But don't worry about a penalty, because if every site that contains duplicate content were dropped from Google's index, the index would be empty.

Chapter 10

Finding Traffic Through Local-Search Marketing

*I*ncreasingly, the Internet is being used as a tool for finding local resources. You can find not only information or buy online, but you can also find homes for sale in your neighborhood, compare local independent insurance agents, and shop at stores close to you that sell the products you need. Thus, it's increasingly important to keep *local-search marketing* in mind when optimizing for search engines — that is, to target by not only a searcher's keyword but also by the searcher's geographic location.

Wait! Before you skip this chapter because you have a purely online business, you need to understand the *two* basic reasons you should consider local-search marketing:

✔ You have a local business.

✔ Your prospects — your target customers — search locally.

Say you are a local business. You sell insurance in your town or own a local health-food store or are a personal trainer with clients within a 5-mile radius. Clearly, you don't need to rank well on the terms *insurance, health food,* or *personal training*. You need to rank well on the terms *insurance denver, health food waco,* or *personal training paducah*. There's no point in competing for general terms against hundreds of thousands of other companies when you're interested in a fraction of the searches; in fact, the really good news is that it's much easier to rank for a local term than a nonlocal term. The work required to rank on Page 1 for the term *personal training* will be *far* more than the work required for *personal training paducah*.

But, say you're not a local shop for local people. You sell to anyone, anywhere. You may find that the people you want to reach don't search for generic terms — they search for generic terms *in combination with local terms.* You may discover this concept if you do a good keyword analysis, which I describe in Chapter 5. Most people don't search for lawyers, for instance; they search for lawyers in a particular city. They don't search for insurance; they search for insurance in a particular state or city. They don't search for mortgages — they search for mortgages in a particular city.

You may find then, that if you want to reach the largest number of people, you *have* to consider the local aspect even if you sell nationally. Large online businesses targeting home buyers, for instance, often create *local-search–targeted* pages designed to reach people in thousands of different locales.

Understanding Local-Search Marketing's Importance

The local aspect of search is hugely important. Remember, for all the e-commerce hype, e-commerce accounts for only a small portion of the overall economy; in other words, most sales are made *offline.* Forrester Research, early in 2010, claimed that e-commerce accounted for 6 percent of the U.S. economy in 2009, and would account for 7 percent in 2010; even by 2014, the company believes, e-commerce will still account for only 8 percent. So offline sales are still hugely important, but they undoubtedly are often affected by online activities. For instance, research has uncovered these gems about Internet users:

- Most are *off-channel, Web-to-shop (W2S),* or *ROBO (Research Online, Buy Offline)* buyers. That is, they research products online before buying offline.

- When in the brick-and-mortar stores, almost half of Internet users spend extra dollars on products they didn't research.

- More money is spent offline after online research than is spent online after online research.

- Forrester Research estimated, in 2010, that in 2009 more than one-third of all offline sales were influenced in some way by the Web; they believe that almost half of all offline sales will be Web influenced.

- Forrester Research expects that by 2011, "online influenced offline sales" will reach $1 trillion. Thus, many businesses are trying to target people in their own areas, to get them to walk into their brick-and-mortar stores. Local-search marketing helps you find those people.

Click and mortified

Studies carried out by ShopLocal.com and reported in January 2008 show that

✔ The Web sees dramatic increases in traffic immediately before big retail shopping days, such as late in the evening on Thanksgiving Day (right before the "Black Friday" shopping mayhem).

✔ In particular, retail store Web sites see huge increases in traffic before big shopping days.

✔ Ninety-two percent of American consumers research products online; yet 95 percent of all purchases are, of course, made offline.

✔ A consumer who researches a product online and then goes to an offline retail store to purchase the product spends an average of $154 on additional, incremental, purchases.

A great deal of money and activity are involved in these "online-influenced offline sales"! One study in 2005 found that 25 percent of all Web searches made by people researching products are shoppers looking for local merchants.

Looking Through Local Search

All four of the major search engines — Google, Yahoo!, MSN/Bing, and Ask. com — now have local search features, sometimes incorporated into their map systems but still accessible from regular search. (Google Local became part of Google Maps, for instance). You can see an example of local-search results, from Google Maps, in Figure 10-1, and in Figure 10-2 you can see the type of results that can be displayed for a particular business.

Local search is the generic term given to the ability to search for information related to a particular location — a state, a city, or even a ZIP Code. In some cases, there's a Local link immediately above the Search box; you click this link and then tell the search engine what you're looking for and where, and it finds the best matches it can. But local searches are carried out if you provide localization information directly into the regular Search box (*pizza denver* or *tax attorney rhode island*, for example).

However, the local search engines also have a good idea where you are (I explain how next), so for many types of searches, they automatically assume that you want a local search. Search any of the big three search engines for *pizza,* for instance, and they'll assume that you're likely looking for a pizza place, so they include local search in the results. Search for *car insurance*, *japanese restaurant*, or *hair salon*, and you'll get local results.

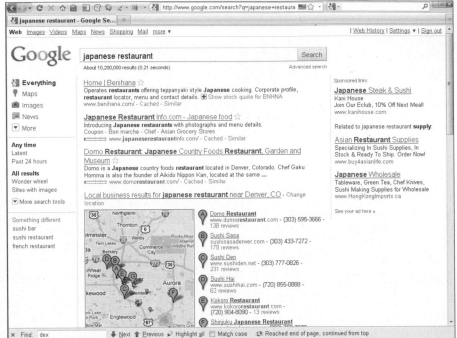

Figure 10-1:
Google
Maps
provide
local-search
results,
including
business
details, cou-
pons, and
menus.

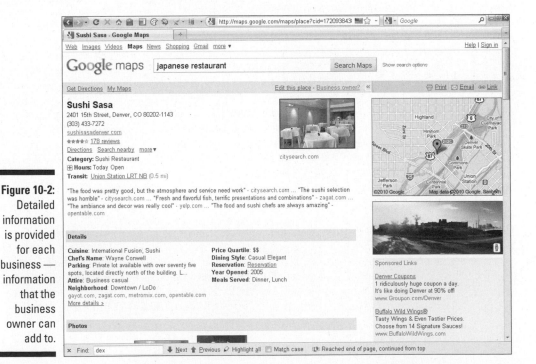

Figure 10-2:
Detailed
information
is provided
for each
business —
information
that the
business
owner can
add to.

How Does Local Search Work?

Local search is based on several different methodologies, including the science known as *geolocation,* the science of trying to figure out where the heck a computer *is,* geographically speaking. Say, for example, that a computer contacts a search engine and says, "Hi, I'm computer 67.176.77.58; can you search for information about *rodent racing* and send me the results?" How does the search engine figure out whether that computer is in Colorado and thus wants information about the famous Rocky Mountain prairie dog racing, or is in Florida and is interested in the famous African Gambian pouch rat races?

Local search generally works in a few basic ways. Different services use different combinations of these methods.

Search terms

If someone types *dentist new york,* the search engine can be pretty sure that the person is looking for a dentist in New York, not a dentist in Oklahoma City. Simple, eh? I can be in Denver, Colorado, but if I type *dentist new york,* the search engine will display a map of New York.

Partner and localized sites

Search services can guess at a location based on the Web site someone is using. If someone is searching at www.google.fr, it's a good bet that the person is in France; if someone searches at www.yahoo.co.uk, that person is probably in the United Kingdom. In other cases, partner sites can be even more specific, and related to a particular region or even city.

IP numbers

Internet Protocol (IP) numbers identify computers on the Internet. Every computer connected to the Internet at any moment has a unique IP number.

With information being sent to and fro — from your computer to Web sites and back — there has to be a way for the information to be "addressed" so that various servers on the Internet know where to deliver the information. Thus, every computer connected to the Internet has an *IP number,* or *IP address.*

In some cases, two or more computers share an IP number, as in a situation in which a house or an apartment is using a cable or digital subscriber line (DSL) connection, with several computers connected through a single router; but for the purposes of figuring out location, this information isn't important, of course.

In some cases, computers "own" a particular IP number: Turn the computer off now and turn it on next week, and it has the same number. This is known as a *static IP number.* Often, however, computers share IP numbers. Log out of a dialup account now and in five minutes dial back in, and your computer is assigned a different IP number (known as a *dynamic IP number*). That IP number is shared among many computers, but only one computer can use the number at any particular time.

Take a look at this IP number: `67.176.77.58`. This number uniquely identifies a particular computer in Colorado. If a server sends a page to that address, the page can go to only one place because at that moment only one computer on the Internet is using that number to identify itself. It's like a telephone number. Every telephone in the entire world has a unique number (when you include the country code). Pick up the phone and dial the full number, and there's only one telephone in the world that you can possibly be connected to.

An IP number is a *hierarchical* system. A block of numbers is assigned to a particular organization or company; that organization or company then assigns blocks of numbers to other organizations or companies, which can then assign their numbers to different organizations or companies, or divisions within a company, and so on.

Consider, again, `67.176.77.58`. This number is "owned" by Comcast Cable Communications, a large American cable-TV company. In fact, Comcast has a large block of numbers: `67.160.0.0–67.191.255.255`. Within that large block lies another block that Comcast uses in Colorado: `67.176.0.0–67.176.127.255`. Clearly, `67.176.77.58` lies within this block.

If you want to see this process at work, a number of sites tell you where you are, or at least where they think you are. I just visited IP2Location (`www.ip2location.com`), and it identified my city — though not my ZIP Code, and it got my latitude and longitude wrong.

Local-search marketing with IP numbers isn't perfect; it's definitely an imprecise science, for a few reasons:

> ✔ **You can't assume that a number assigned to a company in a particular area is being used in that area.** It's possible for two computers using two IP numbers that are just one digit apart — `67.176.77.58` and `67.176.77.59`, for instance — to be thousands of miles apart. An IP number block assigned to an organization in one area can be used

by many different computers in many different locations. For example, a computer in San Francisco assigned a block of IP numbers may use those numbers for computers in branch offices in San Diego, Oklahoma City, and Seattle.

✔ **Dynamic IP numbers are "here today, there tomorrow."** When you dial into a network and are assigned an IP number, you could be in California while the computer that assigned the number is in Virginia. When you log off and someone logs on and takes your number, the new computer might be in Wyoming. In particular, AOL messes up IP location because it assigns IP numbers to dialup users all around the country.

Still, geolocation is getting better all the time. Although the authorities that assign blocks of IP numbers provide very basic geographic information, this information can then be combined with other clues, such as hostnames. For example, it's possible to trace the path from one computer to another and get the IP numbers and hostnames of the servers between the start and destination computers. The following path is from a computer in Australia to `67.176.77.58`:

```
1  FastEthernet6-0.civ-service1.Canberra.telstra.net (203.50.1.65)
2  GigabitEthernet3-0.civ-core2.Canberra.telstra.net (203.50.10.129)
3  GigabitEthernet2-2.dkn-core1.Canberra.telstra.net (203.50.6.126)
4  Pos4-1.ken-core4.Sydney.telstra.net (203.50.6.69)
5  10GigabitEthernet3-0.pad-core4.Sydney.telstra.net (203.50.6.86)
6  10GigabitEthernet2-2.syd-core01.Sydney.net.reach.com (203.50.13.38)
7  i-6-1.wil-core02.net.reach.com (202.84.249.201)
8  sl-gw28-ana-10-0.sprintlink.net (144.223.58.221)
9  sl-bb21-ana-11-0.sprintlink.net (144.232.1.29)
10 sl-bb22-ana-15-0.sprintlink.net (144.232.1.174)
11 sprint-gw.la2ca.ip.att.net (192.205.32.185)
12 tbr1-p014001.la2ca.ip.att.net (12.123.29.2)
13 12.122.10.25 (12.122.10.25)
14 12.122.9.138 (12.122.9.138)
15 12.122.12.134 (12.122.12.134)
16 gar1-p360.dvmco.ip.att.net (12.123.36.73)
17 12.125.159.90 (12.125.159.90)
18 68.86.103.141 (68.86.103.141)
19 68.86.103.2 (68.86.103.2)
20 * * *
21 c-67-176-77-58.hsd1.co.comcast.net (67.176.77.58)
```

The Internet uses IP numbers for addressing, but to make things easier for mere mortals, names (or *hostnames*) can be assigned to computers. Notice something about the hostnames in the preceding code? Some of them have geographic information embedded in them: `Canberra`, `Sydney`, `co` (Colorado), `la2ca` (Los Angeles, California), and so on. Another clue: Some major *Internet service providers (ISPs)* assign blocks of IP numbers geographically, so when you crack the code, you can figure out where people using that ISP actually live. Using clues such as these, geolocation engineers at various companies specializing in this science can fairly accurately locate IP numbers.

From coast to coast

There are other cases in which geolocation doesn't work. To "mask" your location as an example, follow these directions:

1. Search for *anonymous browsing* at any major search engine.

2. Visit one of the anonymous Web-browsing sites.

3. Use one of these systems to visit an IP location site, such as `www.ip2location.com`.

4. See where it thinks you're coming from.

Quite likely, it thinks you're somewhere on the other side of the country or the world.

So the system isn't perfect, but it's close much of the time. In any case, it doesn't usually need to be spot on. If you're searching for pizza in your town, for instance, Google doesn't need to know your exact address; it shows a map with pizza places, and you can zoom in to your specific location if you want.

Two Ways to Reach People Locally

Let me summarize:

✔ People often type location names with their keyword searches.

✔ Search engines are providing local search services, encouraging people to search locally.

✔ Local search services will guess where searchers are.

Now, it's important to understand that the major search engines have two indexes providing "local" data when you do a local search. There are the regular "organic" search results, but the Local results, providing the data such as that shown in Figures 10-1 and 10-2, come from a completely different place.

This type of data is both good and bad. It's good, because it gives you an extra chance of ranking. Perhaps you're not doing too well in the organic results, but you *are* doing well in the Local results, and your site appears high on the page next to the map. Or vice versa. Or, if you do a really good job, your business can turn up in the local search results — up by the map — *and* in the organic results, probably lower down on the page (not always; sometimes the map and Local results are displayed before the organic results, sometimes embedded in them). The bad part is that you have more work to do: They are completely different indexes, so you need to do different things to rank well in each one.

It's also important to understand that the search engines treat each index differently. One is used for true local searches; the other is used solely for keyword searches, so it's searched only "locally" in the sense that if someone types a location term as one of the keywords, the search engine will search for that location term.

For instance, if someone searches for, say, *pizza denver*, Google provides two types of search results:

✔ Local-search results for *pizza* in *denver*

✔ Organic-search results for *pizza denver*

However, if you are in Denver and search for *pizza* — just the product term *pizza* without the local term *denver* — Google returns

✔ Local-search results for pizza in denver

✔ Organic-search results for *pizza*

You see the difference? If the searcher uses a local keyword, Google does a local search *and* searches the organic directory for pages that include that local keyword. If the searcher doesn't use the local keyword, though, Google still does a local search for you using the Local-search directory, based on where it thinks you are, but as far as the organic search goes, Google just looks for the keyword that's entered; it doesn't modify the search based on your location.

So your job, if you want to rank well for local searches, is to know what to do for both of these indexes. I begin with the index I've been telling you about already, the organic-search index, and then I discuss the Local index.

"Localizing" Your Web Pages

I see this all the time with my consulting clients: Web sites that need to rank for local search terms but that haven't the slightest hope of doing so. An example is my rodent-racing client in New York, the owner of the *Big Apple Rodent Racing* track (okay, I made up this client, but bear with me). He came to me saying that he wanted to rank well for *rodent racing new york*, and in fact to rank well for various New York boroughs.

There was one big problem, though. He didn't have a single page with the term *rodent racing* and the name *New York*. The only page that contained *New York* was his Contact Us page, and that page contained only contact information and a map . . . it didn't contain the words *rodent racing*. So my client had not a single page that was a good match for *rodent racing new york*.

So the very first step to take if you want to rank locally is to make sure that you have local terms in your pages. Ideally, have these terms not just in a Contact Us page but on every page.

The problem with putting your location in only your Contact Us page is that while you've probably created dozens, scores, maybe hundreds of lovely keyword-rich pages, you have just removed one of the most important keywords and put it on a separate page. If you want Google to think a page is related to a particular location in addition to finding certain keywords, you need to make sure the location name and keywords appear on the same pages! So, here are a few things you can do:

- ✔ **Include your full address in your Web pages.** Include your street, city, state, and ZIP Code. Although you can put the address in the footer, ideally it should be near the top of the page somewhere. (If you don't know about prominence, see Chapter 6.)

  If you have more than one address, put all the addresses on each page.

- ✔ **Include in all your pages the names of all locations you're interested in.** Include a list of city names, for instance, in your footer or in a sidebar, ideally with links to pages with information about each of those cities.

- ✔ **Create a Contact Us page *for every* location you have.** If you have five office locations, you need five Contact Us pages.

- ✔ **Put important keywords on your Contact Us pages**.

- ✔ **Find other reasons to mention the city and ZIP Code in the body of your text.** If possible, put them in <H> tags; use bold font on some of the references, too.

- ✔ **Include the city name in your** <TITLE> **and** DESCRIPTION **meta tags.**

- ✔ **Include city and state names in link text when linking from other sites to yours.** See Chapter 14 for more information.

You should think carefully about what location names are truly important. Different types of searches use different types of location terms. For instance, when people search for *insurance*, they often search with a state name: *car insurance colorado*, *renters insurance texas*, and so on. For real estate, people usually search with city names or even neighborhood names. For attorneys, people often search using city names but rarely neighborhood names. So you should think about which terms are important and target those terms.

Getting a few keyworded links to your site with the location names in combination with the product or service keywords can be very powerful, so read Chapter 14 carefully. Consider also actually optimizing a few pages for specific locations, using the location and product or service keywords in the <TITLE> and DESCRIPTION tags, in H1 headers, several times in the body text, in links to the page, and so on. My rodent-racing client should probably have a page optimized for *New York Rodent Racing*, one for *Brooklyn Rodent Racing*, another for *Manhattan Rodent Racing*, and so on.

Try these techniques, and there's a good chance that your pages will start appearing in the organic-search results.

Registering for Local Search

In Chapter 11, you read about how to get your site listed in search engine indexes. Let me quickly cover *another* form of search engine submission here: submitting your business to the search engine's local-search indexes.

First note that your business may turn up in the results even if you take no action. The major search engines pull data from a lot of different sources. If you have a business that has been picked up by some kind of business directory, your business has likely ended up on the local-search indexes of the major search engines. For instance, if your business has a business phone listing, you are almost certainly included.

Being in the index doesn't mean that you can rest on your laurels, though. Just because you are in the index doesn't mean you'll necessarily rank well. In any case, there are *lots* of local-search directories, not just the major ones, so you still have work to do. For instance, Google, Yahoo!, and MSN/Bing let you add information about your business directly to the local-search index, increasing the likelihood of being found during a local search and increasing the amount of information that's seen when your information is viewed. Also, you may want to consider the upgrades that some of the search engines sell and that may help push you above your competitors. Table 10-1 summarizes the top four local-search systems.

Table 10-1	The Big Four Go Local	
Site	*Description*	*URL*
Google Maps/ Google Places	Free, including the ability to add video and pictures; if you have more than ten locations, you can submit a data file. To the user, the service appears to be called Google Maps. However, Google is branding the service Google Places in communications with businesses.	`http://www. google.com/ local/add/`
Yahoo! Local	Free or $9.95 per month if you want to add pictures, a "tagline," and a business description.	`http://listings. local.yahoo.com/`
Bing Local Search	Free, including photographs.	`https://ssl. bing.com/ listings/ ListingCenter. aspx`
Ask Local	Ask.com doesn't have its own "local" index; it uses data from Citysearch.com. A basic listing is free.	You can submit data to CitySearch through `www.UBL.org`

A quick word about Yahoo!. As I mention in Chapter 1, the *Yahoo! and Microsoft Search Alliance* brings together Yahoo! and Bing's search businesses. Bing will maintain the organic-search index and the Pay Per Click advertising system and will feed search results to Yahoo!.

At the time of writing, Yahoo! is already getting organic-search results from Bing but is still running Yahoo! Local itself. However, the full *Yahoo! and Microsoft Search Alliance* transition is likely to take a couple of years; at some point you'll probably see both Yahoo!'s and Bing's local-search functions managed in one place.

Grabbing control of (or adding) your business listing

In Table 10-1, in the previous section, I provide the URL of each local service's "ground zero," where you can go to start a new listing or take control of your current listing. Actually, though, you will probably want to start a different way: at the search engine itself. Starting at the search engine shows you where you already stand in the local results, and from there you can grab control of your current listing or add a new one. So, here's what I suggest:

1. **Go to the search engine and search for your product.**

   For instance, if you own a pizza parlor, search for *pizza* along with your town's name (just to make sure that Google searches the correct locale).

2. **If you see your business listed, that's great! If you don't, see whether it's on the full page of results.**

   You should see a link to more local results. Google, for instance, at the time of writing, has a link above the local results that says <u>Local business results for [keyword] near [location]</u>, and a link under the local results that says <u>More results near [location]</u>.

3. **Still can't find your business? Add your business name to the search and search again (*Roddy's Rodent Pie Shop pizza denver*, for instance).**

4. **Still not there? Try searching for the business name and location, with no product or service keyword (*Roddy's Rodent Pie Shop denver*, for instance).**

5. **Still not there? Your business probably isn't listed, so go to the appropriate link in Table 10-1 and add your listing.**

   If you do find your business, though, you need to find your way to the full page of data. In Yahoo and Bing, clicking on the business name link takes you to the information page (see Figure 10-3). In Google, clicking that link takes you to the company's own Web site, which is not what you want — click on the <u>more info</u> or <u>reviews</u> link instead.

   Take a look at what's on your business page; a little sparse? Don't worry, you'll be able to change that soon; you need to look for a way to grab control of your business.

6. **Look for a link or button that says something like <u>Edit Info</u>, <u>Business Owner?</u>, or <u>Change your business listing</u> (see Figure 10-4). Click that and you're on your way to taking control of the listing.**

   The sort of information you provide depends on which system you're submitting to, of course.

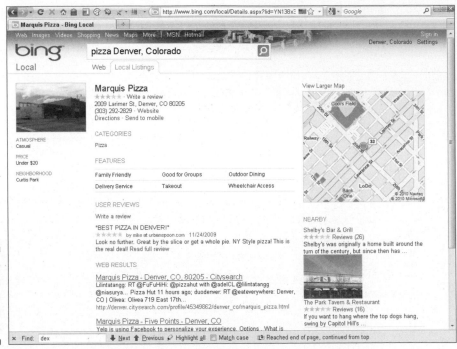

Figure 10-3:
A business
page shown
in Bing
Local.

Yahoo: Look for the tiny *Edit Info* link, or the *Enhance your listing* link

Figure 10-4:
Somewhere,
somehow,
you can
take control
of your busi-
ness listing.

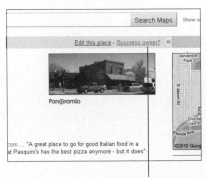

Google: Click the
Business Owner? link

Bing: Click the *Change your
business* listing link

7. **Select some kind of business category and then enter information such as these elements:**

   - Your street address

   - Your phone and fax numbers

   - A link to your Web site

   - A business description

   - The payment methods you accept

   - Your operating hours

   - The year your business was established

   - The languages spoken by your staff

   - The brands you sell

   - Photos (of anything: your staff, your location, your products, and so on)

   - Videos

I recommend that you add as much as possible. Add as much text — with keywords, of course! — as many product and brand names, as many photos as you can, as many videos as possible (Google allows you to include video; you have to upload it to YouTube.com first, then embed it into your listing; see Chapter 18 for more information on video). Adding keywords helps your listing become a match for more possible search phrases, and in any case, adding content to your listing may give your listing a little "oomph" in the search results.

The major systems, such as Google, require, not surprisingly, some kind of verification that you really are authorized to manage the business listing. They typically do this by either phone verification (they send a code to your business phone, which you must then enter into the Web account) or they send a postcard containing a code to your place of business. After you log back in to the system and enter the code, your information is accepted and your changes will go live. (In other systems, such as the ones I talk about next . . . well, there seems to be a degree of trust about who you are.)

Google is now allowing business owners to post "live" to their business listings: messages about special promotions, new products, or whatever else you think might be useful to customers. You can also request that they send someone to your office to take photos (http://maps.google.com/help/maps/businessphotos/) and even request a "Street View" photography session of your business; this is intended for businesses that have large properties that Google Street View camera cars can't reach, such as pedestrian malls, amusement parks, college campuses, race tracks, bike paths in parks, and so on (http://maps.google.com/help/maps/streetview/partners/).

Increasing the odds

Grabbing control of your listing is a great start and may even be a factor that helps your site rank a little higher. But what can you do to increase the odds that your site will rank well in the local results? Here are a few ideas:

- ✔ A huge part of the local-ranking algorithm is based on your location; it's harder to rank for *shoe shop denver* if your shoe shop is somewhere in a suburb. Although many businesses can't do anything about this, some service businesses actually get a mailbox as close to the center of town as possible and register that address as a business location. (It can't be a Post Office box; you need a mail box that you can register as a "suite number.")

- ✔ Get more local directory listings, from other business directories and Yellow Page sites, as I explain later in this chapter.

- ✔ Get links from various other sources directly to your Web site, especially with good location keywords in them (see Chapter 14).

- ✔ If you have multiple addresses, get multiple business listings.

Here's another way to attract attention to your entry (though it won't help with ranking): Use Google Tags. For a flat $25 fee, Google places little yellow tags on the map and under your listing (see Figure 10-5). Clicking the link can lead to photos, coupons, special offers, and so on.

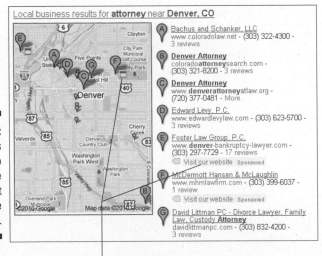

Figure 10-5: Google Tags can help your site stand out from the crowd.

Here are the Google Tags

Finding More Local Systems

More local search systems are out there — many, many more. It's probably a good idea to start with Universal Business Listings (UBL; www.ubl.org). UBL gathers information about businesses and then distributes that information to dozens of different Web sites, such as Internet Yellow Page sites; various business directories such as MerchantCircle and HotFrog; map companies such as MapQuest; search engines; and review sites (such as Yelp). UBL currently has around 150 services on its distribution list.

UBL also distributes data to Google, Yahoo!, Bing, and Citysearch, but that doesn't mean you shouldn't take control of your listings on those services. You should, because UBL doesn't provide these search engines with as much information as the search engines allow you to upload directly. Also, it can take a couple of months for the UBL data to work its way across the distribution network.

In fact, UBL distributes to numerous other popular local search systems, such as iBegin, InfoUSA, InsiderPages, Judy's Book, Kudzu, Localeze, MerchantCircle, MojoPages, Superpages/Switchboard, and YellowPages.com. It's less important to contact these services directly, so you might just let UBL submit data to these places.

But there are more — many, many more. If you have the time, energy, or budget, you may want to work your way down the list of services that UBL currently doesn't reach, such as AboutUs, Angie's List, CitySquares, GoodBoog, Manta, MojoPages, ThinkLocal, and more. I've put a list of these services at www.SearchEngineBulletin.com.

Why do you need to be in all these directories? You'll get links back to your site, and links are always good, especially from "trusted" sources, as many of these local directories are (see Chapter 14). In addition, some of these local directories sometimes come up in the search results, giving you another opportunity to be found even if *your* site hasn't come up on the results for a particular search (or even if it has; see Chapter 23 for a discussion of how to get multiple links on a single search-results page that lead to your site).

And another reason to get into as many directories as possible is that the major search engines are developing partnerships with many different types of local information companies, such as local directories, review sites, menu and coupon services, and so on.

For instance, search for *japanese restaurant san francisco* in Google, and in the businesses you find, Google provides content from UrbanSpoon.com, Yelp.com, OpenTable.com, Gayot.com, Zagat.com, Menutopia.com, and others.

In other words, the major search engines are pulling local data from a large variety of sources, and those sources vary between search engines, locations, and subjects. Do a few searches for your particular phrases and locations, and figure out who's feeding data to whom. Then go to those sources and see how you get listed.

If I ran a restaurant, for instance, I would want to get my menus into Zagat, Menutopia, and MenuPix.com; submit a listing to CitySearch; and figure out how to get reviews into Wcities.com, Zagat, 10Best.com, ViaMichelin, Gayot, and the local papers. Also, though of course I don't condone this type of behavior, let's be honest: Some of your competitors are dropping fake reviews into review sites, to prime the data pump, as it were. But I come to that subject in a moment.

Don't Forget Local-Local Directories

Don't forget local directories that perhaps don't feed data to the major search engines but that are still likely to be important in their own right. For instance, if I owned a restaurant in Denver, I would want to know how to get a review into *5280* magazine, which maintains a popular restaurant guide at www.5280.com. You get a link to your Web site, which the search engines like (see Chapter 14), and because it's a popular site for locals looking for good eats, you will probably get real, live traffic, not just search engine traffic.

Yet another important category of local directories is what I call "local-local" directories. So far, I've looked at just the "local" directories, which cover the entire nation, or even multiple nations. But there are also "local" directories that cover one particular locale.

For instance, if I had a business in Philadelphia, I'd be checking into sites such as these:

- www.philasence.com/
- http://infoaroundphilly.com/
- http://philadelphia-city-directory.com
- http://philadelphiaokay.com/
- http://philadelphia-philadelphia.com/

I'm sure there are others I haven't found in my rather quick search. Again, getting listed in these sorts of directories is good because

✔ You'll get links to your site, and search engines love links (or rather, they reward you for links; see Chapter 14).

✔ These directories will come up in local searches now and then, providing another avenue for people to find your site.

✔ These directories may have a few loyal users who go there looking for businesses. In most cases, probably not many, though; the previous two reasons are probably more important.

The Other Side of Local: Review Sites

There's a very important aspect that you have to know about many of these local sites: the reviews. Plenty of these sites allow anyone to post a review about your service. If you never have disgruntled customers and always have ecstatic clients, that's great. But how many businesses can say that? See Figure 10-6, for instance. How would you like these reviews about your business? There's nothing to complain about "Good and honest folks," but how about "Don't Go Here!" or "Avoid this rip-off joint at all costs"?

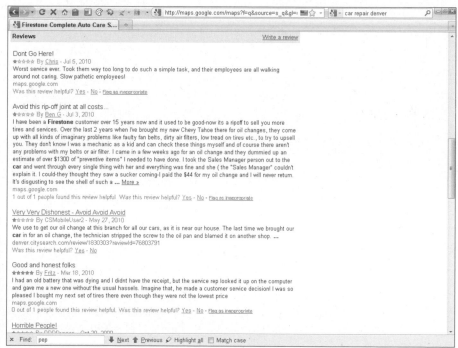

Figure 10-6: Would *you* like these reviews pointing to *your* business?

Why is it important to have good reviews? A couple of reasons.

✔ We don't know for sure, but the number of reviews, or your review "star rating," *may* have some effect on your ranking in the search engines local results. It's clearly not "best reviewed sites get ranked first," but the ranking algorithm may at least take reviews into consideration to some degree.

✔ When a potential customer has to decide which business's site to click, which one do you think will get the click? The business with 10 reviews and 1.5 stars, or the 5-star business with 50 reviews?

Now, it's true that sometimes bad reviews are warranted. But it's also true that sometimes

✔ A single disgruntled customer can start a feud, posting terrible reviews everywhere he can, sometimes using multiple accounts so that he can post multiple reviews to the same service; remember, as the search engines pull data from various different sources, bad reviews at several sites could all end up posted on your business's Google listing.

✔ Angry customers are more likely to complain about you publicly than happy customers are to praise you. Anger "energizes" people more than contentment, so one or two angry clients can totally mess up your review profile.

So it's essential, even if your business is totally dedicated to customer service, that you keep control over the reviews process, and you do that by making sure that people who like you post reviews. Even if you have a few bad reviews, having enough good reviews will dilute the bad ones.

Go check your business in the local listings. Do you have bad reviews pulling your star rating down? If so, what can you do about it? There are two approaches: get the reviews removed or dilute the bad reviews.

Removing bad reviews

Can you get rid of bad reviews? Probably not. It's extremely hard to get bad reviews removed from these review sites. The review sites themselves, in most cases, are protected from prosecution for libel or slander, so your threats probably won't help! On the other hand, Yelp.com — one of the most important review sites — has been sued by a group of small businesses for extortion, the argument being that Yelp's sales staff offers to remove bad reviews if a business pays for advertising. (The lawsuit is currently under way.)

If, however, you have reason to believe the reviews are part of some kind of feud against you, or if they clearly violate the review site's policies, you *may* be able to get them removed, but you would have to have a pretty good argument. (In the case of removing bad reviews from the major search engines, it helps if you have personal contacts inside the companies; if, for instance, you are spending tens of thousands of dollars a month on PPC, you might get some assistance!)

Diluting bad reviews

By far the easier process is to dilute the reviews; that is, to make sure you have enough *good* reviews to overwhelm the bad ones. (Of course, this doesn't work for you if everyone hates your business!) In fact, if you have a large number of good reviews, with a few bad reviews, that's fine; nobody expects perfection. Getting lots of good reviews will, over time, bring your star rating up and make those pesky bad reviews less obvious. It doesn't necessarily take much time. You can often turn things around in a month or two — I've seen a business go from 2.5 stars on Google to 5 stars in about six weeks.

So, how do you get those reviews? Ask your clients! Perhaps give out cards (maybe to the clients who are most clearly happy with your service) asking them to review your site at Google, Yahoo!, Yelp, and so on. (Most won't, but some will). Perhaps you could have a computer terminal actually at the point of sale, and ask people whether they would write a review right there and then. Some businesses collect reviews and post them for their clients, to make sure the reviews get posted. (I am currently working with a company that helps businesses improve their review profile; see www. SearchEngineBulletin.com for information.)

Which review sites?

Which review sites are most important? Clearly, the major search engines themselves are very important, perhaps the most important. But the other review sites that are important to you will depend on your business. For general retail, Yelp.com is hugely important. For many types of service business, Judy's Book (www.judysbook.com) is critical. Medical clinics need to look into Vitals.com and HealthGrades.com. If you're in the travel business, TripAdvisor.com is essential. Other popular sites include Kudzu.com, Local. com, and MerchantCircle.com.

Here's how to figure out what review sites are really important to you. Go to the major search engines and look at the reviews posted to businesses in your industry. Each review shows where it comes from, so you can quickly see the sources of reviews for the major search engines (in addition to the reviews posted directly, of course).

Working with the Yellow Pages

Another form of directory to be considered is the Yellow Page Web sites, which are sites created by the old Yellow Pages companies. The Yellow Page business is in serious trouble, and by now the Yellow Page companies must be worried.

Historically, the (paper) yellow page business has been incredibly profitable; the biggest companies make billions of dollars each year, with profits of many hundreds of millions. They're real cash cows, but they're being steamrolled by the Internet.

Millions of computer-literate, Internet-loving people never pick up a Yellow Pages book or, perhaps, pick one up just once or twice a year, compared with several times a month in the pre-Internet days. The number of people who use the book is declining precipitously as local searches move online. As you see in Chapter 10, all the major search engines provide local search services, and the results are excellent.

More and more, I hear from my small-business friends that they are giving up on advertising in the Yellow Pages; one friend, the owner of a small gym, stopped paying for Yellow Page ads several years ago, telling me that "they just don't work anymore"; he gets more business through his Web site than he ever did from the Yellow Pages.

The Yellow Page companies are definitely in trouble, but they do have one big advantage: *feet on the street*. They have huge armies of salespeople talking to businesses every day, and they've used this sales force to continue selling paper ads as well as to sell businesses *online* yellow page ads.

You rarely hear much about the Yellow Pages sites in discussions about online search, but of course they *are* search systems — search directories, in effect. But how important are they?

YellowPages.com, probably the most important Yellow Page site, claims to have 170 million searches a month; this is a big number, but it's a drop in the ocean when compared to the 10 billion searches a month considered in the Nielsen study I look at in Chapter 1.

Table 10-2 shows the largest Yellow Page sites and their Alexa traffic ranks, indicating the sites' overall popularity. Notice that the most popular of these sites, YellowPages.com, had an Alexa rank of 929 when I checked. Compare that with Google (1), Yahoo! (4), Bing (24), and Ask.com (58).

 Many other Yellow Page sites are not *really* Yellow Page sites. The term *Yellow Pages* is an old term — about 130 years old — and it's not a copyrighted term. Thus, anyone can set up a Web site and call it a Yellow Pages Web site, and many people have done so (see, for instance, YellowUSA.com and MagicYellow.com). What I'm talking about here are the genuine Yellow Pages sites, owned by the real Yellow Pages companies — the guys who dump those huge, yellow books on your doorstep that you immediately throw into the trash (or, one hopes, the recycle bin).

Table 10-2	Largest Yellow Pages Sites	
Site	*URL*	*Alexa Rank*
AT&T YellowPages.com	www.yellowpages.com	929
SuperPages	www.superpages.com	1,273
Yellowbook.com	www.yellowbook.com	4,043
Dex	www.dexknows.com	4,874
Yell.com (in the UK)	www.yell.com	5,162
Yellow.com	www.yellow.com	14,930

According to Alexa, 928 sites are more popular than YellowPages.com, including Boston.com (the Boston Globe) and bit.ly, a URL shorting utility. Google Singapore is more popular than these sites (Singapore has a population of 5 million, by the way). In fact, Alexa claims that Google Singapore (google.com.sg) gets almost twice the traffic of YellowPages.com. Ask.com — the search site I include in my list of the four top search engines, but that I almost don't bother with because it's so small (see Chapter 1) — gets perhaps 15 times the traffic of YellowPages.com. Even My Web Search (www.mywebsearch.com), the seventh most important search site cited in the Nielsen study, has an Alexa rank of 130, and perhaps four times the traffic of YellowPages.com.

These sites are, quite simply, not particularly popular and get relatively very few searches.

That's not to say you shouldn't be in the Yellow Page sites; you absolutely should, and there are several ways to do that:

- ✔ **Get a business phone line.** A business line costs more than a residential line, but you get your free listing in the local Yellow Pages book, which also gets your listing in the online Yellow Pages. As with the book, this is just a simple listing with no extras.

- ✔ **Sign up directly through the Web site.** Some Yellow Page sites allow businesses to create free listings directly through their Web sites; look for an Advertise With Us link or similar.

- ✔ **Buy a listing or ad through your local Yellow Pages rep.** This is the same guy selling you space in the paper book.

- ✔ **Submit to UBL** (as I discuss earlier in this chapter). UBL distributes its data to a number of Yellow Page sites, such as SuperPages.com, Verizon. com, YellowPages.com, and DexKnows.com.

The real question, though, is whether you should *pay* to be in the Yellow Pages, and that's much harder for me to answer. The real disadvantage is that it's expensive, sometimes very expensive.

Does the Yellow Pages work? First, I need to make a full disclosure of a conflict here. I do a bit of "expert witness" work with law firms involved in Internet-related lawsuits, and I've been retained in a lawsuit against a major Yellow Pages Web site. (The suit alleges that the company promises traffic to its advertiser's Web sites that it doesn't deliver; my role is to provide technical information to the plaintiffs.)

So, I want to be balanced here. Let me say that it's a matter of record that many businesses are unhappy with the results of advertising in the online Yellow Pages. That doesn't mean that no companies are *happy* with the service, though.

I recommend that if your company already buys Yellow Pages ads and your business is *location specific* — that is, you're trying to attract buyers in a particular area — you should carefully research using the Yellow Pages. Talk to your rep. The rep should be able to tell you how many searches are carried out in the company's online Yellow Pages, in a particular category and a particular region, each month. With that information, you may be able to decide whether purchasing an ad makes sense.

The online Yellow Pages companies sell a variety of services, such as the following:

✔ A link from the listing in the online Yellow Pages to your Web site. However, in most cases, the search engines do *not* recognize it as a link to your site; some of these directories use *nofollow* links, or they may use redirect links that forward people to your site through the Yellow Page's server. (See Chapter 14 for information on links that are not really links.)

✔ An e-mail link.

✔ A page with detailed information, such as a map to your location, information about your products and services, payment options, and so on.

✔ A link to a picture of your ad that appears in the paper Yellow Pages.

✔ A pop-up promo box that appears when someone points at an icon and that can be modified through an online-management system.

✔ A link to a coupon that customers can print.

Part III
Adding Your Site to the Indexes and Directories

The 5th Wave   By Rich Tennant

@RICHTENNANT

"This is amazing. You can stop looking for Derek. According to an MSN/Bing search I did, he's hiding behind the dryer in the basement."

In this part . . .

Getting your Web site indexed by the search engines and directories should be easy. Let them know the URL and wait for them to add it, right? Wrong. Sure, you can submit information about your site to the search engines, but they probably won't index it.

In this part, I explain how to get your site into the major search engines, including using the new Google, Yahoo!, and MSN sitemap systems. (Hint: You need to make it easy for the search engines to find your site on their own.) I also explain how to work with the two major search directories: Yahoo! (easy; just pay) and the Open Directory Project (easy to submit, and free, but you may never get in!).

This part also tells you how to find important but lesser-known systems and how they can help you. Sure, most searches are carried out through the major systems, but the specialized systems can often provide valuable, highly targeted traffic, as well as valuable links pointing back to your site.

And for those of you selling products, you find out about the shopping directories — specialized systems that index commercial products (and, in a few cases, services) — from Google Product Search and eBay, to Amazon, Shopping.com, and Yahoo! Shopping. If you're selling online, you must know about these systems.

Chapter 11

Getting Your Pages into the Search Engines

. . . .

In This Chapter

▶ Submitting your pages to the search engines

▶ Creating, submitting, and pinging sitemaps

▶ Submitting to secondary search engines

▶ Using registration services and software

. . . .

*Y*ou built your Web pages. Now, how do you get them into the search systems? That's what this chapter and Chapter 12 explain. In this chapter, I talk about how to get your pages into search engines, and in Chapter 12 I explain how to list your site with search directories.

Search engines can find out about and index your site in essentially three ways:

✔ Links pointing to your site

✔ Simple link-submission pages

✔ Sitemap submissions

The most important of these is the first; links pointing to your site lead the search engine to it. The second is worthless. And the third is very important and comes with a number of ancillary benefits. In this chapter, I tell you about these strategies one by one.

Linking Your Site for Inclusion

In Chapters 14 through 16, I talk about the importance of — and how to get — links pointing from other sites to yours. The more links you have pointing at your site, the more important the search engines will think your pages are.

Links are also important because they provide a way for search engines to find your site. Without links, you *might* get your site into search engine indexes, but chances are, you won't. And being included in the most important index — Google's — is much quicker through linking than through registration. I've had sites picked up and indexed by Google within two or three days of having put up a link on another site. If you simply submit your URL to Google (the next method I look at), you may have to wait weeks for it to index your site (if it ever does).

But one or two links sometimes aren't enough for some search engines. They often are for Google: If it sees a link to your site on another site that it's already indexing, it will probably visit your site and index it, too. But other systems are far choosier and may not visit your site even if they do see a link to it. So the more links you have pointing to your site, the better. Eventually, search engines will get sick of tripping over links to your site and come see what the fuss is all about.

It's all about links. The search engines believe that they can maintain the quality of their indexes by focusing on Web pages that have links pointing to them. If nobody points to your site, the reasoning goes, why would the engines want to index it? If nobody else thinks your site is important, why should the search engines? They would rather find your pages themselves than have you submit the pages.

By the way, when I say that a page is in a search engine's index, it doesn't mean that the search engine has read and indexed the entire page. In many cases, the search engine has never even read the page but knows where the page is, based on links it has seen in pages that it *has* read. And even if a search engine has read a page, it may not have read the entire page.

Simple Link Submissions to the Major Systems

The top two search engines — Google and MSN/Bing — provide a very simple way for you to tell them where your site is. Submit your site for free on these pages:

- **Google:** www.google.com/addurl.html
- **MSN/Bing:** www.bing.com/webmaster/SubmitSitePage.aspx

How about Ask.com? It offers no way to submit your Web site. It relies on its searchbots to find pages through links.

However, now that I've given you these links for submitting your site's pages, let me say one more thing: *Don't bother.*

Using these submission pages is unnecessary and may not even work. As Google says, "We do not add all submitted URLs to our index, and we cannot make any predictions or guarantees about when or if they will appear." MSN/Bing is a little more positive, perhaps, but still offers no guarantee: "This change will not be reflected immediately, so please be patient and check back periodically."

I don't bother submitting URLs to search engines using these simple URL submission pages. But I want you to be aware of them because these submissions are one of the biggest scams in the history of SEO (a business that is rife with scams). Hundreds of submission services convinced many thousands of Web site owners to pay to have their sites submitted to the search engines, often repeatedly. It was a totally pointless waste of money.

You don't need to use basic URL submission. You need links to your site, and you should submit a sitemap, which I cover next.

Submitting an XML Sitemap

I *do* recommend one form of site submission. It isn't a replacement for pointing links to your site, but it can, in some cases, improve indexing of your site. I'm talking about creating XML sitemaps and submitting them to the top three search engines, and making it easy for other search engines, such as Ask.com, to find the sitemap on their own.

In 2005 Google introduced a new submission system and was soon followed by Yahoo! and MSN/Bing (and now, of course, Yahoo! and MSN/Bing have partnered, so they act as one system). You can read more about sitemaps in Chapter 6. In that chapter, I recommend creating a sitemap page on your site and linking to it from the home page. The sitemap is a page that visitors can see and that any search engine can use to find its way through your site.

But an XML sitemap is different: It's a special file placed on your site that contains an index to help search engines find their way to your pages. You create and place the file and then let the search engine know where it is. This hidden file (visitors never see it) is in a format designed for those search engines. I think it's worth your time to create this file because doing so is not a huge task and *may* help, particularly if your site is large. Also, after you've submitted a sitemap and "verified" your submission, the search engines give you lots of interesting information about your site.

Sitemap, schmitemap

Don't think that creating an XML sitemap is a magic trick guaranteed to get your site indexed. I've seen, for example, Yahoo! (in the pre-Yahoo!/Bing partnership days) pick up the sitemap file, put it into the search results, come by and pick up 3 pages from the index, ignore the other 20, and leave a whole bunch of old, nonexistent pages in the index. I've also seen MSN/Bing apparently pay little attention to a sitemap. On the other hand, I've seen Yahoo! pick up hundreds of thousands of pages on a large site soon after finding multiple XML sitemaps. The sitemap may help, but you have no guarantee whether or when the search engines will use it. So don't think of the sitemap as an alternative to the hard work of creating links to your site.

In Google's words, "Using sitemaps to inform and direct our crawlers, we hope to expand our coverage of the web and speed up the discovery and addition of pages to our index." If I can help Google by getting it to index my site more quickly, well, that's fine by me.

What does this sitemap file look like? Take a look at Figure 11-1.

Don't worry: XML sitemaps are easy to create; I show you how in a moment.

Figure 11-1: A small XML sitemap.

These sitemaps are typically named `sitemap.xml` (though different names can be used) and placed into the root directory of the Web site — in the same directory as the home page.

Creating your sitemap

You can create a sitemaps file in various ways. Google provides the Sitemap Generator program (`code.google.com/p/googlesitemapgenerator/`), which you can install on your Web server; it's a Python script, so if you don't know what that means, consider creating the file another way.

If you're the proud owner of a large, sophisticated, database-driven site, it's probably a job for your programmers; they should create a script that automatically builds the XML sitemap.

You can find technical details about the formatting of these sitemaps at `www.sitemaps.org`.

What if you own a small site, though, and have limited technical skills? No problem: Plenty of free and low-cost sitemap-creation tools are available.

Note that many of the tools call themselves *Google sitemap* creators, because Google was the first search engine to use sitemaps; all you need, however, is the basic Google XML sitemap format for all the other search engines, so if it creates a "Google" sitemap, it will work fine.

Some of these programs run on your computer, some require installing on your Web server, and some are services run from another Web site. You can find a large list of these sitemap generators here: `code.google.com/p/sitemap-generators/wiki/SitemapGenerators`.

My favorite sitemap generator for small sites is XML-Sitemaps.com. You simply enter your domain name into a Web page and it spiders your site, creating the sitemap as it goes, up to 500 pages. If your site is bigger, you can get the service to install a script on your Web server for $20 (assuming that your server can run PHP scripts).

Sitemap files can be as large as 10MB and contain as many as 50,000 URLs. If you need to exceed either limit, you must create multiple sitemap files and a sitemap index file that refers to the individual sitemap files. Your XML Sitemaps can also be compressed in the `.gz` file format so that they transfer more quickly to the search engine. For specifics of the sitemap protocol, see `www.sitemaps.org`.

Submitting your sitemaps

You can tell search engines about your sitemaps in three different ways:

- ✔ Submit a sitemap through the search engine's Webmaster account.
- ✔ Include a line in the `robots.txt` file telling a search engine where the file is.
- ✔ Ping the search engines.

You need a `robots.txt` file in the root directory of your Web site, with the following line inside it:

```
Sitemap: http://www.yourdomain.com/sitemap.xml
```

The URL should point to your sitemap, of course. The URL tells the search engines that don't provide a Webmaster account — such as Ask.com — where your sitemap is.

Another way to inform search engines of your sitemap's location is to ping them; I describe that process in the next section. But even if you use both a `robots.txt` file and pinging, you should definitely also set up a Webmaster account and submit your sitemap through the account.

Submitting by using the Webmaster account

You should set up an account on both the major systems (Google, and MSN/Bing; Ask.com doesn't currently have Webmaster accounts), and submit your Web site's XML sitemap; then review the various tools that are available. Here's where you can find the Webmaster areas and sitemap-submission pages for the three top systems:

- ✔ **Google:** `www.google.com/webmasters`
- ✔ **MSN/Bing:** `www.bing.com/webmaster`

You don't need a separate account on each system for each Web site you own — you can submit multiple sites through each account, though number of Web sites that you can manage through each account is limited (MSN/Bing limits the number of sites to 125 sitemaps; for Google, it's around 400 . . . enough for most people!).

However, in some cases Web site owners don't want search engines to know that their sites are associated; for instance, if a site owner has three sites, all of which rank on the first page for important keywords, he or she may not want it to be obvious that all sites are owned by the same person. In such a case, of course, the owner would set up separate accounts for submitting each sitemap.

Here's the basic process you use at all these services:

1. Set up an account.

   In each case, you have to set up a password-protected account.

2. Add the URL of your Web site.

3. Tell the search engine where the sitemap is.

   You provide the URL that points to your sitemap; the search engine checks to see whether it can find the file.

4. Create an authentication or verification file and place it in the root of your site.

   You're provided with an authentication or verification code, which is used to create a small text file that's stored on your server. For instance, Google provides you with an `.html` file that you can download and place in your site. The file contains a single line of text, something like this: `google-site-verification: googlec4b99698d01b26f2.html`. (All three systems also allow you to add a special verification meta tag to your home page, if you prefer, rather than create a text file.)

5. Tell the search engine that the file or meta tag has been placed and ask it to "verify" the file.

   After you create the file, the search engine checks to see whether the file is where it should be; if it is, the search engine assumes that you must own or have control over the specified site, and thus is willing to provide you with more information about the site.

Each system is different, so I can't go into detail about how each works. Spend a little time digging around and you'll soon figure it out; remember, the basic process is to add your site URL, add your sitemap URL, and then verify or authenticate.

Pinging search engines

Pinging a search engine means sending a message to the search engine telling it where a sitemap is, and telling it that the sitemap has changed. As of this writing, you could ping all three of the major systems — Google, MSN/Bing, and Ask.com — and some smaller systems, such as Moreover.com.

You can see this process in action for yourself. Create a sitemap and then change the following URL to show the path to your sitemap:

```
http://www.google.com/ping?sitemap=http://www.yourdomain.
         com/sitemap.xml
```

Copy and paste this URL into a browser and press Enter, and you receive this response from Google:

Sitemap Notification Received

Your Sitemap has been successfully added to our list of Sitemaps to crawl. If this is the first time you are notifying Google about this Sitemap, please add it via `http://www.google.com/webmasters/sitemaps` *so you can track its status. Please note that we do not add all submitted URLs to our index, and we cannot make any predictions or guarantees about when or if they will appear.*

These are the sitemap-submission URLS; put the full URL to your sitemap, including `http://`, after the = sign:

```
http://www.google.com/ping?sitemap=
http://www.google.com/webmasters/sitemaps/ping?sitemap=
http://www.bing.com/webmaster/ping.aspx?sitemap=
http://submissions.ask.com/ping?sitemap=
http://www.moreover.com/ping?sitemap=
```

You can manually ping sites each time the search engine is updated. If you have a programmer build your sitemaps automatically by pulling data from a database, the programmer should add a ping function to ping the search engines each time the sitemap is updated. And, some sitemap-creation programs that you can buy have built-in ping functions; the version of the XML-Sitemaps.com program that you install on your server can automatically ping for you.

Are sitemaps bad? I've heard the argument that sitemaps are bad because you might rely on the sitemap rather than create links to your site. This bizarre argument is similar to the one that airbags are bad because you might rely on them rather than drive safely. Sitemaps are *good.* But they're not a substitute for links pointing to your site. You still need links, and many of them.

Webmaster tools, too

As the previous section notes, the two top search engines — Google, and MSN/Bing — now provide Webmaster accounts through which you can submit your sitemap and provide various tools related to your sitemaps. Some of these tools are available even if you *don't* submit a sitemap, but if you do submit a sitemap and then prove that you are the owner of the site (through the authentication or verification process I mention earlier), you'll be provided with more information.

Right now, Google has the best tools and statistics associated with its Webmaster account (see Figure 11-2). Table 11-1 explains some of these tools.

Table 11-1	Google's Webmaster Tools
Tool	***What It Does***
The Site Configuration Menu	
Crawler access	Lets you create and test a `robots.txt` file to make sure that your `robots.txt` file is not blocking areas of your site accidentally. You can also remove pages that you don't want Google to index.
Sitelinks	Indicates which pages on your site Google would use as sitelinks if it decided to present multiple links to your site in the search results. (See Figure 11-2.) If you want, you can block a particular page from appearing.
Change of address	Allows you to redirect one domain to another, telling Google that, for instance, you are using a new domain name.
Settings	Tells Google that you are most interested in searchers in a particular country; that you want Google to assume that *yourdomain.com* points to www.*your domain.com*; that you want to slow down the Googlebot crawl rate; that Google should ignore certain URL parameters to reduce duplicate content.
The Your Site on the Web Menu	
Search queries	Indicates which search queries most often returned pages from your site and which ones were clicked.
Links to your site	Shows links from other sites pointing to your site and indicates which page inside the site they point to (an excellent tool!).
Keywords	A list of keywords that Google found while crawling your site.
Internal links	Shows links between pages within your site.
Subscriber stats	Information about users subscribed to your site's RSS feed, if it has one, using Google services such as Google Reader, iGoogle, or Orkut.
Diagnostics	
Malware	Information about malware on your site (which might happen if your site has been hacked).
Crawl Errors	Shows problems that Google found while crawling your site.
Crawl stats	Information about how quickly and how often Google crawls your site.
HTML suggestions	Problems Google may have found on your site, such as duplicate, long, or short meta description tags, and missing, duplicate, long, short, or noninformative `<TITLE>` tags, and nonindexable page content.
Labs	
Fetch as Googlebot	Fetch a page from your site and see what Googlebot, the Google spider, sees.
Sidewiki	Google Sidewiki is a system by which Google users can, while logged into their Google accounts, see notes about Web pages posted by other Google users. This page allows you to post "page owner" information about your site into the Sidewiki.
Site Performance	Shows how quickly your site's pages load.

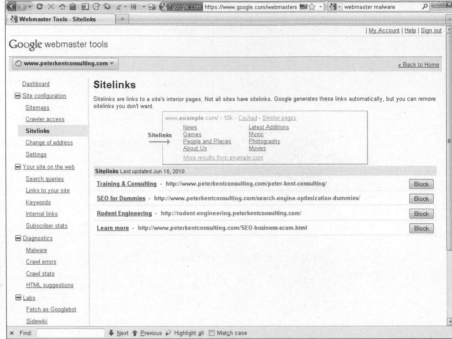

Figure 11-2:
You can see what Google plans to use as your site's sitelinks, and block some if necessary.

This is pretty nifty stuff, eh? Sitemaps are great for big sites; they can really help with indexing. But even if you have a *small* site, submitting and verifying a sitemap is a great way to get some very useful information about your site. (Actually, strictly speaking, you can create a Webmaster account for your site, verify the site, and then access this information even if you haven't submitted a sitemap; however, if you're going to all that trouble, you might as well spend a few minutes with a tool such as XML-Sitemaps.com and submit the sitemap as well.)

Submitting to Secondary Systems

You can also submit your site information to smaller systems with perhaps a few hundred million pages in their indexes — and sometimes far fewer. The disadvantage to these systems is that they're seldom used, compared to the big systems discussed earlier in this chapter. Many search engine professionals ignore the smaller systems altogether. On the other hand, if your site is ranked in these systems, you have much less competition because they're so small.

These secondary systems may be worth submitting your site to:

- **ExactSeek:** www.exactseek.com/add.html
- **Gigablast:** www.gigablast.com/addurl

You can find more, including regional sites, listed on the following pages:

- www.searchenginewatch.com/2156161
- dmoz.org/Computers/Internet/Searching/Search_Engines/
- http://dir.yahoo.com/Computers_and_Internet/Internet/
  World_Wide_Web/Searching_the_Web/Search_Engines_and_
  Directories/

Some smaller search engines encourage you to pay for a submission. Don't. Unless you know for sure otherwise, you can safely assume that the amount of traffic you're likely to get probably isn't worth the payment.

If you plan to submit your site to many search engines, you may want to use a programmable keyboard or a text-replacement utility or macro program, such as ShortKeys (www.shortkeys.com), which can make entering repetitive data much quicker:

- **Programmable keyboard:** You can assign a string of text — a URL, an e-mail address, and so on — to a single key. Then all you need to do, for instance, is press F11 to enter your e-mail address.
- **Text-replacement utility:** Replace a short string of text with something longer. To enter your e-mail address, for instance, you might type just *em*.

A few sites require that you submit your site with a username and password. Most sites require at least an e-mail address; some also require that you respond to a confirmation e-mail before they add your site to the list. *Don't use your regular e-mail address!* Use a throwaway address because you'll receive a lot of spam.

Is it really worth submitting to these secondary search engines? As I mention in Chapter 1, somewhere around 96 percent of all search results are provided by the major search engines, so submitting to the secondary search systems may not be worth the trouble.

Using Registration Services and Software Programs

You can also submit your pages to hundreds of search engines by using a submission service or program. Many free services are available, but some of them are outdated, running automatically for a number of years now and not having kept up with changes on the search engine scene.

Many free services are definitely on the *lite* side. They're provided by companies that hope you'll spring for a fee-based full service.

Some free services also combine links and directory registrations, along with search engine registrations. (I discuss directory registrations in Chapter 12.) By providing links pointing to your site, they can guarantee that your site will be picked up by the major search engines; it's not the submissions to the search engines that are doing the work — it's the links!

Note also that some submission services increase their submission counts by including all services that are fed by the systems they submit to. For instance, if a service submits to Yahoo!, it counts it as multiple submissions because Yahoo! feeds AlltheWeb, Lycos, Terra.com, HotBot, InfoSpace, Excite, and more. Some submission services inflate their numbers by including search engines that don't even exist any more. In fact, I feel that some (many) submission services are little more than scams, charging in some cases very high monthly fees for what's really a service with relatively few benefits.

Still, if you want to try them, here are a couple of services (with more reasonable fees) that you might check out:

✔ **AdPro:** www.addpro.com

✔ **ineedhits:** www.ineedhits.com

There are many, many submission services; search for *search engine submission service,* and you'll find a gazillion of them.

A few submission software programs are available as well. Here are a few of the more popular ones:

✔ **Dynamic Submission,** which you can find at www.dynamic submission.com.

✔ **SubmitWolf** at www.trellian.com/swolf.

The big advantage of these software programs is that you pay only once rather than pay every time you use a service.

You actually have a couple of reasons to use these automated tools. You may get a little traffic out of these small search engines, but don't bank on getting much. In many cases, though, the systems being submitted to are not really search engines — they're search *directories,* and being listed in a directory may mean that major search engines pick up a link pointing to your site. (Several of the systems listed by AddPro, for instance, are directories rather than search engines.) I talk more about submitting your site to search directories in Chapter 12, and you discover the power of linking in Chapters 14 through 16.

Chapter 12

Submitting to the Directories

*I*n Chapter 11, you look at getting your site into the search engines. In this chapter, you look at getting your site into the search *directories*. Submitting to directories can be a great way to get links.

The two major directories are important to a search strategy, although they can be rather frustrating to work with. (One of them you have to pay for, and the other, although free, is incredibly difficult to get into). Also, you may find lots of other, smaller directories you may want to register with.

Pitting Search Directories Against Search Engines

Before you start working with directories, it's helpful to know a few basics about what directories are — and aren't:

✔ Directories don't send searchbots out onto the Web looking for sites to add (though they may send bots out to make sure that the sites are still live).

✔ Directories don't read and store information from Web pages within a site.

✔ Because directories don't read and store information, they don't base search results on the contents of the Web pages.

✔ Directories don't index Web pages; they index Web sites. Each site is assigned to a particular category. Within the categories, the directory's index contains just a little information about each site — not much more than a URL, a title, and a description. The result is a categorized list of Web sites — and that's really what the search directories are all about.

A few years ago, Yahoo! was based around its directory. In fact, Figure 12-1 shows an example of what Yahoo! looked like early in 1998 (courtesy of a wonderful service called the WayBackMachine at `www.archive.org`). The idea behind Yahoo! was a categorized directory of Web sites that people could browse. You could click links to drill down through the directory and find what you needed, similar to flipping through a Yellow Pages directory. Although you could use the Search box to peruse categories, site titles, and site descriptions, the tool was nothing like the Yahoo! search index of today, which can hunt for your term in billions of Web pages.

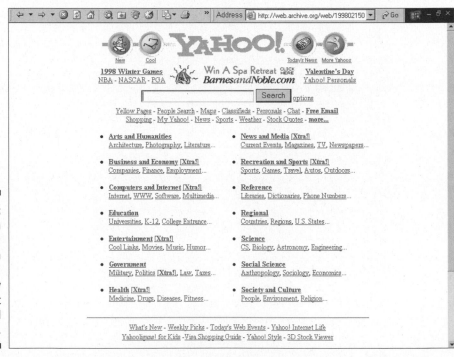

Figure 12-1:
The main Yahoo! page, when Yahoo! Directory was what it was all about.

But Yahoo! made an enormous mistake. In fact, the image in Figure 12-1 is from a time when Yahoo! was at its peak, a time when most of the world's Web searches were carried out through its site — just a few months before Google began operations. Yahoo! evidently hadn't fully realized the weaknesses of the directory system until it was too late. These weaknesses include the following:

- ✔ **Directories provide no way for someone to search individual pages within a site.** The perfect fit for your information needs may be sitting somewhere on a site that is included in a directory, but you won't know it because the directory doesn't index individual pages.

- ✔ **Categorization is necessarily limited.** Sites are rarely about a single topic; even if they appear to be, single topics can be broken down into smaller subtopics. By forcing people to find a site by category and keyword in a very limited amount of text — a description and title — the directories are obviously very restrictive.

- ✔ **Hand-built directories are necessarily limited in size.** Hand-built directories, such as Yahoo! Directory and the Open Directory, add a site to their directories only after a real live human editor has reviewed the site. With hundreds of millions of Web sites, a human-powered system can't possibly keep up.

- ✔ **Hand-built directories get very dated.** Directories often contain some extremely old and out-of-date information that simply wouldn't be present in an index that is automatically recompiled continually. (Yahoo! *spiders* the sites — that is, sends out searchbots to look through the sites — in its index for broken links and dead sites, but if the site's purpose has changed, Yahoo! may not realize that fact.)

The proof of directories' weaknesses is in the pudding: Google took over and now is the dominant search system on the Web. (To be fair, Yahoo! helped Google by integrating Google results into Yahoo! searches, although in the summer of 2004, it dropped Google and began using its own index.)

The old Yahoo! site directory is still there, but it's virtually hidden to many visitors. A few years ago the directory was still on the home page, but so low that you had to scroll to see it; now, the directory isn't even on the home page. You can find it by going to dir.Yahoo.com or by clicking the Directory link on the More menu at the top of the Yahoo! home page.

Why Are Directories So Significant?

If the Yahoo! Directory is hidden away, and if most people have never heard of the world's second most important directory (the Open Directory Project at www.dmoz.org), why do you care about them? They're still very significant for a number of reasons:

✔ Yahoo! Directory is part of the Yahoo! search system, one of the world's most popular search sites. As such, it still gets a lot of traffic. You can access it directly at `dir.yahoo.com`; some people do access it from the Yahoo! main page.

✔ The Open Directory Project feeds results to Google Directory, which is part of the world's *most popular* search site.

✔ The Open Directory Project feeds results to literally hundreds of other sites, large and small. Many of these sites are crawled by the major search engines (such as Google), so a link from the Open Directory Project can show up as a link on many other sites, too.

✔ Yahoo! often uses directory entries for the blurb below a page title in Web search results — the search results page shown when someone searches their indexes, and Google may sometimes grab the site description from the Open Directory Project, so having a directory entry sometimes allows you to control the text that appears on the search results pages for your site.

✔ Links in the major directories help provide context to search engines. If your site is in the Recreation: Pets: Rodents category in the Open Directory Project, for instance, the search engines know that the site is related to playing with rodents. The directory presence helps search engines index your site and may help your site rank higher for some search terms.

✔ Links, as you see in Chapters 14 through 16, are very important in convincing search engines that your site is of value. It's sometimes possible to get links from hundreds of search directories, on pages indexed by the major search engines.

By the way, don't underestimate the Open Directory Project just because you've never heard of it or because the submission forms are often broken or unreliable. Data from this system is widely spread across the Internet and has often been used to kick-start major search systems. Yahoo!, for instance, once used data from the Open Directory Project (which, incidentally, is owned by AOL/Netscape).

Submitting to the Search Directories

Chapter 11 has what some may find an unusual message: "Sure, you can submit to the search engines, but it may not do you any good." Search engines really like links to your site, and having links to your site is often the best way to get into the search engines.

However, the search directories won't find you unless you submit to them. And you can forget automated submission programs for the major directories — there's no way to use them. Submissions must be entered into Yahoo! and the Open Directory Project by hand.

Submitting to Yahoo! Directory

Submissions to Yahoo! Directory used to be very difficult. Surveys showed that people who had managed to get their sites listed in the directory had to try multiple times over a matter of months. It was free, but it was a hassle. Well, I've got good news and bad:

- The good news: You can get your site listed in Yahoo! Directory within about a week. Yahoo! guarantees to review your site within seven business days. They're not guaranteeing to include your site — only to review and add it if it's appropriate. In general, most people don't have many problems. Yahoo! will almost certainly accept your site if it is

  - Functioning without a lot of broken links

  - In the correct language for the particular Yahoo! Directory to which you are submitting (Yahoo! has directories in several languages.)

  - Designed for multiple browser types

  - In an appropriate category

- The bad news: It's probably going to cost you $299 per year for the privilege ($600 for adult sites). It's free if you have a noncommercial site — though it may take some time for your site to be accepted, if it is at all — but for any kind of commercial venture, you have to cough up the cash. (Note, however, that Yahoo! Directory still contains many sites that predate the paid-listing policy and do not require payment.)

Is listing in Yahoo! Directory worth $299? Hard to say, but here are some good reasons to do so:

- It seems likely that getting into its directory ensures that you get into the Yahoo! Web Search, and may even improve your indexing in Yahoo! Web Search. The company actually states that it "can increase the likelihood," but doesn't guarantee inclusion. I've seen a site get fully indexed fairly soon after submitting to the directory, though that could be coincidence.

- It's crawled by other search engines, such as Google, so having a link in the directory helps the search engines find your site and may encourage them to index it.

- Search engines use the directory to help them categorize your site.

- Many people, as I mention earlier, do use the directory.

- If your site is in the directory, you may be able to place a cheap ad at the top of your category. Some category sponsors are paying as little as $25 per month.

The 1-2-3s of getting listed

Here's how to get listed:

1. **Find a credit card.**

   Preferably the card is yours or that of someone who has given you permission to spend $299 (or is it $600?).

2. **Open your browser and go to** `dir.yahoo.com`.

   You're going to make sure that your site isn't already included.

3. **After the page has loaded, type your domain name into the Search box and click Search.**

   If you have total control over your site, this step isn't necessary; of course you'll know whether your site is already listed. But, for example, if you inherited it from another department in the company you work for, who knows, it may already be there. If it isn't, move to the next step.

4. **Return to the Yahoo! Directory main page and browse through the categories looking for the best match for your site.**

   You can find tips on choosing a category in the next section, "Picking a category."

5. **Look for a link that reads something like** *Suggest a Site* **or perhaps a promotional box of some kind.**

   The link is probably somewhere in the top right of the page.

6. **Click the link and follow the instructions.**

   You have to enter a site description, contact and billing information, and so on.

Picking a category

Because of the sheer volume of categories, picking a category is not as simple as it might seem. Yahoo! Directory has 14 major categories, and many thousands of subcategories. But understanding a few points about hunting for and submitting to a category can make the process a little smoother.

You need to choose a fairly specific category. You can't submit to a category or subcategory if it only holds other subcategories. For instance, you can't submit a site to the Business & Economy category; it's just too broad. Rather, you have to drill down farther into the subcategories and find a category that's specific enough to contain actual Web sites.

You'll probably find that your site could perhaps fit into several categories, so you're going to have to dig around for a while and pick the most appropriate. Although discouraged, you can put a single site into multiple categories, but of course you have to pay for each category. (And Yahoo! doesn't like doing this, anyway; it can take time and effort to persuade them.)

One good strategy is to look for your competitors: What categories are they assigned to? If you find a category with a whole bunch of companies similar to yours, you've probably found the right one.

While you move through Yahoo! Directory, you see that some category names have an @ sign at the end, such as Graduate Programs@, Booksellers@, Intranet@, and so on. These cross-references are to categories under different branches of the directory. For instance, if you browse down the directory to Recreation & Sports > Travel, you see a link to Tour Operators@; click this link, and you jump over to Business and Economy > Shopping and Services > Travel and Transportation > Tour Operators. In fact, virtually every Web site that sells or promotes a product ends up somewhere under Business and Economy, even if they're linked from other parts of the directory.

Also, you have to be inside an actual category before you can add a page. This is a little confusing, perhaps. When you first search in the directory, Yahoo! displays a page (see Figure 12-2) that contains a list of categories and a whole bunch of Web sites that match your search but from various different categories. Thus, you're not actually inside a category at this point, so you can't add a page here, but you will see links that take you into specific categories.

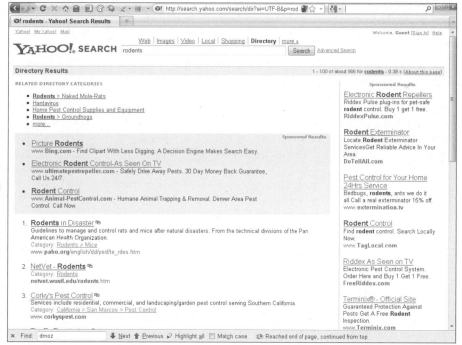

Figure 12-2:
After searching at Yahoo! Directory, you see links to directory categories.

By the way, Yahoo! may not take your advice; it may put your site into a different category. If you're convinced your choice is best, ask them to change. I've successfully requested a change, by pointing out not that the category is best for my client, but that the placement was misleading to searchers because people visiting that category would not expect to see my client's type of Web site.

Should you pay for Yahoo! directory? That is, will you get your 299 dollars' worth? As with much in the SEO field, that's hard to say. If you're a Fortune 500 company, go ahead and pay; let's face it, your company wastes that much every few seconds on everything from ineffective advertising to worthless consultants. If you're on your own and your entire online marketing budget _is_ $299 . . . well, no, there are better ways to spend the money. If you're in between somewhere . . . it's hard to say.

Submitting to the Open Directory Project

Yes, the Open Directory Project is free, and yes, you can submit much more quickly. But the problem is that there's no guarantee that your site will be listed. I've seen sites get into the Open Directory Project within a week or two of submission, and I've seen others that waited months — years! — without ever getting in. Additionally, the submission forms sometimes don't seem to work. Unfortunately, the Open Directory Project — DMOZ, as it's known to search geeks — has more work to do than volunteer editors to do it (each submission has to be reviewed), and although they invite people to become editors, their editor-recruiting process actually discourages editors. Consequently, it's hard to get into the directory.

But don't give up yet. A listing in the Open Directory Project is a great thing to have if you can get it. As I tell my clients, submitting takes only a few minutes, so you might as well try, even if the chance of getting in is low. It's like a free lottery ticket. Here's how to submit:

1. **Read the editor's guidelines at** `dmoz.org/guidelines/describing.html`.

   If you know what guidelines the editors use, you may be able to avoid problems. It's hard to get into the directory, so you may as well give yourself the best chance of getting in.

2. **Go to** `www.dmoz.org`.

   The Open Directory Project home page appears.

3. **Find a suitable category for your site.**

   See the section "Picking a category," earlier in this chapter.

4. **Click the Suggest URL link at the top of the page.**

5. **Follow the (fairly simple) directions.**

Submitting to the Open Directory Project is much easier than doing so to Yahoo! Directory. You simply enter your home page's URL, a short title, a 25–30 word description for the site, and your e-mail address. That's it. Then you wait.

Nevertheless, understand that the editors at DMOZ don't care about your site, they care about the directory; in fact, read the DMOZ forums at www. resource-zone.com and you find that the attitude tends to be "tell us about your site, then go away and forget about it." All sorts of factors are working against you:

- ✔ 8,000 editors are managing more than 700,000 categories.

- ✔ Many small directories might only be reviewed by an editor every six months — or far less frequently.

- ✔ The editors regard a six-month wait, or longer, not particularly excessive.

- ✔ In some cases, editors may even ignore submissions. As one editor explained, "There is no obligation to review them in any order nor is there a requirement to review them as a priority. Some editors find it more productive to seek out sites on their own and rarely visit the suggested sites."

As another DMOZ editor succinctly explained it, DMOZ is "very much like a lottery." The fact is, as important as DMOZ is, you may never get into this directory! If you really, really want to get in, you might consider posting in the DMOZ forums, where you can ask real, live DMOZ editors what's going on: www.resource-zone.com/.

Finding Specialized Directories

For just about every subject you can imagine, someone is running a specialized search directory. Although specialized directories get very little traffic when compared to the big guys, the traffic they do get is highly targeted — just the people you want to attract. Such directories are often very popular with your target audience.

Here's an example of how to search for a specialized directory. Suppose that you're promoting your rodent racing Web site. Go to Google and type *rodent racing directory*. Hmmm, for some reason, Google doesn't find any directories related to rodent racing. Strange. Okay, try *rodent directory*. Now you're getting somewhere! I did this search and found several useful sites:

- ✔ **Ratster.com:** A directory of breeders' links, personal pages, and rescue centers. I'm not sure whether they'd approve of racing rodents, but a link from here would be great.

✔ **ThePetDirectory.us:** You can advertise in this directory; a link would be nice, though I'm not sure it's worth the price. I discuss that a little later. (I don't regard rodents as pets; racing rodents are working animals.)

✔ **NetVet's Electronic Zoo (**`http://netvet.wustl.edu/`**):** This is a big list of links to rodent-related sites, though mostly related to research (the Digital Atlas of Mouse Embryology and the Cybermouse Project, for instance). It's got a good PageRank, too, PR7, so links from here would be valuable. *And* it's on an `.edu` domain, which is valuable (see Chapter 14). Perhaps you can suggest that your site is related to research into cardiovascular performance of rodents under stress.

✔ **Rodent Resources at the National Center for Research Resources:** Hmmm, this is another rodent research site, but with an Alexa traffic rank of 497 and a PageRank of 5, getting listed in this directory would be very useful. (Maybe it's time to apply for a research grant.) Also, because it's at `ncrr.nih.gov`, which is a government domain, links would be valuable (see Chapter 14).

✔ **The Rodent Breeders List (**`AltPet.net`**):** This directory strikes me as one of those "not very pleasant, but somebody's got to do it" things. (How do you breed rodents, anyway? Very carefully I assume.) Still, if you breed rodents for your races, you may want to get onto this list.

When you do a search for a specialty directory, your search results will include the specialty directories you need, but mixed in with them, you'll also find results from the Yahoo! Directory, Google Directory, and the Open Directory Project. If you want, you can clear out the clutter by searching like this:

```
rodent directory -inurl:yahoo.com -inurl:google.com
          -inurl:dmoz.org
```

This search phrase tells Google to look for pages with the words *rodent* and *directory* but to ignore any pages that have `yahoo.com`, `google.com`, or `dmoz.org` (the Open Directory Project) in their URLs.

Note: Some of the specialty directories that you find actually *pull* data from the Open Directory Project. To get into one of these directories, you need to get into the Open Directory Project, as I explain earlier in this chapter.

Hundreds of sites use the Open Directory Project information, so you're bound to run into them now and then. How can you tell when a site is pulling data from the Open Directory Project? Here are a few signs to look for:

✔ Although it's a little-known site, it seems to have a lot of data, covering a huge range of subjects.

 ✔ The directory seems to be structured in the familiar table of categories and subcategories.

 ✔ The real giveaway is usually at the bottom of the page, where you find a box with links to the Open Directory Project, along with a note crediting that organization. See Figure 12-3.

Finding directories other ways

You can use other methods to track down specialty directories. In fact, as you get to know the Internet landscape around your business, you eventually run into these directories. People mention them in discussion groups, for instance, or you find links to them on other Web sites.

With a traffic rank of almost 18,000, Directory.net is definitely not a top-level search system . . .

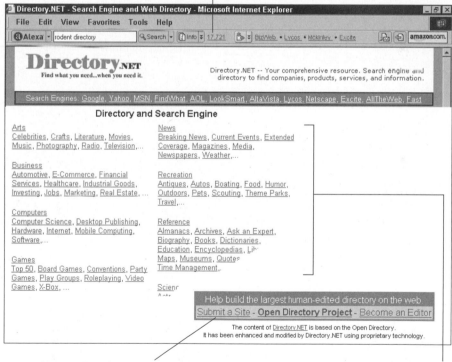

Figure 12-3: Identifying data pulled from the Open Directory Project.

Here's what gives it away — the attribution to the Open Directory Project.

. . . but still, it has a huge amount of information.

Unscientific subcategories

Yahoo! currently has around 1,400 directories subcategories, representing many thousands of directory Web sites. I found links to 13 directories of haunted houses (a number that one might almost imagine is intentional); 13 directories of humor sites; 7 directories of sites that provide electronic greeting cards; and 6 directories of fitness Web sites. This grossly unscientific survey suggests to me that probably almost 14,000 directory sites are listed in Yahoo!. Therefore, chances are good that several may be good candidates for listing your site.

I also like browsing for these directories in the major directories — Yahoo! and the Open Directory Project. Yahoo! Directory (`dir.yahoo.com`) has many subcategories for directories. It doesn't have one for rodent racing, which apparently gets no respect, but it certainly has directories for many other topics, such as the following:

- ✔ Snowboarding > Web Directories
- ✔ Photography > Web Directories
- ✔ Radio Stations > Web Directories
- ✔ Arts > Web Directories
- ✔ Comics and Animations > Web Directories

For some reason, Yahoo! Directory also has subcategories called Directories. (No, I don't know the difference between a Web Directories subcategory and a Directories subcategory.) Here's a sampling of the Directories subcategory:

- ✔ Travel and Transportation > Directories
- ✔ Business and Economy > Directories
- ✔ Reference > Directories
- ✔ Haunted Houses > Directories
- ✔ Ethnic Studies > Directories

The best way to find the Web Directories or Directories subcategories is to go to the Yahoo! Directory and browse for suitable categories for your Web site. Each time you find a suitable category, search the page for the word *directory* to see if the page includes a link to a Web Directory or Directories subcategory. (You can also use the Search box; search for *haunted houses directory,* and one of the resulting links is *Haunted Houses > Directories.*)

The Open Directory Project also lists thousands of directories. Again, browse through the directory (at `www.dmoz.org`) looking for appropriate categories, and then search the page for the word *directories.* Or search for an appropriate directory, such as *golf directories, golf directory, rodent directories, rodent directory,* and so on. (Yes, searching on *directories* and *directory* provides different results.)

When you find a directory, see what's in it. Don't just ask for a link and move on. Dig around, see what you can find. The directory contains links to other sites that may also have their own directories.

Getting the link

After you've found a directory, you need to get the link. In some cases, you have to e-mail someone at the directory and ask. Many of these little directories are run by individuals and are often pretty crudely built. The problem you may run into is that it may take some time for the owner to get around to adding the link — after all, the directory is just a hobby in many cases.

Some directories have automated systems. Look for a Submit Your Site link, or maybe Add URL, Add Your Site, or something similar. The site may provide a form in which you enter your information. Some directories review the information before adding it to the directory, and in other, less common, situations, your information may post directly to the site.

By the way, some of these directories may ask you to pay to be added to the directory or give you preferential treatment if you pay.

Should you pay?

Generally, no.

Why not?

Look, it sometimes seems as though everyone's trying to get you to pay these days. Every time you try to get a link somewhere, someone's asking for money. For example, I recently ran across a portal with all sorts of directories that wanted me to pay $59 (*regularly* $99, though I'm not sure what or when *regular* is). That gets you into the index within seven days and gets you preferential placement.

Of course, that means this portal must have had listings over which I could have preferential placement; in other words, I *could* get in free. I scrolled down the page a little, and found the free Basic Submission.

The term *portal* is an Internet-geek term that, roughly translated, means "We've got all sorts of stuff on our site like news, and weather, and you know, *communities,* and, like, stuff, and we still have some of our dotcom cash left, which should keep us going a few more months while we try to figure out how to make money, and heck, if we don't, Uncle Joe still wants me to come work for him in his furniture store."

I recommend that you do *not* pay for these placements, at least to begin with. In most cases, they simply aren't worth spending $60, $100, or more for the link. It's worth spending a few moments getting a free link, though. If a site asks you to pay, dig around and see if you can find a free placement link. If not, just move on. (If the site can guarantee that you'll be on a page with a high PageRank, the fee may be worth it. See Chapter 14 for more information about PageRank.)

At some point perhaps, it might be worthwhile to *consider* thinking about paying for such placements, but generally, only if you know that the site is capable of sending you valuable traffic or providing valuable links.

You don't have to pay

Luckily, you may find that some of the best directories are free. Take, for instance, the model rocket business. Hundreds of model rocket sites, often run by individuals or families, are on the Web. (See the site shown in Figure 12-4.) Many of these sites have link pages. Although these sites don't get huge numbers of visitors, they *do* get the right visitors (people interested in model rockets) and often have a pretty good PageRank. Most of these sites will give you a free listing, just for the asking. Look for a contact e-mail address somewhere.

Figure 12-4:
It's ugly and doesn't get much traffic, but it does have a reasonable PageRank, and if you ask nicely, the site may give you a link. (It probably won't give me a link now, but maybe you'll get one.)

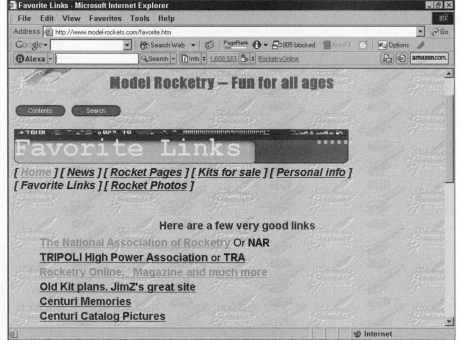

Using "Local" Directories

There are also many *local directories* — directories of businesses sorted geographically. These local directories are often good places to get listed. They're easy to get into and can provide more site categorization clues for search engines, and they often have a high PageRank.

However, this is a subject on its own, so I cover it separately. See Chapter 10 for more information.

Submitting to Second-Tier Directories

Second-tier directories are smallish directories with nowhere near the significance of Yahoo! Directory or the Open Directory Project. They can help you a little if you're willing to spend a few hours registering your site with them.

Unlike search engines, directories can be *crawled* by a searchbot. Directories are categorized collections of sites that you can browse. If you can browse by clicking links to drill down through the directory, then so can a searchbot. In fact, the major search engines index many small directories. If you have a link in one of these directories and one of the major systems sees it, that can help your rank in that search engine, as explained in Chapter 14.

Finding second-tier directories

There are literally thousands of these directories, though you don't want to spend much time with most of them. Many of the directories you find are using data from the Open Directory Project, so you have, in effect, already submitted to them. (You did submit, didn't you?)

Here's the best way to deal with these directories: Find a service that will submit for you. Realistically, these have to be done manually — no automated programs can submit to a huge number of directories reliably — which is extremely time consuming and thus extremely expensive.

However, some firms use Indian labor to make it affordable. For instance, you may be able to find a firm that charges $250 or so to submit to 1,000 Web directories, or perhaps $450 to submit to 2,000. Now, you won't get links in all 1,000, but you may get 400 or 800 over time, so that's a great price. Where do you find these services? Try Guru.com, eLance.com, and oDesk.com.

Some of these firms take screenshots of each submission form, so you can be sure that the submission was completed properly (it uploads the snapshots to a file-sharing site).

I don't want you to go away with the idea that these links are particularly valuable; they're not. I believe they were more valuable in the past, but over time, the search engines have given them less weight. These types of links should be filed under the "they're not great links but they're cheap" category.

Avoiding payment — most of the time

Don't bother paying registration fees to register with these second-tier systems. As with many of the specialized directories, the directory owners are also trying to get site owners to pay for indexing, and in the vast majority of cases, payment is simply not worth it. Regard being listed in these directories as cheap additional links, not as something you need to spend a lot of money on.

On the other hand, you may run across directories that you feel are of *value* — that is, they provide good links back to your site (which helps with search engine rank), or they are likely to provide good traffic to your site. Some of these directories have high PageRanks and do get relatively high traffic. For example, JoeAnt (www.joeant.com) wants a $39.99 one-time fee to list your information; but the home page has a PageRank of 7, and it has an Alexa rank of around 12,000 (meaning that around 12,000 sites on the Web are more popular). That may not sound so great, but it's a big Web, and an Alexa rank of 12,000 is pretty good.

However, before you buy, at least be sure that you know what you're buying. Sometimes a link is not a link. See Chapter 14 for information about links with *no value* — links that look to users like valid links but that search engines either ignore or don't even see as a link to your site.

Chapter 13

Product Search: Remember the Shopping Directories and Retailers

*1*n Chapter 1, I look at *where* people search, focusing on the major search engines, of course, but also giving you a little teaser: "Many, perhaps most, product searches actually begin in sites such as Amazon, eBay, and Craigslist," I write in Chapter 1, referencing you to this chapter.

So what's this all about? It's simple. In this chapter you learn that many, even most, product search results don't come from the major search engines' organic-search indexes; if you sell products and you're focusing only on the major search engines, you're making a big mistake.

So read on, and learn about where people are searching, and how you can get your products, and links back to your Web site, in front of people when they search.

Understanding Where People Search for Products

The Web site comScore claims that in May of 2010, Americans carried out 16 billion searches at the major search engines (Google, Yahoo!, Bing, Ask.com, and associated sites), but another 8 billion or so at other sites. What other sites? Well, YouTube.com accounted for 3½ billion of those searches (see Chapter 18 for more details about them); there's also Facebook (600 million;

see Chapter 17), various other search sites, and map sites. But you should also consider these sites and their search numbers:

- ✔ **Craigslist:** 689M
- ✔ **eBay:** 647M
- ✔ **Amazon:** 280M

That's a total of 1.6 billion searches on these sites, so for every ten searches at the major search engines, a search occurs on one of the preceding three sites.

Do you see where I'm heading? Almost all Amazon and eBay searches are *product* searches, and a huge proportion of Craigslist searches are for products, too. (Craigslist is also the world's most popular "personal ads" site. By the way, by the time you read this, Craigslist will almost certainly have more monthly searches than Ask.com.)

Consider also that many other product indexes exist. How many people search at Buy.com, Overstock.com, PriceGrabber.com, and other similar shopping and price-comparison sites? What about the other "classifieds" sites, such as ePage.com, BackPage.com, and eBayClassifieds.com?

Here's what you can know about searches:

- ✔ Most searches at product retailers, and many searches at classified-ad sites, are for products.
- ✔ Most searches at the major search engines are *not* for products.

That's right, most searches at the major search engines are not product related; they are homework related, news related, celebrity related, politics related, Britney Spears and Paris Hilton related. Sure, 16 billion searches a month is huge, but it covers all aspects of life, not just making purchases.

The simple truth is that *most product-related searches are probably being made outside the major search engines!*

But wait, there's more! The major search engines have their own product indexes. For instance, in this book I discuss various indexes maintained by Google; the PPC index, the organic-search index, and the local-search index (Chapter 10). But Google has one more: the product-search index called Google Product Search. In Figure 13-1 you can see an example; I searched for *binoculars*, and Google displayed some binoculars from its product index, along with a link for *Shopping results for binoculars*.

Yahoo! has a product index, the Yahoo! shopping index, provided by PriceGrabber.com, and Bing has Bing Shopping. (Note that Yahoo! partnered with PriceGrabber.com while at the same time building a search partnership with Bing, so Yahoo! will likely continue using PriceGrabber to provide data to Yahoo! Shopping for some time.) Even Ask.com has a shopping index, provided by a partnership with Pronto.com.

Figure 13-1: Google Product Search results.

So, imagine the following scenario: You sell rodent-racing products, such as harnesses, timers, gates, and the like. You've done a great job getting into the organic search indexes, and you rank well when people search for your products. But you still have one big problem. Most of the search results being presented to your prospective clients don't come from the organic-search indexes; rather, they come from Amazon's index, or Craigslist's, or eBay's, or even one of the major search engine's product search indexes.

The simple truth is this: If you sell products, you *must* consider the product indexes! Most of these directories expect you to pay, though not all do. Google Product Search is completely free, for example. In general, the ones that *do* expect you to pay charge only when someone clicks a link to visit your site, or even when a sale is made, so these directories may be worth experimenting with, too. There are, in effect, three different types of indexes:

✔ **Simple product indexes:** You list your product in the index, and, with luck, when people search for products like yours, your products pop up, the searchers click, and they arrive at your site.

✔ **Classified-ad sites:** You periodically post ads about your products, with links back to your site.

✔ **E-commerce sites:** With this type of index, you are putting your products into someone else's store. It may not even be obvious to buyers that they're buying from a third party; they put your product into the merchant's shopping cart and pay that merchant. Then you ship the product . . . or, as I describe later, in some cases the merchant may stock and ship your products for you.

By the way, you have another advantage to being in these additional indexes, owing to the fact that results from these indexes often turn up in regular search results. The major search engines obviously integrate their own product index results into their organic-search results. But they also index Craigslist, eBay, Amazon, and most if not all of the sites discussed in this chapter. So you get yet another chance (maybe several chances) to rank well in the organic search results.

The following sections look at each of these in turn.

Working with the Product Indexes

The Product Indexes are a simple concept. You get your product listed, so when people search, your product may come up. Just as there is in a search engine's regular search results, there will be a link to your site; in fact, as you've seen, the results may be inserted into the regular search results.

Following is a bunch of product indexes that you might want to check into. Clearly, the most important ones are the indexes used by the major search engines. Go to each one and try to find information about signing up and uploading your data. In some cases, that process is simple — the directory wants you to join, so you find a link that reads something like List Your Products, Sell on Our Site, or Merchant Info. Look in the page footer; you'll often find it there. Sometimes, you have to dig a little deeper because the information is not clearly visible; you may need to use the Contact Us link and ask someone about signing up.

- **Google Product Search:** www.google.com/products
- **Yahoo! Shopping & PriceGrabber.com:** www.pricegrabber.com
- **Bing Shopping:** advertising.microsoft.com/search-advertising/bing-shopping
- **Ask.com & Pronto:** merchant.pronto.com
- **TheFind:** www.thefind.com
- **BizRate & Shopzilla:** www.shopzilla.com
- **NexTag:** www.nextag.com
- **Shopping.com/DealTime.com/Epinions.com:** www.shopping.com
- **PriceSCAN:** www.pricescan.com
- **Pricewatch** (for computer equipment): www.pricewatch.com

Most of these systems expect you to pay if you want to play — generally, you pay each time someone clicks a link to your site. Some let you list your products, and receive traffic, at no cost. Here is a rundown of the three types of systems:

✔ **Free:** You have no direct control over your position, but you don't have to pay for any traffic you get from the site. Google Product Search is the classic example, but Shopmania is free, too, and TheFind is free for basic listings.

✔ **Cost per click; fixed fee:** Yahoo! Shopping is of this type. You don't have any control over position because there's no bidding (as there is with the following type); you pay a fixed fee per click.

✔ **Cost per click; bidding:** Most of the other systems charge per click, but provide bidding systems that help determine your position on search results pages. (As you may expect, merchants with the highest bids are listed first on the page.)

What will you pay for the *cost-per-click (CPC)* systems?

✔ In most cases, CPC systems don't charge a listing fee.

✔ You have to begin by funding your account — typically $50 to $250, which goes toward paying for your clicks.

✔ You pay each time someone clicks your link. Clicks vary in price, generally, from 10 or 15 cents up.

✔ In systems that accept bids, there's a minimum click rate, but the actual rate is dependent on how many people are bidding and their pain threshold; in some cases, clicks could even cost several dollars.

✔ You may be charged other fees, such as a fee to place a store logo next to your listing. (Some of the CPC systems give these logos to the highest bidders free.)

I don't have the space to go into the whole concept of cost-per-click or pay-per-click advertising, but here's a little advice: Be careful! Many people lose a lot of money on the PPC-advertising systems, and there's no reason you can't lose money on these product-directory CPC systems, too.

The product-directory systems probably provide better leads than the more general PPC systems, but nonetheless, you must be careful — you must track results — to ensure that you're not spending more on your clicks than you are making on your sales.

Google Product Search

Google Product Search (www.google.com/products) — formerly Froogle — is Google's product directory. It's been incorporated into the main Google site for years now, and has hundreds of millions of products in the index (Google still labels the service as a beta service, though it's been running for the best part of a decade). I'm sure you've seen Google Product Search, even if you don't realize it. Search, for instance, for *lcd screen* at Google, and Google will,

among the organic-search results, display some product results, along with a
Shopping Results for lcd screen link. Click this link, and Google takes you to the
full Google Product Search directory. The links under the pictures go to specific product pages. Click one of these links, and you see something similar to
that shown in Figure 13-2.

Getting into Google Product Search is easy. Just go to `http://www.google.`
`com/products` and click the Information for Merchants link to find instructions. You can submit a *datafeed* file — a simple text file containing the
product data (which I discuss later in this chapter). In addition, if you have
programmers working on your site, they can use a Google API (Application
Programming Interface) to feed data to Google.

Google Product Search doesn't display a lot of information about each product, so it doesn't require much information from you. You provide a link to
the information page on your site, a link to an image of the product, the name
and description, a price, and a category. Additionally, you can fill various
optional fields, such as author name, model number, size, style, weight, and
so on.

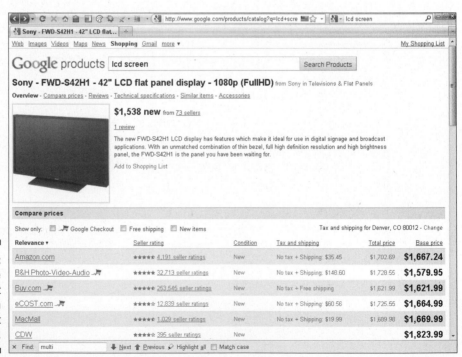

Figure 13-2:
A Google
Product
Search
product
page.

Yahoo! Shopping, PriceGrabber, and PrecioMania

Early in 2010, Yahoo! Shopping dumped its own shopping directory and went into partnership with PriceGrabber (www.pricegrabber.com) and its Spanish-language *hermano* PrecioMania (www.preciomania.com). PriceGrabber was already a major shopping index in its own right, claiming that it has 24 million unique visitors and provides more than a billion dollars in customer referrals each month. PriceGrabber has been a significant shopping directory for a long time because it feeds data to various other shopping directories, and now, with the Yahoo! partnership, it feeds to one of the world's most important shopping directories.

The end result? When you search at Yahoo!, it finds the product you're looking for (see Figure 13-3) and then, when you click the link to the product page, finds merchants that sell the product; see Figure 13-4.

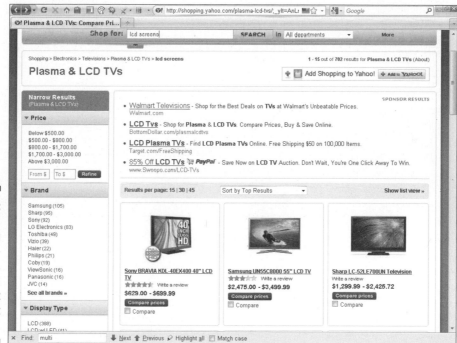

Figure 13-3:
Yahoo!
Shopping
is product-
centric,
taking you
to product
pages, not
merchants.

Figure 13-4:
You can find
links to
merchants
on the
product
page.

So how much does all this cost? That depends on the product category. Unlike some systems, Yahoo! and PriceGrabber charge a fixed fee per click that varies among categories; other systems charge a fee that depends on bidding, as the CPC systems do.

For instance, here are a few click prices:

Appliances	$0.65
Books	$0.15
Computers and Software	$0.75–$1.05
Electronics	$0.65–$1.05
Furniture	$0.35–$0.65
Magazines	$0.75
Sporting Goods	$0.75
Video Games	$0.35

Bing Shopping

Because Bing is the third of the "Big 3" search engines, getting into Bing Shopping could be a very good thing. However, getting into Bing Shopping isn't as easy as getting into Google Product Search or Yahoo! Shopping. You have to contact a sales rep and see whether Bing will take you: `advertising.microsoft.com/search-advertising/bing-shopping`.

Getting into Bing Shopping is, in effect, an advertising buy; Bing has various options, but they're all based on a CPC — cost per click — model. Note that if you're spending less than $500 a month, Bing probably doesn't want to talk to you.

Ask.com and Pronto

Ask.com works with Pronto, so if you want to get into the Ask.com Shopping catalog, go to `www.pronto.com`. As a bonus, your listings will appear on the Pronto site itself, of course, as well as a variety of other Pronto sites — ProntoStyle, ProntoHome, ProntoTech, ProntoKids, and BabyPronto. Your listings will appear on CitySearch, too.

Pronto is also a CPC system and charges you a minimum bid — 20 cents per click for clothing, for instance, and 70 cents for computers — but more if you decide to bid to get a higher position.

TheFind

You may not have heard of TheFind, but apparently plenty of people have; comScore ranks this as the world's number 2 shopping site. I think comScore is wrong — the method it uses to rank shopping sites is flawed. Still, TheFind claims to get 23 million visits a month, so it's still significant. It indexes more than 320 million products from more than 500,000 stores; it goes out and finds the information, but you can "claim" your store so that you can provide a logo and submit datafeeds (which is free), provide coupons, and "optimize" your content. You can pay for better positions.

Shopping.com

Shopping.com (found on the Web at `www.shopping.com`, of all places) is also a pretty important (that is, popular) shopping directory, with around

20 million unique visitors a month. It also charges by the click, and each category has a minimum rate. For instance, the following list shows a few minimum *cost per clicks (CPCs)*, generally based on the value of the product being sold:

Books	$0.05–$0.10
Electronics	$0.20–$1.00
Computers	$0.20–$1.00
Clothing & Accessories	$0.10–$0.45
Furniture	$0.30–$0.50
Travel	$0.05
Kitchen Appliances	$0.20–$0.70

Figure 13-5 shows the Digital Cameras page, a subcategory of Electronics.

Figure 13-5: The Shopping. com directory.

Mergers

Shopping.com was formed by a merger of DealTime and Epinions, the most popular product-comparison sites on the Web. Three separate sites, Shopping.com, DealTime.com, and Epinions.com, now exist; getting into Shopping.com gets you into all three sites. It's worth noting that Epinions listings often rank well in search engines.

Remember, these are *minimums;* your mileage may vary (and almost certainly will); if you want to appear at the top of the search results you'll pay more and, as Shopping.com points out, 50 percent of all clicks go to the top three search results. Unlike with Google Product Search and Yahoo! Shopping, the higher your bid in a system like Shopping.com, the higher you'll initially appear on the product page. However, at Shopping.com, a site visitor can sort the product page by price, store name, and store rating, so as soon as a visitor sorts the page, most of the benefit of the higher bid price is lost. Bids are placed per category, by the way, not per product.

BizRate & Shopzilla

BizRate & Shopzilla (www.shopzilla.com and www.bizrate.com) are two popular per-click sites with common ownership. In addition, Shopzilla owns another *seven* different shopping sites, including six in France, Germany, and the United Kingdom: Beso.com, PrixMoinsCher.fr, SparDeinGeld.de, Shopzilla.co.uk, Shopzilla.de, Shopzilla.fr, and Bizrate.co.uk.

As with Shopping.com, these services charge a minimum fee per category, typically ranging from $0.35 to around a dollar, an extra $0.10 if you have a logo with the product, and the final rate dependent on bidding. Again, merchants with the highest bid are listed first, until the visitor re-sorts the list. Figure 13-6 gives the Shopzilla take on digital cameras — and, no, I'm not necessarily dropping any hints here, although my birthday *is* coming up.

NexTag

NexTag (www.nextag.com), yet another popular site, is also a CPC site with a category minimum and bidding for position. You don't pay a setup fee, but you do have to fund your account before you can get started. That's the norm with all these CPC shopping directories, but NexTag's $150 minimum to start is a little higher than most.

Figure 13-6:
The
Shopzilla
shopping
directory.

NexTag is one of the few shopping systems that lists not only tangible products but also services. If your business sells mortgages or travel services, for instance, you can be listed at NexTag.

You can load data into a Web-form system if you have only a few products. If you have more, you'll want to use a datafeed file. NexTag will take any datafeed file; if you create one for Yahoo! Shopping, for instance, you can use the same one for NexTag. Just send the Yahoo! one to your NexTag account manager, and he or she will handle it.

Pricewatch

Pricewatch (www.pricewatch.com) isn't well known outside geek circles, though it claims to be "The Web's very first price comparison site." Many people in the computer business use Pricewatch to buy their hardware after checking pricing at the site; the site used to be limited to computers, peripherals, and accessories, though it has branched out in recent years. Hey, even UNIX geeks have lives beyond technology . . . well, some of them do.

This crude system (shown in Figure 13-7) appeals to UNIX geeks in particular. It's fast and has few graphics on the search page (or even on the results pages in most cases).

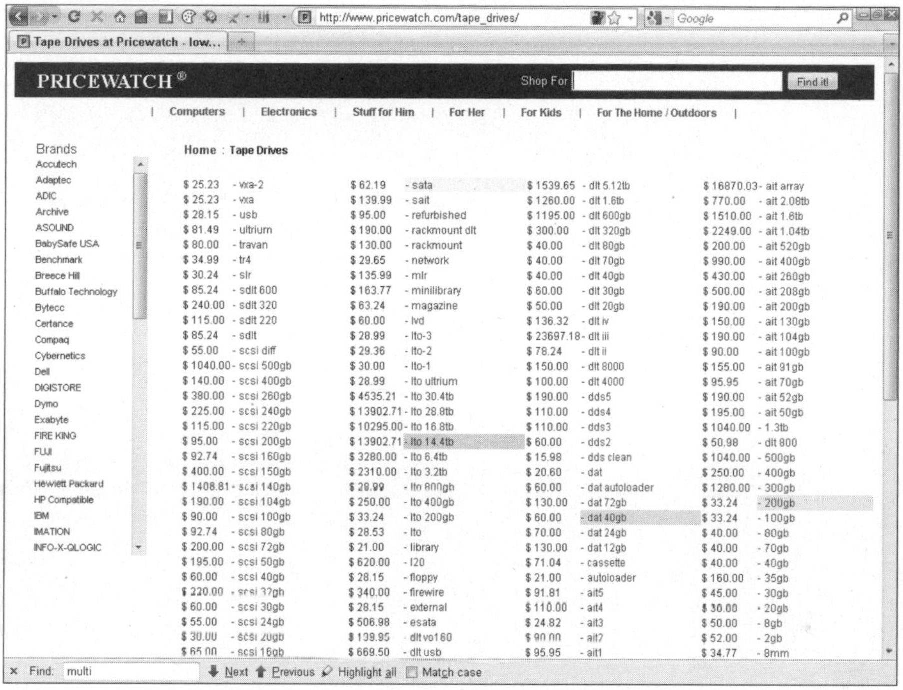

Figure 13-7:
Pricewatch,
a UNIX
geek's
dream
shopping
directory.

The Pricewatch folks claim to serve over 400 million pages each month, so if you have products in their categories, you may want to look into working with them.

PriceSCAN

PriceSCAN (www.pricescan.com) got off to a good start — it was one of the earliest shopping or price-comparison directories — but it seems to have been superseded by the other systems I've mentioned. However, PriceSCAN has one great advantage over most of them: As with Google Product Search, you can list your products for free. The directory does sell advertising, but the price comparisons are intended to be unbiased by fees or CPCs. E-mail the site at vendors@pricescan.com, and who knows, someone might even respond.

More Shopping Services

Yep, there's more, plenty more. Table 13-1 offers a quick rundown of some other places where you can list your products.

Table 13-1	Shopping Services	
Service Name	*URL*	*Description*
AOL Shopping	shopping.aol.com	A very exclusive property; if you want to work with AOL Shopping, you have to negotiate directly.
Become	www.become.com	Created by the founder of mySimon, once a big name in product search.
Best-Price, BuyCheapr	www.best-price.com, www.buycheapr.com	Two comScore top-10 product-comparison sites. These are basically affiliate sites with no way to submit your products.
CoolSavings	www.coolsavings.com	Definitely a smaller site; it claims a million visitors a month.
Dogpile	dogpile.price grabber.com	This popular "metasearch" site uses PriceGrabber for its shopping results.
Kelkoo	www.kelkoo.com	Kelkoo is one of the better-known systems in Europe; in June of 2010, it "beta" launched in the U.S.
Lycos Shopping	shop.lycos.com	Uses PriceGrabber.com.
mySimon	www.mysimon.com	This company was an early and popular product-comparison site. Now it gets its nontech products from Shopping.com and its tech products form CNET's Shopper.com.
PayPal Shopping	www.paypal-shopping.com	This is a comScore top-15 shopping site (it claims 1.5 million visitors a month). To get into the large, searchable index, click the <u>PayPal Shops</u> link under Selling Preferences in your profile. To get into the main catalog that most visitors see, though, you need to call the PayPal merchant services team and apply (it's very selective).

Service Name	URL	Description
PricingCentral	`www.pricingcentral.com`	This is a product "meta search" site; search here, and it pulls up links to various shopping directories.
Shop.com	`www.shop.com`	Originally designed for catalog companies to sell their wares online, this site is looking for merchants with more than 100 consumer-oriented products. Contact `merchantsupport@shop.com`.
ShopCompanion & CatalogCity	`www.shopcompanion.com`. `www.catalogcity.com`	Owned by Shop.com.
Shopper.com	`www.shopper.com`, `shopper.cnet.com`	The technical-product index of CNET.com.
ShopLocal	`www.shoplocal.com`	Claims to have 6.5 billion page views a year. Mostly works with major retailers, so if that doesn't describe you, you may have problems.
Shopmania	`www.shopmania.com`	Listing is free, but it's not a very busy site.
Smarter	`www.smarter.com`	Ranked as one of the top-10 product-comparison sites by comScore.
StreetPrices.com	`www.streetprices.com`	A small CPC site that claims to get 400,000 visitors each month.

The Classified-Ad Sites

Craigslist.com is, of course, the monster, the newspaper killer, of the classified-ads world. You'd never know it from just looking at the site — to call it "minimalist" is being kind — but this site has 20 billion page views a month. Each month, almost 60 million Americans visit Craigslist one or more times; that's almost 1 American in 5. Alexa ranks Craigslist as the world's 33rd most popular Web site, and America's 7th most popular. Ignore Craigslist at your peril!

It's not alone, though. There are several other "significant" classified sites. Significant is in quotation marks because, well, those other sites pale in significance next to Craigslist; nonetheless, some do get significant traffic. I show the following sites' Alexa rankings to give you an idea:

- **BackPage.com:** 904
- **eBayclassifieds.com:** 2,331
- **ePage.com:** 22,593
- **WebClassifieds.us:** 23,794

Perhaps I missed some, but I'm not aware of any other important classified sites, and even the final two of these may not be worth bothering with; the last probably gets under 100,000 visitors a month. (Yes, I know that the home page says "Place your free ads in front of millions of eyes instantly!" but I think the site is using a smidgeon of poetic license; Compete.com estimates that site's traffic at 44,000 visitors a month.) So, it just shows you the state of the classified-ad biz. Craigslist dominates!

How, then, do you use these sites? You post your products in the listings, with links back to your site. The links won't help you; from a search engine ranking standpoint, these are nofollow links (see Chapter 14). You should check the rules because you can't just go in and post a thousand ads or you get blocked. But many businesses promote their products and services very successfully through these classified-ad sites — in particular the first two, of course, Craigslist and BackPage — because they get so much traffic.

By the way, you may run across lists of classified-ad sites, or services that purport to post you to hundreds, nay, thousands, of classified-ad sites (I just saw one promising to post me in 7,000 sites). These are probably not worth your time. Only a very small number of viable classified-ad sites exist.

Working with E-Commerce or Merchant Sites

The last type of product index I want to discuss are the indexes maintained by e-commerce or merchant sites that allow third parties to sell products through their stores.

The two most important, of course, are eBay.com and Amazon.com. eBay's entire business model is based on helping people sell, through auctions, their stuff, whether that stuff amounts to a single item or thousands of items. Amazon.com had people fooled for a few years into thinking that its business model was acting as an online retailer, selling its own stuff, but Amazon's business model, it turns out, is just selling stuff, whoever's stuff that stuff may be. A large part of Amazon's business, certainly more than a quarter of it, is not selling its own stuff but rather selling stuff provided by thousands of other merchants. You could, perhaps, be one of those merchants.

- ✔ With the auction sites, you sell your products, yep, at an auction, and you handle the transactions yourself.

- ✔ With the retail sites, the product is placed into a directory, and if anyone buys it, the retail site handles the transaction, sends you the information so that you can ship the product, and then, a little while later, sends you the money (barring its commission, of course).

Why bother? If you already have a store on your Web site, why work with other stores? Because, as I discuss earlier in this chapter, most people looking for products won't find your site; they'll go through product sites. Amazon gets 280 million searches a month, and some of those are for your products, but you're not getting the sale unless you're working with Amazon.

Are there other such sites, beyond Amazon and eBay? Well, there's Overstock.com, with its tens of millions of visitors each month; you can talk to that company about selling products in its catalog, or quickly set up an account to sell through its Auction site. Another site is Half.com, an eBay-owned, fixed-price retail site that's worth checking into. There may be others, but these few are the biggies.

Working with eBay

eBay is one of the world's three top e-commerce sites, which are as follows: Amazon (Alexa Rank #5), Craigslist (#7), and eBay (#9). It may have more searches than Amazon, though; comScore says it gets around 650 million searches a month, more than twice Amazon's number.

eBay is not just an auction site, though. It hosts thousands of stores, many of which sell fixed-price goods in addition to taking part in auctions. eBay is part of the overall marketing strategy of many different companies. I have one client, for instance, who has his own e-commerce Web site that ranks very well in organic searches and who has an eBay store, too (and who runs Craigslist ads constantly). I don't go into detail about working with eBay; that's a book by itself. But you may want to consider looking into eBay for your own business.

Working with Amazon

Go to Amazon.com and look down the left side of the screen until you find the Selling on Amazon menu. You see the <u>Sell Your Stuff</u>, <u>Fulfillment by Amazon</u>, and <u>Webstore by Amazon</u> links.

Sell Your Stuff takes you to an overview of how to sell products on Amazon, which charges no listing or monthly fee for small merchants. Amazon does charge 99 cents per sale, plus a percentage of the sale. (Media products — books, music, movies, and the like — are also charged a fixed "closing fee" per sale, from 80 cents to $1.35. Larger merchants can pay a $39.99 per month fee and avoid the 99 cents per sale fee. Percentages vary from 8 to 25 percent, depending on the type of product.

The Fulfillment by Amazon link leads to a real eye-opener for many merchants. Amazon will stock and ship your products for you, at really great prices. Whether the order comes from your own Web store, from eBay, from Amazon, or wherever else, Amazon can handle the shipping for you.

This actually gives you a real advantage when selling your products through Amazon itself, but your products are treated exactly as though they were being sold by Amazon itself. In particular, buyers get free shipping on your products (Amazon provides free shipping on most orders over $25). You can actually price your products higher than your competitors do and still have an overall lower price; because Amazon ranks products in its list of vendors by total price, including shipping, your product will rank higher than your competitors'. You'll still have to pay a fee to Amazon to ship your product, but because Amazon is so incredibly efficient at shipping, that fee will be pretty low. (For instance, Amazon charges 90 cents to pick, pack, and ship a book that weighs under 1 pound and costs less than $25. Amazon charges $2.95 if the order was from a non-Amazon sale.)

Amazon is actually out hunting for people to sell products. It has staff looking for successful Web sites with large catalogs of products that are not well represented on Amazon in order to recruit them. (One of my clients was recently recruited and now has thousands of products selling through Amazon.) Check into it; you may be glad you did!

Managing Your Data

To work with the product indexes and e-commerce sites, you need to figure out how to manage your data — that is, all the information about your products. You'll probably need a data file (often called a *datafeed*) containing information about your products. This can be a simple text file carefully formatted, using the correct layout. A datafeed allows you to quickly upload hundreds, even thousands, of products into the directories within minutes.

Although the datafeed file can be a simple text file, creating it is a little difficult for some people. Of course, if you have geeks on your staff, they can handle it for you. The ideal situation is one in which all your product data is stored in a database that is managed by capable, knowledgeable people who know how to export to a text file in the correct format. All you do is give them the data file specification from the shopping directory, and they know exactly what to do. If that's your situation, be happy. If not, I'll help you.

I'm going to explain how to format your data in a spreadsheet program, which is probably the simplest method. If you have a large number of products, you may already have your data in some kind of database format. Unfortunately, you may need to *manipulate* your data — clean it up — before you can use it. I've noticed over the last couple of decades that, for some reason, data is usually a mess — whether the data files were created by small companies or large. Data is often badly formatted — for example, the text files contain the data, but the fields are improperly *delimited* (separated).

I suggest that you use a spreadsheet program to create your data file. Creating the file in a text editor is difficult and error prone, especially if you have a lot of products. Also, remember that each shopping directory is a little different, requiring different information. The spreadsheet file is your source file, from which you can create the various text files as needed.

You may already have a spreadsheet program; Microsoft Excel is hiding on millions of computers around the world, unknown to their owners. (It's part of Microsoft Office.) Or you may have Microsoft Works, which also includes a spreadsheet program. Various other database programs are available — StarOffice and AppleWorks contain spreadsheets, too, and you can get a free spreadsheet program at OpenOffice.org. Microsoft recently released its free Office Web Apps, which includes a pared-down, Web-based version of Excel; see `office.microsoft.com`.

You don't need a terribly complicated program, because the work you do with the file is pretty simple. However, you want to use a program that can have multiple sheets open and will allow you to link from a cell in one sheet to a cell in another.

You can also use a database program to manage all this data. It's just simpler in some ways to use a spreadsheet. Of course, you may already have your data in a database, especially if you have a lot of products.

The data you need

Take a look at the type of data you're going to need for your data file. Google Product Search, Google's shopping directory, requires the following data:

- **product_url:** A link to the product page on your Web site
- **name:** The name of the product
- **description:** A description of the product

- **image_url:** A link to the image file containing a picture of the product
- **price:** The cost of the product
- **category:** The category in which you want to place the product
- **offer_id:** Some kind of product number, such as a *stock keeping unit (SKU)* or *international standard book number (ISBN)*

Those are the basic fields, but there are others you can include, such as instock, shipping, brand, UPC, manufacturer_id, and so on. Each service is different, of course. (For details, you need to check the particular systems into which you want to load the data.)

Here's my suggestion. Begin by creating a spreadsheet file containing *all* the data you have about your products. At the very least, include this information:

- Product name
- Product description
- Product price
- Product category
- A URL pointing to the product's page on your Web site
- A URL pointing to the image file that contains a picture of the product on your site

You also want to include any other information you have — ISBNs, SKUs, EANs, media types, and so on. And, keep the file clean of all HTML coding; you just want plain text, with no carriage returns or special characters in any field.

Formatting guidelines

Some of you may have problems with the product URL. If your site is a framed site, as I discuss in Chapter 7, you have a problem because you can't link directly to a product page. Even if you don't have a framed site, you might have a problem or two. I discuss that in a minute.

Each shopping directory varies slightly, but datafeed files typically conform to the following criteria:

- They are plain-text files. That is, don't save them in a spreadsheet or database format; save them in an ASCII text format. Virtually all spreadsheet programs have a way to save data in such a format (typically as a .csv file).

✔ The first line in each file contains the header, with each field name — product_url, name, description, price, and so on — generally separated by tabs.

✔ Each subsequent line contains information about a single product; the fields match the headers on the first line.

✔ The last line of the file may require some kind of marker, such as END.

✔ In most cases, you can't include HTML tags, tabs within fields (tabs usually separate fields), carriage returns, new line characters within fields, and so on. Just plain text.

Creating your spreadsheet

Take a look at Figure 13-8. This is a simple spreadsheet file containing a number of data fields; it's an example data file from Google Product Search. Each row in the spreadsheet is a product, and each cell in the row — each field — is a different piece of information about the product.

Figure 13-8:
A sample datafeed spreadsheet.

	A	B	C	D	E
		File Edit View Insert Format Tools Data Window Help			_ ☞ ×
1	code	product-url	name	price	shopping-category
2	p12-x	http://www.yourstore123.com/1.html	American Pride Polo Shirt	25	Apparel
3	w345	http://www.yourstore123.com/2.html	Women's Overalls	39.95	Apparel
4	f45	http://www.yourstore123.com/3.html	Carrot Cake	29.95	Flowers, Gifts and Registry > Gourmet and F
5	f46	http://www.yourstore123.com/4.html	Apple Pie	19.99	Flowers, Gifts and Registry > Gourmet and F
6	hg202	http://www.yourstore123.com/5.html	Replacement Blade of Cof	12.95	Home, Garden and Garage > Appliances
7	12kn	http://www.yourstore123.com/6.html	PowerMax Juicer	129.95	Home, Garden and Garage > Appliances > S
8	f235	http://www.yourstore123.com/7.html	Soft Recliner	399.99	Home, Garden and Garage
9	p3002-x12	http://www.yourstore123.com/8.html	Litter box - Gray	14.95	Home, Garden and Garage
10	3exe345	http://www.yourstore123.com/9.html	Handheld power drill	89.95	Home, Garden and Garage
11					

Although the final product will be a text file, you want to save the spreadsheet file in a normal spreadsheet file format. When you're ready to upload data to a shopping directory, *then* you save it as a text file.

Getting those product URLs

To do this spreadsheet business right, you need the URL for each product's Web page. If you don't have many products, this is easy — just copy and paste from your browser into the spreadsheet. If you have thousands of products, though, it might be a bit of a problem! If you're lucky and you have a big IT budget or some very capable but cheap geeks working for you, you don't need to worry about this. Otherwise, here's a quick tip that might help.

Many companies have a source data file that they use to import into an e-commerce program. For this to be useful to you, figure out what page number the e-commerce program is assigning to each product. For instance, one e-commerce system creates its URLs like this:

```
http://www.yourdomain.com/customer/product.php?productid=18507
```

Notice that the `productid` number is included in this URL. Every product page uses more or less the same URL — all that changes is the `productid` number. So here's one simple way to deal with this situation. Suppose you have a data file that looks similar to the one in Figure 13-9, in which you have a product ID or code in one column and an empty column waiting for the URL pointing to the product page.

	A	B	C	D	
1	code	product-url	name	price	shopping-categ
2	803341		American Pride Polo Shirt	25	Apparel
3	803342		Women's Overalls	39.95	Apparel
4	803343		Carrot Cake	29.95	Flowers, Gifts :
5	803344		Apple Pie	19.99	Flowers, Gifts :
6	803345		Replacement Blade of Cof	12.95	Home, Garden
7	803346		PowerMax Juicer	129.95	Home, Garden
8	803347		Soft Recliner	399.99	Home, Garden
9	803348		Litter box - Gray	14.95	Home, Garden
10	803349		Handheld power drill	89.95	Home, Garden

Figure 13-9: Where do you get the URL from?

(Menu bar: File Edit View Insert Format Tools Data Window Help)

Here's how to get these URLs into your product listing:

1. **Copy the blank URL into all the URL fields.**

   Copy the URL without the product ID in it, as shown in Figure 13-10. Some spreadsheet programs try to convert the URL to an active link, one you can click to launch a browser. You may want to leave the URL in that format so that later you can test each link. (*Note:* Working with these active links is often a nuisance because it may be hard to select a link without launching the browser.)

2. **Do one of the following to copy the number in the code field and paste it onto the end of the matching URL with a single keystroke:**

   • *Create a macro.*

   • *Use a programmable keyboard.*

   I love my programmable keyboard! It has saved me hundreds of hours. I use an old Gateway AnyKey programmable keyboard, which you can occasionally buy at eBay.

Figure 13-10:
Place a
blank URL in
the column
and then
copy the
product
code from
the code
column to
the end of
the URL.

	File Edit View Insert Format Tools Data Window Help			_ ᵇ ×
	A	B	C	D
1	code	product-url	name	price	shopping-categ
2	803341	http://www.yourdomain.com/customer/product.php?productid=	American Pride Polo Shirt	25	Apparel
3	803342	http://www.yourdomain.com/customer/product.php?productid=	Women's Overalls	39.95	Apparel
4	803343	http://www.yourdomain.com/customer/product.php?productid=	Carrot Cake	29.95	Flowers, Gifts
5	803344	http://www.yourdomain.com/customer/product.php?productid=	Apple Pie	19.99	Flowers, Gifts
6	803345	http://www.yourdomain.com/customer/product.php?productid=	Replacement Blade of Cof	12.95	Home, Garden
7	803346	http://www.yourdomain.com/customer/product.php?productid=	PowerMax Juicer	129.95	Home, Garden
8	803347	http://www.yourdomain.com/customer/product.php?productid=	Soft Recliner	399.99	Home, Garden
9	803348	http://www.yourdomain.com/customer/product.php?productid=	Litter box - Gray	14.95	Home, Garden
10	803349	http://www.yourdomain.com/customer/product.php?productid=	Handheld power drill	89.95	Home, Garden

Figure 13-10 caption reproduced above.

If you don't have a programmable keyboard (and you should have one!), the spreadsheet you're using may have a built-in macro program that allows you to program actions onto a single keystroke. (MS Excel does, for instance.) Another option is to use a macro program that you download from a share-ware site. If you have only 20 or 30 products, programmable keyboards and macros don't matter too much. If you have a few thousand products, it's worth figuring out how to automate keystrokes!

Creating individual sheets

After you have all of your data in one sheet of the spreadsheet file, you can create a single sheet for each system to which you plan to upload data: one for Google Product Search, one for PriceGrabber, and so on. (A *sheet* is a spreadsheet page, and all good spreadsheet programs allow you to have multiple sheets.)

Remember, each system requires different information, under different headings, and in a different order. So you need to link information from the original sheet to each individual sheet. You don't want to actually copy this information.

Say that you have five shopping directories you're working with and, after you've finished everything, you discover that you made a few mistakes. If you *copied* the data, you have to go into each sheet and correct the cells. If you *linked* between cells, you can just make the change in the original sheet and the other five update automatically.

Here's how this works in Excel. I assume that you have two sheets, one named Yahoo! (with data needed just for Yahoo!/PriceGrabber) and one named Original (containing all your product data). You want to place the information from the *productid* column in the Original sheet into the Yahoo! sheet, under the column named *code*. Here's how you do it in Microsoft Excel:

1. **Click the Yahoo! tab at the bottom of the window to open the Yahoo! sheet.**

2. **Click cell 2 in the *code* column.**

    In this example, this cell is A2, as shown in Figure 13-11.

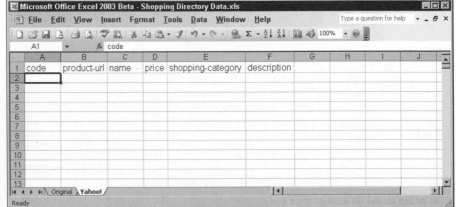

Figure 13-11:
The cursor on cell A2 in the Yahoo! sheet.

3. **Press the = (equal) key to begin placing a formula into the cell.**

4. **Click the Original tab at the bottom of the page to open the Original sheet.**

5. **Click cell 2 in the *productid* column.**

    In this example, this cell is A2, as shown in Figure 13-12.

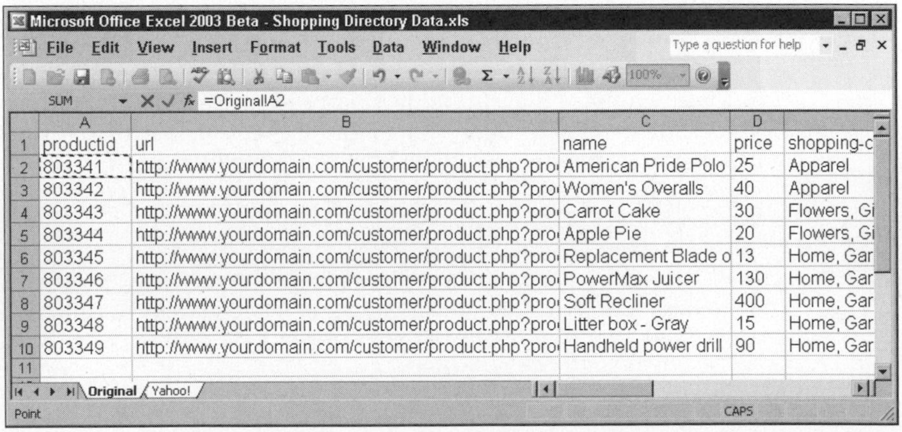

Figure 13-12:
The cursor on cell A2 in the Original sheet.

6. **Press Enter.**

   The program jumps back to cell 2 in the *code* column of the Yahoo! sheet, places the data from the Original sheet into that cell, and then moves down to the cell below.

7. **Click cell 2 and then look in the formula box at the top of the window.**

   You see this formula (or something similar): `=Original!A2`, as shown in Figure 13-13.

   This means, "Use the data from cell A2 in the sheet named Original." You haven't copied the data; rather you're linking to the data, so that if the data in A2 changes, so will the data in this cell.

Here's the formula pulling data from Cell A2 in the Original sheet.

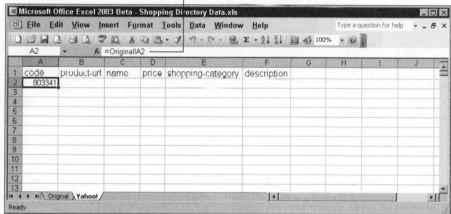

Figure 13-13: Cell A2 in the Yahoo! sheet contains =Original!A2.

8. **With cell 2 in the *code* column of the Yahoo! sheet selected, choose one of the following:**

   - *Press Ctrl+C.*
   - *Choose Edit➪Copy from the main menu.*

   You've copied this data into the Clipboard.

9. **Press the down arrow (↓) to select the cell below.**

10. **Hold the Shift key and press PgDn multiple times, until the cursor has selected as many cells as there are products.**

    For instance, if you have 1,000 products, you want the last selected cell to be cell 1001. (Remember, the first cell contains the header, *code*.)

11. **Choose one of the following:**

    - *Press Ctrl+V.*

    - *Choose Edit⇨Paste from the main menu.*

    The cursor jumps to cell 2 again, and data from the Original sheet — from the appropriate cells — now appears in the cells below cell 2.

12. **Press the Esc key to stop copy mode.**

The cells are now linked. If you change data in a *productid* cell in the Original sheet, it changes in the appropriate *code* cell, too.

Repeat this process for all the columns you need and for all the different sheets you need, and you're ready to export your text files.

Creating and uploading your data files

After you've created your sheets, you can export the text files you need to give to the shopping directories. Each spreadsheet program works a little differently. With some programs, you may find an Export command; in Microsoft Excel, you use the Save As command. Here's how to export the text files from Excel:

1. **Save the spreadsheet file in its original spreadsheet file format.**

   This ensures that any changes you've made are stored in the original file.

2. **Click the tab for the sheet you want to export to a text file.**

   That sheet is selected.

3. **Choose File⇨Save As from the main menu to open the Save As dialog box.**

4. **In the Save As dialog box, choose the appropriate file type from the Save As Type drop-down menu.**

   You generally need to select a text format, such as *CSV (Comma delimited; *.csv)* or *Text (Tab delimited; *.txt)*. Check the shopping-directory specifications, as some may accept other formats.

5. **Provide a filename in the Name field.**

   For example, use Yahoo! if you're submitting to Yahoo!, and so on.

6. **Click OK.**

   You see a message box saying that you can't save the entire file; that's okay; all you want to do is save the selected sheet.

7. **Click Yes.**

   Now you see a message box telling you that some features can't be saved as text. That's okay; you don't want to save anything fancy, just text.

8. **Click Yes.**

   That's it; you've saved the file. It's still open in Excel, with the other sheets, so I suggest that you close the file. (Excel will ask again if you want to save the file — you can just say No.)

   If you want to export another text file, reopen the original spreadsheet file and repeat these steps.

If you want, you can open the file in a text editor like Notepad to see what it really looks like.

After you've created the text file, you're ready to upload it to the shopping directory. Each directory works a little differently, so refer to the directory's instructions.

These data files expire. They last only one month at Google Product Search, for example. Check each system carefully and remember to upload the latest data file before it expires or when you have any important changes.

Other ways to manage data

There are, of course, tools that you can use to do some of the work for you. Search Google for *product data feed* or *feed management* and you find companies advertising a variety of products and services. SingleFeed.com, for instance, can help you feed data to 17 different systems, including Google Product Search, Bing, Become, NextTag, Pronto, Shopzilla, TheFind, and PriceGrabber. Plans start at $99.99 a month.

GoDataFeed works with a huge list — more than 50 sites, including not only product indexes and e-commerce systems but also coupon sites, review sites, and affiliate networks. All this for $99 a month (or $50 a month for a very limited starter plan).

There are also sophisticated services, such as ChannelAdvisor.com and Mercent.com, which charge hundreds, if not thousands, of dollars a month but provide much more sophisticated services, including PPC-campaign management, inventory management, accounting integration, shipping management, and so on. I should also mention SellerEngine.com, a very affordable software program designed to help you manage Amazon.com sales; Zoovy.com, which works with Amazon, eBay, PriceGrabber, and multiple Web stores; Fillz.com, a product designed mainly for selling books, movies, music, and games, so it works with Amazon, Barnes and Noble, and various other media stores; and Monsoonworks.com, another sophisticated system that works with media, textbooks, and consumer goods.

Whatever your products, companies are out there that want to help! So you really should consider working with these other channels. It's where the searchers are!

Part IV
After You've Submitted Your Site

The 5th Wave   By Rich Tennant

"I'm not sure I like a college whose home page
has a link to The Party Zone!"

In this part . . .

Submitting your site to the search engines isn't enough. It doesn't guarantee that they'll include your site, and it doesn't guarantee that your site will rank well. So this part of the book is essential to your success. In particular, you must understand the value of links pointing to your Web site.

Search engines use links to find your site, to figure out what your site is about, and to estimate how valuable your site is. Search engine optimization without a link campaign is like looking for a job without a résumé: You may make contact, but you won't close the deal. In this part, you discover the different ways that search engines use links, and then you find out how to get those all-important incoming links.

You also learn about the role of social networking and video in promoting your site; these are two highly touted but relatively little understood components in a marketing campaign.

Finally, I also look at what happens when the unthinkable happens — Google strikes you down!

Chapter 14

Using Link Popularity to Boost Your Position

*T*housands of site owners have experienced the frustration of being unable to get search engines to index their sites. You build a Web site, you do your best to optimize it for search engines, you "register" with the search engines, and then nothing much happens. Little or no traffic turns up at your site, your pages don't rank well in the search engines, and in some cases you can't even find your pages in the search engines. What's going on?

Here's the opposite scenario: You have an existing site and find a few other sites to link to it. You make no changes to the pages themselves, yet all of a sudden, you notice your pages jump up in the search engines.

There's a lot of confusion about links and their relationship to Web sites. Many site owners don't even realize that links have a bearing on their search engine positions. Surely, all you need to do is register your page in a search engine and it will be indexed, right? Nope. This chapter takes the confusion out of links by showing you how they can help, and what you need to know to make them work.

Why Search Engines Like Links

A few years ago, pretty much all you had to do to get your site listed in a search engine — and maybe even ranked well — was register with the search engine. Then along came Google in 1998 and all that changed. Google decided to use the links from other Web sites as another factor in determining whether the site was a good match for a search. Each link to a site was a vote for the site, and the more votes the site received, the better a site was regarded by Google.

In fact, Google's original name was *BackRub*. No, really. Check out Google's own corporate history (`www.google.com/corporate/history.html`):

> *1996: Larry and Sergey, now Stanford computer science grad students, begin collaborating on a search engine called BackRub.*

> *1997: Larry and Sergey decide that the BackRub search engine needs a new name. After some brainstorming, they go with Google.*

BackRub? As in *backlinks*, links pointing to a Web page. And as in "you rub my back and I'll rub yours," I think, if the original logo is anything to go by. You can see that in Figure 14-1, and again (*no, really*), this is the actual original BackRub/Google logo.

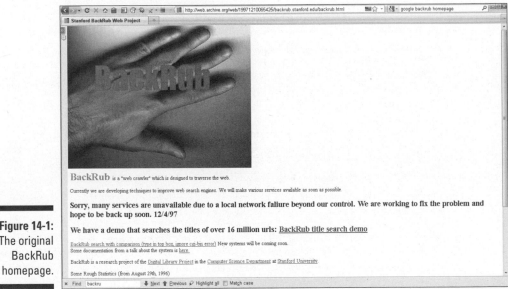

Figure 14-1:
The original
BackRub
homepage.

The founders of Google came up with the original name for a good reason; the original project was all about linking. The research project that led to Google was, according to Wikipedia, "focused on the problem of finding out which Web pages link to a given page, considering the number and nature of such backlinks to be valuable information about that page."

So there you have it. Google was revolutionary *because of the weight given to links*. Google changed the game totally, and now all the major search engines look at links to learn about the referenced pages.

Links pointing to your Web pages do several things for you:

- **Links make it easier for search engines to find the page.** As the search-bots travel around the Web, they follow links. They index a page, follow the links on that page to other pages, index those pages, follow the links on those pages, and so on. The more links to a page, the more likely the page is picked up and indexed by search engines, and the more quickly it happens.

- **Search engines use the number of links pointing to a page as an indication of the page's value.** If lots of pages link to your page, search engines place a greater value on your page than pages with few links pointing to them. If you have lots of links from sites that are themselves linked to by many other sites, search engines conclude that your site must *really* be important. (Google calls this value the page's *PageRank*, but Google isn't the only search engine to use links as an indication of value; Yahoo!, for instance, before the Yahoo!/Bing partnership, was using something called *Web Rank*, and Bing has *Page Score*.)

- **Links provide information to search engines about the page they're pointing to.** The link text often contains keywords that search engines can use to glean additional information about your page. The theme of the site pointing to your site may also give search engines an indication of your site's theme. For example, if you have links from hundreds of rodent-related Web sites, and those links have rodent-related keywords in them, it's a good bet that your site has something to do with rodents.

- **Links not only bring searchbots to a page, but may also bring people to the page.** The whole purpose of your search engine campaign is to bring people to your site, right? Sometimes people will actually click the links and arrive at your site; we often forget that in the SEO world!

Links are very important. Sometimes they mean the difference between being indexed by a search engine and not being indexed, or between being ranked well in a search engine and barely being ranked at all. In this chapter, I delve into this subject, a topic broadly known as *link popularity,* to give you a good understanding of what links from other sites pointed to yours is all about. Then, in Chapters 15 and 16, you discover how to get other sites to link to yours.

Backlinks are an integral part of the optimization of your Web site. A *backlink* — this may surprise you — is a link back to your site. Search engines look at back-links to figure out what your site is about and how important it is. Links aren't something detached from your site; they're an integral part of your site.

Think of your Web site in terms of a regional map. Your site is the major city, and backlinks are the roads bringing traffic into the city. A geographer looking at the map wouldn't regard the city and roads as separate entities; they're all part of the same economic and social system. So don't think of the links pointing to your site as something "out there" — they're a critical part of your site.

Search engines are trying to figure out what site or page is the best match for a search. As you discover later in this chapter, search engines use links as one way to determine this. As with content though (discussed in Chapter 9), using the number of links to and from a site to measure significance is an imperfect method. A page can conceivably be the best page on a particular subject, yet have few links to it. Just because I publish a page today doesn't mean it's worse than a page that was published five years ago and now has many links to it. However, search engines have difficulty figuring out what the searcher needs, so they have to use what information is available to them. Using links is a way of recruiting Web site owners to help point out useful sites and pages. The strategy is imperfect, but that's the search engine world we're living in.

Understanding Page Value and PageRank

Search engines assign a value to your site based on the links pointing to it. The most popular term for this kind of ranking is *PageRank,* which Google uses. The *PageRank* is a value that Google gives to a page, based on the number and type of links into the page.

PageRank is mentioned frequently in the search engine optimization field for several reasons:

✔ Google is the world's most important search engine and will remain so for the foreseeable future.

✔ You don't need a PhD to figure out a page's PageRank. The Google toolbar — the handy little tool I show you how to download in Chapter 1 — shows you the currently loaded page's PageRank. (Okay, strictly speaking that's not true, but it does provide an indication of the PageRank, which I discuss in more detail later in this chapter.)

✔ We also have a basic idea of how PageRank is calculated. Sergey Brin and Lawrence Page, founders of Google, published a paper about the algorithm while at Stanford University. It's almost certain that the algorithm used by Google now isn't the same as the one they published, but it's likely to be similar.

Pulling rank

By the way, you can be forgiven for thinking that the term *PageRank* comes from the idea of, well, ranking pages. Google claims, however, that it comes from the name of one of the founders of Google and authors of the original PageRank document, Larry Page. (The other founder is Sergey Brin.) The truth is probably somewhere in between. Otherwise, why isn't it the PageBrinRank?

Although this section focuses on PageRank, other search engines use similar rankings, and the things you do with links that boost your PageRank also help boost your site with other search engines.

PageRank — one part of the equation

The PageRank value is just one part of how Google determines which pages to show you when you search for something. I want to stress that point because so many people get really hung up on PageRank. A low PageRank is often an indicator of problems, and a high PageRank is an indicator that you're doing something right, but PageRank itself is just a small part of how Google ranks your pages.

When you type a search term into Google and click Search, Google starts looking through its database for pages with the words you've typed. Then Google examines each page to decide which pages are most relevant to your search. Google considers many characteristics, such as what the <TITLE> tag says, how the keywords are treated (are they bold, italic, or in bulleted lists?), where the keywords sit on the page, and are keywords in links pointing to the page (in links both outside the site and within the site). Google also considers PageRank. Clearly, a page with a low PageRank could rank higher than one with a high PageRank in some searches. When that happens, it simply means that the value provided by the high PageRank isn't enough to outweigh the value of all the other characteristics of the page that Google considers.

I like to think of PageRank as a tiebreaker. Imagine a situation in which you have a page that, using all other forms of measurement, ranks as well as a competitor's page. Google has looked at both pages, found the same number of keywords in the same sorts of positions, and thinks both pages are equally good matches for a particular keyword search. However, your competitor's page has a higher PageRank than yours. Which page ranks higher in a Google search for that keyword? Your competitor's.

Here's something else that comes with PageRank, by the way: The higher the PageRank, the more often the page is likely to be re-indexed.

Many people claim that site owners often focus too much on PageRank (that may be true) and that PageRank isn't important. But PageRank (or something similar) definitely is a factor. As Google has said:

> *"The heart of our software is PageRank™, a system for ranking web pages developed by our founders Larry Page and Sergey Brin at Stanford University. And while we have dozens of engineers working to improve every aspect of Google on a daily basis, PageRank continues to provide the basis for all of our web search tools."*

So, Google claims that PageRank *is* in use and *is* important. As long as it includes a PageRank indicator on the toolbar, I have to think it must still be in use, unless Google is playing a huge joke on us (which I wouldn't totally discount, I must admit). But you need to keep its significance in perspective. It's still only part of the story.

It all comes down to what the searcher is searching for. A page that ranks well for one keyword or phrase may rank poorly for another. Thus, a page with a high PageRank can rank well for some keywords and badly for others.

The PageRank algorithm

I want to quickly show you the original PageRank algorithm; but don't worry; I'm not going to get hung up on it. In fact, you really don't need to be able to read and follow it, as I explain in a moment. Here it is:

PR (A) = (1 – d) + d (PR (t1) / C (t1) + ... + PR (tn) / C (tn))

Where:

PR = PageRank
A = Web page A
d = A damping factor, usually set to 0.85
t1...tn = Pages linking to Web page A
C = The number of outbound links from page tn

I could explain all this to you, honestly I could. But I don't want to. Furthermore, I don't have to because you don't need to be able to read the algorithm. For instance, do you recognize this equation?

$$F_{ij} = G \frac{M_i M_j}{D_{ii}^2}$$

Getting details

If you want all the nasty, complicated details about PageRank, you can find a number of sources of information online. One description of PageRank that I like is at the WebWorkshop site (`www.webworkshop.net/page rank.html`). This site also provides a calculator that shows you the effect on PageRank of linking between pages in your site. You might also see the Wikipedia article on the subject (`http://en.wikipedia.org/wiki/Pagerank`), or get the lowdown on PageRank from the horse's mouth: Read *The PageRank Citation Ranking: Bringing Order to the Web* by Sergey Brin and Lawrence Page, the founders of Google. Search on the document's title at Google.

Don't think you can kid me. I know you don't know what this is. (Well, okay, maybe you do, but I'll bet over 95 percent of my readers don't.) It is the Law of Universal Gravitation, which explains how gravity works. I can't explain this equation to you, but I really don't care because I've been using gravity for some time now without the benefit of understanding the jumble of letters. The other day, for instance, while walking down the street, someone shoved a flyer into my hand. After walking on, glancing at the flyer, and realizing that I didn't want it, I held it over a trash can, opened my hand, and used gravity to remove it from my hand and deposit it into the trash can. Simple.

Rather than take you through the PageRank algorithm step by step, here are a few key points that explain more or less how it works:

✔ **As soon as a page enters the Google index, it has an intrinsic PageRank.** Admittedly, the PageRank is very small, but it's there.

✔ **A page has a PageRank only if it's indexed by Google.** Links to your site from pages that have not yet been indexed are effectively worthless, as far as PageRank goes — actually, as far as *any* linking benefit goes in the Google index. If it's not in the index, it can't confer any kind of benefit to your site.

✔ **When you place a link on a page, pointing to another page, the page with the link is voting for the page it's pointing to.** These votes are how PageRank increases. As a page gets more and more links into it, its PageRank grows.

✔ **Linking to another page doesn't reduce the PageRank of the origin page, but it does increase the PageRank of the receiving page.** It's sort of like a company's shareholders meeting, at which people with more shares have more votes. They don't lose their votes when they vote; next time a meeting takes place, they have just as many votes. But the more shares they have, the more votes they can place.

✔ **Pages with no links out of them are wasting PageRank; they don't get to vote for other pages.** Because a page's inherent PageRank is not terribly high, this isn't normally a problem. It becomes a problem if you have a large number of links to dangling pages of this kind. Though rare, this could happen if you have a page that many external sites link to that then links directly to an area of your site that won't benefit from PageRank, such as a complex e-commerce catalog system that Google can't index or an external e-commerce system hosted on another site. Unless the page links to other pages inside your Web site, it won't be voting for those pages and thus won't be able to raise their PageRank.

✔ **A single link from a dangling page can channel that PageRank back into your site.** Make sure that all your pages have at least one link back into the site. This usually isn't a problem because most sites are built with common navigation bars and often text links at the bottom of the page. Of course, the links have to be readable by the search engines (see Chapter 7).

✔ **You can increase a site's overall PageRank two ways:**

• Increase the number of pages in the site, although it's a small increase because the inherent PageRank of a new page is low.

• Get links to the site from outside.

✔ **The page receiving the inbound link gets the greatest gain.** Thus, ideally, you want links into your most important pages — pages you want ranked in search engines. PageRank is then spread through links to other pages in the site, but these secondary pages get less boost.

It's important to understand that Web sites don't have a PageRank; Web pages have a PageRank. It's possible for a site's home page to have a high PageRank, although its internal pages rank very low.

Here are a couple of important implications from this:

✔ **You can vote large amounts of PageRank through your site with a single link.** A page with a PageRank of 5 can pass that to another page as long as it doesn't split the vote by linking to other pages.

When I use the term *pass,* I use it in the sense of passing on a virus, not passing a baton. You can pass PageRank from page to page. Linking from page A to page B passes PageRank from A to B in the same way that person A may pass a cold to person B. Person A doesn't get rid of the cold when he passes it to B; he's still got it. Likewise, page A still has its PageRank when it passes PageRank on to page B.

✔ **You can ensure that PageRank is well distributed around your Web site by including lots of links.** Linking every page to every other page is the most efficient way to ensure even PageRank around the site.

Huge sites equal greater PageRank

Because every page is born with a PageRank (as soon as Google finds it, anyway), the more pages in your site, the greater the site's intrinsic PageRank. If you create a linking structure that links all your pages well, you'll be providing your pages with a high PageRank simply because you have many pages.

However, don't think of creating pages as a search engine strategy. You'd need a huge number of pages to make a difference. If you own or manage a site that already has hundreds of thousands of pages, consider yourself lucky. But don't build hundreds of thousands of pages just to boost PageRank.

This fact provides another reason for Web sites to retain old pages, perhaps in archives. A news site, for instance, should probably keep all news articles, even very old ones. Of course, a massive repository of data often has a high PageRank for another reason — many other sites link to the data. Remove pages and you lose the links.

However, I also believe that in the last couple of years the PageRank algorithm has been adjusted from this original more-pages-means-higher-PageRank concept. I think that very large sites actually have a penalty of some kind. The new algorithm says, in effect, "if you're going to have hundreds of thousands of pages, well, you're going to have to work harder for your PageRank." While a small site might increase its PageRank rapidly with a few links from high PageRank sites, large sites may need many more links to have the same effect.

Measuring PageRank

How can you discover a page's PageRank? You can use the Google toolbar. (In a moment, I explain why you can never find out the *true* PageRank.) As I mention in Chapter 1, you should install the Google toolbar, which is available for download at `www.toolbar.google.com`. Each time you open a page in Internet Explorer or Firefox, you see the page's PageRank in a bar, as shown in Figure 14-2. If the bar is all white, the PageRank is 0. If it's all green, the PageRank is 10. You can estimate PageRank simply by looking at the position of the green bar, or you can mouse-over the bar, and a pop-up appears with the PageRank.

If the PageRank component isn't on your toolbar, click the Options button on the right of the bar and then select Options from the menu that appears so that you can open the Toolbar Options dialog box. Click the Tools button at the top of the dialog box, select the PageRank check box, and click the Save button.

If you don't have the Google toolbar, you can still check PageRank. Search for the term *pagerank tool* to find various sites that allow you to enter a URL and get the PageRank. Mozilla's Firefox browser also has add-ons that display the PageRank in the status bar of every page.

Figure 14-2:
The PageRank bar on the Google tool-bar shows PageRank.

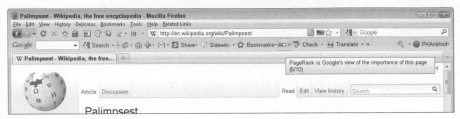

Here are a few things to understand about this toolbar:

- **Sometimes the bar is gray.** Sometimes when you look at the bar, it's grayed out. Some people believe that this means Google is somehow penalizing the site by withholding PageRank. I've never seen this happen, though. (And I have seen the PageRank indicator white after loading a site I'm pretty sure has been penalized.) I believe the bar is simply buggy, and that PageRank is just not being passed to the bar for some reason. Every time I've seen the bar grayed out, I've been able to open the Web page in another browser window (you may have to try two or three) and view the PageRank.

- **Sometimes the toolbar guesses.** Sometimes the toolbar guesses a PageRank. You may occasionally find it being reported for a page that isn't even in the Google index. It seems that Google may be coming up with a PageRank for a page on the fly, based on the PageRank of other pages in the site that have already been indexed.

  Also, note that Google has various data centers around the world. Because they're not all in sync and have data varying among them, it's possible for one person looking at a page's PageRank to see one number, while someone else sees another number.

- **A white bar is not a penalty.** Another common PageRank myth is that Google penalizes pages by giving them a PageRank of 0. That is, if you see a page with a PageRank of 0, something is wrong with the page, and if you link to the page, your Web page may be penalized, too. This is simply not true. Most of the world's Web pages show a PageRank of 0. That's not to say that Google won't take away PageRank if it wants to penalize a page or site for some reason (see Chapter 19). I'm just saying that you can't tell whether it's a penalty or simply a page with few valu-able links pointing in.

✔ **Zero is not zero, and ten is not ten.** Although commonly referred to as *PageRank,* and even labeled as such, the number you see in the Google toolbar is not the page's actual PageRank. It's simply a number indicating the approximate position of the page on the PageRank range. Therefore, pages never have a PageRank of 0, even though most pages show 0 on the toolbar, and a page with a rank of, say, 2 might actually have a PageRank of 25 or 100.

The true PageRank scale is probably a logarithmic scale. Thus, the distance between PageRank 5 and 6 is much greater than the difference between 2 and 3. The consensus of opinion among people who like to discuss these things is that the PageRank shown on the toolbar is probably on a logarithmic scale with a base of around 5 or 6, or perhaps lower.

Suppose for a moment that the base is actually 5. That means that a page with a PageRank of 0 shown on the toolbar may have an actual PageRank somewhere between a fraction of 1 and just under 5. If the PageRank shown is 1, the page may have a rank between 5 and just under 25; if 2 is shown, the number may be between 25 and just under 125, and so on. A page with a rank of 9 or 10 shown on the toolbar most likely has a true PageRank in the millions. With base 5, for instance, the toolbar PageRank would represent a true PageRank as shown in Table 14-1.

Table 14-1   Pure Conjecture — What Toolbar PageRank Would Represent if PageRank Were a Logarithmic Scale Using Base 5

Toolbar PageRank	True PageRank
0	0–5
1	5–25
2	25–125
3	125–625
4	625–3,125
5	3,125–15,625
6	15,625–78,125
7	78,125–390,625
8	390,625–1,953,125
9	1,953,125–9,765,625
10	9,765,625–48,828,125

The maximum possible PageRank, and thus this scale, continually changes as Google recalculates PageRank. As pages are added to the index, the PageRank has to go up. Periodically, Google recalculates PageRank Web-wide, and PageRank drops for many sites, perhaps most.

How can you be sure that the numbers on the toolbar are not the true PageRank? The PageRank algorithm simply couldn't work on a scale of 1 to 10 on a Web that contains billions of Web pages; it just wouldn't make sense. It's not logical to assume that sites like Yahoo! and Google have a PageRank just slightly above small, privately owned sites. I've had pages with ranks of 6 or 7, for instance, whereas the BBC Web site, one of the world's 40 most popular Web sites according to Alexa, has a PageRank of 9. It's not reasonable to assume that its true PageRank is just 50 percent greater than pages on one of my little sites.

Here are two important points to remember about the PageRank shown on the Google toolbar:

✔ Two pages with the same PageRank on the toolbar may actually have a very different true PageRank. One may have a PageRank that is a quarter or a fifth of the other.

✔ It gets progressively harder to push a page to the next PageRank on the toolbar. Getting a page to 1 or 2 is pretty easy, but to push it to 3 or 4 is much harder (though certainly possible). To push it to the higher levels is very difficult indeed — 8 or above is rare.

Leaking PageRank

It's possible for PageRank to *leak* out of a site, despite the fact that pages don't lose PageRank when they link to other pages. Here's how: Each time you link from one page to another, the origin page is voting for the recipient page. Thus, a link from one page in your site to another page in your site is a vote for that other page. If you link to a page on another site, you're voting for another site's page rather than your site's page.

Suppose that you have a page with a PageRank of 10,000 and it has 40 links on it. Each link is getting a PageRank vote of 250 ($250 \times 40 = 10,000$). Now suppose that half the links on the page are external. In that case, you're taking 5,000 votes and pointing to pages out of your site rather than inside your site. So PageRank leaks in the sense that the PageRank of some pages in your site is lower than it could be.

Generally, you should worry more about getting backlinks to your site from appropriate Web sites than about how much PageRank is leaking through your outgoing links. You can build PageRank quickly by using the techniques in Chapters 15 and 16, and in most cases, worrying about outgoing links won't save you much PageRank. Still, you can do two simple things to help reduce rank leak:

- ✔ If you have a page with lots of outgoing links, make sure that it also has links to the other pages in your site. You'll be splitting the vote that way between outgoing and internal links, rather than passing all of it on through outgoing links.

- ✔ Ideally, you want the page with the external links to be one with a low PageRank, reducing the outgoing votes. You can do that by minimizing the number of links from other pages on your site into the link page.

- ✔ You could also use the `rel="nofollow"` link attribute (see later in this chapter for information) so that outgoing links don't pass on PageRank.

There are other theories on how Google figures out which pages rank above others. One is the PigeonRank system described by Google in a technical document that you can find in Google's technology area. Google suggests that "low-cost pigeon clusters (PCs) could be used to compute the relative value of Web pages faster than human editors or machine-based algorithms. By collecting flocks of pigeons in dense clusters, Google is able to process search queries at speeds superior to traditional search engines, which typically rely on birds of prey, brooding hens, or slow-moving waterfowl to do their relevance rankings." Find details at `http://www.google.com/technology/pigeonrank.html`. No, really.

Page Relevance

The problem with PageRank is that it's independent of keywords. The value is a number derived from links pointing at a page with no relation whatsoever to a specific keyword. A page may have a high PageRank, but that doesn't mean it's the type of page you're looking for when you search for a particular keyword.

Thus, search engines add something else to the mix: *relevance* or *context.* The major search engines are attempting to do this sort of analysis by matching keywords. In effect, search engines are trying to create a context-sensitive PageRank or *topic-sensitive* PageRank. A topic-sensitive PageRank is dependent on a particular topic. Instead of counting any and all links, only links from relevant Web sites are included.

Page relevance is harder to measure, though. The concept of page relevance is that a link from a page related in some way to your page is more valuable than a link from an entirely unrelated page. A link to your rodent-racing site from a Web site that is also related to rodent racing is more valuable than, say, a link from your Aunt Edna's personal Web site.

One way search engines are probably trying to do this is by using Yahoo! and the Open Directory Project directory to provide some context. Because Web sites listed in the directory have been put into categories, it gives search engines a starting point to figure out what keywords and sites relate to what categories.

This discussion is getting complicated now, and you really don't need to know the details. However, if you want to read a little geek stuff related to relevance or context, search for a paper, "Topic-Sensitive PageRank," by Taher Haveliwala of Stanford University.

My feeling is that this sort of technology isn't as advanced as many believe or as advanced as search engines want you to believe. Still, people in the search engine business swear that links from related sites are more valuable than links from unrelated sites. To be more precise, links from sites that a search engine *thinks* are related are more valuable than those from sites that a search engine thinks are unrelated. Because the technology is imprecise, search engines don't always get it right. The fact is that no search engine really knows for sure if one site is related to another; it can only guess. As with everything else, relevance is just one ingredient in the mix.

Consider this example. Say you own a rodent-racing Web site. Among the links pointing to your site is one from a blog owned by an insurance agent. Now, most of the content on that site is related to the insurance business, but it just so happens that the owner is also a big fan of rodent racing. So is that link a relevant link? Of course it is! It's from an insurance site but is placed there for good reason by someone who loves your site. That's the real thing, the kind of link Google wants to see.

So don't let anyone tell you that links from "unrelated" or "nonrelevant" sites have no value. A link from an unrelated site helps search engines find your pages, boosts PageRank, can provide information about what your site is about (if you have good keywords in the links, which I discuss later in the chapter), and may even bring visitors to your site. These links just won't have the extra boost provided by relevance, but that doesn't mean they have no value.

Hubs and Neighborhoods

Having said that relevance may be overrated, I still do recognize that relevance can be useful (it's just not everything). The ideal link is one from a related Web site, not just any old Web site you can convince to link to you. The most powerful *link hubs* — networks of interlinked Web sites — are those that are tightly focused on a particular topic. Search engines respect that, want to uncover such situations and rank the target sites more highly, and are probably getting better every day at doing so.

Search engines are looking for what may be thought of as Web *neighborhoods, communities,* or *hubs* — groups of Web sites related to a particular subject, and the sites that appear to be most central to it. If you're positioned in the middle of a *cloud* — a web of Web sites related to a particular subject — that's a good thing.

Imagine a chart showing the world's rodent-racing Web sites and their connections. In this chart, little boxes represent the Web sites and lines show links between the sites. (Figure 14-3 gives an example of such a chart.) Some of the boxes seem to be sitting by themselves — very few links are going out, and very few are coming in. Other boxes have lots of links going out but few boxes linking back. Now imagine your rodent racing site. It's a hub with many links going out, and many links coming in. That would look pretty important on a chart. Don't you think search engines would find that interesting? In fact, search engines are trying to figure out this sort of thing all the time. Therefore, if you can build links to turn your site into a hub, that's a great thing! (That doesn't mean that all you need to do is build lots of pages with outgoing links, by the way — far more important are the incoming links.)

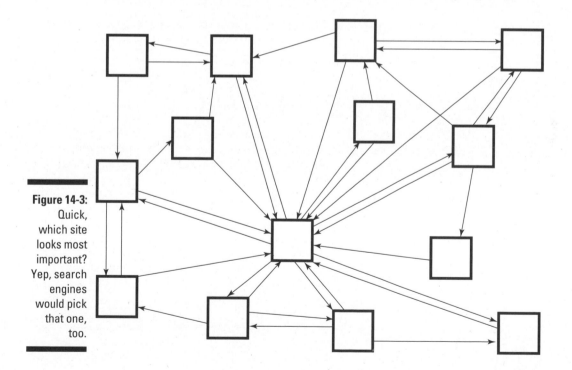

Figure 14-3: Quick, which site looks most important? Yep, search engines would pick that one, too.

Trust in TrustRank

Yet another ranking concept: TrustRank. The idea, from a document written by Yahoo! search engine researchers, is that a small set of "seed pages" is selected manually; someone actually creates a list of Web sites and pages that are likely to be reputable pages that can be trusted.

Then computers measure how far each site is from the seed site, in the sense of how many links away it is. Sites linked to directly from the original list of trusted sites are assumed trustworthy, and sites they link to are probably reasonably trustworthy, and so on. The farther a site is from the trusted sites, the lower the site's TrustRank.

The basic principle, then? Links from reputable sites are likely to be more valuable than links from sites that are not so clearly reputable. A link from CNN.com, for instance, is likely to count for more than a link from TheKentFamilyNewsService.com.

Links from `.edu` (education) and `.gov` (government) Web sites are also likely to be more valuable because such sites are less easily manipulated for SEO purposes.

But remember, this is just one more possible way to weight pages. It certainly doesn't mean that a site can't rank well without lots of trusted links.

Inserting Keywords into Links

As Chapter 5 makes abundantly clear, keywords in your pages are very important. But keywords *outside* your pages can also affect the page results. That is, the keywords in links pointing to your pages are very important.

If you have hundreds of links around the world pointing to your site, with the words *rodent racing* in the links, then search engines will get the idea that your pages are somehow related to rodent racing. It actually makes a lot of sense if you think about it. If hundreds of site owners create links pointing to your site, and, in effect, say, "This site I'm pointing to is about rodent racing," then Google is being given a darn good clue regarding what your site is about. In effect, Google has recruited site owners to tell it what other owners' sites are about.

Link text, in geek terminology, is known as *anchor text*. The link tag is an `<A>` tag, and *A* stands for *anchor*. Thus, if you hang around in geek company, you may hear links referred to as *anchors*. For more on anchors, see the "From the horses' mouths" sidebar.

From the horses' mouths

Read this from the founders of Google, Sergey Brin and Lawrence Page:

". . . anchors often provide more accurate descriptions of web pages than the pages themselves . . . This idea of propagating anchor text to the page it refers to was implemented in the World Wide Web Worm [a search engine that pre-dates Google] especially because it helps search non-text information, and expands the search coverage with fewer downloaded documents. We use anchor propagation mostly because anchor text can help provide better quality results."

The Anatomy of a Large-Scale Hypertextual Web Search Engine, 1998

In other words, Google and other search engines use links to get an idea of what the pages are about. Links can even help search engines figure out what a document is about if they can't read it for some reason (though that's not really the primary concern here).

Now, wait a second. This is important. If a link pointing to your site can describe to a search engine what your site is about, you'd better do all you can to make sure the link says what you want it to say! Even if you don't own the site that points to the one you're trying to optimize (or are trying to get another site owner or site manager to link to your site), it's in your interest to get the right keywords into the link.

While you browse the Web, take a close look at links on the sites you visit. Now that you know how critical it is to add keywords to links, you'll see that many links provide relatively little value to the sites they're pointing to. Sure, a link is better than no link, but a bad link could be better than it is. Here are some of the problems you'll see:

- **Image links, including buttons or banners linking to sites:** Search engines can't read images, so they're not getting keywords from them. (You should add keywords to the ALT attributes in the image tag, but search engines may not value ALT text as highly as link text.)

- **One- or two-word links, such as company names:** In most cases, company names don't help you in search engines. Use the keywords your potential visitors and clients are using.

- **Combinations of descriptions and _click here_ links:** For instance: *For more information on rodent racing — rats, mice, gerbils, and any other kind of rodent racing — click here*. Wow, what a waste! All the keywords are there; they just have no link! Remember, _click here_ links are a total waste of hyperlink space.

The Googlebomb lives

Just how powerful is putting keywords in links? Well, consider the *Googlebomb*.

The most famous example is the *miserable failure* Googlebomb from back in the years 2004 to 2007. Back then, if you searched at the major search engines for the term, the #1 result in all three was President George Bush's bio page on the White House Web site.

This feat was accomplished by a small group of people using links in blog pages. Despite the fact that this page contained neither *miserable* nor *failure,* and certainly not *miserable failure,* a few dozen links with the words *miserable failure* in the link text were enough to trick the major search engines.

Eventually, Google bowed to criticism (after a couple of years) and changed *something* to ensure that the president's page no longer appeared in the search results. Yahoo! and MSN/Live Search (now Bing) did *not* make this change, at least at that time, so this particular Googlebomb, paradoxically, only worked on Yahoo! and MSN/Live. Today George Bush's page still appears near the top of the first page of results on MSN/Bing and its partner, Yahoo!, but it doesn't for Google.

I'm not sure what Google did to remove the George Bush result. Google says that it "came up with an algorithm that minimizes the impact of many Googlebombs." Nevertheless, Google didn't completely throw out the concept of using keywords in links to tell it what the site is about. In fact, its statement suggests just that. It "minimized" the impact of "many Googlebombs"; it didn't completely stop them.

How can you be sure? Well, I can prove it to you. Search Google for the phrase *click here*; what comes up as number 1? The Adobe Reader download page (`get.adobe.com/reader`). Why? Because millions of pages around the world have something like this:

> *The following PDF document can be read with Adobe Reader. To download it, click here.*

Also, visit the Googlebomb page at Wikipedia (`en.wikipedia.org/wiki/ Googlebomb`), where you'll find information about all sorts of Googlebombs.

Note, by the way, that Googlebombing works in both Google and Bing — the Adobe site comes up high for *click here* in both search engines, for instance. However, there are differences between the search engines. The *click here* Googlebomb works on both well, but the *miserable failure* bomb works well on Bing but not on Yahoo!.

Clearly, the way Googlebombs work has changed over time. Perhaps, for instance, in response to complaints about the original *miserable failure* search, Google changed its algorithm to say something like, "If we see *x* number of links of type *y* pointing to the site using keywords that don't appear in the site, then ignore the links."

In any case, though, the fact is the basic principle behind Googlebombing remains valid: Putting keywords in links tells search engines what a referenced site is about, and the more links with keywords the better.

I often have clients ask me why a competitor ranks so well, also stating, "Their pages aren't better optimized than mine. We have more pages, and more pages with the right keywords. . . ." When I do a link analysis (see Chapter 15), I often discover that the poorly optimized, yet highly ranked, site has a huge number of incoming links, with just the right keywords.

Here's the ideal combination for links and the pages they point to: The keywords in the link match the keywords for which the referenced page is optimized. If you have a page optimized for the phrase *Rodent Racing*, point links with the words *Rodent Racing* to that page.

PageRank versus Keywords

So which is more important, PageRank or keywords? Well, they're both important. But I want to make an important point. Many in the SEO business will tell you that low-PageRank links are worthless, but that simply isn't true. Keywords in links are very valuable because they directly tell the search engines what the referenced page is about. So even low-PageRank links, if they have good keywords in them, can be valuable to you.

Good Links and Bad

Search engines must regard some types of links as more valuable than others. And it seems very likely to me that search engines will, over time, change how they regard links. They have, in fact, over time devalued certain types of links. For instance:

- Links inside paragraphs of text are likely regarded as more valuable than links in large lists or links set apart from text.

- Search engines could compare incoming links with outgoing links, and downgrade a page or site if it appears to do a lot of reciprocal linking from link pages.

- Links pointing to a page inside a site might be valued more highly than links to the home page.

- Outgoing links concentrated on a few pages might be valued less than links spread around a site.

When site owners figured out that links were valuable, they started playing tricks to boost incoming links to their sites. Some tricks were so egregious that search engines decided they were unacceptable. The trick you hear about most often is the *link farm,* an automated system that allows site owners to very quickly create thousands of incoming links by joining with thousands of other site owners to exchange links. Search engines don't like link farms and will exclude link-farm pages if they identify them. Another trick is to create multiple *shadow domains* or *satellite sites* — small, well-optimized Web sites that redirect traffic into a single site — and link them all into one site.

However, as with much in the search engine optimization business, another myth has arisen. You may hear that if a link is found to your site from a link farm, you'll be penalized.

Let me set the record straight: Search engines do not penalize sites for incoming links. They can't, or it would *encourage* dirty tricks. Want to push a competitor's site down so that your site can beat it? Then link to it from as many link farms as you can. Obviously, it wouldn't make sense for search engines to encourage this sort of thing, so links from such pages won't hurt your site — though they won't help it, either.

On the other hand, links *to* such sites really can hurt you. Because you do have control over links from your site to others, if a search engine decides that you are linking to a bad neighborhood, it may penalize you.

The bottom line is that you should avoid working with link farms because they can potentially harm you, and they won't help you, anyway.

Do search engines ever penalize? Sure. However, with billions of Web pages in the large indexes, most penalties are automated (although Google also has a team that reviews sites for spam — often, sites that have been reported). To automate penalties, search engines have to create a very loose system that penalizes only the very worst offenses, or they risk penalizing innocent people. The proof is that if you spend time searching through the major search engines, you'll find many pages that clearly break the rules yet are still included in the indexes. See Chapter 19 for more information.

Recognizing Links with No Value

Some links have no value:

- If a page isn't in the search-engine index, the links from the page have no value. Search engines don't know about them, after all.

✔ If a page is regarded as a *link farm* (described in the preceding section) or some other kind of "bad neighborhood," as Google calls it, the search engine may know about the page but decide to exclude it from the index.

✔ Some links to your site just *aren't* links to your site; they appear to be, but they're not. I explain in a moment.

✔ nofollow links are a special form of link that don't bring any value. I look at them later in this chapter.

Identifying links that aren't links

How can a link not be a link? I've seen this happen many times. Someone gets a link to his site from another site with a high PageRank, perhaps a perfectly related site, and is excited. That's a great vote for his site, isn't it? Then some jerk, perhaps me, has to burst his bubble and point out that, actually, no, it won't have the slightest effect on his site because it turns out that the link is not a link.

When is a link not a link? In cases such as these:

✔ The link has been created in such a way that search engines can't read it or will intentionally ignore it.

✔ The link points somewhere else, perhaps to a program on someone else's Web site, which then forwards the browser to your site.

Here's an example:

```
http://ad.doubleclick.net/clk;6523085;7971444;q?http://
            www.yoursite.com
```

This link passes through an ad server hosted by an advertising company called DoubleClick. When someone clicks this link, which may be placed on a banner ad, for instance, a message goes to a program on the `ad.doubleclick.net` ad server, which logs the click and then forwards the browser to `www.yourdomain.com`. You may think this is a link to `www.yourdomain.com`, and it may work like one, but as far as the search engine is concerned, it's really a link to `ad.doubleclick.net`. This is also a common situation with affiliate programs through services such as Commission Junction; the links to your site go through the affiliate-service servers first, so they don't count as links to your site.

Here's another example: Suppose the person creating a link to your site doesn't want the search engine to be able to read the link. This person may be trying to get as many incoming links as possible while avoiding outgoing links, so she does something like this:

```
<SCRIPT LANGUAGE="JavaScript">
<!--
document.write("Visit <A HREF='http://www.yourdomain.
        com/'>
Joe's Rodent Racing site here</A>.")
//-->
</SCRIPT>
```

The author is using JavaScript to write the link onto the page. You can see the link, other visitors can see it, and the link works when clicked, but search engines probably won't read the JavaScript, so they won't know there's a link there. What appears to be a perfectly normal link on a Web page is invisible to search engines; therefore, it does your site no good as far as PageRank or any other link-popularity algorithm goes.

Here's another form of link that search engines can't read:

```
<A HREF="#" class=results onclick="window.
        open('searchresult-
temp1.php?CS=cddzdzdrzfzpzpdc&SRCH=134893378&YD=0.88&RK=
3&PID=16&URL=yourdomain.com','merch','Height=' +
screen.availHeight + ',Width=' + screen.availWidth +
',left=0,top=0,scrollbars=yes,status=yes,toolbar=yes,
directories=yes,menubar=yes,location=yes,resizable=yes',
false)";>Everything About Rodent Racing!</A>
```

This is a real <A> link tag. However, it doesn't use the HREF= attribute to point to a Web page. Rather, it uses a JavaScript onClick event handler to make it work. The JavaScript runs a program that, in this case, loads the page into another window. Again, the link works in most browsers, but search engines won't see it.

Incidentally, it's also possible to do the reverse: make links appear to search engines to be links to your site when actually they're links to another site. For instance, look at the following link:

```
<A HREF="http://www.yourdomain.com?cid=33003&refid=
139782&link=www%2Eyourdomain%2Ecom" onClick="return
rewrite(this);" class="">Joe's Rodent Racing</A>
```

This link starts off well, showing yourdomain.com as the page being linked to. In fact, if you took the URL from the HREF= and pasted it into a browser, it would work properly. However, when someone clicks the link, the JavaScript onClick event handler runs, taking the domain and passing it to a JavaScript function called rewrite. Because search engines don't read JavaScript, they don't see what really happens when someone clicks the link. (In this example, the click runs through a program that tracks how many people use the link.)

Search engines think it's a link to your site, and I guess it is in a sense, but it has to pass through a program on a different site first.

Identifying nofollow links

There's a simple way to tell search engines to ignore links; use the `rel` attribute, like this:

```
<a href="http://www.domainname.com/page.html"
        rel="nofollow">Link Text</a>
```

You can also block all links on a page by using the `robots` meta tag, like this:

```
<meta name="robots" content="nofollow">
```

Tell the search engines not to follow the link — *nofollow* — and what exactly do they do? They ignore the link. It's as though the link were nonexistent. They don't bother following the link to the referenced page, and they don't use the information to index the page. That is, you get no PageRank, Web Rank, or equivalent benefit, and no benefit from the keywords in the link. (That's the theory, anyway; you can read my alternative theory in Chapter 17.)

More and more sites are using `nofollow` attributes to stop people from placing links purely to help their search engine rank. Here's a classic example: Craigslist. The hugely popular Craigslist.com classified-ad site used to be a great place to put links; businesses would drop ads into the system and include links back to their sites to help boost their search position. So, in 2007, Craigslist decided to put a `nofollow` attribute into all links placed on the site in order to discourage this behavior.

If you use Firefox, download the NoDoFollow plug-in. After you've installed it, you can right-click a Web page and select NoDoFollow, and all the links on the Web pages you view will be colored; follow links will be gray, and nofollow links will be pink. (For this reason, nofollow links are occasionally called *pink links*.)

Recalling a Few Basic Rules about Links

So far in this chapter, I've explained why links are valuable and how they can help boost your position in the search engines. But I've covered a lot, so here's a summary:

✔ Links from sites related to yours are often more valuable than links from unrelated sites. (Because the relevancy software is almost certainly imprecise, this isn't always the case.)

✔ Links from pages with a high PageRank are more valuable than those from pages with a low PageRank.

✔ Virtually all incoming links to your site have some kind of value, even if the pages have a very low PageRank or are not contextual. It may not be much of a value, but it's there.

✔ The higher the number of outgoing links on a page that has a link pointing to your site, the lower the value of the link to your site. This is because the vote is being shared. Thus, in some cases, a link from a low-PageRank page with no other links may actually be more valuable than a link from a high-PageRank page with many links.

✔ Links are even more valuable when they include keywords because keywords tell search engines what the referenced site is about.

✔ A link strategy that positions your site as an authority, or a *hub,* in a Web community or neighborhood can be a powerful way to get the attention of the search engines.

✔ And don't forget that, as discussed in Chapter 6, even *internal links —* links from page to page within your site — are valuable because the keywords in the links tell the search engine what the referenced page is about.

Chapter 15

Finding Sites to Link to Yours

· ·

· ·

1n Chapter 14, I explain the value of linking — why your site needs to have *backlinks* (links from other sites pointing to it). Now you have the problem of finding those sites.

Chapter 14 gives you some basic criteria. You need links from pages that are already indexed by the search engines. Pages with high PageRanks are more valuable than those with low PageRanks. Links from related sites may be more valuable, and so on. However, when searching for links, you probably don't want to be too fussy to start with. A link is a link. Contrary to popular opinion, links bring value — even links from unrelated sites.

It's common in the SEO business to say that only links from "relevant" sites have value, but I don't believe that's true. How do search engines know which sites are relevant and which aren't? They don't. Sure, they can guess to some degree. But they can't be quite sure. Therefore, my philosophy is that every link from a page that's indexed by search engines has some kind of value. Some will have a higher value than others, but don't get too hung up on relevance. And don't worry too much about PageRank; sure, if you can go after sites with high PageRanks first, do it, but often it makes sense to simply *go get links* — links with keywords in the text @md and not worry too much about the rank of the linking page.

Use this chapter to get links, and things will start happening. Your site will get more traffic, the search engines will pick it up, and you should find your pages rising in the search engine ranks.

Controlling Your Links

Before you run off to look for links, think about what you want those links to say. In Chapter 14, I talk about how keywords in links are tremendously important. The position of a page in the search engines depends not only on the text within that page, but also on text on other pages that refer to that page — that is, the text in the links. In fact, even a link from a low PageRank page can bring real value, if it has good keywords in it.

For instance, suppose your rodent-racing company is called Robertson Ellington. (These were the names of your first two racing rats, and they still have a special place in your heart. And you've always felt that the name has a distinguished ring to it.) You could ask people to give you links like this:

> **Robertson Ellington**
> Everything you ever wanted to know about rodent racing — rodent-racing schedules, directions to rodent-racing tracks, rodent-racing clubs, and anything else you can imagine related to rodent racing

You got a few useful keywords into the description, but the link — Robertson Ellington — is the problem. The link text contains no keywords that count. Are people searching for *Robertson Ellington*, or are they searching for *rodent racing*?

A better strategy is to change the link to include keywords. Keep the blurb below the link, but change the link to something like this:

> **Rodent Racing — rats, stoats, mice, and all sorts of other rodent racing**

Here are some strategies for creating link text:

- ✔ Start the link with the primary keyword or keyword phrase.
- ✔ Add a few other keywords if you want.
- ✔ Perhaps repeat the primary keyword or keyword phrase once in the link.

You need to control the links as much as possible. You can do this a number of ways, but you won't always be successful:

- ✔ Provide a Link to Us page in your Web site. On this page, provide suggested links to your site — include the entire HTML tag so people can grab the information and drop it into their sites.

   Remember that although links on logos and image buttons may be pretty, they don't help you in the search engines as much as text links do. You can add ALT text to the image, but ALT text is probably not as valuable as link text. Some site owners now distribute HTML code that creates not only image links but also small text links right below the images.

✔ When you contact people and ask them for links, provide them with the actual link you'd like to use.

✔ As soon as someone tells you he or she has placed a link, check it to see whether the link says what you want. Immediately contact that person if it doesn't. He or she is more likely to change the link at that point than weeks or months later.

✔ Use a link-checking tool occasionally to find out who is linking to you and to see how the link appears. If necessary, contact the other party and ask whether the link can be changed. (I mention some link-checking tools later in this chapter.)

Whenever possible, you should define what a link pointing to your site looks like, rather than leave it up to the person who owns the other site. Of course, you can't force someone to create links the way you want, but sometimes if you ask nicely . . . .

Always use the www. portion of your URL when creating links to your site: http://www.yourdomain.com and not just http://yourdomain.com. Search engines regard the two addresses as different, even though in most cases they are actually pointing to the same page. So if you use both URLs, you are, in effect, splitting the vote for your Web site. Search engines will see a lower link popularity. (See Chapter 14 for a discussion of how links are votes.)

Many sites use a 301 Redirect to point domain.com to the www.domain.com form. For instance, type **google.com** into your browser's Location bar and press Enter. Where do you go? You go to www.google.com because Google's server admins have "301'd" google.com to www.google.com. If you want to do this on your site, search for the term *301 redirect* for instructions. Also, the Google Webmaster console (see Chapter 11) provides a way for you to tell Google to use www.*yourdomain*.com as the primary address for your site; select Site Configuration⇨Settings and you see the following option buttons:

✔ Don't set a preferred domain

✔ Display urls as www.*yourdomain*.com

✔ Display urls as www.*yourdomain*.com

You want the middle option, of course. The Google Help text says that "if you specify your preferred domain as http://www.example.com and we find a link to your site that is formatted as http://example.com, we follow that link as http://www.example.com instead."

Doing a Link Analysis

One of the first things you may want to do is find out who is already linking to your site. Or perhaps you'd like to know who is linking to your competitors' sites. How do you do that? You can do it in a number of ways, as described in the next few sections. I list the methods in order of the number of links that you're likely to find, from the least to the most.

Google

In theory, Google shows you links pointing to a particular URL. I explain this only because many people know about it, and thus someone at some point will probably tell you to use it. It's pretty worthless, for two reasons:

- It shows links to a particular page, not to the entire site.
- It shows *some* of the links to the page, not all.

You have two ways to use this Google search syntax. The Google Toolbar has a Backward Links command. (I show you how to download the toolbar in Chapter 1.) Open your competitor's home page, click the PageRank button on the toolbar (see Chapter 14), and then choose Backward Links from the drop-down list.

The other way is to simply search for `link:domainname.com` in Google or in the search box in the Google Toolbar.

These Google methods are not worth the energy you expend to type the command or select from the toolbar. I rarely use them because the information is pretty much useless.

Yahoo! search

Yahoo! often provides good link results. Here's how to use it (yes, the Yahoo! search results come from Bing, but this technique works at Yahoo!, but not at Bing):

1. **Go to** `www.yahoo.com`.

2. **In the search box, type** `linkdomain:domainname.com`.

3. **Click the Search button**

   You see something like that shown in Figure 15-1.

4. **From the Show Inlinks drop-down box, select Except from This Domain.**

   Yahoo! reloads the page. You now have a list of pages that contain links to the specified domain.

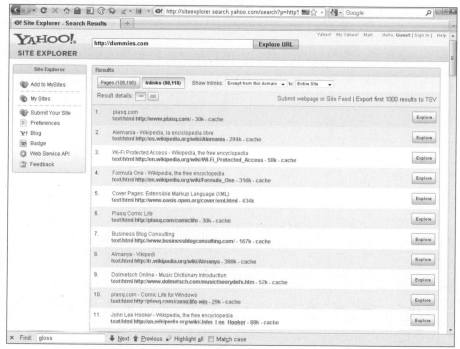

Figure 15-1:
The Yahoo
linkdomain
search
syntax in
action.

Here's an example. I searched Google for *link:dummies.com* and got 289 results. I searched Yahoo! for *linkdomain:dummies.com* and got 80,110 — a much more likely number!

A few things to consider: Yahoo! includes in its list pages that have nofollow links to the domain specified (see Chapter 14). Also, Yahoo! lets you download some of this data. Look for the <u>Export first 1000 results to TSV</u> link near the top. Only 1,000, unfortunately, so with a big result, you lose most of the data. (I've no idea why Yahoo! exports in the nuisance TSV format, rather than in something convenient such as CSV. With CSV, you can open the file directly in a spreadsheet program such as Excel. With TSV, you need to create a new spreadsheet and then import the data into the spreadsheet; in Excel 2007, you open the Data bar, click the From Text button, and select the TSV file.)

Free link popularity sites

Various free online tools exist, such as LinkPopularity.com, that help you find links. However, these sites mostly just search the major search engines for the results. LinkPopularity.com simply creates links to Google, Yahoo!, and MSN/Bing searches for you.

Many such tools are available. Search for *link popularity tools*, and you'll find them. Or don't. The next type of link-analysis tool is far more useful.

Link popularity software

Numerous sophisticated link popularity software tools are available to run on your computer, or as a Web service. However, most have a significant problem; they rely for their data on information that is initially pulled from the major search engines.

My current favorite, however, takes a different approach. MajesticSEO (`www.majesticseo.com`) works with a huge index of Web pages. Rather than ask the major search engines for data, MajesticSEO taps right into the data from the Majestic-12 Search Engine (`www.majestic12.co.uk`), an experimental, community-driven search engine that's been using "distributed computing" since 2004 to build a vast index of pages — currently more than 2 *trillion* pages!

This is a sophisticated tool with a lot of data. I can't explain it all here, so I just hit the highlights.

First, consider that MajesticSEO will probably return many more links than any of the other methods, *except* in one condition. I've found that if a big link campaign has been undertaken recently, MajesticSEO may take more time to catch up than Bing (which feeds data over to Yahoo!). Thus, for a while you may find more links reported by Yahoo! than MajesticSEO, because Bing reindexes the Web faster than Majestic does and passes that data over to Yahoo!. (On the other hand, you can't get to all that data directly from Yahoo!, anyway; it reports the number but lets you download only the first 1,000 pages.)

Look again at dummies.com. Remember the number of links pointing to dummies.com I found from Google and Yahoo! earlier in this chapter? How do their numbers compare with MajesticSEO?

- ✔ **Google:** 289
- ✔ **Yahoo!:** 80,110
- ✔ **MajesticSEO:** 450,795

So if you're looking for the most data, Majestic is definitely the way to go. But what does it do with this data? In Figure 15-2 you can see the first results page. Just look at the information — and keep in mind that this is only the start. Here's what you find on this page:

- ✔ **Domain:** The domain to which the links point
- ✔ **Subdomain:** The number of subdomains within that domain; `www.dummies.com`, `etips.dummies.com`, and so on
- ✔ **Indexed URLs:** The number of pages within the domain that MajesticSEO has indexed

- **Backlinks (EDU/GOV):** The number of links pointing to the domain from pages on other sites; in parentheses, the number of links from pages on `.edu` and `.gov` sites

- **Domains (EDU/GOV):** The number of domains that have Web pages linking to the analyzed domain; in parentheses, the number of `.edu` and `.gov` domains

- **IP addresses (Class C subnets):** The number of different IP addresses that have Web pages linking to the analyzed domain; in parentheses, the number of different Class C IP numbers

- **Images:** The number of links that are image links

- **NoFollow:** The number of links that are nofollow links (see Chapter 14)

- **Redirects:** The number of links that are redirected in some way to the analyzed domain

- **Redirects:** The number of links that are inside frames or iframes (see Chapter 7)

- **Redirects:** The number of links that were removed since Majestic crawled the site the previous time

- **Mentions — Domains:** The number of pages containing the analyzed domain written in plain text (nonlink pages)

Figure 15-2: The first results page from Majestic SEO.

And that's just the beginning. Click the link on the domain name you are analyzing to go to the full reports. You find plenty of data here, enough for the biggest link geek. In fact, one problem with this system, for inexperienced SEO people, is that it has so much data you don't know where to start. So, what *is* important? Here's what you should care about:

✔ **Where do links come from?** What sites are linking to yours, or your competitors? You can get ideas for where to ask for links to your site.

✔ **What is the anchor text** — the text in the links? Links with keywords are powerful. When analyzing competitors, for instance, you can often get an idea of how hard you have to work by seeing how well the links are keyworded; the more links with good keywords, the harder you have to work.

✔ **How valuable are the linking pages?** What PageRank do they have, for instance? (Majestic doesn't use PageRank but has something similar called ACRank.)

There's plenty more information for advanced users, too. Play around and see what you can find. In fact, if you "verify" your Web site (Majestic gives you a file to place in the root of your Web site), you get free reports about your site; to check links to other sites, you have to pay (from £9.99 — around $15 — a month).

Majestic is not the only game in town. Another service that does something similar — that is, maintains its own Web-page index — is SEOmoz Open Site Explorer (www.opensiteexplorer.org). This service has a very nice, slick user interface, but the problem is that it has less data than both Majestic and Yahoo!; at the time of writing, the index it maintains is about a fifth of the size of the Majestic SEO service.

There are also many services and software programs that provide link data by querying the major search engines. One of the best is SEOElite (www.SEOElite.com), a $167 program that looks for links to a site in various search engines, visits each of the pages containing the links, and then returns a report with the following information:

✔ The URL of the page linking to the site

✔ The Internet protocol (IP) number of the site on which the page is held

✔ Whether the link that the search engine *thinks* is on the page is still there

✔ The PageRank of the page

✔ The Alexa rank of the page

✔ The <TITLE> tag text from the page

✔ The *anchor* text — that is, the link text

✔ The number of outbound links on the page

✔ The total number of links on the page (outbound plus internal site links)

✔ *Whois* information — data about who owns the site on which the page sits

✔ The link value — an estimate of the value of the link, based on the PageRank divided by the number of links on the page

✔ A contact e-mail address pulled from the page

This is a great little program, with nifty tools, such as the ability to find potential link partners and e-mail them, and a way to search for potential link-submission pages and quickly submit information to them. You can export your results to an Excel spreadsheet.

There are many link popularity programs out there; search and you'll find them. Be aware, though, that link popularity analysis is difficult, and there's no perfect tool. My current favorite is MajesticSEO, but it *is* complicated and for a new user may provide too much information, so you may also want to look at Open Site Explorer, SEOElite, or perhaps another tool you run across.

Generating Links, Step by Step

Here is a quick summary of various ways to get links; I explain them, and their advantages and disadvantages, in detail next:

✔ **Register with search directories.** The Open Directory Project and the specialty directories aren't only important in their own right but often also provide links that other search engines read.

✔ **Ask friends and family.** Get everyone you know to add a link.

✔ **Ask employees.** Ask employees to mention you.

✔ **Contact association sites.** Contact any professional or business association of which you're a member and ask for a link.

✔ **Contact manufacturers' Web sites.** Ask the manufacturers of any products you sell to place a link on their sites.

✔ **Contact companies you do business with.** Get on their client lists.

✔ **Ask to be a featured client.** I've seen sites get high PageRank by being linked to from sites that feature them.

✔ **Submit to announcement sites and newsletters.** This includes sites such as URLwire (www.urlwire.com).

✔ **Send out press releases.** Sending out press releases, even if distributed through the free systems, can often get you links.

- ✔ **Promote something on your site.** If you have something really useful, let people know about it!

- ✔ **Find sites linking to your competition.** If other sites link to your competition, they may link to you, too.

- ✔ **Ask other sites for links.** During your online travels, you may stumble across sites that really should mention your site, as a benefit to their visitors.

- ✔ **Make reciprocal link requests.** Ask other site owners to link to you, in exchange for a link to them.

- ✔ **Respond to reciprocal link requests.** Eventually, other people will start asking you to link swap.

- ✔ **Search for** *keyword add url.* You can find sites with links pages this way.

- ✔ **Use link-building software and services.** Try using a link-exchange program or service to speed up the process.

- ✔ **Contact e-mail newsletters.** Find appropriate e-mail newsletters and send them information about your site.

- ✔ **Mention your site in discussion groups.** Leave messages about your site in appropriate forums, with links to the site.

- ✔ **Promote to blogs**. Blog sites are often well indexed by search engines.

- ✔ **Pursue offline PR.** Getting mentioned in print often translates into being mentioned on the Web.

- ✔ **Give away content.** If you have lots of content, syndicate it.

- ✔ **Apply for online awards.** Sign up for site awards.

- ✔ **Advertise.** Sometimes ads provide useful links.

- ✔ **Use a service or buy links.** Many companies sell links; Google doesn't like this, but encourages it at the same time.

- ✔ **Just wait.** Eventually links will appear, but you must prime the pump first.

These link-building strategies are ranked by priority in a very general way. One of the first things you should do is to ask friends and family for links and one of the last is to wait. However, in between these strategies, the priority varies from business to business, or person to person. You may feel that a strategy lower on this list is important to do right away.

The next sections look at each of these link-generation methods. But before I start . . . how quickly should you create these links? Some in the SEO business believe that links shouldn't be created too fast because a sudden huge increase in links to your site looks unnatural. Imagine a situation in which your site gets a link or two a month and then suddenly starts getting several thousand a month; that might suggest something odd going on, eh?

I can't give you a number; I can't say "never create more than x links a month," or "y links a week are far too many." It all depends. It depends on what your site has been doing in the past and how many links it already has. If Wikipedia got a thousand links one day, this might not be at all out of the ordinary. If you got 1,000 links one day, it might be unreasonable. (Wikipedia has 5½ *billion* links pointing to it, so actually 1,000 a day is probably nothing.) Just keep in mind that too fast may look suspicious to the search engines.

Register with search directories

In Chapter 12, I discuss getting links from directories, the Yahoo! Directory, and the Open Directory Project, as well as getting links from specialty directories. Links from directories are important not only because people can find you when searching at the various directories but also because search engines often spider these directories.

Google, for instance, spiders both Yahoo! and the Open Directory Project. And the Open Directory Project results are syndicated to hundreds of smaller search engines, many of which Google reads. These links are also highly relevant because they're categorized within the directories; as you find out in Chapter 14, the search engines like relevant links. Therefore, if you haven't registered with the directories, consider that the first step in your link campaign.

Ask friends and family

Ask everyone you know to give you a link. Many people now have their own Web sites or blogs — *Weblogs* (which I discuss in more detail in Chapter 9 and later in this chapter). Ask everyone you can think of to mention your site. Send them a short e-mail detailing what you'd like them to say. You may want to create a little bit of HTML that they can paste straight into their pages, perhaps with a link to a logo stored on your Web site so the logo appears in their pages. If you do this, you get to control the link text to ensure that it has keywords in it: *The best darn rodent racing site on the Web,* for instance, rather than *Click here to visit my friend's site.*

Ask employees

Employees often provide, by accident, a significant number of links back to their employer's Web site. In particular, employees often mention their employer in discussion groups that get picked up by the search engines. So why not send an e-mail to all your employees, asking them to link to the company's site from their Web sites and blogs and to mention you in discussion groups? Again, you might give them a piece of HTML that includes an embedded logo.

Also, ask them to always use a signature with the link when posting to Web-based discussion groups.

Of course, some employers don't want their employees talking about them in discussion groups because they're scared about what the employees will say. If that's your situation, I can't do much to help you, except suggest that you read *Figuring Out Why Your Employees Hate You For Dummies,* by I. M. N. Ogre.

Contact association sites

Association sites are a much-overlooked source of free and useful links. Contact any professional or business association of which you're a member and ask for a link. Are you in the local Better Business Bureau, the Lions Club, or Rotary Club? How about the Rodent Lovers Association of America, or the Association for Professional Rodent Competitions? Many such sites have member directories and may even have special links pages for their members' Web sites.

Contact manufacturers' Web sites

Another overlooked source of links is manufacturers' Web sites. If you sell products, ask the manufacturer to place a link from its site to yours. I know one business that sold several million dollars' worth of a particular toy that it got from a single retailer. For several years, the company was the primary seller of the product referenced by the retailer, which at the time didn't sell directly to consumers; the link brought the retailer *most* of its business at the time. The manufacturer is a well-known national company that gets plenty of traffic, and the manufacturer's Web site has a PageRank of 6 on its main page. (See Chapter 14 to see why that's impressive.) The link to the retailer was on the manufacturer's home page, so not only did the link bring plenty of business, but it also got plenty of attention from the search engines.

Contact companies you do business with

Many companies maintain client lists. Check with all the firms you do business with and make sure that you're on their lists.

Ask to be a featured client

While looking at a competitor's Web site for a client, I noticed that the competing site had a surprisingly high PageRank even though it was a small site that appeared to be linked to from only one place, www.inman.com, which is a site that syndicates content to real estate sites. It turned out that the competitor was linked to directly from one of Inman's highest PageRanked pages. Inman was using the client as an example of one of its customers.

If you're using someone's services — for Web hosting, e-mail services, syndication services, or whatever — you may want to contact the site and ask whether *you* can be the featured client. Hey, someone's going to be, so it may as well be you.

Submit to announcement sites and newsletters

There used to be scores of "announcement" services, Web sites and newsletters that published information about new Web sites. Most have gone.

The only one I'm aware of now is URLwire (www.urlwire.com). This service, which has been around since the beginning of the Web, claims to have more than 125,000 readers, of whom 6,500 are journalists and site reviewers who get the e-mail newsletter. It costs $495, but the impact can be significant, if you can get accepted. (It doesn't take just anyone; you have to have a good story.) Not only do you get a link from a page with a PageRank of 5, but you probably also get picked up by many other sites and newsletters.

Send out press releases

Does your company publish press releases? You should distribute these as widely as possible. Even if you submit press releases through a large service, such as PR Newswire (prnewswire.com), you should also distribute them through the free and low-cost distribution services, which will quite likely get them placed onto other Web sites. You may want to write a few quick press releases and send them through the free-distribution services, just to see if you can generate some links.

This is the list of services I'm currently using when I send releases, with the cost:

- **PRWeb:** www.prweb.com, $200 ($180 if you buy ten at a time)

- **EmailWire:** www.emailwire.com, $49.92 (assumes two releases per month on a $599, six-month subscription)

- **PR Leap:** www.prleap.com, $49 – $149

- **Free Press Release:** www.Free-Press-Release.com, and it's *almost free;* you have to pay $1 to get links in the body of the press release

- ✔ **PressBox:** www.pressbox.co.uk, Free
- ✔ **I-Newswire.com:** www.I-Newswire.com, Ten press releases a month for $47
- ✔ **PRLog:** www.prlog.org, Free
- ✔ **PR.com:** www.pr.com, $39.95
- ✔ **PR-GB.com:** www.pr-gb.com, Free
- ✔ **openPR:** www.openpr.com, Free
- ✔ **TransWorldNews:** www.transworldnews.com, $41.67 (based on two releases per month on an annual, $1,000 subscription)

Distribute to this list and you get very wide distribution — you *will* end up in Google News, Yahoo! News, MSN News, and many, many other sites.

You may also want to create your own list of press-release distribution e-mail addresses and Web pages. For instance, look for industry journals in your field that accept press releases.

Of course, you need to get links into your press releases. All the above services allow you to add at least one link in the "About" area of the press release; many of them allow multiple links throughout the release. Some also allow you to create keyworded links. Therefore, you can create a link that says *Rodent Racing Scores* instead of just putting your URL in the release.

So, go to each site and find out how to create press releases, including how to code links inside them. This varies from service to service. For instance, on PRWeb you'd create a link like this:

```
Robertson Ellington's http://www.RobertsonEllington.com/
          [rodent racing__title__ Rodent Racing] Web site
          ...
```

On PR Leap, on the other hand, you create the same link like this:

```
Robertson Ellington's [url=http://www.RobertsonEllington.
          com/]Rodent Racing[/url] Web site ...
```

In addition, some services use regular http URLs. So you have to know how links are created on each service. But it's worth it. I've done it; I've seen it work. Press releases are a very powerful way to create links back to your site. I'll help you out a little; at http://www.SearchEngineBulletin.com, you can find a document explaining how to create press releases.

By the way, if your company uses a PR firm, you can almost guarantee that the firm has no idea about this, and although it will probably submit your press releases online, it won't put keyworded links into them. Even if the firm tells you that it does proper linking from press releases it sends out, remember: "Trust, but verify"! You need multiple links in the body of the press release, on keywords, not just a link to your site at the bottom of the release.

Create a little "linkbait"

One of the most powerful link-building techniques is to place something very useful on your site and then make sure that everyone knows about it. I've included a little story in the "How links build links" sidebar at the end of this chapter. It shows how links can *accumulate* — how, in the right conditions, one link leads to another, which leads to another, and so on. In this true story, the site had something that many people really liked — a directory of glossaries and technical dictionaries. Almost 17,000 Web sites link to this site now, all because the site owner provided something people really wanted and appreciated.

This, by the way, is something known these days as *linkbait* — something so valuable to others that they link to it. It can be something fun, something useful, something weird, something exciting, something cool, or something important. Just something that provides so much value to other people that they link to it from their blogs and Web sites, and within discussion forums; something they want to tell others about. Matt Cutts, well-known SEO blogger and Google employee (see Chapter 22), defines link bait as anything "interesting enough to catch people's attention."

Find sites linking to your competition

If a site links to your competition, it may be willing to link to you, too. Find out who links to competing sites and then ask them if they can link to yours. In some cases, the links are link-exchange links (which I look at in the later section, "Make reciprocal link requests"), but in many cases, they're just sites that provide useful information to their readers. If your competitors' sites are useful, and (I'm assuming) yours is too, you've got a good chance of being listed.

On the other hand, when you do a link analysis on your competitors, you'll often find that many of the links are *purchased* links, which I talk about later in this chapter, in the "Use a Service or Buy Links" section.

Asking for the link

When you find sites linking to your competitors, you discover that some of them may be appropriate for a link to yours; directories of products or sites, for instance, may want to include you. So how do you ask for the link? Nicely.

Send an informal, chatty message. Don't make it sound like some kind of form letter that half a billion other people have received. This should be a personal contact between a real person (you) and another real person (the other site's owner or manager). Give this person a reason to link to your site. Explain what your site does and why it would be of use to the other site's visitors.

Ask other sites for links

During your travels online, you'll run across sites that provide lists of links for visitors — maybe your site should be listed, too. For instance, while working for a client that had a site related to a particular disease, I found sites that had short lists of links to sites about that disease; obviously, my client should also have been in those lists.

Approach these sites the same way you approach the sites linking to your competitors: Send an informal note asking for a link.

Don't forget the blogs, by the way. Blogs exist on virtually any subject, and most bloggers provide links to sites they like, often in the "blog roll" or "favorite sites" box on one side of every page on the blog.

Make reciprocal link requests

A *reciprocal link* is one that you obtain in exchange for another. (It's often also referred to as a *link exchange*.) You ask site owners and managers to link to your site, and you in turn promise to link to theirs.

In theory, reciprocal linking, if done right, can help you in two ways:

- ✔ The search engines see nice, keyworded links coming into your site from appropriate, relevant sites.

- ✔ You link to appropriate, relevant sites too. (In Chapter 14, I discuss the concept of hubs or value networks.)

- ✔ You may get some traffic through the links themselves (though I doubt you'll get much).

Reciprocal linking is different from asking to be added to a list, although plenty of overlap exists. With the latter, you don't need to offer a link in exchange because the link list is a service to the other site's visitors. However, sometimes site owners respond with, "Sure, but will you link to us, too?" In this case, you've just found yourself in a reciprocal linking position.

Before I go further, though, I need to address a couple issues. First, you may hear that reciprocal linking can get your site penalized; is that true?

If reciprocal linking caused Google to penalize sites, half the Web would disappear. If it's true, why does Google index so many reciprocally linked pages? Why do sites that use reciprocal linking often rank so high? In addition, why would search engines penalize people for using a technique that they have in effect encouraged over the years — a technique so common that, for good or bad, it's part of the "landscape" of the Web?

I admit that some talk has been bandied about concerning MSN's penalizing sites for using reciprocal linking — specifically when sites link to nonrelated sites. (You can read the story at `http://www.seroundtable.com/ archives/006742.html`.) But there's a little unsubstantiated talk here and there, and a lot of conjecture. Again, regardless of the talk, I come back to my questions: If reciprocal linking gets you banned, then why . . . ?

Far more likely is that when search engines decide they don't like reciprocal linking, they'll start downgrading the links, just as, in fact, Google has done over the last few years.

Which brings me to the next major question: Does reciprocal linking actually work? My answer is, it certainly used to work, and work well . . . but these days it has much less value. Reciprocal linking was truly powerful a few years ago; I've seen sites rank first on Google in very competitive markets, based almost entirely on reciprocal linking (and, by the way, at a time when many in the SEO business were saying that reciprocal linking didn't work!).

Today, however, reciprocal links carry much less weight; I don't use them these days, and I certainly wouldn't base a search engine campaign on reciprocal linking alone. Why bother mentioning reciprocal linking at all, then? Because it's still a big thing in linking, owing more to momentum than logic; people have been exchanging links for years, and plenty of reciprocal-linking services are still out there.

Dump the links pages

Also, one of the bad things about reciprocal linking is the "link page," pages stacked with link after link. Some reciprocal linkers use a more reasoned approach; although they still do link exchanges, they spread the links around the site rather than just dump them onto link pages.

You've undoubtedly seen *links pages* all over the place — pages with titles such as "Useful Links," "Useful Resources," "Visit Our Friends," and so on. To be honest (I say that when I'm about to upset people), these pages don't generate much traffic to your Web site. How often do you find useful links useful, or useful resources particularly, er, resourceful? Not very often, I bet.

People simply don't use them. And having tested link-exchange software that measures the amount of traffic going through the links pages, I can tell you that they don't generate much traffic to Web sites. (I discuss link-exchange software later in this chapter.)

You may hear the term *link exchange*. In many quarters, this practice is frowned upon because it implies that the site owners simply want to accumulate as many links as possible and don't really care about the type of sites they're working with. It also implies the use of a links page. On the other hand, *reciprocal linking* implies a more circumspect methodology, in which links are carefully considered and placed throughout the site.

You're far better off *not* using links pages because of the following problems:

- ✔ **Search engines almost certainly already downgrade links from such pages.** A link from an ordinary page is likely to be more valuable than a link from a links page.

- ✔ **Links pages often have dozens or even hundreds of links on them.** Remember that the more links on a page, the lower the vote for each outgoing link.

The ideal situation would be to:

- ✔ Scatter links to other sites around your site in locations that make sense.

- ✔ Encourage site owners linking back to you to do the same. Start educating the other sites you work with! (In fact, tell them to run out and buy this book; better still, tell them to buy ten copies of this book for colleagues, friends, and family.)

- ✔ Avoid having large numbers of links on one page.

- ✔ Avoid calling a page a *links* page. You might try using *resource* page, although I suspect this title is also overused.

On the other hand, the major search engines *do* still index many, many links pages:

- ✔ Go to Google and search for these terms, making sure to include the quotation marks:

  - *"visit our friends"* (I found more than a million pages)

  - *"link exchange"* (more than 30 million)

  - *"links page"* (more than 8 million)

Sure, not all the pages you find are links pages, but many are. On the other hand, when I did this a couple of years ago, the respective numbers were

2.3 million, 64 million, and 8 million; perhaps the new numbers indicate that many links pages have been flushed from the Google index.

✔ Go to some links pages and check to see whether they're in the Google cache, or go to Google and search for the URLs of the pages to see whether they're in the Google index. They often are.

✔ When you visit links pages, look at the Google Toolbar. You often see that they have a PageRank. However, I should reiterate: Links from links pages probably do not have the value of links from normal pages.

Three-way and four-way linking

Many people are using a more complicated form of reciprocal linking these days. The idea is that instead of linking from site A to site B, and back from site B to site A, you create a three- or four-way link, as shown in Figure 15-3. (You may actually see this described as a *one-way link exchange,* but it's the same concept; the person you link to doesn't link back.)

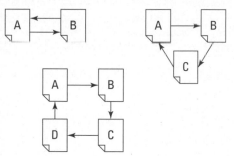

Figure 15-3: Traditional reciprocal linking (top left). Three- and four-way linking is probablymore beneficial.

It's easy for the search engines to recognize reciprocal linking, which is why I, and many others in the business, believe that the value of such linking has been downgraded.

If a search engine sees a link from one site to another, and then sees a link coming back, there's a good chance it's a reciprocal link. (I'm sure it's more complicated than this but the basic principle remains. For instance, does the site have lots of outgoing links, to sites that link back, on the same page?) So it's pretty easy for search engines to recognize reciprocal linking, and because they're aware that such linking is used as an artificial way to boost ranking, they can lower the value of these links.

Say, however, you have a large collection of sites that want to trade links. Rather than have every site link to every other, you might try a more complicated structure where site A links to B, B links to C, and C links back to A, as shown in Figure 15-3. Instead of getting two incoming links, each site only gets one, but it's probably of more value because it's not so obviously a reciprocal link. Or maybe you link site A to B, B to C, C to D, and D to A; in this case each site gets one link instead of three, but again, the links are likely to be more valuable than simple A-to-B-to-A reciprocal links. Some companies that perform SEO work for large numbers of clients use this technique, or even combine traditional reciprocal links with three-way or four-way linking. There are also services that provide three-way linking, but thanks to the software complexities involved in managing a three-way process, not many services are doing this.

Search for keyword add url

Go to Google and search for something like this:

```
"rodent racing" + "add url"
```

Google searches for all the pages with the term *rodent racing* and the term *add url*. You find sites that are related to your subject and have pages on which you can add links, as shown in Figure 15-4. (For some inexplicable reason, you don't find much with *"rodent racing"* +*"add url"* but you find plenty with, for instance, *"boating"* +*"add url"* or *"psychology"* +*"add url".*)

You can also try these searches:

```
"rodent racing" + "add a url"
"rodent racing" + "add link"
"rodent racing" + "add a link"
"rodent racing" + "add site"
"rodent racing" + "add a site"
"rodent racing" + "suggest url"
"rodent racing" + "suggest a url"
"rodent racing" + "suggest link"
"rodent racing" + "suggest a link"
"rodent racing" + "suggest site"
"rodent racing" + "suggest a site"
```

However, these aren't always high-quality links. Generally, the search engines don't really like this sort of linking, and the word on the street is that links from such pages probably don't have the same value that you get from links that are personally placed. On the other hand, they may be easy to get; it's a trade-off.

Incidentally, SEO Elite, which I mention earlier, includes a tool to carry out one of these types of link campaigns, searching for pages with submission forms related to whatever keywords you define, and then helping you submit these forms; see Figure 15-5.

Figure 15-4:
Searching for a keyword or keyword phrase along with *+"add url"* uncovers sites that are just waiting for you to add a link to your site.

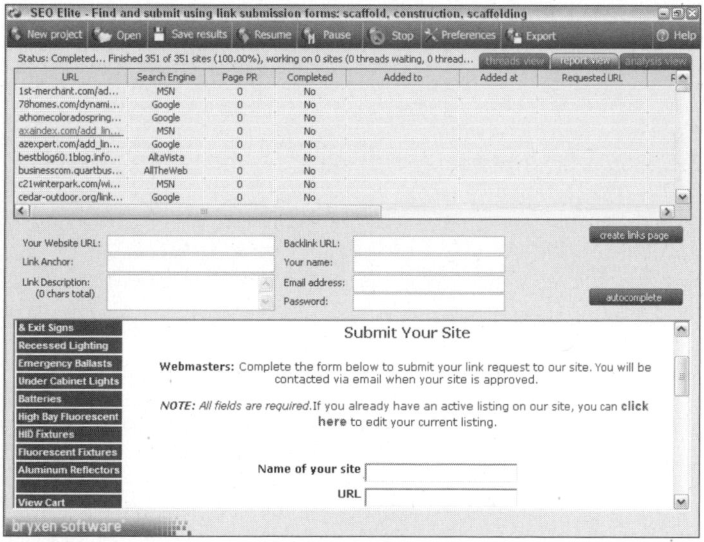

Figure 15-5:
SEO Elite has a tool that helps you submit information on Add URL pages.

Mention your site in discussion groups

Search engines index many Web-based discussion groups. Whenever you leave a message in the discussion group, make sure that you use a message signature that has a link to your site and also include the link in the message itself.

Sometimes URLs in messages and signatures are read as links, and sometimes they aren't. If you type **http://www.yourdomain.com** in a message, the software processing the message can handle the URL in one of two ways:

- ✔ It can enter the URL into the page as simple text.
- ✔ It can convert the URL to a true HTML link (`<A HREF=" http://www.yourdomain.com"> http://www.yourdomain.com/ </A>`).

If the URL is *not* converted to a true link, it won't be regarded as a link by the search engines.

Another strategy is often employed with discussion groups. Seek out questions that you can answer, answer them, and put keyworded links in your message. For instance, say you have a rodent-racing site; you dig around in the rodent-racing forums, answering questions when possible. Someone asks about where to find scores from recent races, and you respond by saying something like, "Well, I may be biased, but I think my site is the best place to find rodent-racing scores!" and by putting a link on rodent-racing scores, of course. (Have I mentioned how important keywords in links are?) Don't be pushy, and don't just post ads. Provide value in your answers, and nobody will mind.

Now, a couple of things to consider. First, many discussion groups create nofollow links (see Chapter 14) in posts; on the other hand, many don't. So you'll get search engine value from many of the links, perhaps even most, but not all.

However, you may get *indirect* search engine value from the nofollow links, too. Many of these discussion groups will turn up when people search, so even if someone searches and doesn't find your site, he or she may find the discussion group and then click the link to your site.

Another quick tactic you can use: search for your primary keywords and then scroll through the search results looking for the discussion groups that come up. Those could be great places for links to your site.

Working with blogs

The Internet holds literally billions of blog pages, and some of them have to be related to the subject served by your Web site. Many blogs allow visitors to respond, and in fact you may find services offering to post responses into blogs for you as a way to create links back to your site.

Don't bother. Apart from the fact that most of these services pollute the blogs with meaningless, worthless messages, most blog software uses nofollow links, so you won't get any value from them.

The best way to work with blogs is to find something the bloggers may be interested in, some kind of PR-story hook, and get them to write about your site.

Pursue offline PR

Getting mentioned in print often translates into being mentioned on the Web. If you can get publications to write about and review your site, not only do many people see the link in print — and perhaps visit your site — but often your link ends up online in a Web version of the article.

Give away content

Many companies have vast quantities of content on their Web sites. It's just sitting there, available to anyone who visits. So why not take the content *to* the visitors before they reach your site? Placing the content on other Web sites is a powerful way not only to build links back to your site but also to get your name out there — to "brand" yourself or your company.

In Chapter 16, I cover this topic in more detail because you need to be aware of several technical issues.

Advertise

You may want to consider advertising in order to get links to your site. However, you need to consider a couple of issues first:

- ✔ Advertising is often grossly overpriced. It may be much too expensive to justify just for a link.
- ✔ Advertising links often don't count as links to your site. Rather, they're links to the advertising company, which runs a program that forwards the visitor's browser to your site. Search engines won't see the link as a link to your site. (See Chapter 14 for more information.)

In some cases, buying ads on a site to get a link does make sense. For instance, if many of your clients visit a particular Web site and you can get a low-cost ad on that site, buying an ad to both brand your company and to get a link that the search engines can read may be worthwhile. And remember that it's a very relevant link because it comes from a site that's important to your business.

How links build links

I want to share a story that provides a wonderful illustration of how a link campaign can work. It shows how you can build links, PageRank, and traffic, all at the same time, the old-fashioned way. I found this story in one of WebmasterWorld's discussion groups. As the author of the post put it, you should remember how the "Internet started and what it was supposed to be all about: sharing information." The search engines want you to remember this, too.

The story is about an Aussie called Woz. Once upon a time, Woz had a site called Glossarist (`www.glossarist.com`), a directory of glossaries and topical dictionaries. This was a hobby for Woz, and he had done little to promote the site. However, one sunny day — July 26, 2003 — he noticed a 4,000 percent increase in traffic. (For the math challenged among you, traffic on that day was 40 times greater than the day before!) The site had been mentioned in the ResearchBuzz e-mail newsletter and Web site (`www.researchbuzz.com`), by the fairy godmother, Tara Calishain. Not surprisingly, ResearchBuzz is a resource for people interested in research. It's the sort of site that would be interested in a directory of glossaries and topical dictionaries.

The very next day, a wonderfully bright and sunny day, Glossarist was picked up by The Scout Report (`scout.wisc.edu/ Reports/ScoutReport/2001/scout- 010727.html`) which, perhaps a little more surprisingly, is a "weekly publication offering a selection of new and newly discovered Internet resources of interest to researchers and educators."

Then on August 9, a *really* sunny day, the site was mentioned in USAToday.com's Hot Sites (`www.usatoday.com/tech/2001-08- 09-hotsites.htm`). I've had one of my sites mentioned in *USA Today,* and believe me, your traffic really spikes when that happens!

By the middle of August, Woz wuz able to identify links from over 200 sites — "libraries and student-resource pages from schools and universities, translation sites, business reference sites, writers sites, information architecture sites, and so on." He also got a lot of traffic from newsletters that had been forwarded from subscribers to friends and colleagues. (Both *ResearchBuzz* and *The Scout Report* are very popular e-mail newsletters.) Not only did site owners find out about him through these e-mails, but many visitors also came to his site through the e-mail links.

All this publicity was great, providing his site with a lot of traffic through those links and making it more likely that his site would be found and indexed by search engines. It also boosted his site's PageRank. By mid-August, the Glossarist PageRank had reached 3; by the end of August, it was 8, which is an excellent PageRank for a hobby site created by a single person without a marketing budget! (I just checked, and it's currently showing a PageRank of 7, which is still very good. It's also likely that Google has adjusted PageRank in the intervening years so that higher PageRanks are now harder to attain.)

By the end of August, Woz had around 300 links. And, as Woz claims, he didn't request a single one of these links. Today? Well, today, around seven years later, I checked using MajesticSEO and found more than 149,000 links from almost 17,000 Web sites, including more than 400 `.edu` and `.gov` Web sites.

Use a service or buy links

I can't stress enough that link campaigns can be very laborious, tedious, and time consuming. That's why many people decide they are better off paying someone to perform the work. Some of these services simply run a link-acquisition campaign for you. Others already have an inventory of ad space on thousands of sites and charge you to place a link on a set number.

One company I've seen is selling almost 800 links for $30 per month. Another company I've seen claims that it can put links on 250 sites for $99. Some companies sell links from pages of a particular PageRank, too. One company, for instance, claims to be able to sell you a link on a PageRank 8 site for $799. (A PageRank 4 page is just $29.)

The vote from a page is shared among all the pages it links to, so the more ads that are sold, the less the value of each ad. You should know exactly what page the link will be placed on, and you should be able to view the page. Consider buying links as a form of advertising that should be evaluated as such. How much of an impact will the ad have on bringing more visitors to your site?

Many, many companies are doing this sort of work. You can find them by searching online (search for *buy links*, *text links*, *purchase links*, *link popularity*, and *link building* at a major search engine) or in the freelancer sites, such as Guru.com, eLance.com, and oDesk.com.

Make sure that you understand what you're getting into. As you've seen, you can use many methods to get links to a site, but they don't all provide the same value. Are you working with a company that can find good links from popular sites that are relevant to yours or a company that uses an automated link-exchange tool to gather links from anywhere it can? There's a real difference! Also, are the links on pages that are actually indexed? One company I know has been effectively banned from at least one of the major search engines; the links it places are thus never seen by that search engine.

Caution! Google doesn't like purchased links!

It's important to understand, though, that Google doesn't like purchased links. In fact, none of the major search engines would be pleased to know that you were buying links pointing to your site. On the other hand, the major search engines have actually (albeit indirectly) *encouraged* link buying for years. How? When the owner of a site decides that she's going to do something about her search-results positions, she may check the links pointing to her competitors. What will she find? *Many high-ranking sites are succeeding thanks to the purchase of links*!

I did an analysis for a client just a few weeks ago and discovered that the competitor he was worried about, a site that had come out of nowhere to a number two position in just four months, had around 300 links, the vast majority of which were purchased in one form or another.

That's why people often buy links: Because it works! Furthermore, it's hard for search engines to deal with this problem for a couple of reasons. First, how do search engines know the link is purchased? Yes, there are highly automated systems that place purchased links, and the search engines may be able to find a *signature* — some kind of characteristic that identifies the link as purchased. However, how will a search engine know whether you ask Fred over at ReallyFastRodents.com, "Fred, if I give you $20 a month, will you link to my site?"

Additionally, if they penalize site owners for purchasing links pointing to their sites — well, how much is it worth to you to push your competitor out of the search engines? Sure, *you* may be too ethical to play this game, but plenty of people aren't. So, say you're tired of seeing ReallyRapidRodents. com ranking above your rodent-racing site month after month. Perhaps you could buy a bunch of links pointing to his site, report him to Google, and see Google drop him from the search engine. Therefore, search engines have to be very careful about penalizing sites for buying links. The more likely scenario is that when search engines identify the links as purchased, they downgrade or ignore them, not penalize the referenced site.

When you buy links, make sure that you buy the right type. You don't want links dropped onto a page using JavaScript, or ads served through an ad server. In the first case, the search engine probably won't read the link at all; in the second case, the link probably points at the ad server, not at your Web site. For instance, AdBrite (www.adbrite.com) sells text ads on a wide range of Web sites, but the link points to AdBrite, not to your site.

Here's an example showing you how to figure whether the link points to your site; an ad I found on one of their advertising sites:

```
Gastric Bypass Pill
Approved! FREE Samples
```

Now, pointing to a link displays one of two things in the browser's status bar:

- ✔ The URL the link points to
- ✔ A fake URL, which is placed there using JavaScript in the Web page

In this case, when I point at the link and look at the status bar in my browser, I see this URL:

```
http://www.zetacap.com
```

However, when I right-click the link, I see the real URL in the status bar:

```
http://click.adbrite.com/mb/click.php?sid=19822&banner_id=
        10235529&cpc=302e3030303030303030&ssc=08862a24b
        01e87aa1498dbcafcda01de
```

When I click the link, that's also the URL I see (for a second or two) before the ad server forwards me to the Zetacap.com Web site. As you can see, the link doesn't point to the advertiser's site — www.zetacap.com — it points to the click.adbrite.com ad server. I'm not suggesting that AdBrite is misleading people, by the way; they don't claim their links can help you with search engines; they're simply selling ads. But when you go looking for pages on which to place links, you must be aware of this issue.

I'm not endorsing the purchase of links. I also recognize, though, that a link campaign can be incredibly LTT — you know, laborious, tedious, and time consuming — and thus I know that many, many people are buying links. (Hey, don't shoot the messenger!) You can find expensive links — dozens of dollars a link — and you can find inexpensive links: a few cents a link. And you can find everything in between.

Just wait

I'm not really recommending that you sit and wait as a way to build links, but if you're doing lots of other things — sending out press releases, getting mentioned in papers and magazines, contacting e-mail newsletters to do product giveaways, and so on — you'll gather links anyway. You've got to prime the pump first; then, things seem to just take off.

Fuggetaboutit

Don't bother getting links in guest books, Free for All pages, and link farms, for the following reasons:

- ✔ Many Web sites contain guest book pages, and one early link-building technique was to add a link to your Web site in every guest book you could find. The search engines know all about this technique, so although many guest books are indexed, links from them probably have very little value in most search engines.

- ✔ *Free for All (FFA)* pages are automated directories that you can add a link to. They bring virtually no traffic to your site, are a great way to generate a lot of spam (when you register, you have to provide an e-mail address), and don't help you in the search engines.

✔ *Link farms* are highly automated link-exchange systems designed to generate thousands of links very quickly. Don't get involved with link farms. Not only can they not help you, but also, if you link to one or host one on your site, you may be penalized in the search engines.

Search engines don't like these kinds of things, so save your time, energy, and money.

Be careful whom you link to!

In general, links to your site can't hurt you. The link may have no value, but it's unlikely to lead to some kind of penalty. It's with *outgoing* links — links from your site to other sites — that people sometimes get themselves into trouble. There are essentially two ways people cause problems:

✔ In attempts to get incoming links, they sign up with some kind of Free for All program or link farm. To be part of one of these programs, they have to link to other sites in the program, thus showing the search engines that they are in fact taking part in such link games. As Google puts it, you shouldn't link to "bad neighborhoods."

✔ They sign up with a program to sell links to other Web sites on their Web pages. Although the search engines can't recognize a purchased from a free link in most cases, they can in some, and may penalize the site owner.

Don't underestimate the power of this kind of grass-roots promotion. It can be tremendously powerful. One link can set off a chain reaction, in the way that a single link in ResearchBuzz did.

Chapter 16

Even More Great Places to Get Links

*L*inking is tough. It's hard to get the links you need. In the previous chapter, I list a whole bunch of different ways to get links, some of which may work for you and some of which may not. But there's a simple maxim in linking: "You can't have too many links!"

Actually, you may reach a point at which you're ranking really well for all the keywords you need to rank for, and you just seem to stick there. I've seen sites that, with very little additional link work, sit at the top of the search results for literally years. But those of you who are not yet in that happy situation still have more link work to do. So, dive right in to this chapter and find out more great places to get links to your site.

Got Content? Syndicate It!

I discuss one aspect of syndication in Chapter 9 — using syndicated content to bulk up your Web site. Now I look at the flip side — syndicating your content to other Web sites and e-mail newsletters. The basic concept? You write something (something interesting or useful or entertaining, I hope) and then provide the information to other Web site owners so that they can post it on their site. In return, you get links from the article back to your site.

Some site owners use this form of syndication as the *only* type of promotion they do — and it can sometimes work well. They write articles and distribute them as widely as possible. But many sites already have a lot of content. Why not give it away and use it as a technique to grab more search engine positions, generate links to your site, and brand your site and company?

Another huge advantage to using syndication is that the links you get back to your site are from relevant sites. Remember, the search engines like *relevant*. If you write articles about rodent racing and get them posted on other sites, what are those other sites likely to be about? Quite likely, rodent racing.

Four syndication technologies

Before I explain how to distribute these articles, you need to know a little geek stuff related to the technology used to syndicate content. You can syndicate content in basically four ways; two of these methods are good, but two of the methods don't help you with search engines at all. Use the wrong methods, and it doesn't matter how widely you distribute your content; it won't bring any search-engine benefit (it could still bring traffic through the links in the articles, though).

The following list details the four main syndication technologies:

- ✔ **Browser-side inclusion:** Many syndicators employ browser-side content inclusion through the use of JavaScripts; a *JavaScript* in a Web page pulls the article off the syndicating site. The problem is that the Web browser runs the JavaScripts when the page loads. Searchbots, however, don't run JavaScripts. Googlebot, when indexing the page, will probably ignore the content pulled by the JavaScript and thus will not see the content or the link to your site in the content. Although site visitors will see the links (and some may click), you won't get the benefit of the link popularity in the search engines.

- ✔ **Hosted content:** Some content syndicators, generally those *selling* content, host the content on their own servers, and the sites using the content link to it. The problem with this method is that if you host content for, say, 50 sites, you don't get the benefit of 50 links in the search engines. Google sees that you have the same article 50 times and ignores 49 of them.

- ✔ **Manual inclusion:** This method works well for search engines; they see the content and the links to your site. The problem, however, is that you're relying on the other site's owner to manually place the content into the page.

✔ **Server-side inclusion:** You can do server-side inclusions a number of ways, such as by using INCLUDE commands, running PHP or ASP scripts (server-side scripts), or using RSS feeds. The advantage is that the search engines *will* see your content and the links back to your site. The disadvantage is that the methods are more complicated to use than either manual or browser-side inclusion.

To ensure that search engines see links to your Web site, you simply can't use the first or second methods. That leaves the last two, of which the third, manual inclusion, is easiest and by far the most common.

It's possible to make a JavaScript-style syndication give you at least one link that is readable by the search engines. Typically, syndicators ask users to drop a piece of JavaScript into their pages. Of course, you can ask them to drop a piece of HTML that includes a JavaScript inside, along with a link out-side the JavaScript. For instance, rather than use

```
<SCRIPT LANGUAGE="JavaScript" src="http://www.
        ronaldsrodents.com/content/article.js"></
        SCRIPT>
```

you can use

```
<SCRIPT LANGUAGE="JavaScript" src="http://www.
        ronaldsrodents.com/content/article.js"></
        SCRIPT><P><STRONG>Article provided by <A
        HREF="http://ronaldsrodents.com>Ronald's
        Rodents</A>. Visit us for more great articles
        on rodent racing.</P>
```

Getting the most out of syndication

If you intend to syndicate your work, consider the following points when cre-ating your articles:

✔ Every article should contain your site name near the top of the article. When possible, you should also put a site logo near the top and include a link on the logo back to your site.

✔ Try to work a link to your site into the body of the article. You can do it a couple times, maybe, but don't overdo it. Perhaps link to another arti-cle on your site for more information. Make sure that the link text has useful keywords. (Note, however, that most syndication services don't allow links in the body; I look at syndication services in a moment.)

✔ At the bottom of the article, include an attribution or bio box, including a keyworded link back to your site and a logo with a link on it.

If you have a lot of traffic to your site, and plenty of content that you can share and think that people may want to use, set up a library on your Web site where people can access the articles. In the library, you should post certain conditions:

- ✔ Consider putting limits on the number of articles that can be used without contacting you first. For example, site owners can use up to five articles, and if they want more, they must get permission.

- ✔ State clearly that you retain copyright of the article and make clear the following conditions:

    - *The user cannot change the content.*

    - *All logos, attributions, copyright notices, and links must remain.*

    - *Links must remain as standard HTML <A> tags and cannot be converted to another form of link.*

Getting the word out

When you have your articles ready, you need to get them into the hands of people who can use them. There are actually hundreds of article libraries in which you can post your articles, bringing two benefits. First, the article sits in the article library, which may be indexed by the search engines (many are), and thus the links to your site will be picked up by the search engines. Second, if you're lucky, the article will be picked up by site owners who need content for their sites; if so, your article then appears in *those* sites, gets indexed by the search engines, and provides more value.

Here are just a few of these article libraries:

- ✔ www.amazines.com
- ✔ www.articlealley.com
- ✔ www.articlecity.com
- ✔ www.articlesbase.com
- ✔ www.authorconnection.com
- ✔ www.ezinearticles.com
- ✔ www.freesticky.com
- ✔ www.goarticles.com
- ✔ www.greekshares.com
- ✔ www.ideamarketers.com
- ✔ www.searchwarp.com

Check them out; but you may not want to post directly to them. There are hundreds of article syndication libraries, and you need to get your articles into as many as possible, so you should consider using one of the syndication services, as discussed in the aptly named "Syndication services" section, coming up next.

Syndication services

A number of syndication services and software programs can help you distribute your articles. For example:

www.submityourarticle.com

www.distributeyourarticles.com

www.contentcrooner.com

www.articlesender.com

www.articlesubmitterpro.com

These services and programs help you distribute your articles as widely as possible. Submit Your Article, for instance, claims to distribute to "hundreds" of article libraries and "other sites and niche-focused blogs," dozens of e-zine publishers, several article-announcement lists, and a number of content-syndication feeds.

You may even want to use several of these services. Follow this general procedure:

1. Write an article, putting keyworded links in the "resource" box at the bottom of the article (but not in the article itself).

2. Modify the article slightly so that you have a different version for each service.

3. Submit the article through each service. When using submitYOURArticle, use its ArticleLeverage system, which modifies each article slightly so that each one it submits to an article library is slightly different.

4. If using the Article Submitter Pro software, add keyworded links within the article and then submit to only the article directories that allow keyworded links inside the articles.

Who will write your articles?

Of course, you come to the old question: Who can you get to do this work? Perhaps you can write these articles yourself. Perhaps an employee in your company fancies himself an author. Or perhaps you can hire someone.

It's off to Guru.com, eLance.com, or oDesk.com you go, where you'll find countless people willing to write articles for you for $10 to $20 an article — some of whom can even speak a few words of English! Still, you're not looking for poetry or Nobel-prize-winning literature; you're looking for short articles with good keywords in them, and you really can find people who can write short articles — 200 to 400 words — very cheaply.

High-value article sites

The form of syndication I've just described is, let's face it, low quality. If you've spent a little time in the article libraries I pointed you to and read some of the articles, you know by now that many of the articles are written by people who are not English speakers or not writers, and in many cases by people who are neither English speakers nor writers. They are, to speak bluntly, terrible. No, really, *absolutely terrible*. Of course, what do you expect a $10 article to look like? I'm betting that Salman Rushdie and Scott Turow are not writing these articles as a side business.

These are articles written for one purpose only: to get links. In many cases, all you can expect the article to simply sit in the article libraries and never be syndicated to other Web sites; you are in effect buying the value of the links from the article libraries themselves.

However, another class of article marketing exists. This class consists of high-quality article sites that you can't just submit any old junk to; instead, you can write for them only after you've been approved.

For instance, Examiner.com (www.examiner.com) is a major news site — it has 19 million pages indexed by Google — with around 40,000 writers around the United States. Each writer has been through an approval process; writers have to show some writing ability and knowledge about the subject area they want to write about. Thus, the articles on Examiner.com are of a *much* higher quality than those of *Joe's Super Huge Article Library* and its ilk. The advantage to you is that you can place follow links in articles in a site with many high PageRank pages. (You may also get paid a little, a share of the ad revenue from your pages, but don't leave your day job quite yet.)

There are other sites that don't allow just anyone to post. Instead, they try to filter out the garbage and allow only quality writing. These sites are likely to provide better links to your site than the links from "Joe's" site. Two examples are Suite101.com and AssociatedContent.com; you may be able to find more. Oh, and don't overlook Knol (`knol.google.com`), Google's article site that almost nobody knows about. Google doesn't make joining it particularly hard, but it does use various techniques to encourage quality, such as verifying the identity of authors and allowing community feedback related to article quality. So don't try to dump your $10 article written in English by someone who writes English poorly. It won't last.

Syndicating utilities

A number of companies do a tremendous job at building truly huge numbers of incoming links by giving away Web utilities. The basic concept is that you create something useful and let people place it on their Web site if they include a link back to your site.

Here's an example. You've probably seen those dreadful "page counters" at the bottom of many Web pages, a number showing how many people have visited the page (and essentially say to visitors, "the owner of this site is an amateur")? Many of those page counters are given away to create links back to the site that is giving them away. The code provided to people placing them on their sites includes a small piece of text with a nicely keyworded link, and I've seen this strategy work very well. Sometimes the counter links back to the site giving away the counter; sometimes it links back to a completely different site and is promoting a different site owned by the owner of the counter site or perhaps a site the owner has been paid to promote.

A strategy involving giving something away can work in many different ways with a little imagination. Whatever you give away — clip art, videos, flash animations, calculators — make sure you include links back to your site. For instance, your rodent-racing site could distribute a utility for handicapping mice and rats. (I don't mean to damage them physically; I mean to calculate the race handicap — *what do you think I am!*) The utility would have a link back to your site — nicely keyworded — providing you with lots of great backlinks for search engines to read.

And More . . .

A few more ideas for building links:

- ✔ Carry out traditional PR (public relations) campaigns, targeting blogs and newsletters, to promote your site. You need a good "story," but if you contact enough sites, you can get people to talk about you.

✔ You can find a variety of services connecting people who need links with people willing to sell links on their blogs — services such as `www.blogsvertise.com`, `www.loudlaunch.com`, and `www.payperpost.com`. Of course, as discussed in Chapter 15, the search engines don't want you buying links. And watch out for bloggers claiming a higher PageRank than they really have.

✔ Dozens of "Question and Answer" sites exist, such as BlurtIt.com, Askville, Yahoo! Answers (answers.yahoo.com), Answers.com, and so on. Some have follow links; some have nofollow links. Some SEO people seek out questions about their sites and answer them, including a link to their site, of course.

✔ Keep your eyes open, and do a few link analyses (see Chapter 15) now and then; you'll be surprised at some of the link tricks you can learn from competitors.

The nofollow Curse

A quick note about the `nofollow` tag mentioned earlier. This tag — `rel="nofollow"` — tells search engines to ignore a link. Strictly speaking, it tells them not to follow the link, but more important, it tells them not to give any credit to the referenced Web site. That is, a link to your site, with `rel="nofollow"` in the link, is as good as no link at all from a search engine perspective.

This tag was created to stop *blog spam*. When blogs first became popular, many people, trying to push their sites up in the search engines, were visiting blogs and posting messages in the blog with links back to their sites, solely to boost their sites in the search engines. Thus, blogs became inundated with absolute garbage. You could even hire Indian companies to place links in blogs for you or buy programs that hit thousands of blogs in a few hours. (Still can.)

So, the major search engines came together to figure a way to put a stop to it. They figured that if blog spam had no real benefit, it would stop. Therefore, nofollow was born.

What's happened over the last few years though is that, gradually, other sites have started using the `nofollow` tag. Wikipedia used to be a great place to put links back to your site until it started coding every link with `nofollow`. Craigslist, too, was a very popular place to post ads with links back until it began using nofollow.

So, if you discover a good place to put links to your site, first check to see whether the links are genuine links; that is, make sure they don't have `nofollow` in the link itself, or `nofollow` in a meta tag at the top of the page. Second, check periodically. A site that allows regular follow links today may not tomorrow.

Who's Going to Do All This Work?!

Wow, finding sites to link to yours is a lot of work. It's very LTT (laborious, tedious, and time consuming). It's also not, shall we say, high-rent work. How do you get all this done? Assuming that you're not using a link-acquisition firm, here are some options:

- Do you have kids? If not, get some. It's a little drastic, but after you've spent a week or two doing this stuff, it may not seem so bad.
- Do your neighbors or employees have kids?
- Do your siblings have kids?
- Local schools and colleges definitely have kids, so you may want to find one or two who will do a few hours of work each evening.
- India and the Philippines have many, many kids willing and able to do this sort of work, and they're just waiting for you to hire them on Guru.com, eLance.com, and oDesk.com.

Chapter 17

Social Networking — Driven by Drivel

In This Chapter

▶ Understanding social networking

▶ Avoiding the hype

▶ The SEO benefits of social networking

*I*s there a place for social networking in a book on SEO? Well, to some degree, yes. But I don't go into great detail about social networking, because many of the benefits (when there are benefits) are not related to SEO. Social networking can be used in various different ways to market a product or service, or an associated Web site, but that's not all about SEO.

Before I go any further, though, I should answer a basic question: What *is* social networking?

A social-networking service is one that helps people communicate together. Consider for a moment a basic, informational Web site. Clients come to the site, read about the products or services being promoted by the site, perhaps take some kind of action — make a purchase, sign up for a newsletter, or whatever — and go away. The communication flow is all one-way.

Of course you could add two-way communication to a Web site; a chat system that allows customers to chat online with customer-service staff, for instance. But it's still fairly limited communication.

A social-networking service, though, provides multichannel communications; members of the service's "community" can communicate with any other member who wants to communicate. Facebook, the world's largest social-networking service, had 500 million active members in July 2010. If Facebook were a country, it would be the world's third most populous nation. Any of those 500 million members can communicate with any other member, assuming the other member is interested in communicating.

Social networking is more than, that, though. Social network sites often encourage people to set up their own minisites or profiles, on which they can post information about themselves, such as photos and messages. They can search for and connect with other members with similar interests, or members they know out in the real world.

The social-networking landscape is large and amorphous. You can certainly argue that discussion groups are part of social networking, and there are many tens of thousands of discussion groups. Blogging is also often considered a part of social networking. I think one important characteristic of social-networking sites is that they make publishing easy for people with no technical skills. All of a sudden, through the power of social networking, virtually anyone can be an online publisher, rather than merely a consumer of online information.

Social networking is a relatively new term; even most of today's Facebook members probably didn't know the term until relatively recently. (Facebook didn't open to the public until September 2006.) But social networking is actually an old concept, going back at least to the late 1970s or early 1980s. Online services such as CompuServe might be thought of as proto-social-networking services, allowing one-to-one communication between members, group communications in forums, the sharing of digital materials (text documents, images, software), and so on.

Today, though, what are the really important social-networking sites? The two most important are definitely Facebook and Twitter. In June 2010, Twitter announced that it had 190 million individual users each month, "tweeting" (that is, for those of you who have been held hostage in a cave somewhere, sending short Twitter messages) 65 million times a day. (Is Twitter *really* a social-networking service? Yes, because it *allows* multichannel communication; however, the majority of Twitter users never send a message, they use it to *receive* information, so for most users it's really more of a message-delivery service than a social network.)

Many other social-networking services exist, of course. Here are a few of the biggies in North America:

- **MySpace**: Almost 70 million users, and dropping; it used to be the world's #1 social-networking site. Many teenagers use MySpace until they decide they're old enough to switch to Facebook.

- **LinkedIn**: A business-networking site (based on the "six degrees of separation" concept), with around 70 million users and growing.

- **Windows Live Spaces**: Microsoft claimed several years ago to have 120 million users, though some estimates are much lower.

- **Flickr**: A photo-sharing network with tens of millions of users.

> ✔ **Orkut**: Not so popular in North America, actually, but I need to mention this because it's owned by Google and has perhaps 100 million members (mostly in India and Brazil). Also, rumor has it that Google plans to launch a *Google Me* service, based on Orkut, to rival Facebook.

There are many, many social-networking sites, including "social-bookmarking" sites (such as Delicious and Stumbleupon), sites related to particular interests, sites designed to help people find old friends (Classmates.com, for instance), and so on.

Beware the Social-Networking Hype

Social networking, properly used, can most definitely be a very valuable marketing tool. Having said that, I want to warn you that there's a lot of social-networking hype out there, and it's easy to get swept up into social networking only to find you have wasted a lot of time and money.

First, consider that social networking will work better for some companies than others. For instance, take Twitter. This service can be a great way to communicate with people for some businesses. ShopAtHome.com has around 16,000 followers of its Twitter feed. This company provides shopping discounts, so a Twitter feed is a natural fit for it; people like deals! Groupon, a "deal of the day" service, has dozens of separate feeds, one for each city it works in; the GrouponChicago feed currently has about 12,000 followers.

But what about a company that provides air-conditioning installation service? How many people want to hear from them every day? I'm not saying that it's not possible for such a company to benefit from a Twitter feed, but I am saying that the chance they will succeed is much lower.

Also, social-networking campaigns need to be well thought out and well managed. Plenty of companies are happy to take your money for setting up some kind of generic, "me, too" social-networking system that hasn't a hope in Hades of working.

Here's an example. Way back when — say, four or five years ago — I would hear from new clients who said things like, "My friend Joe [my nephew/the last SEO firm I worked with/and so on] told me that if you want to do business online, you *must* have a MySpace account." I even heard this from real estate agents. It was complete nonsense, of course, but the hype was strong, too powerful for many businesses to resists, and wasted millions of dollars.

So before you let someone talk you into a social-networking campaign, make sure you understand exactly how it would work. Why will people join your group or subscribe to your Twitter feed? What do you expect them to do? How will you communicate with them? How will all this turn into a benefit for you?

Before anyone accuses me of being "against" social networking, let me just reiterate. Social networking *can* work well, at least for the right companies that have all their ducks in a row. However, I'm pretty certain that most dollars spent on social networking are wasted.

The drivel factor

If you don't know this already, you need to learn quickly. Most — the vast majority — of social networking is *drivel*. (Drivel: senseless talk; nonsense; saliva, drool; to talk nonsense; to talk senselessly.)

Do I have to prove this, or can we take it as a given? Okay, here's an example. Pear Analytics did a study of randomly selected public Twitter messages and found that

- 40.6% were "pointless babble"
- 37.6% were "conversational messages"
- 8.7% were "pass along" messages, those useful enough to have been forwarded by another Twitter user
- 3.6% were information about news from the mainstream media
- 5.9% were company self-promotion
- 3.9% were spam

What is "pointless babble"? You know the type of message: *I want to eat cereal, but I'm out of milk!!!* or *Where has that postman got to?!* The sort of thing that burns up perfectly good electrons for no good reason.

Taken together, then, the pointless babble, conversational messages, and spam comes to around 82 percent of all messages.

The challenge for the marketer is to somehow cut through the drivel and find the value.

The SEO Benefits of Social Networking

Because this is a book on SEO, I want to get back to that subject: How can social networking help your SEO efforts? There are essentially three ways:

- **Link benefit:** Links from social-networking sites can, in some cases, help boost your pages in the search engines.

✔ **Search engine "real estate":** As the search engines index some social-networking pages (and Tweets), being in social-networking sites gives you another online location, another possibility for being found by the search engines.

✔ **The social networking sites *are* search engines:** What's a search engine? A site where people search. And people search on social-networking sites.

Getting links through social-networking sites

You find out about the value of links in Chapters 14 through 16. Well, Google has indexed almost a billion Facebook pages, and many of those pages contain links to the page owners' Web sites.

Here's the problem, though. These links are nofollow links (see Chapter 14), so, in theory at least, they have no link value. Twitter also uses nofollow links; MySpace currently doesn't, but many other social-networking sites do.

So, do those links have any value? In Chapter 14, I told you *no*. In this chapter, I'm suggesting a theory. I don't know whether this is true , but . . . what if the search engines *do* sometimes read nofollow links? After all, what is the point of nofollow links? The original purpose was to stop people from spamming blog comments by telling the search engines not to follow the links and thus removing an incentive for blog comments. But the purpose of nofollow was not to stop search engines indexing links; that was just the mechanism.

Now, imagine that you are a search engine programmer. You want as much information as you can get to help you rank pages. Aren't all those links on social-networking sites useful? After all, Google was based on the concept of examining links to learn about referenced sites. In the pre-social-networking days, Google recruited a relatively small number of site owners to tell them which sites were important.

Now, with the barriers to entry being much, much lower for social networking and social bookmarking — it's much easier to set up a Facebook, or MySpace, or Digg account than to build a Web site — Google has a much larger army of site reviewers to help it figure out how to rank Web sites. There are quite simply many more social-networking accounts than there are conventional Web sites.

So you, the search engine programmer, know that all this great information is out there to . . . but wait! They are nofollow links! Do you decide not to use the links?

To make nofollow links accomplish their original purpose, search engines don't have to ignore the links; it's good enough if people *think* the search engines ignore the links. But perhaps they don't. Perhaps they do read those links to extract this vast amount of useful information.

That's just a theory; again, I don't know whether it's true. I can tell you that under the commonly accepted nofollow theory, many social-networking links have no SEO value. On the other hand, if my unproven theory is correct, these links *do* have value.

Another way to generate links from social-networking sites is, of course, by engaging your community. If you have a strong social-networking community, you can use various techniques to encourage members to create links to your Web sites, on their own Web sites, their blogs, their social-networking profiles, and so on.

Grabbing search engine real estate

Another way that social networking can help you — perhaps — is to grab "real estate" in the search results. That is, when someone searches for your keywords, your site comes up in the search results *and* some of your social-networking profiles come up in the results.

In practice, this is harder than it seems, because social-networking pages themselves are not given much weight by the search engines. How do I know that? Because they don't often come up in the search results.

You can find significant exceptions, though. For instance, search for names, and often LinkedIn.com pages come up pretty high in the results. Here's another example of a way that Google has just recently started incorporating social-media content into the search engines: Search for a well-known musician (such as Peter Kent), and Google puts links from iLike.com to that musician's music at the top of the search results, as you can see in Figure 17-1. (Okay, so Peter Kent isn't a well-known musician, and the Peter Kent writing this book is not the same Peter Kent who is apparently a musician, which just goes to show that this works with even lesser-known personalities.)

Google has also experimented with incorporating Twitter tweets into search results; you may have seen the small scrolling boxes in the search results, sometimes carrying news links but also sometimes carrying tweets. This is called a "real-time" search and is usually placed into the results with a <u>Latest results</u> link above the scroll box (see Figure 17-2). However, I think it would be exceedingly hard to *target* real-time search positions because the results are so fleeting.

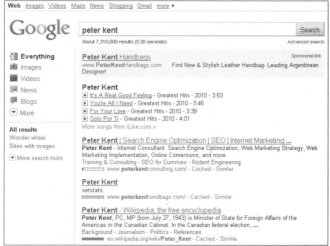

Figure 17-1:
iLike.com
information
displayed
at the top of
the Google
search
results.

Figure 17-2:
Google real-
time search
results.

The Social-Networking Sites Are Search Engines

Okay, back to Chapter 1 and the comScore study I discussed. You'll recall that comScore counted around 25 billion searches; however, almost a billion of those were in Facebook and MySpace. Facebook gets almost as many searches as Ask.com does.

So, social-networking sites *are* search engines. Now, it's true that many of these searches are for people, but many will be for interests and products, too. So another SEO reason for a social-networking strategy is that you have a chance of coming up in the many social-networking site searches.

Social Networking — a Book in Itself

Social-networking marketing is a big and complicated subject that deserves a book of its own. I've outlined in general terms how social networking can be used to help your site from an SEO perspective, but social networking is a form of marketing by itself, independent of any SEO benefits you may derive from it. So I leave it there, and move on, in Chapter 18, to a related subject: using video for SEO purposes.

However, to find out more about using social networking for your business, see *Social Media Marketing For Dummies,* by Shiv Singh (published by Wiley Publishing, Inc.) and *The Digital Handshake: Seven Proven Strategies to Grow Your Business Using Social Media,* by Paul Chaney (also published by Wiley).

Chapter 18

Video: Putting Your Best Face Forward

. . . .

In This Chapter

▶ Understanding the benefits of using video

▶ Optimizing videos on your own site

▶ Getting videos into video hosting sites

▶ Using videos to grab search engine "real estate"

. . . .

Back in Chapter 1, I mention a comScore study of search habits. The study looked at a variety of sites through which around 25 billion searches were made in June 2010. But almost 4 billion of those searches were done through YouTube; in fact, YouTube gets more searches than Yahoo!, and way more searches than Bing.

In the previous month, comScore reported, around 144 million visitors to YouTube watched 14.6 billion videos. (That's right, someone's spending a lot of time in front of YouTube; that's 101 videos per viewer!) In all, 183 million people in the United States watched an online video at least once in the month.

Video's big. But how do you use it from a search engine perspective? This chapter tells you about the SEO benefits of working with video, the best ways and places to upload video, and how to do so most effectively.

The SEO Benefits of Video

So how can you benefit, from an SEO perspective, from video? In these ways:

 ✔ **Providing content on your site that search engines like:** That's the theory, anyway, but the reality is a little different, as I detail in a moment.

✔ **Getting listed in more search engines — the video search engines:** As mentioned earlier, YouTube is a hugely important search engine. So getting videos into YouTube (and other video-search sites) gets you into the video-search game.

✔ **Grabbing search engine real estate:** This is in some ways more important, because Google likes to insert videos into its search results, as you can see in Figure 18-1.

Figure 18-1: Video inserted into the Google search results.

Videos on your site

The most obvious benefit to putting videos on your site, from an SEO perspective, is that it provides content that the search engines like, and you'll often hear that as a reason given for using video on your site. The reality is a little different; videos are *not* particularly good search engine fodder, although you can improve that situation a bit. The proof of the pudding is in the eating, they say; when videos are embedded into the search results, they are almost always from major video sites, such as YouTube.com and Vimeo.com.

Ah, I can hear someone in the back mumbling, "But Google listens to the videos and transcribes them!" That's true. In fact, if you go to YouTube.com and view a video (YouTube is owned by Google, by the way), look for a little

CC button in the bottom-right corner of the video player. Click that button and you see a Transcribe Audio option. Click that option and you can play the audio with "closed caption" transcription shown at the bottom of the video.

Automated transcriptions are problematic, though. Here's a transcription I got from YouTube recently. See whether you can figure out what this is all about:

> *"The fastest antenna began sending its shares that women really didn't take it lightly it's done as on our last segment in one search for the port in ten different times it's been a great night lasting antenna and the big news is we do it again this year in fact that if I think that if back thanks you, but at the time the President indicates that the intent to evade that's a factor that comments in for instance the truth and I think so standby it's"*

Believe it or not, this is a transcription of a promotional video from Coca Cola's Fanta soft drink, promoting a contest to find the fourth "Fantana girl." What, you didn't get that?

So, if you think that the search engines will listen to and transcribe your videos into something that might actually help you, think again. Not this year, anyway, or the next. On the other hand, these transcriptions might be getting better. Here's the same video transcribed a couple of months later:

> *But this is not something audiences for instance and decision on right this second and faint dot com and their pretty amazing yes I always wanted only a lot some may still a year maybe a favorite and your ratings are important they help determine the top ten finalists I think answer is get your friends and family behind and if you think that there's a great privilege to you they say let's everybody was the standard and so then check out those the is a great great great and if you get Iraq ice-cold can separate store*

Hmmm, better, but not quite there yet.

So don't expect a video sitting on your site to do you much good from an SEO perspective, unless you help it along a bit. Like this:

- ✔ **Label it:** Create a nicely keyworded label or short description of the video; use an <H> tag in the HTML around this label.
- ✔ **Describe it:** Include a longer description, again with good keywords.
- ✔ **Transcribe it:** Do a *real* transcription, and post the transcribed text on the page. Services exist that can do this for you very affordably and pretty efficiently.
- ✔ **Name it:** Use keywords in the video's filename and URL.

- ✔ **Link to it:** Create links, on your site and others, to the video page, using keywords and the term *video* in the link. This is very important; providing links into the video page can help a lot.

- ✔ **Tag it:** As usual, use keywords (including the word *video*) in your page's `<TITLE>` tag and `DESCRIPTION` tag.

- ✔ **Add to it:** Add other keyworded content on the page, especially if the transcription is short.

- ✔ **Submit it:** You can include video content in your sitemap (which I discuss in Chapter 11), or create a special mRSS (media RSS) feed, providing the video title, description, a thumbnail URL, and so on. Some video experts believe that submitting both a regular sitemap and an mRSS sitemap is a good idea. You can find details about both in the Google Webmaster Help information.

Use the word *video* throughout; remember, you're trying to tell the search engines that this is a video. Don't overdo it, but you can use the term *video* in the `<H>` tag, the description, the filename, links, `<TITLE>` tag and `DESCRIPTION` meta tag, and so on.

Incidentally, by the time you read this, Google will probably have released Google TV (`www.google.com/tv/`). The basic idea: a television search engine. Imagine your TV set getting TV from wherever you normally get it (cable, satellite, or over the air) *and* connecting to the Internet. Add a search engine — Google, of course — and now you can search and find exactly the show, documentary, funny video, or whatever, and view it from wherever it may be.

Now, because of this, Google is getting more serious about indexing video on the Web. In particular, Google is eager to get your video-sitemap data. As Mr. Google SEO, Matt Cutts (see Chapter 22) said recently, "If you tell us where your videos are, we will try to index them a little bit harder. For example, if you think about things like Google TV. . ., it's in everybody's interest that all the videos that are on the Web be able to be very discoverable and very searchable." Google *wants* your video, so make it easy for Google to get it.

Don't use pop-up video players; embed them into the page. If you do use pop-ups, the danger is that the video isn't found by the search engines, especially if the pop-up is generated by JavaScript. Also, the video will probably be "orphaned" in the search results, much the same way as framed pages become orphaned (as I describe in Chapter 7).

You might also allow other people to embed your video into their sites; this can help create links back to the video, assuming that people actually take you up on the offer.

Playing the video search engine game

Okay, next step: If you go to the trouble of creating videos, why not distribute them as widely as possible, on as many video sites as possible? Remember, these are search engines, too, so being present when someone searches for your keywords would be good. As Woody Allen said, "Eighty percent of success is showing up," and if you're not in the video sites, you're not showing up. So, here are a few tips for you on uploading your videos:

- ✔ **"Watermark" your videos**: Now and then you'll find videos, on the video-upload sites or perhaps embedded into someone's Web site, with no identifying information in the video itself. You need to make sure your videos "stand alone" as a marketing tool for your site, so "watermark" the videos with your site's domain name — at the very least at the beginning and end of the video, but ideally on every single frame so that no one can view the video without knowing where it comes from. (If you have videos that are not watermarked, on YouTube you can use the Annotation tool to overlay text onto the video. Oh, use keywords when you annotate, too!)

- ✔ **Provide plenty of keyworded descriptive info:** The video-upload services provide space for you to supply a title, description, and keywords (or tags). Use them, and use them fully — by entering a long description with plenty of keywords, for instance.

- ✔ **Include a link to your Web site:** Put it in the URL field if the service provides one, or the description if it doesn't. You want people to be able to find your site, after all. Note, however, that most video sites provide nofollow links (see Chapter 10 for details on nofollow links), so you won't get rank-boosting value in the search engines from them.

- ✔ **Put your domain at the top of the description, in particular on YouTube:** YouTube hides your video description, except for the first line, so to ensure that people see your site's URL, you need to put it on the first line.

- ✔ **Include a transcript or caption file:** YouTube allows you to upload time-coded captions, or a plain-text transcription file. (You have to upload the file first, view the file in your Uploaded Videos area, and then click the Captions button.) Google may read these files.

There are literally dozens of video hosting sites to which you can upload your videos. You can find a good list at http://en.wikipedia.org/wiki/List_of_video_hosting_websites. Of course, it'll take you, um, forever to upload to all of them. So you should consider using a video-upload service, which works by having you load the video once into the distribution service so that the service can then upload to a variety of different sites. For instance, TubeMogul.com will upload your video to 30 different services. Another distribution service is TrafficGeyser.com, which can upload to a similar number (and has some other advantages, which I discuss in a moment). Yet another is HeySpread.com, and you might find others.

Incidentally, the ranking of videos on the upload sites is not just a matter of keywords and links to the page. On YouTube, for instance, other aspects may be taken into consideration, such as

- ✔ The number of times the video is viewed
- ✔ The ratings given to the video by viewers
- ✔ The number of times the video was shared
- ✔ The number of comments
- ✔ The number of people subscribing to the video publisher's channel after viewing the video
- ✔ The number of times the video is embedded into viewers' own Web sites

Grabbing search engine real estate

So, you've got your videos uploaded to the video-upload sites. You now have a chance of being found in what are, in effect, video search engines. But as the search engines index some of these video sites, you also now have a chance of your videos turning up in the regular search results (as you see in Figure 18-1).

But there is a bit more to the game, if it's played right. If you want to encourage the search engines to rank your videos well, you really need links pointing to the videos. That's right, you need to create links from various places to the video-upload sites; as Chapter 14 notes, links help pages rank, so it makes sense that your videos on a video-upload site might need a few links to help them rank. TrafficGeyser.com actually automates this process, uploading videos to the video hosting services *and* posting links to the videos on social-networking sites.

Chapter 19

When Google Bites Back: A Guide to Catastrophe

Imagine that Google decided it didn't want to play with you anymore. Imagine an enterprise rolling along nicely, bringing in plenty of business on the Web, perhaps even most or all of its business, and most of that business came through the search engines, when, all of a sudden . . . the site just drops in the search results. All of a sudden, you can't find your site anywhere through any of the great keywords for which you were ranking well.

A frightening thought, eh? But it happens, and has happened to many. Why? And what can you do about it? Well, that's the subject of this chapter, which gives you a look at what search engine penalties are all about, how to avoid them, and what to do if the worst happens.

How, and How Much?

There are, in a broad sense, two types of penalties, and Google can impose them in two ways. The types of penalties are as follows:

✔ **Total:** Your site is completely dropped from the search engine. It's no longer in the index, and the search engine will probably stop visiting your site. (This is often called *de-indexing* or a *ban*.) Assuming that you've been penalized (and, as I discuss a little later, your site can be dropped for reasons other than a penalty), you've *really* annoyed Google!

> ✔ **Partial**: Your site is still in the search engine, but it just doesn't seem to be ranking well; plus, some other symptoms are appearing (which I discuss in this chapter) that also suggest a penalty. But the site is still in the Google index, and Google even returns periodically to crawl more pages. This is still bad, of course, but not as bad as a total ban. Google's saying, in effect, "We don't like what you've done, but we're willing to give you another chance." *Phew!*

By the way, a partial ban probably has different grades, different "levels" of penalty. In fact, the SEO community has come up with all sorts of names, such as a –30 penalty (Google has adds 30 positions to your site every time it comes up in the search results, pushing it down three pages); a PageRank penalty (Google reduces your PageRank); a –950 penalty (you drop so far that you just can't be found); and so on. Google almost certainly has some kind of obscenity filter that is intended to drop porn sites from the regular results and that says, in effect, "We're not going to drop you from our index because you haven't necessarily done anything wrong, but we don't want your site coming up for regular search results." These penalty types are conjecture, though — Google doesn't state what the penalties are, beyond saying, in effect, "Yes, we penalize, and we have different grades of penalty."

Now, the two processes by which a penalty can be imposed are the following:

> ✔ **Algorithmically:** The Google "algorithm," the complex piece of software that evaluates sites and decides how to rank them, has found something on your site egregious enough to penalize your site.
>
> ✔ **Manually:** Google has a "spam team" that employs real, live human beings to examine Web sites. If the team finds something it doesn't like, it can impose a penalty.

Relatively few sites actually get penalized; in fact, if you pay attention during your travels around the Web, you'll find all sorts of sites that really should be penalized. These are sites that play all sorts of nasty SEO tricks yet somehow are still in the index. Why?

First, with a trillion or so pages in the Google index, there's simply no way to manually examine all of them for spamful intent. On the other hand, to automatically or algorithmically apply penalties, search engines have to create a very loose system that penalizes only the very worst offenses or they are bound to penalize innocent sites. I know that Google's search engine engineers are trying to not penalize innocent parties. This fact is obvious because so many indexed pages clearly break the rules.

I know a little about the spam team, too, by the way. I know, for instance, that you can submit sites to be checked for spam. If you have a competitor that is quite clearly playing significant SEO tricks that "break the rules," you can actually tell Google (and the other search engines) about that site. I provided links to the search-engine spam-report pages near the end of Chapter 8.

I also have an idea of what the spam team does, partly from the "leaking" in 2007 of the *Google Spam Team Quality Rater Guidelines*, a PDF document that apparently provides information to team members on how to examine a site to see whether it's playing unacceptable SEO tricks. This leaked book is generally accepted in the SEO community as being genuine, and if you do a search (at Google!) for that title, you should be able to find it. (At this writing, it's posted here: `www.scribd.com/doc/2299019/Google-Quality-Rater-Guidelines`.) It makes fascinating reading, at least for search geeks.

Here's what worries me about the spam team: How often does it make mistakes? Everyone makes mistakes, of course, and plenty of those mistakes are made during work hours. (Have you worked in corporate America? Let's face it — it's not exactly a mecca of efficiency and competence.) A simple statistical analysis indicates, in fact, that people make somewhere around 30 percent of all their mistakes during working hours. And, just perhaps, tomorrow one of those mistakes will be made by the Google Spam Team, and your site (or mine) will be hit with a penalty.

Still, having read the Quality Rater Guidelines, I must say that they seem reasonably lenient. I come back to them a little later.

So, from the perspective of the site owner with the "damaged" site, two big questions are of concern:

 ✔ Has the site been penalized? It may seem obvious — the site has disappeared, so obviously it has been penalized — but the situation is actually more complicated than that.

 ✔ If so, then what can be done about it?

So, start at the beginning and first determine whether your site has *really* been penalized.

Is It Really a Penalty? A Little Analysis

It may seem counterintuitive, but just because your site appears to have been penalized doesn't mean that it has. In fact, it seems to me that in most cases when a site owner thinks his site has been penalized, it really hasn't. You see, when your site drops in the search results, a number of reasons could be behind it. A few (I'm sure there are more) are as follows:

 ✔ You've done something to damage your site, telling Google not to index it anymore.

✔ Someone else, perhaps a hacker, has done something to damage your site.

✔ Google has changed its algorithm, and all the great little SEO tricks you were using in the past no longer work, so your site is dropping in the ranks.

✔ Google is in the middle of an upheaval, and your site is dropping for no particular reason and will probably come back in a few days . . . and then perhaps drop again and come back later.

✔ You really have been penalized. Google's algorithm has identified something it doesn't like in your site.

✔ You really have been penalized. A Google Spam Team member has seen your site (perhaps because it was reported by a competitor), didn't like something you were doing, and penalized the site.

Before you can figure out which of these possibilities is true, you have to determine what is really going on with your site. "It's dropped in the search results" isn't enough; you need more detail.

Here are a few things to consider when trying to figure out whether your site has been penalized:

✔ Is the site still indexed?

✔ Has Google flagged your site as "suspicious"?

✔ Has the number of pages in the index significantly changed?

✔ What happens when you search for your domain name?

✔ What happens when you search for the domain name minus the TLD (Top Level Domain; the .com piece, for instance)?

✔ What happens when you search for a text string in your <TITLE> tag?

✔ What happens when you search for a text string in your home page?

✔ Does your Google Webmaster console contain a message?

✔ Is Google still crawling your Web site?

✔ Have you done a Penalty Checker?

In the following pages, I look at each of these items.

Is the site still indexed?

Go to Google and ask it how many pages are indexed, like this:

```
site:domain.com
```

For instance, if you type `site:cnn.com` into Google and press Enter, Google displays a list of pages from cnn.com and shows a number at the top, under the Search box. It will be something like `About 84,500,000`.

Now, say that you do this for your site, and it comes back with a list of pages. That's good news; clearly you haven't been hit with the most serious penalty. You may still have been partially penalized, though.

However, let's say Google returns a message like this:

```
Your search - site:domain.com - did not match any
          documents.
```

Now you know that you have definite problems. Has the site been penalized? Perhaps, but before you can say for sure, you have to rule out other possibilities. Anyway, some of the following questions are now irrelevant to you. I suggest that you skip forward to the "Does your Google Webmaster console contain a message?" section.

Has Google flagged your site as "suspicious"?

If your site is no longer indexed, Google may have found some kind of "malware" on the site, bad software such as Trojan horses or viruses. This sometimes happens when a site has been hacked. So, try this little check (in fact, try it even if the site *is* still indexed; doing so takes only a moment). Type the following into your browser's Location bar and press Enter:

```
www.google.com/safebrowsing/diagnostic?site=youdomain.com
```

Google will return a page telling you whether your site is listed as suspicious. If so, there's your problem! You need to figure out what's on your site that Google doesn't like and get rid of it. By the way, in the response page, if your site is not infected, you may see something like this:

```
Google has not visited this site within the past 90 days
```

Just ignore this line; it does *not* mean that your site has not been indexed for 90 days. (It's probably referring to the bots that are sent out to examine a site for malware.)

This data actually comes from a service called StopBadware.org, so see `www.stopbadware.org/home/reviewinfo` for information on fixing your site.

Has the number of pages in the index significantly changed?

If your site *is* still indexed, how many pages does Google say it has in the index? Has it dropped considerably? If so, this fact doesn't mean anything in isolation. Google's index numbers fluctuate a lot of time, after all. However, if you come back a few days' running, or over a couple of weeks, and the number seems to be in free-fall, you may have a problem. On the other hand, even if the number is fairly solid, you could still be under some kind of penalty.

What happens when you search for your domain name?

Go to Google and search for your exact domain name in this format: *domainname.com*. What happens? Does Google return pages from your site? Good. Does it return the following?

```
Your search - domainname.com - did not match any
            documents.
```

If so, that's bad. Really bad.

What happens when you search for the domain name minus the TLD?

Say that you searched for your domain and Google did return the page. In that case, you might try searching for the domain name without the TLD (Top Level Domain); that is, don't search for *domainname*.com but search for *domainname* instead.

Don't bother if your domain name is a short, common term. But if it's a string of two or three terms, in a sequence that is unlikely to appear except in your domain name, then Google should bring up your site. If it doesn't, that's not good.

What happens when you search for a text string in your <TITLE> tag?

So, things are going okay so far; or maybe you've got bad news, but you want a little more confirmation. Copy a line of text from a <TITLE> tag in a page on your site that you know to be indexed.

Next, search for that term like this:

```
site:domainname.com "The text from the title tag"
```

Does Google find this? It should find it if the page you picked is definitely in the index and you typed it all correctly. Okay, now search for the string of text, in quotation marks, *without* site:*domainname.com* in front of it.

Google now doesn't find it? If you pick a distinct enough phrase, very few pages should come up in the results, perhaps even fewer than ten, so you should be able to find the results if they're there. If Google *doesn't* return it — wow, that's bad.

What happens when you search for a text string in your home page?

You can try a similar test by searching for a particular string of text that you know is in a page that is definitely in your site. First, test like this:

```
site:yourdomain.com "The text from the home page"
```

When the page appears in the search results (and if it doesn't, that's very unusual, and very, very serious; are you sure you entered the text correctly?), you'll see that your search string is shown in the Search box. Just delete the site:*yourdomain.com* piece and press Enter to search again.

If you get a "No results found for" message at the top of the page, or if that message doesn't appear, but you just can't find your page in the search results, that's a serious problem.

Does your Google Webmaster console contain a message?

If any of the following is true:

- ✔ Your site is still indexed.
- ✔ Your site doesn't contain malware.
- ✔ The number of pages in the index has not significantly changed.
- ✔ When you search for your domain name, you find it.
- ✔ When you search for the domain name minus the TLD, you find it (assuming that it consists of more than one word or uncommon string of words).
- ✔ When you search for a text string in your <TITLE> tag, you find it.
- ✔ When you search for a text string in your home page, you find it.

. . . then it's unlikely that you have been penalized. Still, you may want to log into your Google Webmaster account (see Chapter 11 for information) and check a couple of things; and if the tests in this bulleted list *didn't* turn out so well, you definitely want to do that.

Log into your account and see whether Google has sent you a message about a problem in your site. Newly received messages should appear at the top of the page when you log in, but you can also click the <u>Messages</u> link to go to your inbox.

Nothing there? That doesn't mean anything, either way. You may have been penalized, you may not, but sometimes Google will send messages to site owners about simple problems. I've heard of people receiving messages about hidden text on their sites, but this doesn't seem to be a common occurrence. Google also sends messages to sites that have been hacked, or even sites that are running old server software that leaves them open to being hacked.

Is Google still crawling your Web site?

Here's another thing to check while you're in the Webmaster account: Is Google still crawling your site? Go to the Webmaster account home page and click the name of your site. The site's Dashboard page appears. Click the <u>Diagnostics</u> link and then the <u>Crawl stats</u> link. If you're lucky, a page with information like that shown in Figure 19-1 appears. If not, your site is no longer being crawled; in other words, the Googlebot is no longer visiting your site and downloading pages. That's what we in the SEO business call A Very Bad Thing.

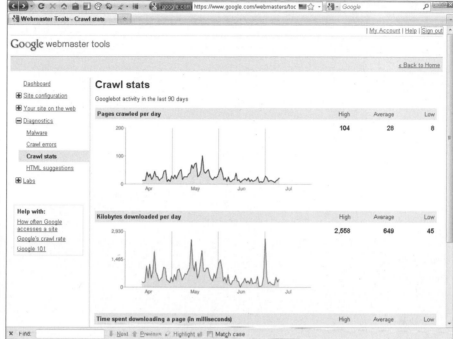

Figure 19-1:
Google
Webmaster
account
shows you
Googlebot
activity on
your site.

Still, even if Google *is* still crawling your site, it doesn't mean you have not been penalized. You may have a partial penalty, and Google is waiting for you to fix the problems.

Try a penalty checker

For further confirmation, you may want to try a "Google penalty checker"; you can find one by doing a search. For instance, you may be able to find one at `tools.lilengine.com/penaltychecker` and perhaps `www.seo penalty.com`.

The tool creators generally don't tell you exactly how they determine whether your site has been penalized; they probably just run through some of the tests that I have looked at in this chapter already. Still, they may provide a little confirmation of what's going on, a sort of "second opinion." (See Figure 19-2.)

You may get different results from a penalty checker than you get when you perform these checks yourself; for instance, things may still look bad to you — Google won't return your site in the result when you search for text in your home page's <TITLE> tag or page content, perhaps — and yet the penalty checker says there's no penalty. That result *may* be because of the difference between Google data centers; different locations get results from different Google data centers, and it takes time for changes to propagate all the way across all data centers.

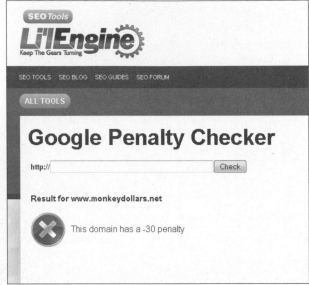

Figure 19-2:
The Li'l
Engine
Google
Penalty
Checker in
action.

Some of these penalty checkers are no good; I've seen one that says Google. com is penalized. But Li'l Engine seems okay, and perhaps they're getting better in general. Still, they don't have any secret channel to Google; they're just using the sorts of checks I describe here.

Pulling It All Together: Have You Been Penalized?

So what do you do with all this information? Here's a review.

- ✔ **Is the site still indexed?** If so, great; if not, either you've been penalized or there's a problem with your site. See the upcoming section "Why Aren't You Indexed?"

- ✔ **Does Google say your site has malware?** If so, there's your problem. If not, proceed.

✔ **Has the number of pages in the index significantly changed?** If so, not a good sign. On the other hand, this number does tend to fluctuate in Google, so it doesn't prove you've been penalized.

✔ **What happens when you search for your domain name?** If you can't find it, that strongly suggests that you've been penalized.

✔ **What happens when you search for the domain name minus the TLD?** Again, if you can't find it, you've likely been penalized. (But this search works only with unusual combinations of words in your domain name.)

✔ **What happens when you search for a text string in your `<TITLE>` tag?** Yet again, if Google doesn't return your site, you've likely been penalized.

✔ **What happens when you search for a text string in your home page?** Again, if your site isn't in the search results, you've probably been penalized.

✔ **Does your Google Webmaster console contain a message?** Clearly, if you get a message saying you've been penalized, well, you've been penalized! Few people ever get this message, though.

✔ **Is Google still crawling your Web site?** If so, that's a great sign; you may still be penalized, but you've got another chance. If not, you've quite likely been penalized.

✔ **Try a penalty checker.** The penalty checker says what it says; it's just another bit of information, one way or the other.

It's never totally clear whether you've been penalized or not; Google generally doesn't say. So, what can you do now?

✔ **If you are no longer indexed, and Google has stopped crawling your site:** You need to check to see whether your site is "damaged" in some way (see the upcoming section "Why Aren't You Indexed?"), and then, if everything seems okay, consider what you may have done to be banned. (On the other hand, you probably know whether you've been playing egregious SEO tricks; you may not know whether a company you hired to work on your site has, though.)

✔ **If you are still indexed okay but all indications suggest that you've been penalized:** See the "Digging Your Way Out of the Hole" section, later in this chapter.

Of course, another possibility is that you don't seem to have been penalized but your site is not ranking well for your keywords. This scenario could be the case for one of two reasons:

✓ **Google is in the middle of some kind of update:** This happens now and then. Sites jump up and down in the search results for a period of a few days or even weeks, and then things settle down to more or less where they were before.

✓ **Google has changed its algorithm, and you site no longer appears to be a good match for your keywords:** In other words, the content and links that you had before worked okay, and now Google has adjusted its algorithm so that they don't. For instance, many people have been hit over the years by adjustments in the algorithm related to reciprocal linking. Although reciprocal linking used to be very powerful, now it's pretty weak, and therefore many sites relying on that technique don't rank well anymore.

Why Aren't You Indexed?

If you've been dropped from Google's index, the first thing to consider is whether you have, in effect, told Google to drop your site. I've seen this happen on a number of occasions, and the mistake can be minor. A few mistyped characters in your `robots.txt` file, for instance, can tell Google that you don't want to be indexed. (I've even seen a site sabotaged by someone intentionally changing the `robots.txt` file.)

That's where I recommend that you start: by checking your `robots.txt` file (see Chapter 6 for more about this file), in particular the Disallow lines. For instance, the following is fine:

```
User-agent: *
Disallow: /includes/
```

On the other hand, the following removes your site from the search engines:

```
User-agent: *
Disallow: /
```

A small, simple mistake, and you're dead in the water!

Google Webmaster account (see Chapter 11) provides some nice tools that help you check your existing `robots.txt` file. These tools can tell you what the effect of a change you make will be, and they can even create a new file based on what you want to do. You can even specify a directory in your site and ask what effect the `robots.txt` file has on that directory (whether it is accessible to search engines or blocked to them). To find these tools, click the Site configuration link in the Dashboard and then click the Crawler access link.

You can also block a search engine using the `robots` meta tags in individual pages. If, for instance, you have the following:

```
<META NAME="robots" CONTENT="noindex">
```

you've just told the search engines not to index that page.

These are the most common problems, although there are other, far less likely, possibilities, such as the server being unresponsive to search engines. (You would have that problem only if you have a particularly incompetent or malicious server administrator.)

Digging Your Way Out of the Hole

So, say that you've decided that you have indeed been banned or penalized. Reversing a ban may be very difficult, though not impossible; you did something very naughty. A penalty under which you are still indexed, and possibly even crawled by Googlebot, is likely to be less of a problem.

You need to figure out what you did to make Google mad. Note that it *could* be accidental — you did something that Google doesn't like, but you did it innocently. For instance, you may have a medical Web site that contains sufficient density of sex-related terms to trigger a Google obscenity filter. Or maybe you have been using cloaking or hidden text (see Chapter 8) for perfectly good reasons, yet Google has interpreted it as a trick.

Or perhaps you hired a Web-development team that implemented various tricks without your knowledge, or maybe your company gave you a site to look after long after the tricks were used. Or you might have purchased a domain name that was penalized because of dirty tricks in the past. (Just changing owners isn't enough to automatically lift the penalty.)

So, here's what I suggest. You should review various materials and write a list of possible items that Google objects to. Here are a couple of places to check:

Google's Webmaster Guidelines (`www.google.com/support/webmasters/bin/answer.py?answer=35769`): You can ignore much of what's here; you're interested only in things that will be interpreted as mal-intent (such as "sneaky redirects"), not things that simply hurt your search engine ranking (such as poor `<TITLE>` tags).

The Google Spam Team Quality Rater Guidelines (`www.scribd.com/doc/2299019/Google-Quality-Rater-Guidelines`): Read this, in particular "Part 4: Webspam Guidelines," to see the sort of things the spam team is looking for.

You might also go into the SEO forums (see Chapter 22) and ask for help. But be warned: Many of the responses you get will be just plain *wrong!* (In particular, forum members seem to see spam on just about every page they look at.) So sometimes working with the forums can lead you in the wrong direction, and at the least can raise your frustration level during a difficult time.

Finding on-page problems

Start with on-page problems, which are the most likely issues to be causing a penalty. Read through the Webmaster guidelines and Spam Team guidelines, and check your site, issue by issue.

Here are the items that the spam team looks for:

- **PPC Pages:** Pages created purely for the sake of placing Google AdSense PPC ads on them, with little or no useful content

- **Parked Domains:** A Web site that has no real value beyond being a placeholder for sponsored links

- **Thin Affiliates:** A page that has no purpose but to deliver a visitor to another Web site

- **Hidden Text and Hidden Links:** Text and links placed on a site so that they are visible to search engines, but not to visitors

- **JavaScript Redirects:** JavaScript used to automatically redirect someone to another site so that the search engine sees the page content but the visitor doesn't

- **Keyword stuffing:** A page overstuffed with keywords, often repeated many times

- **100% frame:** A trick in which the main frame, seen by the search engine, contains one set of content, while another frame, that covers the first one, shows different content to the visitor

- **Sneaky redirects:** Another redirect trick, in which a page redirects through multiple Web sites, often ending up at a merchant site such as eBay or Amazon

Of course, there are sure to be other things the spam team looks at now; this document dates back to 2007. You might also check for outgoing links, in particular these three forms:

- **"Injected links":** Sometimes hackers break into a site and insert hidden links to "bad neighborhood" sites such as link farms.

- **Sold links:** Did you sign up with a firm that pays you to place links on your site to other sites? You might get penalized for that.

- **Links to "bad neighborhoods":** Have you joined some kind of massive link-exchange program in which you link to a service that automatically creates links to thousands of sites? That could be a problem. (You might want to try this "bad-neighborhood" link checker to find clues: www. bad-neighborhood.com/text-link-tool.htm.)

Finding link problems

Next, check your off-page issues, that is, links from other sites to yours. You often hear people in the SEO world talk about these links as a potential problem, but in fact they rarely are. Google has to be very careful about penalizing sites for links pointing to a site, unless it can find links on the site itself pointing back to the "bad neighborhoods," as I discuss in the previous section. Otherwise, Web site owners with few scruples would "attack" competitors by linking to their sites from bad neighborhoods in the hopes of getting those competitors kicked out of the search engines.

So consider external link problems, but be aware that in most cases they are not a problem, unless something indicates a relationship between the two linked sites.

Finding domain name problems

Sometimes a domain name may be damaged goods. For instance, perhaps you purchased a domain name that has been penalized in the past. The site currently contains nothing that is causing problems, but the domain itself has a penalty applied to it that hasn't been lifted.

This isn't the case, of course, if you have owned and operated the domain name successfully and have just been hit with a penalty. If you need to check a domain that you purchased, though, you might look in the WayBackMachine (www.archive.org), to see whether it has a record of what the site looked like in the past; was it a spammy-looking site? Also, search for the domain name in Google and see whether it has been discussed on other Web sites in the past. Finally, you might look at other domains owned by the previous domain owner; are some of those domains damaged goods, too? In the case of egregious Web spamming, Google may penalize all of a domain-holder's domains at one time.

Submitting a Request for Reconsideration

Having gone through the process recommended in the previous sections, you may end up with a list of items that may be at odds with ranking well on Google. If you're lucky, some are quite obviously a problem; there's hidden text on your pages, clearly intended to be hidden from readers, or someone hacked into your site and "injected" links to link farms. I call this being lucky because you know the cause of the penalty and can remove it and move on.

More problematic is when you're just not sure. For instance, the Google Spam Team Quality Rater Guidelines talks about hidden text being used to mislead search engines (which it often is) but also says that "hidden text is not considered to be Spam if there is no intention to trick the search engine"; so, what happens if you had no intention to trick the search engine? Could the Google staff member be misinterpreting your use of hidden text? (For instance, many sites use links to open more areas of text on the page.)

You have two ways to deal with these sorts of ambiguous issues. You can fix the worst problems and leave the ambiguous things, submit a reconsideration request (which I explain in a moment), and hope that Google *wasn't* misinterpreting the ambiguous items. Then you wait to see whether the penalty is lifted. Or you can change even the ambiguous items before doing your reconsideration request.

What if you've found the problem and fixed it? You need to ask Google nicely to remove the penalty, using what's called a "Request for Reconsideration" in the Google Webmaster account.

Log in to your account and then click the Site reconsideration link on the left side of the page that appears when you log in. Then, in the Help page that appears, click the Request reconsideration of your site link. (Or just log in and go directly to www.google.com/webmasters/tools/reconsideration.)

A form appears that allows you to explain what happened and what you've done. Explain, for instance, if an SEO firm you used did some bad things, or if something you've done may have been misinterpreted by Google.

How long does it take to receive a response? Google says "several weeks," and I've seen a response in as little as two weeks. Your mileage may vary. After some time, though, you may see this:

> *We received a request from a site owner to reconsider how we index the following site: http://www. domainname.com/.*

> *We've now reviewed your site. When we review a site, we check to see if it's in violation of our Webmaster Guidelines. If we don't find any problems, we'll reconsider our indexing of your site. If your site still doesn't appear in our search results, check our Help Center for steps you can take.*

That's it. Don't expect an explanation, and don't expect to hear whether the penalty has been lifted. All Google will do is tell you it has received a request and reviewed your site, and even that's ambiguous; Google *has* reviewed the site, and if it *doesn't* — future tense — find problems, it will *reconsider* the indexing of the site. Wow, nothing like clarity, eh?! Even this is an improvement; a year or two ago, you would submit a request and never get any kind of response, it just dropped into a big hole.

If you get one of these responses, don't expect a sudden change. Over the next week or two, recheck your site as explained earlier in this chapter, and see whether the situation improves. If not, rinse and repeat!

Are there other avenues you can pursue? I have been told by someone who spends good money on PPC that if you have an account manager, that person can sometimes contact the right person at Google to get an answer. On the other hand, I have a client in this happy situation: Despite spending literally hundreds of thousands of dollars on PPC each month, and despite the fact that when he ran into a problem he *did* get answers from Google, those answers were so vague as to be useless. It's next to impossible to get a good, solid, "this is the problem" answer from Google on these issues. (Unless, that is, Google sends a message to you in the Webmaster console describing a problem.)

So, that's it. It's a very scary experience and no really good answers exist. However, for all this talk of penalties, I want to reiterate that you have probably not been penalized. Just because your site has dropped in the search results doesn't mean that you're being punished. In most cases, it means that Google has changed the algorithm it's using and it no longer gives your pages, or the links pointing to your pages, the same weight it did in the past.

If you find all this confusing and frustrating — well, welcome to the world of SEO!

Part V
The Part of Tens

The 5th Wave   By Rich Tennant

"So far our Web presence has been pretty good.
We've gotten some orders, a few inquiries,
and nine guys who want to date our logo."

In this part . . .

After you get the basics of search engine optimization under your belt, this final part of the book gives you one last push in the right direction.

I begin by trying to answer the age-old question, "How do I pick an SEO firm?" Then I talk about a number of myths and mistakes that are common in the search engine business. (No, you're *not* getting a number one position on Google for $25; and yes, you should start thinking about search engines before you build your site.)

This part also points you in the direction of some great information resources, places where you can find out more about search engine optimization or get info on a particular search engine technique. I also tell you about useful tools to help you in your endeavors, from programs that help you analyze the traffic coming to your Web site to link checkers and search-rank tools.

Chapter 20

Ten Things to Know and Do When Picking an SEO Firm

The SEO business is 80 percent scam. There, I said it. Too late to take it back.

But plenty of you know that, anyway. In my consulting business I hear all the time from firms large and small that have worked with SEO companies, sometimes paying many thousands of dollars, and received little in return. In fact, I'm often asked, "Can you check my site and see what they did?" and on doing so discover that "they" did very little.

I won't go into detail here about my 80 percent scam contention (if you care to read the details, visit www.PeterKentConsulting.com); I'll just state that picking a good SEO firm is a little like picking a good multilevel-marketing firm. You might get lucky and get rich, but far more likely is that you'll waste a lot of time and money.

In fact, one of the most common questions I'm asked is, "How do I hire an SEO firm?" So, here are ten things you need to know and do when looking for an SEO firm that is worth the money you'll be paying.

Read This Book

Step 1: Read and understand this book! Even if you don't intend to do the work yourself, it's essential that you, or someone on your team, understands SEO. Most people buying SEO services really don't understand what they are getting for their money, so they're buying blind, crossing their fingers, and hoping it will all turn out okay.

A better strategy is to understand what SEO firms do so that you can understand what the prospective firms are telling you and check up on them to see that they really do what they claim.

Why You Don't Need an SEO Firm to Optimize Your Site

You actually don't need an SEO firm to optimize your site. Ideally, the people *building* the site should be doing that.

Remember, SEO is essentially about two different things:

- On-page optimization
- Linking

In most cases, when you sign up for a third-party SEO service to optimize your site, very little gets done, and some really important page-optimization issues are ignored. It's hard for a third-party firm to come in and restructure your site, creating good keyworded URLs, for instance, or rebuilding your page templates to use H1 tags, or implementing extensive internal linking. . . and thus, they don't. Instead, they tweak a few things here and there, such as by fixing title tags and description tags (usually badly) and creating keyword meta tags (mostly pointless). I'm not sure that I've *ever* seen a third-party SEO firm do a good job of page optimization.

Hiring a third-party firm to optimize your site is, in most circumstances, a *bad* strategy. Rather, the team that is building and maintaining the site needs to understand optimization, and optimize as it builds.

So what's the role of an SEO firm? In my mind, it's all about linking. I don't think it make sense to hire an outside firm to do page optimization, so that leaves the other part of the equation, linking. My advice is that if you plan to hire an SEO firm, focus on linking.

There is one exception: a situation in which an SEO firm is going to come in and take over your entire Web site for you. Then that firm has control over everything and can make all the necessary changes. This doesn't mean it'll do a good job, necessarily, but a *good firm* could, in such a situation, do a good job. The average SEO firm, without having full control but instead just tweaking a few on-page issues here and there, won't do a good job.

Find Firms Through Referrals

Perhaps the best way to find an SEO firm is through referrals. Do you have friends of colleagues who have worked with a good SEO firm, one that actually did help their sites rise through the search ranks? If so, that firm's a good place to start.

Unfortunately, considering the 80 percent scam factor, you probably *don't* have a friend or colleague who has successfully hired a good SEO firm, so you're going to have to dig a little deeper.

Look for Niche Services

I only said that the SEO business is 80 percent scam; there *are* some good firms, and some of the better firms focus on particular areas, such as the legal business, insurance firms, or medical clinics.

So, you might look around and see whether you can find any firms working in your particular business. However, beware: Many firms focusing on a particular niche *don't* do a good job.

Understand What It Is Providing — Specifically

SEO firms love to blind with science. It's easy to do, because most people don't understand SEO. You, however, are different. Armed with your new knowledge from this book, you know what SEO is all about, and what an SEO firm should be doing.

For instance, when a firm says, "We'll get you blog links," you know enough to ask, "What does that mean?" What kind of blog links? Are they follow or nofollow links (see Chapter 14)? Are they on sites that are indexed by Google? How *many* links? How *many* different blogs? And so on. All too often, I have clients admit to me, "Well, I'm not *exactly* sure what they were going to do." Don't be one of them!

One client I worked with was paying $2,700 per month to a firm without fully understanding what that firm was doing. It turned out that it was doing some (pretty worthless) on-page optimization, along with creating somewhere around 25–30 new links pointing to the site every month. After the client understood what he was getting, he also understood that he was paying way too much.

Understand What the Firm Expects of You

Here's a common SEO scam. You sign up for an SEO program, the SEO firm does a little work for you, but then it starts sending you e-mails telling you what *you* should be doing. Eventually, you realize that the service you signed up for involves *the firm* telling *you* what to do!

"Here are some good blogs related to your business," an e-mail from the SEO firm states. "You should get links from them." Following is a list of blogs, something that took the firm all of ten minutes to put together. That's its work for the month.

As a journalist from a major business magazine told me after an interview, when we started talking about her own startup Web site, "I thought that's what I was paying for, for them to get me links, and now it turns out I'm paying them to tell me where to get links from. I could have figured that out for a lot less than $800 a month!"

So, before you sign up to spend your hard-earned money, make sure you understand what your prospective firm is going to expect *you* to do.

Look at Samples

Before you start, make sure you see examples of the firm's work. If you are (against my best advice) hiring a firm to do on-page work, take a look at sites it has done before. What did it do? Did it do it well? Are the title and description tags good? Are the URLs well keyworded? Do the pages use H1 tags, and have good keywords scattered throughout, and so on. (After you've taken a look, you'll probably agree that I'm right and *not* hire a firm for on-page optimization.)

If you're using a firm to create links, do a link analysis on sites it has worked for in the past, using one of the tools I discuss in Chapter 15. See what sort of links it's creating, and how many. Are they good links? That is, well key-worded, follow (not nofollow) links, ideally from sites with some PageRank (although, as explained in Chapter 14, that's not always essential). Are the sites the links come from indexed in Google? Is there a range of different types of links?

Whatever you do, do not hire the firm until you've seen, and evaluated, what it can do for you.

Ask for References

You should also ask for references, or simply call the owners of sites you know the SEO firm has worked for and ask them how their experience was. Did their site's rank improve in the search engines? Did the firm do what it said it would?

SEO work can be expensive, so a little time spent checking references can save you a lot of money.

Compare Dollar for Dollar

After you understand what you are getting, services become easier to compare. If you're *not* paying for on-page optimization especially, you can even figure out pricing per link.

For instance, consider the service I mentioned earlier: $2,700 a month for 25–30 links a month. I'm ignoring the value of the on-page work, because quite frankly, it was close to worthless. So the monthly price works out at $90–$108 per link. They'd better be *really* good links. (They weren't.)

On the other hand, it's often possible to get good keyworded links from sites with a PageRank of 2–4 for $3–$6 per link, or low-value links (low PageRank links, for instance) for as little as 10 cents a link. This $2,700/mth service was *way* overpriced (and my client dropped it, in fact).

Will It Provide Reports?

Make sure you'll get reports; ask to see an example, and make sure they provide useful information and that you can understand them. Many millions of dollars have been spent on SEO without the clients knowing what they are getting in return. (I call this *faith-based SEO*.)

It's an old management adage that *you can't manage what you don't measure*. If you don't get reports, you're not measuring, you're not managing — and you're quite possibly being scammed.

Chapter 21

Ten-Plus Myths and Mistakes

. . . .

In This Chapter

▶ Understanding common mistakes made by site developers

▶ Deconstructing harmful myths

▶ Knowing the problems that hurt your search engine rank

. . . .

A lot of confusion exists in the search engine world — a lot of myths and a lot of mistakes. In this chapter, I quickly run through a few of the ideas and omissions that can hurt your search engine positions.

Myth: It's All about Meta Tags and Submissions

This is the most pervasive and harmful myth of all, held by many Web designers and developers. All you need, many believe, is to code your pages with the right meta tags — KEYWORDS and DESCRIPTION, and things like REVISIT-AFTER and CLASSIFICATION — and then submit your site to the search engines. I know Web designers who tell their clients that they'll "handle" search engine optimization, and then follow nothing more than this procedure.

It's completely wrong for various reasons. Most meta tags aren't particularly important (see Chapter 6), if they're even used by search engines at all. Without keywords in the page content, search engines won't index what you need them to index. (See Chapters 6 and 7.) Submitting to search engines doesn't mean they'll index your pages. (See Chapter 11.) Moreover, what about links? (See Chapters 14 through 16.)

Myth: Web Designers and Developers Understand Search Engines

I'm a geek. I've worked in software development for almost 30 years. I still work closely with software developers (these days, mostly Web-software developers) and Web designers; I build Web sites for my clients (so I work with developers and designers on these sites); my friends are developers and designers, and I'm telling you now that most developers and designers do *not* understand search engines to any great degree.

Most Web-development companies these days tell their clients that they know how to handle search engines, and even that they're experts. In most cases, that's simply not true; no more than it's true that I'm an expert in neurosurgery. This makes it very hard for business owners when they hire a Web development team, of course, though I hope this book will help. It will give you an idea of the sorts of questions you should ask your developers so that you can figure out whether they really *do* understand search engine requirements (see also Chapter 20 and 22).

In addition, many Web developers don't enjoy working with search marketing experts. They think that all search engine experts want is to make the site ugly or remove the dynamism. This is furthest from the truth, and a Web developer who refuses to work with an SEO expert may just be worried for his or her job.

Myth: Multiple Submissions Improve Your Search Position

As far as the major search engines go, multiple submissions, even automated submissions, don't help. Someone recently told me that he was sure it did help because his position improved in, for instance, the Open Directory Project when he frequently resubmitted. This is completely wrong — in the case of the Open Directory Project, there's no way it could possibly help, because all entries have to be reviewed by a human editor, and submitting multiple times is more likely to annoy the editor rather than convince him to let you in!

As you just read, *submitting* to search engines — requesting that they index your pages — often doesn't get your page indexed anyway. Far more important is a link campaign to get plenty of links to your site; see Chapters 14 through 15. And you should definitely be working with XML sitemaps (see Chapter 11). Perhaps multiple submissions to smaller search engines might help with those, but it won't help with the major systems. Some of these multiple-submission services are little more than a scam; in fact, on a number of occasions, I've reviewed the "here's where we submit your site to" lists for some of these services and found out-of-business search engines included.

Mistake: You Don't Know Your Keywords

This is also a major problem: The vast majority of Web sites are created without the site owners or developers really knowing what keywords are important. (That's okay, perhaps, because most sites are built without any idea of using keywords in the content anyway.) At best, the keywords have been guessed. At worst — the majority of the cases — nobody's thought of the keywords at all.

Don't guess at your keywords. Do a proper keyword analysis. (See Chapter 5.) I can almost guarantee that two things will happen. You'll find that some of your guesses were wrong — people aren't often using some of the phrases you thought would be common. You'll also discover very important phrases you had no idea about.

Just recently, I talked with a company that ranked *really* well for the keywords it was interested in. The only problem was that there was another group of keywords the company simply hadn't considered, which were almost as important as the ones it had. . .and for this second group of keywords, it didn't rank at all. So it doesn't matter how well you play the SEO game — if you didn't consider keywords, you might as well not bother.

Mistake: Too Many Pages with Database Parameters and Session IDs

This is a surprisingly common problem. Many, many sites (in particular, sites built by big companies with large development teams) are created these days in such a manner that search engines won't read them. Search engines don't like database parameters or session IDs in a URL. (See Chapter 7.)

My favorite example used to be CarToys.com, a large chain of electronics stores. This site had thousands of products but fewer than 100 pages indexed by Google, and most of those were Adobe Acrobat files, pop-up ads ("Free Shipping!"), or links to dynamic pages that wouldn't appear when a searcher clicked a link in the search results. Luckily for CarToys.com, someone at the company figured it all out, fixed the problem, and Google then picked up tens of thousands of pages.

Mistake: Building the Site and Then Bringing in the SEO Expert

Most companies approach search engine optimization as an afterthought. They build their Web site and then think, "Right, time to get people to the site." You really shouldn't begin a site until you have considered all the different ways you're going to create traffic to the site. It's like starting to build a road without knowing where it needs to go; if you're not careful, you'll get halfway there and realize "there" is in another direction.

In particular, though, you shouldn't start building a Web site without an understanding of search engines. Most major Web sites these days are built by teams of developers who have little understanding of search engine issues. These sites are launched and then someone decides to hire a search engine consultant. And the search engine consultant discovers all sorts of unnecessary problems. Good business for the consultant; expensive fixes for the site owner.

Myth: $25 Can Get Your Site a #1 Position

You hear a lot of background noise in the search engine business from companies claiming to be able to get your site into thousands of search engines and rank your site well for $25 a month. . . . Or a $50 flat fee . . . or $75 a month . . . or whatever.

The truth is that it's more complicated than that, and everyone I've spoken to who has used such services has been very disappointed. They often don't get into the major search engines at all, and even if they get included in the index, they don't rank well. Search engine ranking is sometimes very easy — but other times it's complicated, time consuming, and tedious. Most of the offers streaming into your Inbox in spam e-mail messages or displayed in banner ads on the Web aren't going to work.

Myth: Google Partners Get You #1 Positions

If you receive a spam e-mail telling you that the sender has a "special arrangement" with Google and can get you a #1 position within hours or days, delete it; it's nonsense — a scam. It's true that you can buy a top position on Google through its AdWords PPC (Pay Per Click) program, though you'll be bidding against your competitors. However, this scam refers to something different — to Google's having a special program that allows certain privileged companies to sell top positions in the organic-search results.

Don't believe it; it's nonsense.

Mistake: You Don't Have Pages Optimized for Specific Keywords

Have you built pages optimized for your most important keywords? I spoke recently with a firm that ranked pretty well — #5 in the search results — for his most desired keyword phrase, but not well enough (obviously, the site owner wanted #1).

The funny thing was that he was doing very well considering the fact that he didn't have a single page optimized for the keyword phrase he desired. Sure, he had pages close, pages that had the individual words in the keyword phrase scattered throughout the page, but not a single page that was fully optimized for the phrase.

Therefore, think about your most important phrases. Do you have pages *fully optimized* — that is, you have the phrase at the beginning of the `<TITLE>` tag, at the beginning of the `DESCRIPTION` tag, in `<H1>` tags, scattered throughout the page, and so on — for all these phrases? If not, maybe you don't *deserve* the #1 spot!

Mistake: Your Pages Are Empty

This one is a huge problem for many companies; the pages have nothing much for search engines to index. In some cases, the pages have little or no text that a search engine can read because the words on the page are embedded into images. In other cases, the words may be real text but are very few and aren't the right keywords.

Remember, search engines like — *need* — content. To a search engine, *content* means text that it can read and index. Whenever you provide text to a search engine, it should do the most for you — help you to be found in the search results. And the more content, the better.

Myth: Pay Per Click Is Where It's At

Pay Per Click (*PPC;* the small "sponsored" ads you see at the top of the search-results pages) can be a very important part of a Web site's marketing strategy. It's reliable, predictable, and relatively easy to work with. But it's not the only thing you should be doing. In fact, many companies cannot use PPC because the clicks are too expensive for their particular business model (and click prices are likely to keep rising as search marketing continues to be the hot Internet marketing topic).

The growth in PPC has been partly caused by the lack of search engine optimization knowledge. Companies build a site without thinking about search engines and then don't hire professional expertise to help them get search engine traffic, so they fall back on PPC. Many companies are now spending hundreds of thousands of dollars on PPC each month; they could complement their PPC campaigns with natural search engine traffic for a small fraction of that cost.

The wonderful thing about PPC advertising and SEO is that the two work hand in hand. If you want to know whether a word is important enough to optimize, get a hundred clicks from your favorite search engine through PPC and look at the conversion rates and the return on investment (ROI). Want to expand your PPC keyword list? No problem; look at the words that people are already using to find you as a baseline, and grow your list from these words. (For example, if they are using *rodent racing* to find you, buy ads triggered by the words *mouse rodent racing, rat rodent racing,* and so on.) Many companies are using PPC profitably; just don't assume it's the only way to go.

Many companies actually use PPC and SEO in combination. One client of mine has high organic-search positions, yet still buys PPC positions. Overall, he gets more business than he would if he did only one or the other.

Mistake: Believing Everything You Read

Just because something's "in print" — or on a Web site — doesn't mean it's true! I see all sorts of incorrect information on this subject all the time. This field is full of misinformation, ambiguousness, and outright nonsense. I often hear my clients say, "Well, I read x the other day," and I have to convince them that x is quite simply wrong. It's hard to do, though, because so many people think that if someone said something in a forum, or on a blog, or even in a book on SEO, it *must* be true. Let skepticism be your byword.

When I'm told that something is undoubtedly true, I want to see the evidence. Did Google say it, for instance? If not, and if it doesn't seem to make sense, then it's probably not true.

Chapter 22

Ten-Plus Ways to Stay Updated

The naysayers said it couldn't be done, that a book about search engine optimization couldn't be written because the technology is changing so quickly. That's not entirely true — I wrote the first edition of this book five years ago, and the basics are still the same: creating pages that search engines can read, picking good keywords, getting lots of links into your site, and so on.

But some details do change. Where are people searching these days? What tricks are search engines really clamping down on? Why did your site suddenly drop out of Google (as many thousands do now and then; see Chapter 19)?

You may also need more detailed information than I can provide in this book. Perhaps you have a problem with dynamic pages and you need to know the details of URL rewriting for a particular Web server, for instance. You need to know where to go to find more information. In this chapter, I provide you with resources that you can use to keep up-to-date and track down the details.

Let Me Help Some More

Visit my Web site at www.SearchEngineBulletin.com. I point you to important resources, provide links to all the Web pages listed in this book (so that you can just click instead of typing them), and provide important updates. I also have bonus chapters on pay per click, copyright law, and Google search techniques.

I also provide consulting services, including phone consultations. I can examine a company's online strategy from not just the perspective of search engines but also a wider view; I've been working online for 26 years now and have experience in Web design, e-commerce and online transactions, traffic conversion, non–search engine traffic generation, and so on. An hour or two of advice can often save a company from the huge expense of going down the wrong path!

The Search Engines Themselves

One of the best ways to find information about search engines is by using carefully crafted search terms at the search engines themselves. Say you want to find detailed information about dealing with session IDs (see Chapter 7). You can go to Google and search for *search engine session id*. Or perhaps you have a problem with dynamic URLs and know that you need to use something called *mod_rewrite*. Go to a search engine and search for *mod_rewrite* or *mod rewrite*. (The former is the correct term, although many people talk of *mod rewrite* in the vernacular.)

It's amazing what you can find if you dig around for a little while. A few minutes' research through the search engines can save you many hours of time wasted through inefficient or ineffective SEO techniques. I suggest you read the bonus chapter posted at `www.dummies.com/go/seofd4e`, which explains various techniques for searching at Google. A good understanding of how to use search engines will pay dividends.

Google's Webmaster Pages

Google is happy to tell you what it wants from you and what it doesn't like. No, it won't tell you exactly how it figures out search result rankings, but good information is there nonetheless. It's a good idea to review the advice pages Google provides for Webmasters. You can find them at the following URLs:

- ✔ **Google Webmaster Guidelines:** `www.google.com/webmasters/guidelines.html`
- ✔ **Google Webmaster Help Center:** `www.google.com/support/webmasters/`

Google's Search Engine Optimization Starter Guide

Late in 2008, Google finally decided, "If we can't beat them, join them," and published its own SEO guide.

It's basic but useful stuff, and I find it particularly handy when I'm arguing with Web developers. For instance, when a Web developer says, voice dripping with skepticism, "Why should we bother using H1 tags; nobody does anymore," I can say quite simply, "Because Google says so," and end the conversation right there.

You can find the guide here: `www.google.com/webmasters/docs/search-engine-optimization-starter-guide.pdf`.

MSN/Bing SEO Tips

You can find information about optimizing pages for submission to MSN/Bing (and, through their partnership, inclusion in the Yahoo! search results) at `www.bing.com/docs`. You'll find a wide range of information, from how the MSNbot works to how to handle a site move.

Yahoo!'s Search Help

Yahoo!'s search engine is the world's second most important, but it is now powered by Bing, as discussed in Chapter 1.

However, Yahoo! still provides information about how to use the system, even if the information on how to work with it to get your pages indexed might be a little dated. If you want to know more about how to use Yahoo!'s search engine, go to `http://help.yahoo.com/l/us/yahoo/search/basics/`, where you'll find links to Search Tips, Advanced Search, Search Shortcuts, and more. (There are dozens of shortcuts, allowing you to search for airport information, exchange rates, gas prices, patents, U.S. Post Office, FedEx, UPS packages, and so on.)

Search Engine Watch

The Search Engine Watch site gives you a great way to keep up with what's going on in the search engine world. This site provides a ton of information about a very wide range of subjects related to not only search engine optimization but also the flip side of the coin — subjects related to searching online. In fact, perhaps this site's greatest weakness is that it provides *so much* information; it's really intended for search engine optimization experts rather than the average Webmaster or site manager. The site is divided into a free area and a paid-subscription area.

Visit the site at www.searchenginewatch.com.

The Official Google Webmaster Help Group

Google Groups hosts a very useful resource, the *Official Google Webmaster Help Group,* which has tens of thousands of members and hundreds of thousands of archived messages. It's a great way to find out what people in the business are saying about, well, just about anything. Find it at www.google.com/support/forum/p/Webmasters.Google's Inside Scoop

Here are a couple of great ways to peep into the mind of Google:

✔ **Google Webmaster Central Blog:** A very useful site, with information from actual employees of Google providing the Google view of search engine optimization. Visit googlewebmastercentral.blogspot.com.

✔ **MattCutts.com:** Matt Cutts is a well-known employee of Google (well known in SEO circles, that is) who works for the Search Quality team. He maintains a blog about a wide range of issues, including many related to SEO issues. I like to use Matt's blog to find out the *real* answers; when I hear an SEO tip that I think is perhaps unlikely to be true, yet oft quoted, I sometimes think, "Let's see what Matt has to say on the subject." It's also a great way to shut up Web developers. For instance, when someone says, "Why use hyphens in URLs rather than underscores?" I can shut him or her up with a quick "Because Matt Cutts says so!"

Go to www.mattcutts.com/blog to see what he has to say.

WebMaster World

WebMaster World (www.webmasterworld.com) is a very good discussion group, with many knowledgeable people. It'll cost ya, though: $89 for six months, or $149 for a year.

HighRankings.com

Hosted by a search engine optimization consultant, HighRankings.com is a pretty busy forum (free at this time) with discussions covering a wide range of subjects. Check it out at www.highrankings.com/forum.

Get the Search Engine Buzz

If you want to find out what people are doing with search engines — popular searches, for instance — check out some of the services in this section.

Google Zeitgeist is an analysis of what people are searching for, when, and where. You can find the most popular brand-name searches, charts showing how searches peak for particular keywords during news events or in response to TV shows, the most popular searches for particular men, women, and fictional characters, the most popular movie searches in Australia, the most popular brands in Italy, and so on. Google provides weekly, monthly, and annual reports. Check it out at www.google.com/press/zeitgeist/.

Here are some other tools that provide information about how people are searching:

- ✔ **Google Trends:** This is a very cool tool; enter a list of search terms, separated by commas, and Google displays a chart showing how often the terms have been searched over a particular time range, along with news stories correlated with particular peaks. You can even select a particular country (www.google.com/trends).

- ✔ **Google Insight:** "Compare search volume patterns across specific regions, categories, time frames and properties" (www.google.com/insights/search/).

- ✔ **Wordtracker:** Wordtracker provides free reports of the top 500 searches — with or without sexually explicit terms, both long-term and short term (freekeywords.wordtracker.com/top-keywords/).

✔ **Ask.com IQ (Interesting Queries):** A service showing you the top search terms and the top *advancing* search terms — the ones that are growing most quickly (`sp.ask.com/en/docs/iq/iq.shtml`).

✔ **Yahoo! Buzz:** Yahoo! figures out what people are searching for the most and then selects the most popular result pages within those searches (`buzz.yahoo.com`).

What I find depressing about these lists is just how obsessed people are with sports and celebrities! Oh, and pornography. The Wordtracker list is a real eye opener; view the full, uncensored list, and you may be surprised at just what your neighbors are searching for!

Chapter 23

Ten-Plus Useful Things to Know

*I*n this chapter, I describe a number of useful little things to know, from 301 redirects to Google's enhanced image search; from various information sources to how Google creates multiline search result entries.

Managing Sitelinks (Multiline Search Results)

You've probably seen multiline search results, such as those shown in Figure 23-1.

How does this happen? More important, how can you make it happen for your site?

Google calls these internal site links, um, *sitelinks,* and they're intended to help users find their way into popular pages within popular sites. They are typically displayed only when Google is almost certain that you're looking for that particular site. Search for *dummies,* for instance, and the Dummies.com site appears, with sitelinks; search for *search engine optimization for dummies,* though, and none of the sites in the results, including Dummies.com, have sitelinks.

Google actually analyzes the site and tries to figure out which pages are significant. At the time of writing, there's no *direct* way for you to tell Google which pages to use (Google said long ago that it may allow Webmaster input in the future, but the future's already here and Google still doesn't.).

Figure 23-1:
Google adds sitelinks to the results for some popular sites.

In the early days Google created sitelinks for only very popular sites, but these days, many, many sites have sitelinks displayed in the search results now and then. So how can you tell Google which pages to use? You do so indirectly, through site structure. Google looks at the site's link structure, and if you have lots of links saying <u>Contact Us</u> that point to a particular page, that page may be picked up for a sitelink. Google may also look at folder structure. If you have a <u>products</u> link pointing to a /products/ folder, it may give even more of a hint.

However, if you're fortunate enough to be in the happy situation of having sitelinks, but don't like one of the pages that Google is using, you can tell Google not to use it. Log into your Webmaster account (see Chapter 11), click the Site Configuration link in the left navigation bar, and then click the Sitelinks link. It may take "some time" for the blocked sitelink to no longer be used. And there's one idiosyncrasy you should be aware of. Google says that "Once you've blocked a sitelink, it won't appear in the Google search results for 90 days. This period will be extended every time you visit the Sitelinks page on Webmaster Tools."

Checking Your Site Rank

How do you know how well your site ranks in the search engines? You can go to a search engine, type a keyword phrase, and see what happens. If you're not on the first page, check the second; if you're not there, check the third.

Then go back and do it for 50 search terms on several search engines. It will take a while.

Another problem with manually checking position is that if you're logged into a Google account, Google will start "personalizing" your search results to what it thinks is most appropriate for you; you won't see what the average user sees.

Luckily, you can get help. Many programs can check your search engine position for you. You tell the program which keywords you're interested in, which search engines you want to check, and which Web site you're looking for in the search results. Then you let the program do its work.

Traditionally, search engines have "banned" such tools. In fact, Google still has text referring to one of the most popular of these tools, WebPosition (www.webposition.com), as "unauthorized software." In theory, if Google notices that a computer is using one of these tools excessively, it may ban search queries from that computer. That doesn't mean it hurts your Web site, of course, because the queries are not coming from your Web site.

On the other hand, Google now provides a special application programming interface (API) that programs such as WebPosition can use to send queries directly to Google, bypassing the search page. Such access *is* okay. (You can find information about the Google API at www.google.com/apis.) As for WebPosition, it recently changed from Windows-based software that you purchase to a monthly Web service, so the software runs on WebPosition's servers, and accessing the data is its problem, not yours.

You can see a typical keyword report, showing positions for each keyword in several search engines — in this case, produced by WebPosition — in Figure 23-2. Many other programs can create site-ranking reports for you — both through programs that are installed on your computer and through Web-based services, such as WebCEO (www.webceo.com) and Rank Tracker (www.link-assistant.com/rank-tracker), and even a few free services, such as GoogleRankings (www.googlerankings.com).

Here's a quick tip for a quick rank check. Go to Google and click the Advanced Search link. Select 100 Results from the drop-down box at the top of the page that appears, enter your keywords into the top text box, and then click the Google Search button. You see 100 search results rather than the normal 10, and you can search the page looking for your site.

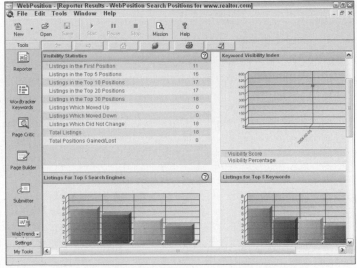

Figure 23-2:
A page rank report generated by Web Position.

Checking for Broken Links

Link checkers are always handy, whether you're interested in optimizing your site for the search engines or not. After you've created a few pages, run a link check to make sure you didn't make any mistakes in your links.

Again, many, many link checkers are available, including paid services, such as LinkAlarm (`linkalarm.com`), that will automatically check links on your site and send you a report. I'm currently using a little Windows program called Xenu's Link Sleuth, as shown in Figure 23-3 (`home.snafu.de/tilman/xenulink.html`). It's free, which is always nice! (The creator of Link Sleuth requests that if you like the program, support some of his favorite causes.) This program is very quick — checking tens of thousands of links in a few minutes — and very easy to use. It produces a report, displayed in your Web browser, showing the pages containing broken links. Click a link, and the page opens so you can take a look. You can use the program to check both internal and external links on your site.

Note also that your Web design software package may include a built-in link checker.

Figure 23-3:
A report created by Xenu's Link Sleuth; it checked over 17,000 links in fewer than ten minutes.

Alexa Toolbar

The Alexa toolbar (`download.alexa.com`) can be handy, too. I sometimes use it to assess the traffic of Web sites I may want to work with. For instance, if someone approaches you trying to sell advertising space on a site, how do you know whether it's a good deal? So many sites get almost no traffic that it may not be worth the expense.

The Alexa toolbar can give you a very general idea of whether the site gets any traffic at all; you can view traffic details for the site, such as the *traffic rank,* an estimate of the number of visitors to the site out of every million Internet users, and so on. Reportedly, Alexa's numbers are pretty good for the world's most popular sites, but rather inaccurate for the average site. However, you can still get a general feel. If the site is ranked 4,000,000, you can bet it doesn't get much traffic at all. If the site is ranked 4,000, it's far more popular. Alexa also provides a list of the most popular sites in thousands of categories; a good way to track down affiliates, for instance, or link partners.

Alexa isn't the only company providing this sort of information, though. Sites such as www.compete.com and www.quantcast.com, popular competitors to Alexa, provide estimates of traffic and rank. Note, however, that none of these numbers are accurate; they are just estimates.

Install Firebug

Firebug (shown in Figure 23-4) is a fantastic Firefox browser add-on. It allows you to quickly analyze a Web site. That is, to look into the site code while looking at the Web page. Right-click a page component and select Inspect Element, and you see the code that creates it — great for seeing exactly how links are coded, for instance. You can also edit the code to immediately see how the page would look with the modifications.

Figure 23-4:
Firebug is a great tool for analyzing Web pages.

If you're not using Firefox, you probably should anyway. It's a great browser. So, once installed, choose Tools⇨Add-ons and then click the Get Add-ons button in the Add-ons dialog box. Search for *firebug* and then, when the results appear, click the <u>See all results</u> link.

Finding Your Keyword Density

As I explain in Chapter 5, you don't need to get too hung up on keyword density. You can analyze to the *n*th degree, and everyone has a different opinion as to exactly what the density should be. But it's sometimes interesting to check your pages for keyword density, and many tools are available to help you do so. WebPosition, mentioned earlier in this chapter, has a built-in density tool, and you can find various online tools as well, such as the following:

✔ **SEO Tool's Keyword Density Analyzer:** `http://www.seochat.com/seo-tools/keyword-density/`

✔ **KeywordDensity.com:** `www.keyworddensity.com`

Analyzing Your Site's Traffic

You really should track traffic going to your site. At the end of the day, your search engine position isn't terribly important — it's just a means to an end. What really counts is the amount of traffic coming to your site. And it's important to know *how* people get to your site, too.

The two types of traffic-analysis tools are those that read server logs and those that tag your Web pages and track traffic by using a program on another server. In the first case, the tool analyzes log files created by the Web server — the server adds information each time it receives a request for a file. In the second type of tool, you have to add a little piece of code to your Web pages — each time a page from your site is requested, the program is, in effect, informed of the fact.

You quite likely have a traffic-analysis tool already installed on your site — ask your server administrator how to view your logs. Otherwise, you can use a tag-based traffic-analysis tool, and these days you don't even have to pay.

Analysis tools show you all sorts of interesting (and often useless) information. But perhaps the most important things you can find are

- How many people are reaching your site, and from what areas
- Which sites are sending visitors to your site
- Which search engines are sending visitors to your site
- What keywords are people using to reach your site

You may find that people are reaching you with keywords that you hadn't thought of, or perhaps unusual combinations of keywords that you hadn't imagined. This doesn't replace a real keyword analysis, though, because you see only the keywords used by people who found you, not the keywords used by people who *didn't* find you but were looking for products or services like yours. See Chapter 5 for more information about keywords.

These days, it seems that almost everyone but the largest companies are using Google Analytics. A few years ago, Google purchased one of the top independent traffic-analysis firms, Urchin, and then started *giving away* traffic-analysis accounts. Visit `analytics.google.com`.

This is a very sophisticated tool, and to fully understand what can be done with the system, you need to spend a few dozen hours with a good book, such as Brian Clifton's *Advanced Web Metrics with Google Analytics* (which I'm mentioning not just because it's published by Wiley, the publisher of the fine tome you are currently reading, but because it's a good read, too; well, as good as a book about Web analytics can hope to be; I mean, it's not John Grisham, but still. . .you know what I mean). Still, Google analytics can be set up to run a few minutes and provide useful information "right out of the box."

Traditionally, the traffic-analysis companies were big believers in blinding their customers with science. They didn't understand that sometimes less is more and focused on throwing as much complicated information at the client as possible. Things are getting better, though, and Google Analytics isn't too bad. Whatever route you take, you really need to install analytics.

Thanks to Google Analytics, it's now hard for a Web analytics company that targets the small-business market to make it, and some of these firms have died out. You might want to look at `www.crazyegg.com,` though, which I think has a "we'll survive through the power of *cool*" strategy that seems to be working for it. It's a simple-to-setup system that provides very cool "overlays," like the one in Figure 23-5.

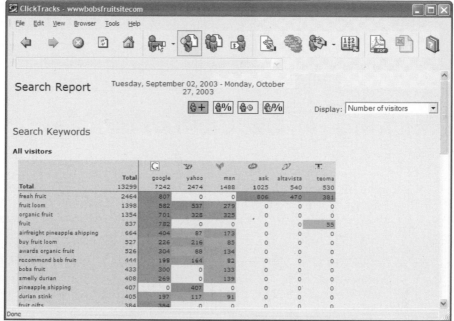

Figure 23-5:
A demo of
Crazy Egg's
neat traffic
analysis
overlay.

Phone Call Tracking

Many companies have a significant problem in tracking business. The business comes through the phone, not through the Web directly. Prospective clients come to the Web site and then, rather than submitting a lead through a submission form or making a purchase on the site, they pick up the phone.

As an example, doctors' offices and medical clinics are likely to get a very high proportion of phone leads. If your phone number is prominently displayed on the site, most people — perhaps 95 percent or more — will call you rather than use your submission form.

How, then, do you track this traffic? Use a call-submission service. Such a service, which can be very affordable at around $10 a month, provides you with a phone number to place on your site. Then it tracks all the calls through the number; some services even record the calls. You get reports showing these calls, of course, but some services can even integrate with Google Analytics, so you can see the number of calls that way, too.

I've used www.hostednumbers.com, which is good for small businesses (you can get a single link for $8 a month), but various other service may be more appropriate for larger companies needing more numbers. The company dial800.com, for instance, provides 25 numbers for $225. To find these services, search for *phone call tracking*.

Checking for Duplication and Theft

Copyscape (www.copyscape.com) is an interesting tool that allows you to see whether anyone has stolen your site content, and to see how closely your content matches other sites. For instance, if you're quoting documents or using syndicated content, the less duplication, the better. The concern is that search engines may downgrade pages that they know duplicate other pages, so you don't want your pages to match others too closely.

Enter a URL into Copyscape, and it searches for pages that match the page referenced by the URL, to varying degrees. Copyscape returns the results, and when you click the links, you see the page with the matching text colored and, at the top, a Copyscape banner telling you how many words match.

Here's a particularly useful application for this tool. When you pay for someone to write articles for you, whether for your site or for syndication (see Chapter 16), run the articles through Copyscape. One way to make writing $10 articles profitable is not to write them, so you may find that the writer isn't the writer, but he copies really well. Copyscape can track down this kind of perfidy in seconds. An interesting little toy; experiment and see.

Using 301 Redirects

301 redirects tell search engines that a particular URL really points to another URL. Google uses a 301, for instance, to point google.com to www.google.com. (Try it; you'll see.)

301s are especially useful when moving pages or changing domain names. They're very easy for server administrators; about the only time you have problems with 301 redirects is when your site is a shared hosting account on a Windows server. You should also use a 301 redirect from the non-www version of your domain name; that is, from *yourdomain.com* to www.*yourdomain.com* (go to google.com and see what happens; it 301 redirects to www.google.com).

Search for *301 redirect* in Google, and you find plenty of information.

Getting Multiple Results on the Search Results Page

How would you like three, four, five, or more results on the search-results page? It can be done; I've seen it done and done it several times myself.

Getting two results on the first page is common; as you know by now, Google often returns two pages from a single site, one indented below the other. But how about more? People use a couple of strategies to do this:

✔ **Create multiple sites:** Some companies create two or more totally independent Web sites in an attempt to grab more "real estate" on the search-results page, and if done right, this strategy can work well. If you want to be paranoid, though, and ensure that the sites are never identified as belonging to the same business, the domain names can't have the same contact information. To this end, many people use a domain-privacy system to block exposure of ownership information. In addition, you need to make sure that the domain names have completely different IP numbers — not just the set of numbers at the end of the full set, but a different "C" block or higher. (The bold number in the following IP number is the C block: 98.137.**149**.156).

✔ **Get into the pages that rank alongside yours:** Take a look at the other pages ranking high for your keywords. If you're lucky, you can get onto those pages. I've seen situations in which numerous other links in the first page of search results point to directories, and you may be able to buy a position in those directories. Another possibility: Affiliate companies that rank well may be willing to sell your products.

✔ **Buy a PPC ad:** Many companies rank well in the search engines *and* buy PPC ads. Many searchers go straight to the PPC ads rather than organic results; on the other hand, many ignore the PPC ads and use only the organic results. Thus, many companies decide to cover all bases and position themselves in both areas.

The problem with the first strategy is that you now have two or more sites to work on — which you have to create links to in order to get them to rank well. Still, it's a strategy that does work for companies that do it right.

Here's an example. Search for *free credit report*, and, at the time of writing, you find, among others, these results:

PPC Ads

FreeCreditReport.com

Experian.com

FreeCreditScore.com

Organic Results

FreeCreditReport.com

Experian.com

Five results on one page, including two in the organic results . . . and all are owned by Experian. I've seen better, though; I've seen as many as seven organic results pointing to the same company through its own sites and directories.

Identifying Fake PageRank

Here's a little trick that was popular a few years ago and was sometimes used to scam people buying domains, or buying links to their site. I haven't seen it work lately; perhaps Google has found a way to block it. Still, I haven't found any discussion on the subject, so just in case the problem's still there, here's what it's all about.

People playing this dirty little trick would do a 301 redirect from a site with little PageRank to one with much higher PageRank. The fraudster would wait until Google came by, indexed the site, and then assigned a high PageRank to it (Google would pick up the PageRank from the site to which the low-rank site was 301 redirected). Then the trickster would drop the redirect and try to sell the domain or sell links. Because Google takes a few months to change PageRanks, even though it re-indexes more frequently, the site would appear to have a higher PageRank for some time.

How can you check whether this trick is being played? A couple of ways:

✔ Search Google for *info:yourdomainname.com*; Google will return information about that site. If it returns information about a *different* site, the site is, or was, redirected to that other site.

✔ Go to the site and then use the Google toolbar to look in the cache: Click the PageRank button and select Cached snapshot of page. If Google shows a different site, the original site was recently redirected to the one being shown.

You Need an Attractive Site

This isn't directly related to SEO, but it's so important and is such a big issue with small companies I consult with that I need to mention it. You see, it doesn't matter how well your site ranks: If your site is grotesquely ugly, you're not going to sell much!

I don't understand why people don't get this. I often show clients a competitor's site in one browser tab and their site in another tab (I use Web meeting software so that we can both see the same thing while talking on the phone). I jump between the two and ask, "Now, which company would *you* buy from?"

Still, even when someone understands, it's often difficult to find good design. So, here are some tips:

- Web design is *not* a pure commodity, like sugar or memory chips. Many businesses seem to think that design is design is design, and they buy the cheapest design they can find. You should buy design only from an individual or company that has already created something that looks good.

- Never buy design from a firm without knowing that it has the designer of the work you liked available for your project. Just because that firm has done good work in the past doesn't mean that it will for you, especially if it assigns a different designer to your project.

- Here's a great way to find designers: Go to 99designs.com and look at the project winners (99designs.com is a design-contest site with some really great work). Find work you like and then contact the designer directly to discuss your project. Other places are Guru.com, eLance.com, and oDesk.com.

- Understand that no direct correlation exists between price and quality of graphic design. You can spend a lot of money on garbage or get quality work for very little. (It reminds me of the Pepsi and Nike logos. Pepsi reportedly paid a million dollars for the 2008 redesign of its logo; Nike's swoosh logo cost the company $35.)

- Don't get hung up on beautiful Web design. Most companies need *professional*, not *award-winning*, design. Many designers want to create something cool, but what you want is usable — something that looks good and lets people get the task at hand done.

- Speaking of usability, few designers understand this concept. You might want to read *Don't Make Me Think*, by Steve Krug (New Riders Press); it's an excellent book on the subject.

- ✔ Never, never, *never* create a Web design with white text on a black background! (Well, a few headers here or there don't create a problem, but you should *never* do this to body text.) White text on a black background says to people, "Don't read this!" The proof? None of the world's top sites use light text on a dark background. So, if you see a designer who likes this type of layout, move on to someone else.

More Tools

If you're looking for more useful SEO tools, try these sites:

- ✔ **SEO Help:** `www.seo-help.com/seo-reference/seo-resources.html`
- ✔ **Webconfs.com:** `www.webconfs.com`
- ✔ **Pandia SEO:** `www.pandia.com/optimization`

Don't Forget the Search Engines

Don't forget that you can find just about anything through the search engines themselves. If you have a tedious procedure to work through, chances are good that someone has built a program to automate the procedure. So head to your favorite search engine and spend a little time tracking it down!

Index

• **Q** •

• **R** •

• T •

• X •

• Y •

• Z •

...ple & Macs

...ad For Dummies
...8-0-470-58027-1

...hone For Dummies,
...h Edition
...8-0-470-87870-5

...acBook For Dummies, 3rd
...dition
...8-0-470-76918-8

...ac OS X Snow Leopard For
...ummies
...8-0-470-43543-4

...siness

...okkeeping For Dummies
...8-0-7645-9848-7

...b Interviews
...r Dummies,
...d Edition
...8-0-470-17748-8

...sumes For Dummies,
...h Edition
...8-0-470-08037-5

...arting an
...line Business
...r Dummies,
...h Edition
...9-0-470-60210-2

...ck Investing
...r Dummies,
...d Edition
...8-0-470-40114-9

...ccessful
...ne Management
...r Dummies
...3-0-470-29034-7

Computer Hardware

BlackBerry
For Dummies,
4th Edition
978-0-470-60700-8

Computers For Seniors
For Dummies,
2nd Edition
978-0-470-53483-0

PCs For Dummies,
Windows
7 Edition
978-0-470-46542-4

Laptops For Dummies,
4th Edition
978-0-470-57829-2

Cooking & Entertaining

Cooking Basics
For Dummies,
3rd Edition
978-0-7645-7206-7

Wine For Dummies,
4th Edition
978-0-470-04579-4

Diet & Nutrition

Dieting For Dummies,
2nd Edition
978-0-7645-4149-0

Nutrition For Dummies,
4th Edition
978-0-471-79868-2

Weight Training
For Dummies,
3rd Edition
978-0-471-76845-6

Digital Photography

Digital SLR Cameras &
Photography For Dummies,
3rd Edition
978-0-470-46606-3

Photoshop Elements 8
For Dummies
978-0-470-52967-6

Gardening

Gardening Basics
For Dummies
978-0-470-03749-2

Organic Gardening
For Dummies,
2nd Edition
978-0-470-43067-5

Green/Sustainable

Raising Chickens
For Dummies
978-0-470-46544-8

Green Cleaning
For Dummies
978-0-470-39106-8

Health

Diabetes For Dummies,
3rd Edition
978-0-470-27086-8

Food Allergies
For Dummies
978-0-470-09584-3

Living Gluten-Free
For Dummies,
2nd Edition
978-0-470-58589-4

Hobbies/General

Chess For Dummies,
2nd Edition
978-0-7645-8404-6

Drawing
Cartoons & Comics
For Dummies
978-0-470-42683-8

Knitting For Dummies,
2nd Edition
978-0-470-28747-7

Organizing
For Dummies
978-0-7645-5300-4

Su Doku For Dummies
978-0-470-01892-7

Home Improvement

Home Maintenance
For Dummies,
2nd Edition
978-0-470-43063-7

Home Theater
For Dummies,
3rd Edition
978-0-470-41189-6

Living the
Country Lifestyle
All-in-One
For Dummies
978-0-470-43061-3

Solar Power Your Home
For Dummies,
2nd Edition
978-0-470-59678-4

...ilable wherever books are sold. For more information or to order direct: U.S. customers visit www.dummies.com or call 1-877-762-2974.
. customers visit www.wileyeurope.com or call (0) 1243 843291. Canadian customers visit www.wiley.ca or call 1-800-567-4797.

Internet

Blogging For Dummies,
3rd Edition
978-0-470-61996-4

eBay For Dummies,
6th Edition
978-0-470-49741-8

Facebook For Dummies,
3rd Edition
978-0-470-87804-0

Web Marketing
For Dummies,
2nd Edition
978-0-470-37181-7

WordPress
For Dummies,
3rd Edition
978-0-470-59274-8

Language & Foreign Language

French For Dummies
978-0-7645-5193-2

Italian Phrases
For Dummies
978-0-7645-7203-6

Spanish For Dummies,
2nd Edition
978-0-470-87855-2

Spanish
For Dummies,
Audio Set
978-0-470-09585-0

Math & Science

Algebra I
For Dummies,
2nd Edition
978-0-470-55964-2

Biology For Dummies,
2nd Edition
978-0-470-59875-7

Calculus For Dummies
978-0-7645-2498-1

Chemistry For Dummies
978-0-7645-5430-8

Microsoft Office

Excel 2010 For Dummies
978-0-470-48953-6

Office 2010 All-in-One
For Dummies
978-0-470-49748-7

Office 2010 For Dummies,
Book + DVD Bundle
978-0-470-62698-6

Word 2010 For Dummies
978-0-470-48772-3

Music

Guitar For Dummies,
2nd Edition
978-0-7645-9904-0

iPod & iTunes For
Dummies, 8th Edition
978-0-470-87871-2

Piano Exercises
For Dummies
978-0-470-38765-8

Parenting & Education

Parenting For Dummies,
2nd Edition
978-0-7645-5418-6

Type 1 Diabetes
For Dummies
978-0-470-17811-9

Pets

Cats For Dummies,
2nd Edition
978-0-7645-5275-5

Dog Training For Dummies,
3rd Edition
978-0-470-60029-0

Puppies For Dummies,
2nd Edition
978-0-470-03717-1

Religion & Inspiration

The Bible For Dummies
978-0-7645-5296-0

Catholicism For Dummies
978-0-7645-5391-2

Women in the Bible
For Dummies
978-0-7645-8475-6

Self-Help & Relationship

Anger Management
For Dummies
978-0-470-03715-7

Overcoming Anxiety
For Dummies,
2nd Edition
978-0-470-57441-6

Sports

Baseball
For Dummies,
3rd Edition
978-0-7645-7537-2

Basketball
For Dummies,
2nd Edition
978-0-7645-5248-9

Golf For Dummies,
3rd Edition
978-0-471-76871-5

Web Development

Web Design
All-in-One
For Dummies
978-0-470-41796-6

Web Sites
Do-It-Yourself
For Dummies,
2nd Edition
978-0-470-56520-9

Windows 7

Windows 7
For Dummies
978-0-470-49743-2

Windows 7
For Dummies,
Book + DVD Bundle
978-0-470-52398-8

Windows 7 All-in-One
For Dummies
978-0-470-48763-1

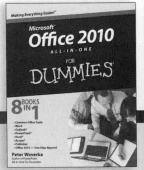

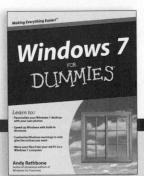

Available wherever books are sold. For more information or to order direct: U.S. customers visit www.dummies.com or call 1-877-762-2
U.K. customers visit www.wileyeurope.com or call (0) 1243 843291. Canadian customers visit www.wiley.ca or call 1-800-567-4797.